THE STEPHEN KING UNIVERSE

# WITHDRAWN

# THE STEPHEN KING UNIVERSE

*A Guide to the Worlds of the King of Horror*

---

STANLEY WIATER, CHRISTOPHER GOLDEN,
AND HANK WAGNER

RENAISSANCE BOOKS
*Los Angeles*

Library of Congress Control Number: 2001088642

10 9 8 7 6 5 4 3 2 1

*Design by Lisa Lenthall*
*Typeset by Susan Shankin*

Published by Renaissance Books
Distributed by St. Martin's Press
Manufactured in the United States of America
First edition

*To Iris and Tanya, for fighting off the wolves so long, so well. I love you both. And to Stephen King, for inviting me to your party in 1979 and allowing me to stay.* **S.W.**

*To Connie, Nicholas, and Daniel, my fellow explorers. And to the man himself, Stephen King, who always holds the lantern high to light the path, and yet rejoices in the shadows cast by its illumination.*

**C.G.**

*To my parents, who endured my antics as a child, and to Nancy and the kids, who endure my antics now that I'm "allgrownup." And to Stephen King, for all his wonderful stories.* **H.W.**

# Acknowledgments

---

*We would like to thank those people who had a hand in the creation of this book. First, our agent, Lori Perkins, who can truly say she was the mother of this particular (sometimes very particular) baby. And . . .*

| | |
|---|---|
| *Arthur Morey* | *Kathi Kamen-Goldmark* |
| *Richard Chizmar* | *Dave Hinchberger* |
| *Bill Walker* | *Misty Jenese* |
| *Marsha DeFilippo* | *Micol Ostow* |
| *Julie Eugley* | *James Robert Parish* |
| *Stephen Spignesi* | *Allan Taylor* |
| *Alan Clark* | *Kathi Kamen Goldmark* |
| *Claudia Carlson* | *Lisa French* |
| *Beth Gwinn* | *Lisa Lenthall* |
| *Suzanne Moss* | *Susan Shankin* |

# Contents

---

SECTION EIGHT

Tales from Beyond

APPENDIX A

A Stephen King Chronology

APPENDIX B

The Fiction of Stephen King

# *Introduction*

---

**W**ELCOME TO *The Stephen King Universe.* It is an incredible place of grotesque terror, dark magic, and fearsome wonder, a great multiverse conjured from one individual's imagination. A vast and still-growing kingdom, its many pathways can veer off into the darkest regions, where it's all too easy to get lost without guidance.

That's why we're here. To be your guides.

And what about you? Why are *you* here? Are you one of the faithful, one of those to whom Stephen King refers as the Constant Reader? Have you read his writings only casually, or have you paid closer attention and seen a pattern emerge? Perhaps you've only recently begun to explore what we respectfully call "the Stephen King universe." If so, you may not have realized that there is so much more to know: connections implied or revealed, stories hidden within stories, tales spun within tales.

No matter how involved you are with this master storyteller, how many excursions you have made into his short stories, his novels, or the films he's written and those that have been made from his works, you are likely to find a great deal of interest within these pages. You may even—dare we say it—find certain observations and revelations that are startling or controversial.

The Stephen King universe—though it might be more precisely called a multiverse (a cluster of universes existing in parallel dimensions)—is a truly wondrous and monumental creation. This volume of the same name is not, however, a concordance or an encyclopedia, nor is it a critical examination. More accurately, it is a guidebook. King's body of fiction can be, in large part, broken down by category based on the world or reality in which each story takes place: the world of the *Dark Tower* series or *The Stand*, the world he created under his pseudonym, Richard Bachman, or the world in which most of his work has taken place—the reality in which Derry and Castle Rock and *'Salem's Lot* exist, which we call herein the prime reality.

All are interrelated. Characters and stories cross over from one to the next. More important, there is a seemingly eternal struggle between good and evil, chaos and order, taking place throughout the Stephen King universe and its myriad parallel realities or dimensions.

In this book, organized according to the parallel realities, you will find descriptions of the significant action of nearly every story, novel, or original screenplay King has written, along with discussion of the themes that recur throughout the author's work. In addition we have created a sort of bible that references every major individual and setting in the Stephen King universe, including notes about the various characters' current whereabouts or activities.

The implications are vital.

Why would you need to know the current whereabouts of Ben Mears from *'Salem's Lot?* That novel is more than two decades old. Simply put, *'Salem's Lot* truly isn't over yet. It exists within the Stephen King universe, an ever-changing fictional landscape. It is constantly being altered because it is all of a piece. King has created—with a large portion of his audience not realizing it at the time of publication, or even now—an entire multiverse, a fully realized cosmology wherein every story and book is *somehow connected to every other story and book by the author.*

For example, *Firestarter* (1980) is connected to *The Tommyknockers* (1987), which is connected to *The Talisman* (1983), which is connected to the *Dark Tower* series, which just happens to be connected to literally everything else penned by King. There are dozens upon dozens of subtle (and sometimes not so subtle) connections within King's work, but that is still only the tip of the iceberg.

Ever since he began working on *The Dark Tower* epic while in college in the 1960s, King has been feeding into one, larger, greater narrative: that of Roland the gunslinger. Simply put, *The Dark Tower* is the core of the Stephen King universe. Works as seemingly diverse as *IT* (1986), *Insomnia* (1994), *Hearts in Atlantis* (1999), *The Eyes of the Dragon* (1987), *The Stand* (1978), and *The Talisman* (1983) are all vitally and directly connected.

King has been choosing sides for decades. He has been inventing (and occasionally reinventing) his heroes and villains on a cosmic scale, across time and space and dimension, painting in broad strokes the outline of a battle for the fate of the multiverse—of the Stephen King universe itself. Admittedly, he has yet to make precisely clear to his readers where that battle will take place and which of his characters will be involved. There is no doubt, however, that Roland and his *ka-tet* (the group of characters whose destiny is bound together in the *Dark Tower* series), Ralph Roberts from *Insomnia*, the kids from *IT*, Dennis and Thomas from *Eyes*, Ted Brautigan from *Hearts in Atlantis*, Mike Anderson from *Storm of the Century* (1999), the cast of *Desperation* (1996), and so many others are allied, perhaps unwittingly, against the evil forces that also inhabit the Stephen King universe. These dark beings include the Crimson King, Flagg, It, Tak, Leland Gaunt, Andre Linoge, and many, many others.

Such theories and ideas, certainties and possibilities, the connecting of various pieces to the puzzle, are the fabrics of *The Stephen King Universe*. In addition to the exploration of the author's work herein, this volume has been constructed to examine that coming overall battle. Be assured, it is coming.

Like no other modern author, King has crafted a massive fiction, comparable in some ways to the great universes of Marvel and DC Comics—which, of course, sprung from the minds of hundreds of story tellers and artists. Yet, amazingly enough, the Stephen King universe is the work of *one person*. In appendix A, we provide a timeline of King's life and work. We also provide lists of recommended further reading and preferred Web sites dealing with this bestselling author and his work. For the most part, however, our primary goal is to present both the Constant Reader and the casual fan with the first overview of the creations of one of the most important writers in American history.

In any undertaking of this magnitude, some hard and practical choices must be made. For one thing, no one involved wanted a book that would be too large to lift off a desk without injury to the reader. Scattered herein you will find the words *apparently, presumably,* and similar terms. Such hypothetical terms were necessary, as no confirmation from our subject was available.

More important, however, were our discussions about what to include or exclude, how to present the information, how much space to devote to an individual work, and so on. We focused on several fundamental questions:

*1. What deserves inclusion?* Of course, all of King's published novels are included in this volume, but there are some gray areas, as follows:

- The original scripts for *Storm of the Century, Golden Years* (1991), *Cat's Eye* (1985), and *Sleepwalkers* (1992) are covered in individual entries. Though the book includes discussions of film and television adaptations, we considered only the original print version as part of the official continuity of the Stephen King universe. For instance, the film *Cat's Eye* is based on stories that were previously published except for one segment, which was written specially for the film. Following our format, the original segment would be considered part of the Stephen King universe, but the adapted segments would not. Thus, *Sleepwalkers* and *Storm of the Century* are also part of the official continuity, because they also had not previously appeared in another form. *Golden Years* proved a special challenge (see section five for further explanation). Four books have already been written on the numerous film and television adaptations of King's works.

- Conversely, in the case of *The Stand* and short stories such as "Blind Willie," which appeared some time *after* their initial publication in an altered form, we consider the most recent versions as being in official continuity, since they were updated by King himself.

- The author's unpublished or most obscure or unavailable works are not included.

- King's early, short work is covered here only if he deemed it significant enough to be included in one of his collections. Later short stories and novellas not yet gathered into a collection are addressed at the end of section six.

• Though Tabitha King's novels include references to her husband's universe, and Peter Straub co-wrote *The Talisman*—making the entire works of both authors tangentially a part of the Stephen King universe—we limited our coverage to works actually written by, or as in the case of *The Talisman,* co-written by, King himself.

*2. How shall we break down the discussion of each book?* Although we certainly wanted to examine the books themselves in open-minded fashion, we also deemed it important to discuss all of the significant characters and major elements of the Stephen King universe (or SKU) as if the reader truly were entering that multiverse. In this way, we hoped to provide the proper feel, texture, and setting to those entries.

(*Note:* Since such characters as *The Dark Tower*'s Eddie Dean are drawn into the Stephen King universe from the world in which King himself exists, it follows that Dean is from our real, flesh-and-blood world. And if Dean is part of that universe, so, by extension, are you. You are a character of Stephen King's imagination. He may not have created you, but he has certainly co-opted you.)

• • •

For three decades, Stephen King has been creating worlds that are enthusiastically visited by literally millions of readers. According to *Entertainment Weekly,* he is the most significant novelist of the second half of the twentieth century. While Tom Clancy and John Grisham have challenged and briefly even surpassed his position as America's most popular author at one time or another, no writer in modern times has had his staying power. His accomplishments in terms of worldwide book sales and motion picture and television miniseries adaptations are, to say the least, extraordinary.

So phenomenal is his stunning success that his literary accomplishments are frequently relegated to a position of lesser importance due to the staggering statistics on his endeavors (that is, the number of novels he has written, the total number of his books in print, and his personal finances and charitable activities). Though many critics would disagree that he has a place in the lofty halls of literature or art, others have lionized him as the greatest writer of purely American fiction of his generation, comparing him to such masters as Mark Twain. Others consider him the contemporary version of the nineteenth-century British novelist Charles Dickens.

And what does Stephen King himself think of his work?

He has been known in the past to mockingly refer to his brand of fiction as "the literary equivalent of a Big Mac and fries." It is safe to dispense with those words as the modest self-image of a writer who realizes the best defense against harsh critics is a good offense. (Unless, of course, King was referring to the universal popularity of McDonald's, with billions and billions sold, in which case the brand-name reference might be more accurate. It has been estimated that there are to date more than 300 million copies of his books in print worldwide.) But that off-handed comment implies a lack of greater literary ambition on behalf of the author, an assertion that simply is untrue.

There is a *great* deal more going on in the works of Stephen King—on several levels—than at first seems apparent to the casual reader. You will discover this for yourself.

# SECTION ONE

## The Worlds of
## *The Dark Tower* and *The Stand*

*The Dark Tower: The Gunslinger*

*The Dark Tower II: The Drawing of the Three*

*The Dark Tower III: The Waste Lands*

*The Dark Tower IV: Wizard and Glass*

*The Eyes of the Dragon*

*The Talisman*

*Hearts in Atlantis*

*The Stand*

Related Tales

EW CONSTANT READERS would disagree that the *Dark Tower* series is the core of the Stephen King universe, and the axis on which our entire thesis for this book rotates. Though the majority of the author's work takes place in the parallel-reality dimension that is home to the fictional towns of Castle Rock, Derry, and others, the parallel reality of Roland the gunslinger—and, by extension, that of *The Stand*—is much more fundamental. Stephen King has been working on the *Dark Tower* series for three decades, weaving it in and out of his other writings, and yet a great many of his readers are likely to have missed its prominence.

Just as the Dark Tower itself is the point of time, space, and reality where all dimensions meet—the spindle of creation—so are all of King's works an outgrowth of the *Dark Tower* series, which was conceived as early as 1970. All of King's heroes and villains, scattered across the various parallel realities, are involved in a single, cosmic conflict, with the Tower as the ultimate prize.

· · ·

It all started with a poem.

King read Robert Browning's "Childe Roland to the Dark Tower Came" (1855) for a class assignment in his sophomore year (1967/68) at the University of Maine at Orono. In March of 1970, the year he graduated, he began the first installment in the series, *The Gunslinger*. Over the next twelve years, he continued to work on it even while turning out some of his best-loved works, including *'Salem's Lot* (1975), *The Shining* (1977), and *The Stand* (1978).

Did he realize, then, at the start of the process, that it would be all bits of a single story? In *Dark Tower*'s fourth volume, *Wizard and Glass* (1997), he at last came to that conclusion. In the afterword, he states:

> I have written enough novels and short stories to fill a solar system of the imagination, but Roland's story is my Jupiter— a planet that dwarfs all the others. . . . I am coming to understand that Roland's world (or worlds) actually *contains* all the others of my making; there is a place in Mid-world for Randall Flagg, Ralph Roberts, the wandering boys from *The Eyes of the Dragon*, even Father Callahan, the damned priest from *'Salem's Lot*.

It is all of a piece. Herein we discuss the books in this series and those related to it, how they are interrelated and interconnected, and how they touch upon and are likewise touched upon by the author's other works.

· · ·

The story of *The Dark Tower* unfolds as follows: In a place called Mid-world—which might be the future of a world much like our own, or a separate reality entirely—the land is divided into baronies, some ruled by an honorable rank of men called gunslingers, much like knights. One of the jewels of Mid-world is Gilead, whose lord is Steven Deschain, a gunslinger descended from the bloodline of Arthur Eld, who had united much of Mid-world in ancient times. (This is a parallel to the legend of King Arthur, of course.)

But during Steven's time, a new threat arises. John Farson, called "the good man," has begun to instigate a rebellion among the peasantry and some members of nobility against the Affiliation, the governments of the various baronies that have banded together. Traitors and spies abound. Marten, a wizard adviser to Steven, seduces the lord's wife and flaunts their intimacy in front of their son, Roland, a gunslinger-in-training. (In order to become gunslingers, students must best their teacher in battle.) Marten hopes to force Roland to an early test against his teacher, so that he will fail and be killed or banished from Gilead. Marten succeeds, but Roland defeats his instructor in single combat.

Roland is shocked to find that his father is aware of Marten's machinations. Steven prevents his son from going after Marten and tells him that Marten is working with Farson. To keep Roland safe, Steven sends his son incognito to a seaside barony called Mejis, along with his two best friends, Cuthbert and Alain, neither of whom is a full-fledged gunslinger yet. There, however, they find Farson's plans have advanced even further, and the local authorities are in league with the rebellion. It is evident that Farson, though pretending to be a hero of the people, has had sinister intentions all along. While the relationship is unclear, it is possible that he is working for Marten, rather than the other way around. Both are served by a lesser magician called Walter, who shows up in Mejis.

In Mejis, Roland falls in love with Susan Delgado, and though their love is doomed (as is Susan), it is the one true love of Roland's life. During his time by the sea, Roland comes into possession of a glass ball that is part of Maerlyn's rainbow, a powerful magical tool. In it, he sees a vision of the future, much of which he cannot remember later, but one thing remains clear to him: the Dark Tower at the center of all things, the spindle on which reality turns, has been somehow tainted. It is being corrupted, and Roland decides instantly that he must devote his life to saving the Tower.

First, he returns to Gilead, where he is tricked by a witch into killing his own mother. The time subsequent to that is shrouded in mystery. All that is known is this: Farson's efforts cause the destruction of the Affiliation and the devastation of Gilead, which only hastens the changes that are coming to the entire world—the world, as Roland says so often, is moving on. It is growing barren and empty. The only way to stop that decline is to save the Tower; and so Roland and his friends set off on a quest to find the Tower. During that mission, all of his associates, his ka-tet, die, until only he remains.

Many years later, Roland catches up with Walter, the man in black, and learns more about the true nature of the Tower. Thereafter, he begins gathering a new ka-tet from various worlds connected to his own: Eddie and Susannah Dean and Jake Chambers become gunslingers in their own right over the course of the quest. They have many adventures and hardships during their travels. Susannah becomes pregnant, though it is uncertain if the father is her husband, Eddie, or the demon that raped her. The group crosses over from one world to another and then back, through thin places between those worlds. In the New York City that Jake hails from is a rose that may be the physical embodiment of the Tower before it became tainted. The agents of chaos, or of the Beast who now guards the Tower, want it destroyed, and Roland and the others must save it.

They meet Randall Flagg on their journey, and it is revealed that he is also Marten and Maerlyn, whom Walter once said was the source of all magic in the world, and who serves the Beast. It seems likely that the Beast is also the being known as the Crimson King, who will be Roland's ultimate enemy.

That is what we know. But that is only part of the story.

As noted, the specific chronicle of Roland is the centerpiece of the series, but a great many of King's other works have direct or indirect ties to it. Flagg originally appeared in King's landmark novel *The Stand*, still widely considered to be among his best. In that book, a U.S. military research facility investigating biowarfare accidentally unleashes a virus that kills 99.9 percent of the population on Earth. In America, the survivors are plagued with dreams of a kindly old woman who serves the side of light and a dark man with blazing red eyes who serves the cause of darkness. The latter is Flagg. Over the course of the novel, the survivors join one side or the other, and eventually those who serve light must make a final stand against those who serve darkness. Flagg is defeated, and society and civilization begin anew.

At the time of *The Stand*'s publication, Flagg's part in Roland's story had yet to be revealed. In fact, the next time Flagg appeared as a major figure was in *The Eyes of the Dragon* (1987). In that fairy tale–like story, Flagg is a wizard serving a king in a medieval landscape filled with magic, a land that seems somewhat similar to but not necessarily the same as that of Roland the Gunslinger. Flagg is noted to have returned to that particular city many times over the ages. The heroes of that tale eventually defeat Flagg, but he escapes, prompting two of them, Thomas and Dennis, to embark on a hero's quest to destroy the wizard. That is a story as yet untold.

In the novella "The Little Sisters of Eluria," King clearly connects Roland's world with that of *Eyes of the Dragon*, unmistakably making them one and the same. In *The Dark Tower IV*, Roland and his ka-tet pass through a parallel dimension which is clearly that of *The Stand*, just before they finally meet Flagg face-to-face.

It remains unclear if Flagg and the being called the Crimson King are one and the same, or if Flagg serves that creature. If the latter is true, then the Crimson King is likely the same creature referred to in *The Dark Tower* as the Beast or Maerlyn, even though Flagg himself has claimed to be Maerlyn in the past. In any case, there is no doubt that Roland is a central player in service to light, and Flagg a major force for darkness.

A major theme of the *Dark Tower* series is that due to the machinations of the Crimson King (or perhaps, as noted below, a desperate act by *The Talisman*'s Jack Sawyer), the "beams" of power that emanate from the Tower and hold time, space, and all realities together are being corrupted. This phenomenon has affected all of those realities, causing the barriers between them to begin breaking down and allowing for travel from one to the next, as detailed below.

- In *Insomnia* (1994), which takes place in the parallel universe in which most of King's work unfolds, a boy sees a vision of Roland, and the main characters find themselves up against the Crimson King. They save the life of that boy, who is supposed to be important to Roland's battle against the Crimson King. According to this book, if Patrick Danville dies, the Tower will fall. Thus, Ralph, Lois, and Patrick are allied with Roland against the forces of chaos represented by the Crimson King and Flagg, among others.

- In *The Talisman* (co-authored with Peter Straub, 1983), Jack Sawyer finally gets his hands on the talisman, which is believed to represent all reality. When he removes it from the building in which it is housed, all realities flash around him, and in one of them, the building becomes a Dark Tower. Jack's removal of the talisman may have allowed the Crimson King to gain influence over the Tower. At present, King and Straub are working on a sequel to *The Talisman*, which Straub has stated will be much more specifically tied to the parallel reality of *The Dark Tower*.

- Roland recalls having met Dennis and Thomas from *The Eyes of the Dragon*, who are on a mission to destroy Flagg. King has implied that we will see them again.

- King has noted that Father Callahan of *'Salem's Lot* will play a role in the ongoing saga. Interestingly, Roland and his ka-tet are now approaching a land of darkness called Thunderclap, where it is always night and the dead roam the land. Given that Callahan will show up in Thunderclap, these dead are likely vampires. This is yet another way in which the parallel realities of the Stephen King universe infringe upon one another.

- In *IT* (1986), there is a great deal of discussion about the Turtle (a benevolent being as opposed to the Crimson King) and the Way of the Beam, both references to Roland's saga. Also, it is possible that the creature in *IT* is the Beast itself (the Crimson King), or at least one of his servants.

- In *Hearts in Atlantis*, it is revealed that the Crimson King employs humans with psychic abilities as breakers, forcing them to use their mental powers to aid in the shattering of the beams that bind the worlds together, the center of which is the Dark Tower. Once the beams are shattered, the Tower would come completely into the Crimson King's control, and he would then be able to manipulate all realities to his liking. There is also a very oblique reference in the book indicating that Randall Flagg himself is interfering in the lives of its characters. His purpose is unclear but is likely related to the characters' relationship to the breaker they meet early in the story. The protagonists may also find themselves allied with Roland and his comrades in the final battle.

• In *Rose Madder* (1995), the world that exists inside the painting is likely to be Roland's world, as there are references to the city of Lud.

This interweaving of characters and events reinforces the idea that all beings in the various parallel realities of the Stephen King universe—his main protagonists and antagonists in particular—are involved in one enormous struggle for the fate of the Dark Tower. Within the *Dark Tower* series, King introduces the idea that the beams have cosmic guardians whose avatars are animal in nature, including the Turtle, a cosmic being who actually plays a part in *IT*. There is as yet no indication that these guardians will take further part in this battle for the Tower, if they even still live.

With all of the above connections in place, one might then move further out into King's works, making links to the various stories set in Castle Rock, Derry, and Haven. Take, for instance, *The Tommyknockers* (1987). Jack Sawyer's appearance in this novel connects it to *The Talisman*. Its references to John Smith of *The Dead Zone* (1979) ties it to all of the Castle Rock books and stories. Derry is mentioned, creating a link to *IT* and *Insomnia*, and therefore to *Dark Tower*. There are more associations, but the foregoing simply serves to illustrate that all of King's stories are indeed of a piece, and that the *Dark Tower* series is the center. Almost all of King's central characters are merely soldiers and pawns, or at the very least innocent bystanders, in the grand battle for the Tower.

As for Roland's story, where will it go? Previous to the injuries King suffered in the summer of 1999, he announced his intentions to write all three of the final volumes in the series back to back, and release them simultaneously. It now appears the fifth volume to be titled *The Black House,* will be published sometime in 2001. What these books may contain is anyone's guess.

For comparison, however, we return to whence we began: the epic poem. Browning's poem concerns Roland, a knight and adventurer on a quest to find the Dark Tower. Though he never reveals the true nature of the Tower itself, Browning creates many images that King paralleled. During his quest, Roland meets a malicious being who "lied at every word." He is a devious, devilish man, and considering his placement in the poem, it seems likely that King took his inspiration for Walter, the man in black, from this character. For just as Walter gives King's Roland the drive to sally forth on his quest, so the malicious man does to Roland in the Browning poem. Why does Browning's Roland (and King's Roland) take him at his word when he seems so insidious? Simply put: the quest has been long. Trap or no, he wants it to end, wants the final battle to come, even if it should result in failure. Roland says:

> *If at his counsel I should turn aside*
> *Into that ominous tract which, all agree,*
> *Hides the Dark Tower. Yet acquiescently*
> *I did turn as he pointed: neither pride*
> *Nor hope rekindling at the end descried,*
> *So much as gladness that some end might be.*

Browning's hero longs for a conclusion, for if that means his death, he hopes to join his fallen comrades, members of "the Band" of knights, who were also on the same quest. They have all passed on, just as King's Roland has seen all of his own comrades, his ka-tet, die on the quest for the Tower. The poem also illustrates Roland's crossing of a barren wasteland where "nothing throve," a clear inspiration for King to create the landscape of *Dark Tower III: The Waste Lands* (1991). In addition, Roland's best friend is a fallen knight named Cuthbert, a relationship King echoes in *Dark Tower*.

Indeed, Browning's stanzas have been his guide all along, though King has created something infinite and grand from the inspiration he received from the British poet. Yet, if one keeps the poem in mind when pondering where the series will go from here, a fascinating and disturbing possibility presents itself. Roland approaches Thunderclap, a dark land filled with vampires, on the other side of which is End-world, where the Tower stands. In Browning's poem, Roland comes to a place where he is surrounded by hills. From that small valley, he can see the Tower. He remembers, in that last moment before the final battle, those friends he has lost. He then observes:

> *There they stood, ranged along the hillsides, met*
> *To view the last of me, a living frame*
> *For one more picture! In a sheet of flame*
> *I saw them and knew them all.*

As he is about to approach the Tower, Roland finds himself surrounded by his long-dead friends. Whatever Browning's intention might have been, this stanza inspires wild speculation. It is never revealed how Cuthbert and Alain died. When Roland reaches the Tower, will they be there in the dark, waiting for him, blood on their lips?

Whatever the ending, when King completes the saga of the Dark Tower, he will have brought closure to a creative vision unparalleled in twentieth-century fiction and in more than thirty years' worth of stories. If he desires, he can begin again with a clean slate.

What follows is a guide to each individual work in the Stephen King universe that contains the parallel realities of the *Dark Tower* series and *The Stand*. Each segment includes a discussion of a work in question and a guide to the key characters, as well as places or items where appropriate.

# 1

## *The Dark Tower: The Gunslinger*

---

"THE MAN IN BLACK fled across the desert, and the gunslinger followed." So begins Stephen King's longest work to date. Not *The Gunslinger* itself, but *The Dark Tower*, the series of which this novel is the first installment. Within its pages, the many threads of the Stephen King universe are drawn together. The quest of Roland— whose journey and epic significance to his world gives him numerous opportunities to explore other parallel universes, traveling through space and time—mirrors our own quest to understand the Stephen King universe as a whole.

As the story goes—becoming its own sort of myth, in a way— King began the saga of Roland in March 1970, and continued to return to it when the tale called to him over the course of the ensuing twelve years. He was inspired by Robert Browning's epic romantic poem, "Childe Roland to the Dark Tower Came" (1855), which was itself inspired by the legends surrounding the death of the real-life Count Roland, nephew of the emperor Charlemagne.

*The Gunslinger* is composed of five long chapters, all of which were published in the *Magazine of Fantasy and Science Fiction* between 1978 and 1981. The story defies genre classification, melding horror, fantasy, science fiction, and mystery together into what King designed as a sort of romantic epic.

Roland's world may once have been similar to our own, but what civilization there once was has been all but forgotten. The old society crumbled so long ago that it has become little more than myth, replaced by a feudal system reminiscent of mythical England before Arthur brought unity to that land. Now even that has disintegrated. The world is deteriorating rapidly, and much of what remains is barren wasteland.

It is evident that King is on a journey, just as Roland is. The author is marching forward on a quest of discovery, putting the pieces together as they are revealed to him, just as the oracle and the man in black, in their turn, reveal things to Roland. But King is also hinting, even perhaps to himself, at the greater significance that Roland must eventually play in the Stephen King universe.

> In book form, The Gunslinger was originally published in a high-priced hardcover edition limited to 10,000 copies. Perhaps because King deemed it so different from his other work, years passed before it became available in any other edition.

As a hero, Roland is perhaps King's most single-minded, implacable creation to date. When we first meet him, he has long since lost everything that ever meant anything to him. The world, as we are reminded time and again, has moved on (though it will be some time in the series before King begins to explain precisely what that means). Roland pursues the sinister man in black, the wizard named Walter, not merely to punish him for his offenses, but to learn more about the Tower itself. The Tower is revealed to be the cornerstone of all existence, holding the meaning to life and the universe (or the multiverse). Roland hopes that at the Tower, he will find . . . what? Answers? Enlightenment? It's an odd thing for such a stolid and hardened hero to seek enlightenment, to search for the secrets of the universe. Yet that is what we have here. King doesn't let Roland dwell too much on the metaphysical nature of his quest, but it's there just the same.

And Roland is effective. It is only logical to extrapolate from the dialogue between Roland and Walter at the end of *The Gunslinger* that a powerful entity has recognized in Roland the potential to do precisely what he plans. Interestingly enough, however, the force does not appear determined to stop him. Why should it? Nothing can interfere with *ka*, the word, in Roland's world, for destiny. There is more to Roland than even he knows.

As the narrative evolves, Roland must struggle to find some balance between the focus and callousness he was taught as a gunslinger, and his great capacity for love, a part of him that he regularly denies. Still, he places his quest above all else, even at the cost of the life of the boy, Jake Chambers, a member of his ka-tet.

Roland is a product of his world, a place that had already "moved on" (begun to deteriorate, suffering greatly from natural—or perhaps forced—entropy) since he was a boy, but now has broken down even further. All that is good and noble seems to have gone out of the world. Just as another modern version of the romantic epic hero, Luke Skywalker of *Star Wars,* is the last of the Jedi knights, so is Roland the last of the gunslingers, until, like Skywalker, he ventures out and begins to prepare himself for his destiny. But whereas George Lucas's creations take place a long time ago in a galaxy far, far away, King's characters feel much closer to home. There are startling similarities between Roland's world and the "real world," what we call the prime Stephen King universe, in which novels such as *The Shining* (1977) and *'Salem's Lot* (1975) take place. Sometime in the past—as evidenced by old songs and artifacts and the words of Walter—Roland's world was almost identical to the prime parallel reality of the Stephen King universe, the one that includes Castle Rock and Derry.

*King's boyhood home, Durham* | DAVID LOWELL

It is possible that Roland's world *is* the same world in which most of King's novels and stories take place, but far into the future of that world. Even more likely is that Roland's adventures take place in the future of the splinter universe (as opposed to the prime Stephen King universe) established in *The Stand* (1978, a possibility hinted at more specifically in the fourth *Dark Tower* book, *Wizard and Glass*, 1997). Roland's adventures may take place in yet another splinter universe, separate from the various other realities in which King's stories have unfolded.

Consider the similarity between Walter and the ubiquitous Randall Flagg. Though it is made perfectly clear later in the *Dark Tower* series that the two are not one and the same, they share a certain attitude and presence and seem to have a similar facility with magic. In truth, there is a great deal of confusion about the many evil mages that populate King's work—Flagg, Marten, Walter, and Maerlyn among them. Flagg and Marten turn out to be the same individual, but it is never quite clear what their relationship is to the others. Since Flagg is a walker-between-worlds—a being who can travel from one dimension/reality/universe to another—as revealed in *The Stand* and *Eyes of the Dragon* (1987), one wonders if Walter may have that talent as well.

Just as the *Dark Tower* stories are unique among King's writings, so is Roland singular among the author's protagonists. His world is one bedecked in the trappings of fantasy fiction, and yet in King's other excursions into fantasy realms, he nearly always uses children as his protagonists. Roland shares a great deal with the boys from *Eyes of the Dragon*, particularly Thomas, whose father was also a ruler named Roland, and who set himself on a quest to destroy a wizard who had brought ruin to the land of his birth. In Thomas's case, the villain was Flagg. In Roland's case, it was a sorcerer named Marten. (Later in the *Dark Tower* series, King will reveal that Marten *is* Flagg.)

There are also similarities between Roland and young Jack Sawyer of *The Talisman* (written with Peter Straub, 1983). Both seek the Tower—Roland for vengeance and truth, Jack to save his ailing mother— and both embark on an epic quest. Both have mothers who are queens in more than one way, although Roland's mother is already dead, while Jack's is ill. Both saw their parents betrayed by a trusted adviser who turned out to be a dark magician.

But the major differences between the two offer an explanation. The first is obvious: Jack reaches the Tower and retrieves the talisman. Given what we know of the Tower from the man in black and from Roland, this should be a complete impossibility. (It may be this act of Jack's that corrupted the Tower to begin with, the removal of the talisman having left it unprotected.) Jack goes to the Tower to take from it, while Roland seeks it out to restore its integrity. What Roland will find, and how it will affect the rest of the Stephen King universe, remains to be seen.

## PRIMARY SUBJECTS

*ROLAND*. A member of the warrior caste called gunslingers, Roland is the son of Gabrielle and Roland the Elder, the apparent rulers of Gilead, the realm in which Roland grew up. Thanks to civil unrest and the machinations of the sorcerers Marten and Walter (the man in black), Gilead was all but destroyed. The world moved on, suffering the predations and deterioration of entropy. The gunslingers died off or were killed, and Roland is the last of them.

Roland's quest is twofold. First, he endeavors to find the man in black and have vengeance upon him for his evil doings. Second, he must journey to the Dark Tower, where he will uncover the answers to the questions of the universe, including the very nature of reality itself. During this journey, Roland meets and later sacrifices a boy named Jake, and later spends ten years (at least, ten years pass for Roland; it might be one night for the rest of the world) entranced by the man in black on a mountaintop, after having his fortune told by the sorcerer. His quest, though he has already been at it for a very long time, is merely beginning.

*WALTER*. A powerful sorcerer who manipulates and topples rulers, Walter spreads his influence and perpetuates evil all at the command of an even more powerful being called Marten (a.k.a. Maerlyn, the Ageless Stranger, Randall Flagg). Walter leads Roland on a chase across the desert and to the mountains, where he reads Roland's fortune and gives him a psychic vision revealing the true nature of the secrets within the Tower. He then dies, having served his purpose.

*MAERLYN/MARTEN/FLAGG.* Also known as the Ageless Stranger, Maerlyn is a being of extraordinary power and magic. He lives backward in time, yet exists in all times simultaneously. It has been implied that he is also the Merlin of Old England in the days of King Arthur. Yet even Maerlyn is not his own master, for he serves the Beast, guardian of the Tower. As Marten, he was a sorcerer and enchanter. He manipulated Roland's father, Steven Deschain, and seduced Steven's wife, which led to the ruin of Gilead. As Randall Flagg, he has performed many heinous deeds throughout the multiverse and will recur in story after story.

*THE BEAST.* "To speak of the Beast," Walter tells Roland, "is to speak of the ruination of one's own soul." This creature, whatever it may be, is guardian of the Tower and is purported to be in some way the creator of all magics and enchantments.

*JAKE CHAMBERS.* Jake is not from Roland's reality, but from some other dimension. In his own reality, his life comes to an end when he is pushed in front of an oncoming car. Instead of dying, however, Jake is somehow transported to Roland's world. Briefly, he joins Roland on his quest. When Roland is forced to choose between catching the man in black or letting Jake fall to his death, Roland lets the boy die.

*STEVEN DESCHAIN/ROLAND THE ELDER.* Lord of Gilead, father to Roland, husband to Gabrielle, he is betrayed by his wife and his confidante, Marten, and it costs him his life. How he came to be sometimes called Roland the Elder is yet unknown.

*CORT.* Cort is the instructor who teaches the boys of Gilead everything they need to know to become gunslingers. He instructs them in weaponry, as well as in hand-to-hand combat and strategy. In order to "graduate," a gunslinger must defeat Cort in single combat. Roland becomes the youngest gunslinger ever to do so. Cort later dies, but the manner of his death is as yet unrevealed.

*CUTHBERT.* During their youth, Cuthbert was Roland's best friend. In time, he became a gunslinger. As Roland is the last of the gunslingers, it must be presumed that Cuthbert is dead.

*DAVID.* In order to defeat Cort and take his place among the ranks of gunslingers, Roland must choose a single weapon. He selects his falcon, David.

*GABRIELLE.* Roland's mother, Gabrielle, is the bride of the ruler of Gilead, but she betrays her husband by sleeping with Marten, the enchanter. She is later accidentally killed by her own son.

*HAX.* A cook in the service of Roland's father, Hax turns out to be a traitor and is hanged by the Gilead authorities. Roland attends the execution.

*SUSAN.* The only woman Roland ever loved, Susan was a part of his life some years ago. She was burned to death, but at this time no other circumstances of her fate are known.

*THE TOWER.* Almost impossible to define, the Tower seems to be time and space incarnate. It is perhaps some kind of order placed on the necessary and infinite chaos of the multiverse. Within the physical existence of the Tower lies all the knowledge, magical and otherwise, in existence. Roland is determined to find it.

## 2

## *The Dark Tower II:*
## *The Drawing of the Three*

---

I N THE FIRST VOLUME of the *Dark Tower* series, 1982's *The Gunslinger,* King introduced his readers to Roland of Gilead. At the time of its release, in a limited edition, the first book was an oddity, a fantasy novel with a western motif by the acknowledged master of horror. Five years later, *The Drawing of the Three* was released, also in a limited edition, readers remained unaware that King had embarked on the greatest literary journey of his career and had invited them along on the trip. In many ways, the series is the fundamental work on which all of the author's other writings, before or since, are built.

As detailed in the comparatively brief first volume, *The Gunslinger,* Roland is on a quest to find the Dark Tower, which others have insisted is only a myth. Roland believes the Tower is not only real but holds the secrets of the universe. There he believes he will find an explanation for the manner in which his world has fallen apart or "moved on," as he so often thinks of it.

In *The Drawing of the Three,* King accomplishes something intriguing. Roland uses magical portals to enter other worlds and draws from them two individuals who will go on to become a new generation of gunslingers, replacing his dead comrades. One of them is Eddie Dean, whose presence creates a fascinating twist to the Stephen King universe. While King's various writings take place in a multitude of realms—all of which we posit herein are connected to one another—the world Eddie Dean comes from is the real world. In Eddie's world, for example, there exists a film called *The Shining*, directed by Stanley Kubrick and based on a novel by Stephen King. It is an obvious extrapolation to posit that King and Eddie live in the same world. Therefore, since King exists in our world, it is possible to say that all of us, including your brother and mother and third cousins, also exist in the same world with Eddie. And that world is part of the Stephen King universe.

*King's West Broadway mansion in Bangor* | VINTAGE POSTCARD

Thanks to the presence of Eddie Dean in this story, we are all, you and I and Stephen King himself, a part of the Stephen King universe. A part, then, of the imminent final battle for control of the Tower and the fate of all reality.

•   •   •

*The Drawing of the Three* was first released in 1987 in a limited edition from Donald M. Grant Publishers—which has published the hardcover editions of each of the books in the series—and sometime later in a trade paperback version from Plume.

While *The Gunslinger* introduced us to Roland, his quest, and the basic concepts of his world, this second volume does not advance him substantially along his journey. Rather, King spends time doing precisely what the title implies, drawing together Roland's team in the same way that bands of adventurers have gathered around heroes throughout myth and popular fiction—Robin Hood's merry men, the Apostles, the X-Men. They are ka-tet.

That is what *The Drawing of the Three* really is about, though we as readers don't quite understand that early on. In Roland's world, *ka-tet* means a great many things, one of which is family. It can be a group of people—usually without actual blood relation—bound together by duty, obligation, love, and common objectives. But in many ways, it is more vital and real even than family, because there are other definitions of *ka-tet*, specifically that it is a group of people bound together by destiny. Fate has inextricably linked them together, for better or worse. This may define an alliance, or it may explain the hatred of sworn enemies—they are destined to destroy one another. In this case, we are speaking of the former.

Over the course of this volume, Roland travels from his reality (or dimension) into others through mystical portals that appear inexplicably on the beach, placed there by some unknowable, benevolent force. By way of these portals, he enters the minds of individuals in other worlds and can assert control over them physically. He is even able to bring things—and people—back from those worlds. He visits three variant realities in this fashion, or quite possibly three different time periods of the same reality. During these trips, Roland abruptly abducts two people who will in time become part of the new order of gunslingers. Eddie Dean comes from New York City circa 1987. Odetta Holmes, a legless woman with multiple-personality syndrome, comes from New York City circa 1963. The last of the three is apparently Susannah, the woman who eventually comes forth when Odetta's two personalities merge.

Roland visits a third reality, however. There he jumps into the mind of a murderer named Jack Mort—whose last name, of course, means death—mentally inhabiting his body just as he did Eddie's and Odetta's before drawing them through. Mort thinks of himself as "the pusher." But it isn't drugs he pushes, it's people. In fact—and here is the kind of thing that in the world of *The Dark Tower* cannot be coincidence—Mort is responsible for the injury that caused Odetta's multiple personalities to develop, as well as a second incident that led to the loss of her legs. Further, Mort is responsible for the death of Jake Chambers in *The Gunslinger*. Jake is a young boy from a parallel-reality Earth (which we later discover is the same reality from which Eddie Dean hails) who dies in his reality, only to somehow awaken in Roland's. Forced to decide whether to save Jake's life or finally catch up with the man in black, Roland lets Jake die, a deed over which he agonizes.

In *The Drawing of the Three*, Roland has a chance to undo that wrong. When Jack Mort moves to push Jake in front of the car that will kill him, Roland is psychically along for the ride. At the critical moment, he commandeers control of Mort's mind and prevents Jake's death. This redemptive action will set up a maddening incongruity between the two dimensions that Roland must deal with in volume 3. There is an implication that Jake will become a member of the newly developed ka-tet; indeed, he will. Already it seems that the members of this ka-tet are intrinsically linked to one another.

Through Roland's intervention, Odetta is able to unify her two disparate personalities, merging to become one woman named Susannah Dean, as she now considers herself Eddie's wife. This is another link in the chain that binds them together. Though Roland's quest seems to halt during the events of this story, Roland himself continues to grow as an individual. He is a cold, practical, single-minded man, and yet the presence of Eddie and Susannah and the forming of a new ka-tet begins to bring about a change in him. Roland does not become softer—that would be the death of him. He does, however, become more aware of what is happening around him, and the feelings of those with whom he is now forever linked. Still, it is clear that his quest for the Tower supersedes any such humane concerns. Nothing is too precious to be sacrificed in favor of the quest. We are told this time and again, and it will prove true often.

We have suggested that the quest does not truly advance in this story. This is not entirely true. Volume 2 opens with Roland on the beach, and he spends most of the story there, walking along the shore in a direction his instincts tell him is the right one. At intervals along the way he comes upon the doors through which the three are drawn. Thereafter, they continue on their way. Though they travel many miles, their external progress is only in the building of Roland's ka-tet with Eddie and Susannah. The real progress in this tale is almost entirely internal, in the *preparation* to reach the Tower. The team is molded; bonds are formed, almost as though these were necessary rituals leading to the inward transformation of the characters.

What this accomplishes, in a more concrete way, is the formulation of identity for all three characters. Roland, the last gunslinger, seeks to redefine himself in a world that has moved on and has no more use for his kind. He seeks to find the truth about his virtue, the answer to his own questions about what kind of man he truly is in the aftermath of Jake's death. Eddie, for his part, strives to find the identity at his core, beneath the despicable surface of a drug-addicted loser so dependent on an enabling relationship with his brother. He strives to find within him the man he knew he could be, and he succeeds. Odetta/Susannah's quest for identity is, of course, the most obvious of the three. Her split personalities—the erudite, wealthy Odetta Holmes and the vulgar, furious, and uneducated Detta Walker—are both aspects of her self, but she is not a whole being until those aspects are united in Susannah Dean.

The characters' identity quests are individual, but each could not be realized without the other. This is yet another facet of ka-tet. Separately, their paths are unclear, their wills—with the exception of Roland's—wavering. But together they become strong, the whole process feeding strength and purpose back into the parts.

Finally, within *The Drawing of the Three*, we actually learn very little about the Tower itself and the nature of the Stephen King universe as a whole. This is, perhaps, to be expected in what is only the second volume of a much longer story. Where Roland's quest will finally lead, only King himself knows.

## PRIMARY SUBJECTS

*ROLAND.* Last survivor of an order of warriors called gunslingers, Roland is also prince of Gilead, a realm that is no more. Though the destruction of Gilead and the circumstances surrounding the deaths of many of his family and friends are unclear at this point, Roland is on his own, and must begin anew by gathering a new breed of gunslingers that he himself must train.

In volume 2, he encounters doors into other dimensions, from which he brings back both Eddie Dean and the woman who will become known as Susannah Dean. They are to be the new gunslingers and members of Roland's ka-tet, who join him on the quest for the Dark Tower. The quest is his fate and his destiny. Roland presses forward with his new companions, drawing ever closer to the Tower.

*EDDIE DEAN.* The first to be drawn into Roland's world, Eddie is a junkie living in New York City. He seems weak at first, due to his addiction and his fear of drug lord Rico Balazar. But the death of his brother and his experiences in Roland's world strip away that outer shell to reveal a strong and dangerous man within.

Eddie goes through a torrent of emotions brought on by the other new arrival, a woman who suffers from multiple-personality disorder. He begins to fall in love with one of her personae, Odetta Holmes, even though he is terrified—and rightly so—of her other, Detta Walker. Eventually, however, the two personalities of the woman are merged into Susannah, who becomes Eddie's wife. Eddie comes to terms with his destiny and now dedicates himself to the quest for the Tower.

> *Balazar the drug dealer is purportedly involved with a Mafioso thug named Ginelli, who appears in a much more prominent role in* Thinner *(1984).*

*SUSANNAH DEAN.* Susannah began her life as Odetta Holmes. When she was a young girl, Jack Mort dropped a brick on her head. As a result, she developed a second personality, that of a crass, vicious woman named Detta Walker. Later, after Mort pushes her in the path of a subway train and she loses her legs as a result, her condition worsens. Through the efforts of Eddie and Roland, Odetta is able to merge her two selves into the woman named Susannah Dean. She now considers herself married to Eddie, and has also dedicated herself to the quest and to the ka-tet that the three have formed.

*JAKE CHAMBERS.* A boy from an alternate New York City, Jake dies in his own world, only to awaken mysteriously, and later die, in Roland's reality.

Later, Roland travels in mind and spirit to Jake's reality. Arriving before the boy's first death, Roland psychically enters the body of Jack Mort, "the pusher." Roland soon realizes that Mort is the man who will later push Jake in front of the car that kills him. Roland kills Mort, creating a glitch in the time-space continuum. If Mort is dead, then Jake will not die in this reality, and thus, will not come to Roland's world, where he dies a second death. It is a paradox that will later cause a great deal of trouble for both Roland and Jake.

*JACK MORT.* Mort is a twisted man who is a sort of "serial pusher," shoving people into the path of speeding cars or subway trains. Some of his victims, including Jake Chambers, die. Others, such as Odetta Holmes, aren't as fortunate. Mort is one of the three people Roland mentally "enters" and is able to control. Just before he leaves Mort's body, Roland forces the killer to jump in front of a speeding train. Thus, Mort faces death in the same manner as had his victims.

*FLAGG.* A creature of magic, Flagg appears to be a sorcerer, though Roland believes he might actually be a demon disguised as a man. Years earlier, Roland saw Flagg near the end of the chaos that destroyed Gilead, but that story has yet to be told in full.

## 3

# *The Dark Tower III: The Waste Lands*

---

WHILE PREVIOUS VOLUMES in the *Dark Tower* series concern themselves almost exclusively with Roland's quest, in *The Waste Lands* King at last begins to elaborate on the world of Roland's birth. There is, of course, a great deal more than that going on in volume 3, chief among them the solidifying of the relationships among the main characters and their development as gunslingers. However, the bits and pieces supplied to readers regarding the nature of this world are also vital.

*The Waste Lands* first appeared in 1991 in a limited-edition hardcover from Donald M. Grant Publishers, but this time there was a shorter wait before the trade paperback appeared. This new speed seems to be reflective of the quickening pace at which King returns to the story of the last gunslinger. Though there are still years between each book, they are coming forth more quickly. To quote King, "The Tower draws ever closer."

Which is odd, considering King's revelations about Roland's world in *The Waste Lands*. It is, in fact, an extraordinary domain. Thousands of years earlier, when the world first began to break down, it was apparently repaired and maintained by the civilized race of that time, remembered in Roland's era as the Great Old Ones. They did not create the world, but seem to have re-created it. To do this, they built a technological marvel, apparently tapping into the natural—and perhaps supernatural—energies of the planet. With the Tower as the focal point, or nexus, the old ones built twelve portals to other dimensions—apparently the source of the power needed for their Herculean task—so that the invisible beams or circuits between each pair of opposing poles would intersect at a central point: the Tower.

Once upon a time, the twelve portals were at equal distances all around the world. But since that time, the world has moved on. Which brings us to the most mind-boggling element of all this. The portals and beams and the huge cyborg animal guardians left to guard those entrances are farther away than they once were, and they are all breaking down. Entropy is winning the day. As a result, the power of the beams is waning, and the very thing that they were created to prevent is happening at an accelerated pace.

Like those mechanical constructs, the world is running down, rusting. At the same time, it is spreading. Impossible as it may seem to us, Roland's world is quite literally growing and expanding. A distance that was once a thousand miles might now be twenty times that. This is apparently a direct result of the Tower weakening or being tainted by the machinations of the forces of darkness or chaos represented by the Crimson King. (As noted, it is a process that may have begun with Jack Sawyer removing the talisman from the Tower in the book of the same name.)

Due to this expansion, to the world "moving on," Roland has been on his quest for more than twenty years. In that time, we discover, he has lost all his remaining friends. It seems that when he set about his task, he was not alone. Which of his former comrades-at-arms were with him is unclear, but they are dead now. Or are they? Certainly they have passed on physically. But King is at pains here to tell us that Roland's new ka-tet is almost a reincarnation of the original. Eddie reminds Roland very much of his best friend Cuthbert, while Susannah's passion reminds him of another gunslinger and friend, Alain.

In this installment, King introduces us to fascinating and complex ideas about this world, and implies connections and relationships without ever slowing down the pace of the quest itself. In addition to the bizarre nature of the world's condition, there is the time paradox, which is slowly driving Roland insane. By killing Jack Mort in the previous volume, Roland prevented the death of Jake Chambers, which means that Jake was never transported to Roland's world, never met Roland, and never was sacrificed by Roland.

Though Roland once allowed Jake to fall to his death, he has now seemingly redeemed himself. However, Roland and Jake, in their respective worlds, are being driven mad by the fact that they each retain two sets of memories from the dual realities in which Jake both died and did not die. Once again, King takes a complex idea and turns it into yet another obstacle on the road to the Tower.

*King's home, Bangor* | DAVID LOWELL

But ka is more powerful. To save Roland from going insane, Jake must be drawn back into Roland's world. When we see Jake, ka is drawing him inexorably toward the place where he will cross over into Roland's world once more. He comes to an empty lot wherein grows a single, perfect rose. This flower seems destined to play a major role in the story, as Jake is convinced that the rose must be protected. Roland seems to believe that the rose is somehow an incarnation of the Tower itself. But that is a story that is sure to be told to us later.

Jake at last is drawn into Roland's realm again, and he and Roland finally are at peace. Yet the ka-tet is not complete. That is achieved only with the arrival of Oy, a furry little creature whom Jake takes to right away. Oy is a billy-bumbler, a species of animal known in Roland's world for their ability to mimic human speech in an almost parrotlike fashion. Yet Oy seems to know what he's saying at times.

Together, the five forge ahead, and we learn more about Roland's world—this land that is moving on, apparently to its eventual demise. Few children are born. Memories of the past have grown vague and unclear. Those who survive respond in a variety of ways. Some, like those at the River Crossing settlement, exist in peace. Others, like the Pubes and Grays in the city of Lud (also discussed in *Rose Madder*), continue to feud decades after they have forgotten what the conflict is about.

Before they reach Lud, however, Roland's ka-tet comes upon a downed airplane. Within that craft they find the remains of David Quick, a widely renowned outlaw prince of local legend. But the plane is even more interesting, coming as it does from the World War II Germany of Jake, Eddie, and Susannah's world. Crossing over is not nearly as uncommon as we might once have believed.

We also learn more about the nature of ka-tet, in that all three of Roland's gunslingers-in-training have at one time read a book called *Charlie the Choo-Choo*, which, unbeknownst to them, is directly connected to this grand adventure they now share. Also, though Eddie doesn't remember, he and Jake crossed paths once before, when Eddie was not much older than Jake is now. That kind of time paradox is the nature of the Tower, but it also establishes one fact for certain. Jake, Eddie, and Susannah all come from different times in the same world or dimension, or the same "level of the Tower," as Blaine the Mono (the psychotic, split-personality train) notes later.

The city of Lud is a nightmarish place, where the last remaining residents are split into two groups. The Grays are led by the Tick-Tock Man, later revealed to be Andrew Quick, descendant of the outlaw David Quick. The Tick-Tock Man's followers include the vicious Gasher, who steals Jake away from the ka-tet briefly. While Roland and Oy are rescuing Jake, Eddie and Susannah seek the Cradle, or train station, of Lud, wherein they finally meet Blaine the Mono. On the way, they are forced to deal with the Grays' enemies, the Pubes, who are killing themselves off in a mournful, despairing kind of lottery. The Grays are nearly all dead, including Gasher, but unbeknownst to Roland and Jake, the Tick-Tock Man survives and is recruited by a mysterious demon-sorcerer who introduces himself as Richard Fannin, and also states that he has been known as Maerlyn or the Ageless Stranger.

It is at that moment that the dominoes begin to fall, when the tale of the Dark Tower begins to draw together with all the other chronicles in the Stephen King universe. For Richard Fannin is clearly the same being as Randall Flagg of *The Stand* (1978) and *The Eyes of the Dragon* (1987).

> *In a small bookstore, Jake meets the proprietor, a man with the suggestive name Calvin Tower, and buys a copy of* Charlie the Choo-Choo. *Tower congratulates Jake on his willingness to "saddle up and light out for the territories," most certainly a reference to* The Talisman.

Fannin notes that one of his other followers worshiped him with the words "my life for you," which is right out of *The Stand.*

In the first volume of the series, Walter describes the Ageless Stranger as being the agent of the Beast that guards the Tower. Therefore, it seems clear that Flagg and Roland are destined to confront each other. King also implies in his afterword that Walter may in fact *be* the Ageless Stranger, a.k.a. Flagg, meaning he was Roland's enemy from the very start.

This installment concludes with a cliffhanger, as the ka-tet are traveling along the path of the beam toward the Tower, aboard a suicidal train who will carry them to their deaths if they cannot stump him in a game of riddles.

## PRIMARY SUBJECTS

*ROLAND.* The gunslinger, son of the last lord of Gilead, Roland, has been on a quest for the Dark Tower over the course of many years and has lost everything and everyone most dear to him. He has gone on to gather a new ka-tet, those who will become a new rank of gunslingers, and with them his quest continues. As this portion of his tale comes to a close, he and his friends are trapped onboard Blaine the Mono, a sentient, insane monorail train.

*EDDIE DEAN*. Eddie was a drug addict on his world before Roland fetches him through dimensions, and now participates in Roland's quest against his will. Now, though, Roland's search has become Eddie's. He is the husband of Susannah. Eddie does not realize it until much later, but when he was a boy he came into contact with Jake Chambers, establishing that Eddie and Jake are from the same dimension, though not from the same time. Despite his fears and reservations, Eddie is becoming a gunslinger.

*SUSANNAH DEAN*. Like her husband, Eddie, Susannah is drawn from another time and place to become part of Roland's quest. During an attempt to distract an invisible demon from their efforts to bring Jake Chambers over into Roland's world, Susannah is raped by the monster. Legless, bound to her wheelchair, she nevertheless is becoming a gunslinger.

*JAKE CHAMBERS*. The first time they met, Roland let Jake die. Later, by traveling through time, Roland saved the boy before that death ever occurred. This created a time paradox that nearly drove them both mad. With help from Eddie and Susannah, Roland draws Jake back into his world, eliminating the paradox. Jake is now an integral part of the ka-tet and the quest for the Tower.

*OY*. One of a breed of creatures called billy-bumblers, Oy becomes part of the group by sheer accident. Later, he saves Jake's life and possibly Roland's as well, in battle with the Tick-Tock Man and Gasher.

*BLAINE*. An insane monorail train with a fondness for riddles, Blaine is currently racing toward destruction, with Roland and his ka-tet aboard.

*LITTLE BLAINE*. The "sane," smaller voice of Blaine the monorail, another personality of its artificial intelligence.

*RICHARD FANNIN.* Fannin is also known as the Magician or the Wizard, Merlin, Maerlyn, and, quite obviously, given his conversation with the Tick-Tock Man, as Randall Flagg. A being of as yet undefined evil power, he is Roland's nemesis.

*THE TICK-TOCK MAN.* The Tick-Tock Man is Andrew Quick, son of the legendary giant David Quick, who apparently originated in another world and came to Roland's. He controlled most of the city of Lud before Roland, Jake, and Oy came his way. Oy and Roland did him some damage, and he appears to have been dead until Flagg discovers him. Currently, the Tick-Tock Man serves Flagg.

*SHARDIK and THE GUARDIANS.* Like the Turtle, Shardik the Bear is one of the guardians of the portals of the beam. The beam or beams are bands of invisible energy that hold the world, and possibly all worlds, together. At their epicenter is the Tower. Each of the beams has a guardian at its termination point. In Roland's world, cybernetic guardians have been built to represent their more cosmic counterparts. One of these is Shardik, who goes mad and is destroyed by Roland's ka-tet.

*CUTHBERT.* Cuthbert was a childhood friend of Roland's and later a gunslinger. Cuthbert is dead, but the manner of his demise has yet to be revealed.

*ALAIN.* A childhood friend of Roland's who later also became a gunslinger. The circumstances of Alain's death have yet to be revealed.

# 4

## *The Dark Tower IV: Wizard and Glass*

D ONALD M. GRANT Publishers released the fourth volume of
*The Dark Tower* in 1997. Here, King once again returned to the
fantastic world of Roland of Gilead. This time, however, the trade
paperback edition quickly followed. The clamor for the next segment
in the story—the tale that increasingly appears to be at the center of
the Stephen King universe—had grown so loud that getting it into
readers' hands had become vital.

Before the 1999 automobile accident that sidelined King from
writing for a brief period, the author announced a plan that seemed to
speak to the enthusiasm for the series. He would write the final three
volumes of the *Dark Tower* series back to back and release them
simultaneously. At this writing, there is no word on when those volumes will actually be written or published. Meanwhile, the demand
grows ever stronger. One might imagine that the clamor is not merely
in the voices of his readers, but in the mind of King as well. Roland's
world is moving on.

King's universe is moving on too. The skeins of his fictions have
been drawing together for some time, and they seem to be gathering
speed as they approach an ending. How long his injuries will delay the
author remains to be seen.

In the meantime, however, *Wizard and Glass* remains a fascinating book, though a frustrating place to stop Roland's story. The book
continues the journey of Roland's new ka-tet, but perhaps more

important, it tells the tale of his very first ka-tet, composed of his good friends and fellow gunslingers (though they were but children at the time), Cuthbert and Alain, and the only woman he ever truly loved, Susan Delgado.

*Wizard and Glass* is a history, then, but it is also very much a western. In truth, only by reading this fourth volume does one realize that *all* of Roland's stories are westerns. The slow mutants or Blaine the Mono or robot bears or demons and sorcerers might throw one off the track of the sagebrush genre but in the end, they really are all components of classic western stories, the kind of thing John Ford might have directed if he and King had ever had the opportunity to work together.

While *Wizard and Glass* is the fourth installment in the series, in so many ways it is also the true beginning of everything. It is here that we learn more of Roland's backstory than we might ever have hoped King would share. Roland's father, Steven Deschain, was a gunslinger, a member of the elite ruling class of the many baronies that made up the Affiliation, which itself had descended over many centuries, so legend had it, from King Arthur himself. Arthur, Maerlyn, Excalibur—all are known to Roland's world.

Believing Roland to be a roadblock to the plans he shares with John Farson, the would-be usurper of the Affiliation, the wizard Marten seduces Roland's mother and allows the boy to discover them. Marten knows that the angry Roland will try to "graduate" early, and win the title and weapons of a gunslinger. He hopes Roland will fail and be sent west. Roland does not fail, and becomes the youngest gunslinger in Gilead's history. He is horrified to learn that his mother's infidelity has not escaped Steven's attention, and that his father has allowed it to go on because of the greater issues at hand. A dark time is coming in which Farson will bring war to the land, and Steven wants his son out of danger.

Roland is dispatched, along with his friends Cuthbert and Alain, to the oceanside town of Mejis for their safety. There they discover a plot against the old ways, and in favor of John Farson. Over the course of the conflict that ensues, they find a glass ball with great power, one of the last surviving pieces of Maerlyn's rainbow. The great enchanter had once owned a great many of these powerful objects, in all the colors of the rainbow.

It is when the ball is in Roland's possession—and he in its (for the ball has a horrible hold on those who behold it)—that he has his first real glimpse of the Dark Tower, and the future that awaits him and his ka-tet. Most of the vision he forgets. But from that point on, he knows there is a sickness at the Tower. Only by curing that sickness and destroying whatever had tainted it can he right all the wrong with the world. If he succeeds, he can pull the skeins back together and reverse the process by which the world is "moving on."

In the end, having triumphed over their enemies in Mejis—and paying the horrible price of Susan Delgado's life—Roland and his friends move on, poised for the quest that Roland will pursue for the rest of his life. But before that search begins, Roland suffers a horrible blow. In a cruel twist of fate—manipulated by magic—he ends up murdering his own mother, a sin for which he can never forgive himself.

*Wizard and Glass* combines many genres. Tragedy is one, western another. It is also a love story. The romance and passion of Roland's relationship with Susan is related so powerfully that their rightness for each other is undeniable. "Ka like a wind" is a statement repeated time and again in this book. King's romantic relationships—such as that between Ben and Susan in *'Salem's Lot* (1975) and between Fran and Stu in *The Stand* (1978)—are always sweet, natural, and real, but never so real as here, never so intense and undeniable as within these pages.

With the sacrifice of Susan, the murder of his mother, and his vision of the future, we truly begin to see the heart of Roland the gunslinger, Roland of Gilead, who had once, in the village of Tull, slaughtered the entire populace and seemed so inhumanly cold. We see, also, that in order to be more than a cold-hearted killer, to be human, Roland must surround himself with friends, with ka-tet, with those doomed to join him on his quest. There are previous comparisons, but now we see why Eddie Dean, with his sharp wit and hot temper, reminds Roland so much of Cuthbert, and why Susannah, with her gentle smile belying her cold steel mind, recalls Alain. Then there is the boy, Jake, who appears, even more than the others, destined to a fate of unspeakable pain and horror.

A great deal is contained in *Wizard and Glass;* it offers much detail and establishes the foundations of the chronicle that will bring King's multiverse together. When Roland's ka-tet pass through a "thinny," a place where the barrier between parallel worlds is thin, they wind up in the world of *The Stand.* It is not the world Jake, Eddie, or Susannah come from, but because the world is moving on, because the Tower is being slowly corrupted, the barriers between worlds are thinning even further. Which means that the superflu, Captain Trips, can begin to make its way through those barriers.

King's worlds, his universes, are imploding and merging. Nowhere is this more evident than in the presence here of Randall Flagg. His identity was hinted at in *The Waste Lands* (1991). Here, all pretense is dropped. Flagg, it appears, has been Roland's enemy all along. Not only is Flagg also Marten the enchanter, but he is Maerlyn as well. And if Walter, the man in black, is to be trusted (and if he is not also Flagg in some way), then Maerlyn is the servant of the Beast that guards the Tower.

Flagg is far more than we ever imagined. "All hail the Crimson King," say some of the graffiti in the world where people are torn between Mother Abagail (see p. 86) and Randall Flagg. Although it is not entirely clear, it seems possible that Flagg himself is the Crimson King. In *Insomnia* (1994), we are told by a small boy that Roland is also a king, and that he will come into final conflict with the Crimson King. This seems to be inevitable now, for Roland is, after all, the last descendant of King Arthur, and if the Crimson King is Flagg . . . well, Flagg, of course, is Maerlyn.

In the end, Roland and his ka-tet are back on the path of the beam, back on the road west, heading for the Dark Tower. King tells us that they will come to a dark land called Thunderclap, where other threads, other stories, other universes may intertwine.

The world moves on again.

The final conflict is yet to come.

## PRIMARY SUBJECTS

*ROLAND.* The gunslinger, whose last name seems to be Deschain, has now completed the gathering of his new ka-tet, a band of raw gun-slingers drawn from other worlds who join him for the final leg of his quest. Roland, we have learned, is the son of the last lord of Gilead, a descendant of Arthur Eld, an ancient king who united the baronies as an Affiliation.

Sent to Mejis as a teenager by his father, Roland met and fell in love with Susan Delgado. In Mejis, he and his friends foil a plot by the locals to aid the efforts of John Farson to destroy the Affiliation. It is also there that he comes into contact with the powerful glass ball that is part of Maerlyn's rainbow, and it gives him glimpses of the future, launching him on his quest for the Dark Tower. Many years later, with his new ka-tet, Roland begins to learn just how serious the threat of the Dark Tower's corruption is, not merely to his world, but to all worlds. He finally meets Flagg, his true enemy, face to face. He remains on the road with his ka-tet.

*EDDIE DEAN.* Eddie is the member of the ka-tet who figures out how to destroy Blaine the Mono, saving all of their lives just in time. He is drawn out of another time and place to become part of Roland's quest. At first he is pulled in against his will. Now, though, Roland's quest has become Eddie's.

*SUSANNAH DEAN.* Like her husband, Eddie, Susannah is drawn from another time and place to become part of Roland's quest. However, Susannah holds a dark secret from her husband that only Roland knows: she is pregnant, and her offspring might be Eddie's, or it might be that of the demon that raped her.

*JAKE CHAMBERS.* Despite his extremely complicated personal history with Roland, Jake is now an integral part of the ka-tet.

*OY.* Thanks in part to the actions of Flagg, Oy is an important part of the ka-tet.

*BLAINE.* An insane monorail train, Blaine runs from Roland's world into another dimension where a plague called Captain Trips has decimated most of the population. It has a fondness for riddles. Eddie eventually drives it even more insane, and Blaine is destroyed.

*LITTLE BLAINE.* The "sane," smaller voice of Blaine the monorail, another personality of its artificial intelligence.

*STEVEN DESCHAIN.* Son of Henry the Tall, Steven is descended from Arthur Eld himself. He was rightful Lord of the Barony of Gilead at the time of its destruction and his death. The details of those dark times are still unclear.

*CUTHBERT.* One of Roland's closest friends, they are together in Mejis when Roland first learns of the Dark Tower, and the danger to all things posed by its deterioration. Cuthbert joins Roland on his quest, but dies before completing it.

*ALAIN.* Another of Roland's closest friends, Alain also accompanied Roland to Mejis. It seems likely that Alain later joins Roland on his mission, but dies before completing it.

*SUSAN DELGADO.* A young girl living in the village of Hambry in the barony of Mejis, Susan falls in love with Roland, though she has been promised to the mayor of Hambry, Hart Thorin. She breaks that promise by becoming Roland's lover. In the end, thanks in great part to the hideous actions of her cruel aunt, Cordelia Delgado, Susan is burned to death by the townspeople for actions impugned to her.

*RHEA.* A witch who lives on the outskirts of Hambry, Rhea is keeper of one of the pieces of Maerlyn's rainbow for a time. Despite her magic, it corrupts her, sucking the life out of her. That is not what kills her, however, and the circumstances of her death have yet to be revealed. After the events in Hambry, she uses her magic to manipulate Roland into murdering his own mother. He sees her again, but those events have yet to be revealed.

*ELDRED JONAS.* The leader of a trio of hired guns called the Big Coffin Hunters, Eldred once dreamed of being a gunslinger. He failed the final test, however, and, like all those who did, was sent west, excommunicated from the Affiliation. Though he is eventually killed by Roland, it is interesting to note that according to his associates, Jonas bragged of having traveled to other worlds through "special doors." These must have been thinnys, but the circumstances of such travel have yet to be revealed.

*SHEEMIE.* A slow boy who lives in Hambry, Sheemie is a friend to Roland, Susan, and the others and part of their ka-tet. When they go in search of the Dark Tower, he accompanies them. His fate is yet unrevealed.

*JOHN FARSON.* A mysterious figure, always referred to but thus far unseen, Farson leads the revolt against the Affiliation. It seems Farson either is not what he seems, or serves a dark force far greater than himself.

*WALTER.* A magician and apparently a servant of Flagg's (though that relationship is still unclear), Walter at least appears to be a servant of John Farson's, and first crosses paths with Roland (or nearly does) in Hambry. Later, of course, it is Walter whom Roland pursues across the desert. He dies on the mountain after giving Roland visions of the future.

*MAERLYN'S RAINBOW.* It is said that Maerlyn has thirteen objects of power, one for each of the twelve guardians of the portals, and one for the nexus point of the beams that connect those portals. The nexus point, of course, is the Dark Tower. These objects are glass balls, most of which have apparently been destroyed. By looking into one of them, Roland is given a vision of the Dark Tower and of the future.

# 5

## The Eyes of the Dragon

---

**W**ITHOUT A DOUBT, *The Eyes of the Dragon* is a book for young readers. As such it is a strange addition to the canon of Stephen King. As the story goes, King's daughter, Naomi, complained to her father that he never wrote anything she would want to (or be allowed to?) read. King set out to do just that, and dedicated the book to both Naomi and Ben Straub, son of his longtime friend and one-time collaborator, Peter Straub. Indeed, it is obvious who the "Ben" and "Naomi" characters in the book are named after.

This novel is a fairy tale, told in a serious yet whimsical voice. It is a story of long ago, a story told at bedtime, perhaps. It has magic and kings and clever princes, intrigue and poisons and brave young girls. The protagonists are two young princes, Peter and Thomas, who live in the kingdom of Delain. When the court magician, the evil Flagg, kills their father, he makes it appear as though the elder prince, Peter, did the deed. A shrewd young man, Peter would have inherited the throne and likely tossed Flagg out of Delain moments after being crowned. But Flagg has prepared for that eventuality by manipulating young Thomas. Thomas has always felt that in their father's eyes he could not live up to his older brother's example. Flagg plays on that until Thomas is almost entirely his creature. When Peter is framed for the king's murder—though Thomas knows it is Flagg who is responsible—the younger brother does not make any attempt to help the elder.

Thomas becomes monarch, and Peter is imprisoned at the top of the Needle, a narrow tower that stands at the center of the kingdom. With extraordinary patience, Peter forges an ingenious scheme to escape—a plan that could be found only in a fairy tale. Using the tiny loom in his mother's old doll house and a small number of threads stolen every day from the napkin that comes with his lunch, he weaves a lengthy rope. It takes many years to complete, of course.

When the time finally comes for Peter to make his escape, he has help from some of those who still believe in him. At the same time, Thomas is at last tired of living with the horrible guilt of what he knows, and is determined to defy and hopefully destroy Flagg. In the end, the kingdom is at peace once more, with Peter as ruler. His friends Naomi and Ben live "happily ever after." Thomas and Dennis, his butler, go out across the land in search of the fugitive Flagg, determined to find him and put an end to him once and for all. The results of that quest are not revealed in the story (though the author has implied in his *Dark Tower* books that the boys' final battle with Flagg may finally take place within the pages of that series).

Primary among the many interesting facets of this story is this: though Thomas shares the role of protagonist with Peter, and it appears to be a narrative in which the younger brother, falsely made monarch, will rise to the occasion and make all things right, Thomas does *not* emerge the hero. The account does not follow that path, but remains, in Thomas's case, a rather sad one. He may share the role of protagonist, and he may be the one to turn the tables on Flagg, but he is *not* a hero.

> *In* Eyes of the Dragon, *Flagg reads from a book of darkest magic, bound in human skin, which was written by a madman named Alhazred on the Plains of Leng. This is an obvious nod to horror grandmaster H. P. Lovecraft, whose own book of darkest magic, the* Necronomicon, *was also supposedly written by a madman named Alhazred.*

*Eyes* is far more than a fairy tale. Not only does it contain a number of adult elements, including a discussion of the sexual practices of the ruler of Delain, but it also has strong ties to the rest of the Stephen King universe. These links have become stronger over time, as additional material has been added to the Stephen King universe. The most obvious of these links is Flagg. The author's most ubiquitous villain, Flagg also appears in *The Stand* (1978) and the *Dark Tower* series (1982–present), and quite possibly in several other places as well (though disguised), including 1999's *Hearts in Atlantis.* Interestingly enough, though we first spotted him (or at least, first know him) as the Walkin' Dude from *The Stand,*

> *The gunslinger recalls that he saw the creature called Flagg near the end of the chaos that destroyed the realm of his birth, and that Dennis and Thomas were in pursuit of him. This is the first indication that the* Dark Tower *saga and* Eyes *are closely linked.*

in *Eyes* it is revealed that he has spent a great deal of time in *that* world. He has returned, for many decades at a time, century after century, to plague the kingdom of Delain.

Why Delain? What special fascination does it hold for Flagg? We are never told, but his ongoing presence there implies that this world may be his home dimension. That possibility is supported by Flagg's appearance—in several disguises—in the books that make up the *Dark Tower* series, which we come to learn takes place in the same dimension as *Eyes.*

Thomas and Dennis, and their quest in pursuit of Flagg, are remembered by Roland in *The Drawing of the Three.*

But that is not enough to be 100 percent certain that Roland's world and the world of *Eyes* are one and the same. The author went to great lengths to establish that certainty, however, and only recently. For the

> *In the story, King establishes that the witch Rhea has sisters. One of them is likely Rhiannon of Coos, who is mentioned in* Eyes of the Dragon, *which also takes place in the same plane of reality as Roland's story. "The Little Sisters of Eluria" is, therefore, also part of the saga of the* Dark Tower.

1998 novella collection, *Legends,* he penned an entry titled "The Little Sisters of Eluria," in which Roland the gunslinger meets a boy who is from Delain, a kingdom Roland knows of and which he expects to pass through on his quest.

One could also easily look at *Eyes* as a segment of the *Dark Tower* series, and just as important, if not more so, than such other "linked" works as *The Stand, Insomnia* (1994), and *'Salem's Lot* (1975).

## PRIMARY SUBJECTS

**PETER.** The elder son of King Roland of Delain, Peter becomes king briefly upon his father's murder, only to be framed for the crime by Flagg. He spends years as a prisoner until his own ingenious plan for escape and his friends' determination to free him combine not only to give him liberty, but also to reveal Flagg as the true villain and regain the throne. It is presumed that Peter is still king of Delain.

**THOMAS.** The younger son of King Roland, Thomas is disaffected and jealous, and is manipulated into becoming Flagg's puppet after his brother is imprisoned. Thomas proves to be a very poor king, but he eventually rebels against Flagg, almost destroying him in vengeance for the murder of King Roland. When Peter again becomes ruler and Flagg flees Delain, Thomas and his former butler, Dennis, set off after the wizard in hopes of destroying him once and for all. They are still on that quest.

**RANDALL FLAGG.** An ancient wizard, possibly a demon, Flagg has existed for millennia. He has plagued Delain time and again. His latest scheme involved the killing of King Roland, the framing of the king's son Peter, and the attempt to control the kingdom and bring about its ruin through the manipulation of Peter's younger brother, Thomas. Flagg's plan eventually fails, and he flees the kingdom. Though his current whereabouts are unknown, he has continued to plague others across many worlds.

**KING ROLAND.** Once king of Delain, Roland was a good king, but not a bright one. He was the father of Peter and Thomas. His wizard and adviser, Flagg, plotted against him and murdered him.

**DENNIS.** Son of Brandon, Dennis is born into service to the royal family of Delain. As Brandon was King Roland's butler, so Dennis is butler first to Peter and later Thomas. When Peter is eventually freed, Dennis joins Thomas on his quest to find and destroy Flagg.

*BEN STAAD.* Though not of noble blood, Ben Staad has been Peter's best friend since childhood. He is one of the prime movers involved in the effort to free Peter from the Needle. Eventually, he marries Naomi. It is presumed that he still lives in Delain and remains the king's close friend and confidant.

*NAOMI REECHUL.* Daughter of a noble family who have fled Delain in fear of Flagg, Naomi becomes part of the effort to free Peter from the Needle, and falls in love with Ben Staad along the way. They are eventually married. It is presumed that she still lives in Delain.

*ANDERS PEYNA.* Peyna was the Judge General of Delain. It is he who, upon seeing Peter crying at the news of his father's death, believes those tears imply guilt in the king's murder, and orders a trial. But Peyna comes to believe he may have made a mistake, and is instrumental in helping to free Peter. It is presumed that he still resides in retirement somewhere in Delain.

*SASHA.* Queen of Delain and mother to Peter and Thomas, Sasha dies giving birth to her second son. Her death is no accident, but has been engineered by Flagg.

*NINER.* A dragon slain by King Roland, Niner's head is displayed on the wall of the king's private chamber. There is a secret passageway behind the wall from which one can peer into the chamber through the dragon's eyes.

# 6

## *The Talisman*

---

$A$TTEMPTING TO incorporate *The Talisman* into the Stephen King universe is a mind-bending endeavor. In some ways, it should not be done at all. The simple fact that King did not author the book alone but in full collaboration with his friend and colleague Peter Straub—a masterful writer in his own right—should disqualify the novel. But given that the book is connected specifically to at least one other King novel, and tangentially to so many others (through the "black hotel" and many of its concepts), it must be included herein. Also, it should be noted that King and Straub are as of this writing at work on a sequel to be named *The Black House*. Straub has said the new novel will be very directly tied into the parallel reality of the *Dark Tower* series.

By virtue of the logic followed throughout this volume, that means the entire works of Peter Straub could conceivably be connected to the Stephen King universe as well. Furthermore, since there is a character in the Straub novel *Mystery* who is essentially the Shadow, we might include all of the old Shadow pulps. Obviously, we must draw the line somewhere. Logic dictates that it be drawn cleanly between the two authors of this novel. So, while King and Straub co-authored *The Talisman*, it will be in its relation to the overall Stephen King universe that we address that work, and only in that context.

For all its classic Americana—a King trademark—*The Talisman* is a quest novel in the grand fantasy tradition. A teenager named Jack

Sawyer discovers that his mother, Lily Cavanaugh, is dying of cancer. Almost simultaneously, he encounters Speedy Parker, an elderly black blues musician turned maintenance man. Parker reveals to Jack that the teenager's destiny could lead him to find a cure for his mother's ailment.

Jack learns he is supposed to travel across the country, from coast to coast, to find the mystical icon known as the talisman. It is an object of extraordinary power that contains within itself a sort of microcosm of all time and space. With it, Jack can cure his mother. In his travels, Jack is able to "flip" back and forth between the "real" world and a place called the Territories, a parallel reality in which there are many people who are doppelgangers—or "twinners"—of people in Jack's world. The queen of the Territories is also dying, for she is Lily Cavanaugh's twinner.

Traveling between both worlds, Jack must retrieve the talisman and bring it home. In that way, the book is also about a classic journey. The authors are at pains to reveal that one of their major inspirations is the work of Mark Twain. The classic American novelist, Twain's *Tom Sawyer* (1876) and *Huckleberry Finn* (1885) are clearly the precedents on which this book is dependent. Jack's last name, after all, is Sawyer. The novel ends with a quote from Twain. And Lester "Speedy" Parker begins as a character who might easily have been torn from the pages of Twain's stories.

Twain is not the only literary influence on this book. It seems the authors thought to throw in a bit of Charles Dickens as well. His *Oliver Twist* (1839) shares certain elements with sections of *The Talisman* in which Jack and his friend Wolf are forced to become "guests" at a home for wayward boys called the Sunlight Gardener Home. The way the older boys treat the younger kids, and the way Gardener, the preacher who runs the home, deals with the local authorities, is quite Dickensian in nature.

Indeed, there are many classic elements in this novel, right alongside the very new, the very Straub, and the very King. Among the elements that are very King is the talk of multiple dimensions and the thinning of certain places between them. Though in *The Dark Tower: The Gunslinger* (1982), it was clear that Jake had come from another, parallel world, it was not until much later, after *The Talisman*, that the concept of "thinnies," or places where the barriers between dimensions are worn down and can be traveled through, began to show up. Yet this idea plays a significant role here. Even more significant is that this was the place where King (with Straub) first explored in earnest the idea of infinite dimensions. This has become not only a fundamental building block of King's work ever since, but the major premise for the book you now hold in your hands.

Moreover, beyond Jack's universe (which is clearly the prime parallel reality of the Stephen King universe, given that Jack later appears in 1987's *The Tommyknockers*) and the Territories, *The Talisman* also contains thinly veiled references to the Dark Tower. The talisman is located in "the black hotel," which can be entered only by people who are unique in the multiverse (as is the talisman). But when Jack touches the talisman and the world around him rapidly shifts through hundreds of variations, one of those permutations seems to be the Dark Tower.

*Even small details support the connections. The two-headed parrot, East-Head and West-Head, in* The Talisman *might well be the same creature owned by Flagg in* The Eyes of the Dragon *(1987).*

It is possible that Jack's removal of the talisman from the Dark Tower is the act that allowed the corruption of the Tower (talisman and Tower are considered the sum total of space and time, incorporating all dimensions) that led to Roland's world "moving on" in the *Dark Tower* series. Roland and his ka-tet, along with King's other heroes, are attempting to reverse that unraveling of all time and space, and the Crimson King and his forces are attempting to complete it. This is mere conjecture, but it has a basis in the plots and themes which are so central to King's writings.

*Director Steven Spielberg has held the screen rights to* The Talisman *almost since its publication. As of this writing, Spielberg has finally announced plans to produce it as a television miniseries.*

In essence, *The Talisman* is about youth, hope, and innocence that harkens back to the simpler times depicted in Mark Twain's work. That is why it is so stunning when Jack appears on the beach in *The Tommyknockers*. Jack went through hell—in some ways, quite literally—to locate the Talisman and return it to his dying mother's bedside. But in *The Tommyknockers*, one of the main characters meets up with Jack on Arcadia Beach, not far from the town's hotel, and we learn that Jack's mother was killed by a drunk driver. All of his struggles and all of his hopes eventually came to nothing. It is startling that King chose to add such a cynical, despairing coda to such a hopeful book.

## PRIMARY SUBJECTS

*JACK SAWYER*. The son of a Hollywood agent and a movie starlet, Jack Sawyer led a privileged life in California. Even as a child, though, strange things happened around him, including the death of his father, Phil. His mother, Lily Cavanaugh Sawyer, brings him to Arcadia Beach in New Hampshire, to an old hotel called the Alhambra, where Jack learns his mother is dying of cancer.

Jack also meets Lester "Speedy" Parker, who reveals to him (or more accurately, reminds him of) the existence of a place called the Territories, an alternate, almost medieval dimension. Jack learns there are people in the Territories who are essentially alternate versions of people in the real world. Speedy calls those people Twinners. Jack's twinner, Jason, son of the queen of the Territories, Laura DeLoessian, was killed at a young age as the result of the machinations of the villainous Morgan of Orris. Jack soon learns that Queen Laura is also dying.

> *Oatley, the town where Clay Reynolds and Coral Thorin of* Wizard and Glass *meet their eventual end, is also the name of the town where Jack Sawyer is kept almost as an indentured servant by the owner of the local bar.*

Spurred on by Speedy and his fear for his mother's life, Jack sets off to retrieve the magical talisman, which Speedy tells him will save the lives of both of his "mothers." Meanwhile, his father's former business partner, Morgan Sloat, who has been seeking to control the Territories for years, tries to prevent Jack from retrieving the talisman.

"Flipping" back and forth between his own world and the Territories, Jack travels across the United States until he reaches "the black hotel," wherein the talisman is kept. He has many grand adventures along the way, and eventually retrieves the talisman. With it, he saves the lives of both his mother and Queen Laura. Some time later, however, Jack's mother is struck and killed by a car. Jack's current whereabouts are unknown, but he was last seen lingering around the Alhambra Hotel.

*LILY CAVANAUGH.* After the death of her husband, Phil, B-movie queen Lily Cavanaugh raises their only child, Jack, thwarting the plans of her husband's sleazy former business partner, Morgan Sloat. When Lily discovers she is dying of cancer, she takes Jack to the Alhambra Hotel in New Hampshire, where she remains there for some time. Despite her fatal disease, there is always a spark of hope in her. She doesn't understand what her husband and Sloat were up to, but she knows it was something incredible. She also knows Jack is linked to the project somehow. When her son tells her that he is leaving to find a way to cure her, she has faith, or at least hope.

In Jack's absence, however, Sloat does his best to break Lily down, but she refuses to give in. Eventually, Jack brings the talisman back and heals her cancer, but a few years later she is killed by a drunk driver.

*WOLF.* A werewolf from the Territories, Wolf is a gentle soul save for the times when the full moon is upon him. Even then his instinct is always to protect the "herd." In the Territories, the "wolves" are all shepherds, and the herd is sacred. To this particular Wolf, Jack becomes the herd. Wolf dies protecting him.

*MORGAN SLOAT.* A Hollywood agent, Sloat once was the business partner of Phil Sawyer, Jack's father. Sloat is an envious, insidious man who discovers the mystery and magic of the Territories and, by abusing that knowledge, does his best to turn the Territories into his own kingdom. He has even greater ambitions, including the proprietorship of the talisman and the total control of infinite reality. He kills Phil and several other people and would have liked to do away with young

Jack Sawyer if he'd had the chance. Sloat dies in final battle with Jack over the talisman on a stretch of California beach.

*MORGAN OF ORRIS.* Also known as Morgan Thudfoot, this vicious man is the twinner of Morgan Sloat. In the Territories, he is very powerful and intends to overthrow Queen Laura. He dies when his twinner does.

*RICHARD SLOAT.* The son of Morgan Sloat, Richard was Jack's childhood friend. Like Jack, he also saw strange things as a boy, but rather than pursue them as Jack has, he closes his mind off to them and becomes an ultrarealist until Jack draws him into his adventures in the Territories. Richard aids Jack in his quest. Rendered parentless following the death of his father, Richard is taken in by Lily Cavanaugh. His activities after her death are a mystery, and his current whereabouts are unknown.

*LESTER (SPEEDY) PARKER.* Speedy, whose twinner is a man responsible for law and justice in the Territories, is a figure of mystery. He plays an important role in finding Jack in New Hampshire and clarifying his quest, and gives him the potion that allows him to "flip" between worlds. He later provides Jack with advice during the journey. Speedy's current whereabouts are unknown.

*PARKUS.* Twinner to Speedy Parker, Parkus is the marshal in charge of peace and justice in the Territories. It is presumed that he remains there and still retains that position.

*PHIL SAWYER.* Jack Sawyer's father, Phil, an aspiring Hollywood agent, is one of the first to discover the Territories. Phil is murdered on the instructions of his business partner, Morgan Sloat. His twinner is Prince Philip Sawtelle, who dies in the Territories at about the same time Phil does.

*OSMOND.* The right-hand man of Morgan of Orris, he is the twinner of Sunlight Gardener, head of the Sunlight Gardener home for boys. Osmond is a vicious, sadistic man. He dies in the final battle on the beach in California.

*QUEEN LAURA DeLOESSIAN*. Queen of the Territories, Laura is much loved by her people. Thanks to the machinations of Morgan of Orris, she falls ill, and would have died were it not for Jack Sawyer, the twinner of her dead son, who saved her by fetching the talisman. Despite the death of her twinner, Lily Cavanaugh, it is presumed that Queen Laura still rules the Territories.

*SUNLIGHT GARDENER*. Osmond's twinner, Gardener is an evangelist who runs a home for wayward boys, which in reality is nothing more than a slaving operation. The sadistic preacher dies during the final conflict on the beach in California.

*JASON*. The late son of Queen Laura of the Territories, Jason was Jack Sawyer's twinner. It was widely believed that he would return to life again, in messianic fashion, to save the Territories. Those who met Jack during his quest often thought he was Jason reborn.

*THE BLACK HOTEL*. The structure that houses the talisman before Jack removes it, the black hotel might also be an alternate-reality version of the Dark Tower.

# 7

## *Hearts in Atlantis*

AT A POINT in his long career when many authors, dried out creatively, might no longer be capable of producing, Stephen King produced *Hearts in Atlantis* (1999). It was truly a milestone.

In this volume, King has written his most ambitious literary novel—an exploration of the many facets of the Vietnam War era and the way it has tarnished America's idea of itself—yet one that is also filled with wonder, terror, and a significant and tangible connection to his most fantastical and epic work, the *Dark Tower* series (1982–present).

Though still a novel in that it does relate a singular narrative, *Hearts in Atlantis* is also experimental. It begins with a segment called "Low Men in Yellow Coats," which, at 243 pages, is a novel unto itself. Set in 1960, it deals with the coming of age of Bobby Garfield, a Connecticut boy who finds, much to his surprise, that his best pal, Carol Gerber, is in fact his girlfriend. It is also the story of Ted Brautigan, who takes a room on the upper floor of the boardinghouse where Bobby lives with his mother, Liz.

Ted and Bobby form an odd friendship based on their mutual love for books and the fact that Ted doesn't treat Bobby like a kid.

Bobby learns Ted's secret: that he is on the run from the low men in yellow coats. At first, Bobby isn't sure if Ted is sane, and Liz wonders if Ted might be a pervert. (She herself is dealing with a boss who is a sexual predator, and so her cynicism is perfectly understandable.)

Both Bobby and Carol are forced to grow up in this tale. When Carol is assaulted by local bullies, Bobby pays them back in spades. After a confrontation with Bobby's mother, Ted is almost handed over to the low men and is forced to leave town. Tragically, the low men catch up to Ted anyway, and Bobby is given the choice of trying to help, which means being captured along with Ted, or standing by and doing nothing. He chooses not to fight, and his life is changed forever. His youthful spirit and faith in himself are taken away. He becomes a juvenile delinquent, his life on an ugly path. The Garfields move, and Bobby's already damaged relationships with Carol and with his best friend, Sully, wither. For some time, Bobby and Carol write to each other, but even that comes to an end. Bobby believes his destiny is a dark one.

*Two of the books Ted reccommends to Bobby are of interest: William Golding's* Lord of the Flies *(1954) is a favorite of King's and the source of the name of the fictional town Castle Rock, and Clifford D. Simak's* Ring Around the Sun *(1952) may well have influenced King's idea of a multiverse.*

Only when Bobby receives a note from Ted, forwarded by Carol, does he appear to have a change of heart. Bobby learns more about Ted, and here is where the story veers into *Dark Tower* territory and connects with the Stephen King universe. The low men are not human. Rather, they are supernatural shepherds, or trackers, who work for the Crimson King, the evil being who hopes to destroy the tower and, in turn, all reality. The low men bear a red eye upon their persons, the symbol of the Crimson King. The multiverse is bound together by beams (made of energy or possibility or something else entirely), and the Tower's integrity is assured by those very beams. Ted is a "breaker." He has certain mental abilities that when focused could help to shatter the beams. In fact, the Crimson King had enslaved him to do just that, but Ted escaped to Bobby Garfield's world and time. (According to sources close to King, the character of Dinky from the short story "Everything's Eventual" is a breaker just like Ted.)

When Bobby receives Ted's note, he realizes Ted has once again escaped from the Crimson King. There is hope. To illustrate that, Ted includes several rose petals with the note, which have an effect on Bobby even he does not understand. But *we* do. The implication is that those petals are from the rose of creation, which is an incarnation of the Dark Tower (and therefore all reality) itself, and which Roland and his friends must protect in that series.

Though *Hearts in Atlantis* is King's most mainstream book, it also has undeniable connections to his earlier writings and many echoes of others. The relationship between Bobby and Ted, for example, is the sweet mirror image of the horrifying relationship between Todd Bowden and Kurt Dussander in the 1982 novella "Apt Pupil." In both narratives, a boy reads to an old man who has failing eyesight while hiding the truth about the relationship from the boy's parent(s). And yet, the end results in each account could not be more different.

> *The cross-referencing can be seen in seemingly trivial details. Bobby sees a classic western film called* The Regulators, *which King invented for the novel of the same name, written under his pseudonym, Richard Bachman. The fact that this fictional film exists in both Bachman's work and that of King further unifies their worlds.*

Ted's powers are similar in some ways to those of John Smith in *The Dead Zone* (1979). His dialogue is laced with King references, including a joke about the library police (a nod to the novella "The Library Policeman" from *Four Past Midnight*, 1990), a paraphrasing of *The Dark Tower* refrain "there are other worlds than this" and an exact quote from *Storm of the Century* (1999)—"Give me what I want and I'll go away"—which seems quite intentional.

• • •

The Stephen King universe is a tapestry into which new colors are constantly being woven, and yet it is all of a piece. None of the author's works reveals that as completely as "Hearts in Atlantis." At 150 pages, the title story is the second longest piece in the book, and it stands out as one of the most obviously autobiographical works of King's career. That is not to say King wasted a semester of his college career playing the card game hearts, as happens in this tale. This narrative introduces us to

Pete Riley, a freshman at the University of Maine at Orono in 1966. It's no coincidence that King was also a freshman at Orono that year.

We think we lose our innocence when we become teenagers. Perhaps, as this story implies, that loss comes later. In this novella, Pete Riley and his friends get themselves wrapped up in a GPA-destroying obsession that causes some of them to fail academically and be expelled. But there's no safety net for them. Those who are asked to leave are likely to be sent off to Vietnam, with a good chance of coming home in a body bag.

But the game of hearts goes on. The students find enlightenment of a sort and realize the horrible injustice of that war, but almost by accident. Few of the characters in this piece are actively seeking a cause, and yet it finds them. The title novella may be a work of fiction, but it rings all too true. King has re-created this troubled era quite convincingly.

*At the same time that Carol Gerber and Pete Riley were attending the University of Maine at Orono, Bill Denbrough of the novel IT was also on campus as a student. Note, though, that the campus in "Hearts in Atlantis" has been altered for the purposes of the story. "Hearts in Atlantis" is just as much a coming-of-age story as "Low Men in Yellow Coats," but a different kind of age.*

Pete is attracted to Carol Gerber, through whom we learn a bit more about Bobby Garfield. She has lost touch with him, and in high school she and Bobby's best friend, John Sullivan, called Sully, became romantically involved. But Sully is now in Vietnam, and Carol is a vocal antiwar protester. She is inspired by the way Bobby once lifted her up in his arms after she had been attacked by local boys, and carried her up the hill to his house even though she was bigger than he was. She believes somebody has to be there to help when injustice is being done. Though her relationship with Pete does not last, Carol has started on a path that will lead to tragedy.

·    ·    ·

In the third installment, "Blind Willie," the book jumps ahead to 1983 and focuses on Willie Shearman, one of the boys who assaulted Carol back in 1960. Willie never got over the guilt of what they did to her: he had held her while another boy hit her with a baseball bat, hard enough to dislocate her shoulder. As a boy, he also stole Bobby's baseball glove, an item that takes on a talismanic importance.

In Vietnam, Willie saves John Sullivan's life, but in his mind, he hasn't done enough penance. He is later injured and temporarily blinded, but still it isn't enough. Now, in 1983, Willie goes through a complex series of ruses and identities to hide the truth: he suffers from a temporary blindness for several hours *every afternoon*. He has no job, save for begging for money in the guise of a blind vet named William Garfield, and yet he has a life at home with a wife who loves him. Willie writes a message of apology thousands of times, a little each day, and gives a large portion of his income to the church—all to try to make amends for what he did. He pays off the police to leave him alone while he is panhandling, but one of the cops is becoming trouble. By the end of the tale, it appears as though Willie will take on yet another identity to kill the cop. Such a deed would not be his and therefore wouldn't interfere with his penance.

> *The segment "Blind Willie" first appeared, in very different form, in the magazine* Antaeus *in 1994, and later, also in different form, in the small-press collection of the author's work,* Six Stories *(1997).*

In this segment, we learn a great deal more about Carol's fate through newspaper clippings that Willie keeps. She becomes involved with a militant antiwar group that plants a bomb at a college lecture hall. The building is supposed to be empty, but unfortunately it is not. Carol tries to stop the bombing but is pulled away by Raymond Fiegler, the leader of the group and apparently her lover. A number of people are killed in the blast. The group is blamed, and its members are hunted down by the authorities. Eventually, in a confrontation with police, Carol supposedly dies in a house fire.

·     ·     ·

The fourth part of *Hearts in Atlantis*, "Why We're in Vietnam," turns the focus on John Sullivan and takes place in 1999. Saved in battle by Willie Shearman but horribly wounded, Sully has never been the same. In this short tale, we learn he has been haunted since even before that incident by the ghost of an old Vietnamese woman whose life he could have saved but didn't. She was murdered by another American soldier named Ronnie Malenfant (a character who also appears in the novella "Hearts in Atlantis").

One day, Sully is stuck in traffic on the way home from yet another funeral of a fellow veteran. He reminisces about a great many things, including the horrors of the war and the fallout for veterans, both emotional and physical. This story ends with yet another extra-ordinary moment. Things begin to fall from the sky, with no rhyme nor reason as to what exactly is falling: pianos, lawn mowers, ironing boards, anything you can imagine—including Bobby Garfield's old baseball glove, with a note inside.

Only it is revealed that none of that actually occurred. What does happen is that John Sullivan has a heart attack in his car during a traf-fic jam, and dies. But he dies with Bobby's baseball glove on his hand.

· · ·

The book ends with "Heavenly Shades of Night Are Falling," a brief sequence that brings the narrative back to Harwich, the little town where all of the central characters grew up, and to Bobby Garfield. He returns home for Sully's funeral. Bobby is a carpenter now, living in Philadelphia with a wife and children. But he harbors the tiny hope that Carol is alive because he has received a message from Ted Brautigan.

Carol *is* alive, of course, though she teaches at Vassar College under an assumed name and identity. The message is for both of them. Sully's executor sends Bobby his old baseball glove, because on it is somehow inscribed, in Ted Brautigan's handwriting, Bobby's *current* address. Inside the glove is a sheet of paper torn out of a book that Ted and Bobby had loved in 1960, with the words "tell her she was as brave as a lion," referring to the time Ted fixed Carol's dislo-cated shoulder. There is also an inscription familiar to Carol from her Vietnam antiwar days. Translated, it says, "Love plus peace equals information."

This final segment also reveals, albeit subtly, the other connection. Bobby doesn't notice Carol at the service for Sully because she does not want to be seen. Someone—a dangerous and clever someone—taught her, once upon a time, how to remain unseen, how to be *dim.* Being dim, as we know from *The Eyes of the Dragon* (1987), is a trick of the dark sorcerer Randall Flagg, who also appears in *The Stand* (1978) and the *Dark Tower* series. The leader of the antiwar group Carol was involved with was Raymond Fiegler. Flagg has been shown to have had many aliases over the years, and a number of them have been under the initials R. F. Raymond Fiegler is undoubtedly also a pseudonym for Randall Flagg. Not only does this show Flagg stirring up trouble and tragedy yet again, but it implies strongly that Flagg and the Crimson King are *not* one and the same, that in the Stephen King universe Flagg is lower on the hierarchy of evil. For if Flagg is out sowing evil and discord, much like a mythological Trickster, it is then highly unlikely that he could also be the Crimson King, a nearly omnipotent evil being working behind the scenes to manipulate not just individuals, but the universe.

In the conclusion to "Hearts in Atlantis"—thanks to Ted and to Sully's death—Bobby and Carol are reunited to ponder a fundamental question. Earlier, a character laments that once upon a time, we had a chance to change the world, and "we blew it." The sentiment is shared as if it is too late now. Or is it?

"People grow up," Carol tells Bobby firmly in the story's closing sequence. "They grow up and leave the kids they were behind."

"Do they?" Bobby asks.

Not really. Not in their hearts.

## PRIMARY SUBJECTS

***BOBBY GARFIELD.*** Bobby grows up in Harwich, Connecticut. During these formative years, he is best friend to John Sullivan and Carol Gerber, his first love. He and his mother, Liz, live in a boardinghouse. During the summer of 1960, a new boarder named Ted Brautigan moves in. The man and the boy become friends. Bobby's decision not to help save Ted from the low men in yellow coats sours his life for several years. Today, Bobby lives outside of Philadelphia with his family. He is a carpenter by trade.

*CAROL GERBER.* In the summer of 1960, Carol is in love with her best friend, Bobby Garfield. When she is brutally beaten by several local boys, Bobby takes vengeance upon the leader of the thugs. Later, after Bobby has moved away from Harwich, Carol dates his best friend, John Sullivan, for some years. In 1966, she attends the University of Maine at Orono, where she meets Pete Riley. Carol breaks up with Sully and dates Pete briefly, even as she becomes entrenched in the antiwar movement spawned by the crisis in Vietnam. Later, she becomes close to a man named Raymond Fiegler (who is also the creature known as Randall Flagg) and his group of militant antiwar protesters, who plant a bomb that ends up taking lives. Carol becomes a fugitive. She is believed to have died in a house fire with several of her colleagues, but survives, resurfacing some time later with a new identity as Denise Schoonover. Today, under that new name, she lives in Poughkeepsie, New York, and is a professor at Vassar College.

*JOHN SULLIVAN.* As a child, John Sullivan, or Sully-John, is best friends with Bobby Garfield. The events of the summer of 1960 so alter Bobby's behavior that their friendship is irrevocably damaged. After Bobby moves away, Sully dates Carol Gerber. Not long after their breakup in 1966, Sully is shipped off to Vietnam to fight in the military. During the war, Sully witnesses several atrocities including the senseless murder of an old woman by a soldier named Ronnie Malenfant, and the ghost of that old woman haunts him for the rest of his life. Also in Vietnam, Sully's life is saved by Willie Shearman, who also comes from Harwich.

Sully has a heart attack and dies while his car is stuck in traffic one day. Impossibly, when he is found, he wears Bobby Garfield's baseball glove on his hand, a glove that had been stolen from Bobby when they were children, and which neither of them had seen since.

*TED BRAUTIGAN.* Ted is a mysterious figure. It isn't certain to which era or even dimension he truly belongs. He enters Bobby Garfield's life in a year that to Bobby is 1960. But Ted is on the run from the agents of the Crimson King, a force for chaos in the infinite multiverse. Ted had been forced to work for the King as a breaker, someone who has the ability to psychically chip away at the bonds, or beams, holding reality together. Ted is recaptured but later escapes once more, as evidenced by the messages he sends to Bobby. His current whereabouts are unknown.

*LIZ GARFIELD.* Bobby's mother, Liz is widowed young. In trying to make ends meet, she finds herself with an employer who turns out to be a sexual predator. Eventually, she becomes a successful real estate agent in Danvers, Massachusetts. It is presumed that she still resides there.

*PETE RILEY.* As a student at the University of Maine at Orono in 1966, Pete falls in love with Carol Gerber. Though he nearly flunks out of school due to an unending card game of hearts in his dorm, he eventually gets back on track and graduates. During this time, partially due to his relationship with Carol and his exposure to people such as Stokely Jones, he becomes a war protester. Pete's current whereabouts are unknown.

*SKIP KIRK.* Stanley "Skip" Kirk is a college friend of Pete Riley's and also nearly falls victim to the game of hearts. Today, he is an artist of note, residing in Palm Beach, Florida. He has had at least one heart attack.

*NATE HOPPENSTAND.* Nate is Pete Riley's quiet, almost prissy college roommate, but he is also secretly a war protester and helps to open Pete's and Skip's eyes to the horrors of Vietnam. He still exchanges Christmas cards with Pete.

*STOKELY JONES.* Crippled in an auto accident, Stoke is forced to use metal crutches at all times. In 1966 he is the first student at the University of Maine to wear the peace sign. Despite his curmudgeonly persona, he inspires a passionate interest in the crisis in Vietnam among many of his fellow students. He drops out of college to protest full-time but later becomes an attorney, and is a constant presence on various TV network news and political programs.

*RAYMOND FIEGLER.* The mysterious leader of the group of war protesters that included Carol Gerber, Fiegler is supposedly killed in a fire in 1971. However, there is great reason to believe Fiegler is actually the creature known as Randall Flagg, and as such is very much alive. His current whereabouts are unknown.

**WILLIE SHEARMAN.** Willie grows up in Harwich, Connecticut, along with Bobby Garfield, Carol Gerber, and John Sullivan. Unlike them, he attends St. Gabe's, a local Catholic school. Though he doesn't want to, Willie succumbs to peer pressure and becomes a bully. In that role, he steals Bobby Garfield's baseball glove. He also helps his friends beat up Carol Gerber in the summer of 1960, and is haunted with guilt thereafter.

In Vietnam, Willie saves the life of John Sullivan, who had been Carol's boyfriend for a time. Even that is not enough to relieve his self-torment, however. During the war, he is badly wounded and left with an incredible handicap. For several hours each afternoon, Willie is blind. Otherwise, his eyesight is fine. Over the years, he develops a complex multiple-personality system based on his guilt and what he thinks of as penance, which includes begging for money on a New York City street corner, and giving some of that income to the church.

During that time, he uses Bobby's old baseball glove in performing his bizarre acts of penance. In 1983, he is still working on his penance, but it seems likely that some new fate befalls him in 1999, because that same glove appears on John Sullivan's hand at the moment he dies.

**THE CRIMSON KING.** An enormously powerful entity serving chaos, the Crimson King is working to unravel the ties that bind the infinite multiverse together.

**THE LOW MEN.** The low men are supernatural creatures who are employees and enforcers for the Crimson King.

# 8

## *The Stand*

---

THOUGH IT ALMOST exists as a separate universe unto itself, *The Stand* (1978) connections to the *Dark Tower*, particularly the appearance of Randall Flagg, are strong enough that it occupies a subdivision of the *Dark Tower* universe.

*The Stand* is one in a long line of classic postapocalyptic novels, including such seminal tales as Robert Merle's *Malevil* (1972), Nevil Shute's *On the Beach* (1957), and Richard Matheson's *I Am Legend* (1954). However, while *The Stand* is certainly not the first postapocalyptic novel, it is, without a doubt, the one by which all subsequent works in that subgenre will be measured.

One of King's most popular works, *The Stand*—which was translated into an ABC miniseries in 1994—is a novel whose shocking events are ingrained in the consciousness of readers around the world. This is particularly so in America, where even those who have never read the book or seen its television counterpart are likely to be familiar with its basic concepts. One of the things that sets *The Stand* apart is King's trademark fascination with Americana. Both the original version (published in 1978) and the revised, expanded version (published in 1989) are richly layered with pop culture references. But more than merely attracting readers with its intimate familiarity with American lives, the book tells an epic story of good and evil.

Frannie Goldsmith is a young woman pregnant by her unsupportive boyfriend. Harold Lauder is the bitter outcast whose love for her is spurned. Nick Andros is a deaf-mute whose handicap brings out both the best and worst in people. Stu Redman is a quiet man, the classic western hero type. Larry Underwood is a drug- and drink-ravaged rock singer whose shot at stardom falls short. They are characters we understand. This is one of the elements that King does best, and it's a major reason why *The Stand* is the ultimate postapocalyptic tale. Its strength also lies in the horror, the fear, the hope, and the terrifying knowledge that, ultimately, we have a choice whether to help or to hurt. It's all in our hands.

In addition, *The Stand* contains a vital element in the Stephen King universe. It has its beginnings in a short story called "Night Surf," which was originally published in the men's magazine *Cavalier* in August 1974. This tale features the first references to a "superflu" in King's work, and actually uses the name Captain Trips for the illness, a nickname that recurs in *The Stand*. It isn't clear that the two exist in the same

> *In the uncut version of* The Stand, *Frannie Goldsmith reads aloud from* Rimfire Christmas, *a novel by Bobbi Anderson—the main character of* The Tommyknockers *(1987)—which of course exists only within the Stephen King universe.*

branch of King's universe, but since there is no mention of a year in the short story, it isn't unreasonable to presume as much.

But *The Stand* is perhaps most important to the Stephen King universe in that it introduces the demonic Randall Flagg for the first time. Flagg would later reappear in various forms in *Eyes of the Dragon* (1987) and *Hearts in Atlantis* (1999). In *Dark Tower IV: Wizard and Glass* (1997), the hero, Roland, and his friends cross over from their dimension into the reality in which the events of *The Stand* take place—or a world strikingly similar to it—while on their quest.

Let us reflect on the novel for its own sake, rather than on its relationship to the Stephen King universe at large. The popularity of *The Stand* among the author's legions of fans cannot be overlooked. Many consider it the greatest of his early works, primarily because the whole is greater than the sum of its parts, but the parts themselves are extraordinarily memorable. Some of the characters and scenes that linger in the mind include: Frannie dreaming about the coat hanger.

Tom Cullen. Nick Andros. Mother Abagail. The Trashcan Man. Flagg and poor, deluded Nadine in the desert. The sacrifice of the story's heroes in the end. And Larry's solo trek through the Lincoln Tunnel, of course, surely one of the most harrowing passages ever written.

Finally, any examination of *The Stand* would be incomplete without commenting on its religious content. This novel makes certain two things that prevail throughout the Stephen King universe: First, that hope and faith and good will *can* triumph over evil. Second, and quite insidiously, that until the final battle is fought at the very end of all things, evil will always find its way back to test, tempt, and terrorize us again.

## PRIMARY SUBJECTS

*STUART REDMAN.* One warm day in Arnette, Texas, Stu is drinking beer and jawing with some of his close friends at Hapscomb's Texaco station when a car crashes into the station. The driver of the car, Charles Campion, is infected with the superflu, as are his wife and daughter, who have already died. Campion expires shortly thereafter, but not without infecting those at the station with Captain Trips—the nickname for the disease, likely taken from the nickname of Grateful Dead guitarist Jerry Garcia. Stu turns out to be immune—as .06 percent of the population is—and after escaping from a plague center in Stovington, Vermont, he hits the road. He is inspired by dreams of an old woman named Mother Abagail and frightened by nightmares about Flagg, "the Walkin' Dude."

Stu proves himself to be an easygoing yet heroic man. He becomes a leader among the survivors of the plague and is among those who travel to Las Vegas to confront Flagg and his followers. Stu is the only survivor of that trip. In the end, after Flagg's defeat, he and Frannie Goldsmith—another survivor of the plague who is now his wife—return to her native Maine with their son.

*ACE HIGH.* One of Flagg's most trusted men, Ace is part of the inner circle in Las Vegas, along with Lloyd Henreid. He dies in a nuclear explosion in the gaming capital.

*RANDALL FLAGG (a.k.a. AHAZ, ANUBIS, ASTAROTH, RAMSEY FORREST, RICHARD FRYE, NYARLAHOTEP, R'YELAH, RUSSELL FARADAY, SETI, THE WALKIN' DUDE).* Who can say what Flagg really is? A demon or something quite like it, or perhaps even the Devil himself. He has been known by an infinite number of names, and sowed the seed of evil across multiple dimensions. In this incarnation, he is watching carefully as the world dies, as 99.4 percent of the human population is killed off by the superflu. He does his best to take advantage of the situation. He manipulates the survivors, sending them dreams that guide them to him. In Las Vegas, he gathers all those who would heed him and follow him. There he hopes to start a new human race, a breed of people with darkness in their hearts, who will bow to his demands.

A tempter, a liar, a killer, and a maker of ultimate mischief, Flagg is the rot of civilization. He is entropy itself, bringing all things to their eventual destruction. But he is not all-powerful. Like all evil beings, he believes too much in the extent of his own power, and can be tricked. In the end, he must answer to a higher power, as he does in Las Vegas. He is about to execute Glen Bateman, Larry Underwood, and Ralph Brentner when the Trashcan Man arrives with a nuclear warhead scrounged from a nearby U.S. military site. The hand of God reaches down from the sky and detonates the warhead.

Flagg is thwarted, but not destroyed. Shortly thereafter, he finds himself on a beautiful, tropical shore, with a band of mystified natives whom he terrifies into becoming his acolytes. But that is just one tiny shard of Flagg's fascinating story.

*NICK ANDROS.* In his travels after the plague has begun, deaf-mute Nick Andros, who is immune to the disease, drifts into Shoyo, Arkansas. There he is beaten up by the locals and then befriended by the sheriff, a man named John Baker. When Baker and the rest of Shoyo are eliminated by the superflu, Nick moves on and eventually meets Tom Cullen, a retarded man who is also immune, and whose dreams of Mother Abagail are similar to Nick's own. When they finally meet, Nick quickly becomes a favorite of Mother Abagail's but is killed by a bomb planted by the traitorous Harold Lauder. Later, however, Nick's ghost appears to Tom Cullen, guiding him in the proper care for the gravely ill Stu Redman. It is not known whether Nick's spirit is still able to manifest itself.

*GLEN BATEMAN.* A retirement-aged sociology professor from Woodsville Community College, Glen finds himself immune to the superflu. He adopts his dead neighbor's dog, whom he rechristens Kojak when it appears the canine is also a rare survivor of his species. Glen travels with Stu Redman for a while before they all end up in Boulder, Colorado. Along with Ralph Brentner and Larry Underwood, Glen is one of those whose perseverance and sacrifice helps to thwart Flagg's plans. He dies in the nuclear explosion in Las Vegas.

*RALPH BRENTNER.* Like Stu Redman, Ralph is a good and simple man, with a quiet strength towards which others seem to gravitate. After the flu epidemic hits, he hits the road in his truck on a quest to find Mother Abagail, an elderly woman many of the survivors have been dreaming about, picking up Nick Andros and Tom Cullen along the way. In the end, Ralph is among those chosen few whom Mother Abagail instructs to go to Las Vegas and face Flagg. He dies in the nuclear explosion that destroys the city. In Boulder, a large monumental rock is named in his honor.

*CHARLES CAMPION.* Campion works on the classified Project Blue at a top-secret U.S. biological testing site in California. When the superflu germ leaks from its containment unit, Campion and his family are the only ones to survive. However, they quickly fall ill. By the time Campion crashes his car at Hapscomb's Texaco station in Arnette, Texas, his wife and daughter are dead. He lives only a few hours longer.

*NADINE CROSS.* A truly tragic figure, Nadine hooks up with Larry Underwood on the road, and likely because of her attraction to him, chooses Boulder—where Mother Abagail's followers have gathered—as a destination over Las Vegas, where Randall Flagg has set up shop. When her feelings for Larry are not reciprocated, Nadine—lured by dreams of Flagg—heads into the desert to become the dark man's "bride." In the end, however, she sacrifices her life by diving out a window in order to kill her unborn child—which would have been Flagg's heir.

**TOM CULLEN.** A retarded man Nick Andros meets on the road, Tom eventually helps to save Stu Redman's life, aided by Nick's spirit. Tom is presumed to still be residing in Boulder as part of the Free Zone.

**THE TRASHCAN MAN.** Donald Merwin Elbert, better known as the Trashcan Man, was taunted and beaten up as a child, and grew up to become a very twisted individual obsessed with setting fires. His dreams of the Walkin' Dude offer promises of fires beyond his imagination. While on his trek to Las Vegas, he travels for a time with "the Kid," a savage killer who is apparently the reincarnation of 1950s mass murderer Charles Starkweather. The Trashcan Man becomes progressively more insane to the point where, believing Flagg would be grateful, he snatches a nuclear warhead from a military base and brings it to Las Vegas, where it promptly explodes, eliminating everyone there (except Flagg).

**MOTHER ABAGAIL.** Abagail Freemantle, the daughter of a slave, is more than a century old when the world as she knows it comes to an end. More than likely, she is the oldest woman alive when travelers who have been dreaming about her begin to appear on her doorstep in Hemingford Home, Nebraska. Mother Abagail has been gifted with special knowledge, certain prescience, about the people who come to her and the evil they will face. As the focal point for good among the survivors of the world, and as Flagg's "opposite number," she becomes a reluctant leader until she dies peacefully.

**FRANNIE GOLDSMITH.** Frannie grew up in Ogunquit, Maine, an idyllic beach community. Her life, however, has been less than idyllic. Still a teenager, she finds herself pregnant by her boyfriend, who abandons her. At first she is faced with the choice between keeping a child she dares not tell her parents about or having an abortion she doesn't want. The decision is taken from her by the arrival of the superflu and the death of nearly everyone around her. Her baby is the first healthy child born after the plague. It is a cruel irony that the only other survivor in Ogunquit is a neighbor of Frannie's named Harold Lauder, a malcontented misfit who has always lusted after her. The two set off together and end up traveling (against Harold's wishes) with Stu Redman, with whom Frannie falls in love. She later marries Stu, and he becomes stepfather to her son. They settle in Maine after the final battle against Flagg has been won.

*LLOYD HENREID.* A two-bit criminal, Lloyd and his partner, Poke Freeman, hold up a grocery store not long before the superflu attacks. Poke is killed by the store owner and Lloyd ends up in prison, where he is when the flu ravages the town. To survive, Lloyd is forced to eat not only rats, but also bits of the corpse in the next cell. Flagg rescues him from that hellish existence and makes Lloyd one of his most trusted men. Lloyd is killed when Las Vegas is blown up.

*HAROLD LAUDER.* Harold grew up overweight, stricken, sweaty, and lonely in Ogunquit, Maine, and has had a crush on Frannie Goldsmith his whole life. What luck, then, that she is the only other survivor of Captain Trips in his hometown—at least, that's what Harold thinks. When they travel together and meet up with Stu Redman, Harold realizes that even if he *were* the last man on Earth, Frannie would never love him. Always a bit devious, he becomes increasingly bitter and spiteful over time. Though Harold has never been trustworthy, Fran's love for Stu may well be the final straw for him. He plants a bomb that kills Nick Andros, then flees to join Flagg in Las Vegas, where he dies along with the rest of Flagg's followers.

*THE KID.* In 1958, nineteen-year-old Charles Starkweather shot and killed the parents of his fourteen-year-old girlfriend, Caril Fugate, and clubbed her baby sister to death with a rifle butt. The two of them fled, and Starkweather killed a couple out on a date and stole their car. Before his spree was brought to an end, ten people were murdered. The National Guard was called in, and after a high-speed chase, Starkweather was caught and later executed in the electric chair.

At some later date, Starkweather is reincarnated as the Kid, a sadistic, evil young man with a taste for classic cars and Elvis Presley. He meets the Trashcan Man on the road, but unlike so many others, the Kid has an evil that is not tainted by any trace of good. So dark is the Kid that he doesn't want to join Flagg—he wants Flagg's job. This profoundly upsets Flagg. After the Kid tortures the Trashcan Man, Flagg sends a pack of wolves after him, and the Kid is eventually killed.

However, since Charles had been reincarnated once, it is not unreasonable to suspect that the young murderer may return to plague the world again.

> *Charles Starkweather's crime spree—one of the great crime stories of the mid-century, covered in detail in the popular press—apparently haunts King. In addition to giving us the Kid, a reincarnation of the killer, King told* TV Guide *in 1994 that "[Randall] Flagg is like the archetype of everything that I know about real evil, going back all the way to Charles Starkweather in the '50s."*

**LARRY UNDERWOOD.** Larry has lived life in the fast lane. Sex and drugs and rock 'n' roll nearly destroyed him. His one major hit as a musician, "Baby Can You Dig Your Man," is likely also to be his last. Struggling to stay off drugs, Larry returns to New York City to visit his mother. He is there when Captain Trips hits. In escaping the corpse-filled city, Larry undergoes a harrowing journey through a lightless Lincoln Tunnel. Despite the fact that he has a low opinion of his self-worth, Larry finds himself a prominent citizen of the Free Zone, and is one of those who travels to Las Vegas to confront Flagg. He dies in the climactic nuclear explosion.

**THE FREE ZONE.** The name given to Boulder, Colorado, and its environs by the survivors of the superflu who settle there.

**HEMINGFORD HOME, NEBRASKA.** The small town where Mother Abagail lived her entire life before the outbreak of Captain Trips.

**CAPTAIN TRIPS.** Nickname for the superflu created in an American military research facility and accidentally released into the general populace. It kills 99.4 percent of the world's population.

## ADAPTATIONS

For years, King went through draft after draft of the screenplay for *The Stand*. The epic finally came to life on the small screen in an eight-hour ABC miniseries aired May 8, 9, 11, and 12, 1994. It was one of the most ambitious projects ever attempted, with more than one hundred speaking parts and a reported budget of nearly $30 million. Directed by Mick Garris (with whom the author has collaborated on several other occasions), the film boasted a stellar cast of veteran movie and television actors, including Gary Sinise as Stu Redman, Molly Ringwald as Frannie Goldsmith, Jamey Sheridan as Randall Flagg, Laura San Giacomo as Nadine Cross, Ruby Dee as Mother Abagail, Ray Walston as Glen Bateman, Matt Frewer as the Trashcan Man, Rob Lowe as Nick Andros, and King himself in a small role as Teddy Weizak.

King's fans had long been waiting to see the novel adapted to the screen. In an interview conducted before the miniseries was finally made, executive producer Richard Rubinstein noted that he had been taking an informal survey of fans for some years of which scenes in the massive tome were absolutely indispensable to a film or television version. The number one request, the infamous Lincoln Tunnel scene, was indeed terrifying to watch but could not possibly duplicate the novel's intensity. This was mainly due to the fact that in the book, the scene takes place in total darkness.

Ratings were stellar and reviews generally positive, and King, of course, continues to have a creative, productive, and profitable relationship with ABC-TV.

# 9

# Related Tales

---

SEVERAL SHORT STORIES are directly connected to the *Dark Tower* universe. They reveal other aspects of characters well-known from the novels, add to their legends, or reinterpret events that readers learned about elsewhere.

## "NIGHT SURF"
### from *Night Shift* (1978)

First published in the men's magazine *Cavalier* in 1974, the short story "Night Surf" was included in King's first short-story collection, *Night Shift*. A precursor to *The Stand* (1978), this story introduces the idea of the superflu, nicknamed Captain Trips (an ironic reference to Grateful Dead guitarist Jerry Garcia), which kills most of the population of the world. The narrative focuses on Bernie, Corey, Joan, Kelly, Susie, and Needles, a group of rural New England teenagers doing their best to survive in a postapocalyptic world.

## "THE LITTLE SISTERS OF ELURIA"
### (1998)

Though Roland appears—or is at least referred to—in a number of other King works, his primary story had been confined until now to the *Dark Tower* series. First published in 1998 in the massive *Legends*—a collection of fantasy novellas edited by Robert Silverberg—"The Little Sisters of Eluria" reveals a previously untold story of Roland and hints at connections we had only suspected before.

Early in Roland's pursuit of the man in black, which opens the first *Dark Tower* book (1982's *The Gunslinger*), but far enough along in the epic storyline that he is already questing on his own, Roland finds himself in what amounts to a classic western ghost town. There are echoes of King's short story "Children of the Corn" in that situation, but it is a traditional fictional conceit. Of course, the town isn't completely deserted. There are "slow mutants" in the area. They are green-fleshed and horrid to look at; the victims or descendants of victims of radiation exposure from long ago.

*Baseball field built by King, "The Field of Screams," Bangor* | DAVID LOWELL

When Roland is attacked by a band of slow mutants, he is turned over to the Little Sisters of Eluria. They appear, at first, to be a religious organization dedicated to nursing patients back to health. However, that is far from the truth. They turn out to be a special breed of vampire, and they have their sights set on Roland. Sister Mary, their mother superior, particularly dislikes him.

Roland is protected by a chain around his neck that he took from a dead boy whose living brother he finds in the "hospital" with him. It isn't long before that young man succumbs to the vampires' charms. Roland is also protected by Sister Jenna, who appears to hold power over the others. She is, in some way, the chosen one among her kind, the inheritor of "the dark bells," which can summon the black bugs called "the good doctors"—insects that heal the sick. Sister Jenna misses her humanity and falls for Roland. She helps him escape, and Sister Mary is killed. When the sun comes up, however, Sister Jenna meets her fate—she is transformed into an army of black bugs.

Clearly, these are not the vampires of 'Salem's Lot (1975). But the two are related, one might suspect, given King's implication that that novel's Father Callahan will soon make his way, or has long since made his way, into Roland's world.

In addition to presenting a new chapter in Roland's story, this novella also gives us both subtle and overt connections to other King works. The first and most obvious is that the boy in the bed next to Roland's is from the city of Delain, the setting of *The Eyes of the Dragon*. This establishes the probability that Roland visited Delain at least once. Second, mention is made of the nasty, vicious witch, Rhea of the Coos and her sisters, from *The Dark Tower IV*. In this story, Roland thinks about Rhea and her sisters. Given that *The Eyes of the Dragon* mentions Rhiannon of the Coos, this creates another link to tie *Eyes* to the Tower. Finally, Roland recalls that his friend Jamie DeCurry was fond of saying that Roland "could shoot blindfolded, because he had eyes in his fingers." This is likely a reference to the early King story "I Am the Doorway."

# SECTION TWO

## The Prime Reality, Part I: Derry

*IT*

*Insomnia*

*Bag of Bones*

Related Tales

ORE RECOGNIZABLE THAN the world of the *Dark Tower* series—the most familiar reality in the Stephen King universe, is what we have called the Prime Reality. Perhaps as much as 90 percent of King's work is set there. However, with regard to the overall struggle between good and evil, or the Random and the Purpose, as King has sometimes called that battle, the reality of the Dark Tower is more significant. Yet there is no question—as you will find as you read the chapters that follow—that this war rages on within the pages of nearly every one of King's works, and nowhere with more frequency than in the prime reality.

For the sake of clarity and to make it simpler for the reader to envision, we have broken down the prime reality into five areas, each of which is addressed in the parts that follow: Derry, Castle Rock, King's Maine, Tales of the Shop, and Other Prime Reality Tales. Still, it bears repeating that all of these parts form the whole that is the prime reality. In addition, there are only three other realities or parallel dimensions, those of the *Dark Tower* and *The Stand,* and those created under King's pseudonym, Richard Bachman (a complex area covered later in this book).

·   ·   ·

Though perhaps not as "name-branded" for longtime King readers as Castle Rock is, Derry may well prove to be a more important battleground in the cosmic struggle between good and evil that constantly rages within the Stephen King universe. While most of King's settings in the prime reality (or most prominent parallel dimension)—particularly those in Maine—have seen their share of battles in this war, Derry's seem to have been staged on a larger scale. Derry is, after all, the site of *IT* and *Insomnia,* among others, both of which have evil antagonists who are undoubtedly more powerful and grandiose than their counterparts in Castle Rock (such as Leland Gaunt) or Jerusalem's Lot (such as Kurt Barlow).

Derry is also one of the pivotal locations lending itself to our thesis that all of King's worlds and works are connected. There are obvious links between Castle Rock and other locations. Works within the prime reality tales set in Derry have provided some of the most significant links to the other realities that together make up the substance of the Stephen King universe.

Located near Bangor, Maine, Derry appears on its surface to be a typical New England town. Some unsettling statistics tell a different story, however. The murder rate in Derry is six times that of any other town of comparable size in New England. Also, in Derry children disappear inexplicably at the rate of forty to sixty per year. They are never found.

One would think these statistics would alarm the populace, but as Mike Hanlon commented in *IT* (1986), "In Derry people have a way of looking the other way."

Apparently, people have been looking the other way for quite some time. In the chronology below are some significant events in the history of the town, many of which were gleaned from Hanlon's unpublished book, *The Unauthorized History of Derry*. Hanlon, who, along with many of his childhood friends, faced the creature known as "It" twice in his life and survived, knows a great deal about the dark side of his hometown.

*1741.* The entire population of Derry township vanishes. Hanlon states, "The only case remotely like it in American history is the disappearance of the colonists on Roanoke Island, North Carolina." This creates an interesting link between *IT* and the sinister Andre Linoge, who, as we know from his appearance in the 1999 TV miniseries *Storm of the Century*, was responsible for the disappearance of the colonists.

*1851.* John Markson kills his entire family with poison, then consumes a deadly "white-nightshade" mushroom.

*1879.* A crew of lumberjacks finds the remains of another crew that spent the winter snowed in at a camp in the Upper Kenduskeag, at the tip of the modern-day Barrens. All nine had been hacked to pieces.

*1906.* On Easter Sunday, the Kitchener Ironworks exploded during an Easter egg hunt, resulting in 102 deaths.

*1930.* The Black Spot, a Negro social club, is burned to the ground by the Maine Legion of Decency. Dozens perished.

*1958.* One hundred and twenty-seven children, ranging in age from three to nineteen, are reported missing in Derry.

*1985.* Nine children are murdered. Their killer is never apprehended. This is also the year of the Great Flood, which resulted in millions of dollars of damage to the town.

*1994.* Feminist Susan Day is killed when Derry resident Ed Deepneau— driven insane by an otherworldly being named Atropos—launches a kamikaze attack on the Derry Civic Center in which Day is addressing a capacity crowd.

Stephen King aficionados already know many of these tragedies were caused by It, the creature who used the town as its own private killing ground for centuries. (Readers will recall that the events of 1958 and 1985 are chronicled in 1986's *IT*, originally titled *Derry.*) King again used the town as a setting in 1994's *Insomnia*, where Derry resident Ralph Roberts becomes embroiled in a battle between the cosmic forces King has named the Purpose and the Random (order and chaos, essentially), and in 1998's *Bag of Bones*, which presented a less cosmic view of the town.

*Paul Bunyan statue in Bangor* | VINTAGE POSTCARD

The fictional Derry is closely patterned on Bangor, Maine (its neighbor, according to King's invented geography of that state). In fact, a standard map of Bangor would prove useful in identifying many of the landmarks described in *IT*, such as the Barrens, the standpipe, the statue of Paul Bunyan, the Derry Public Library, and West Broadway, where the rich families of Derry make their homes. (Coincidentally, King lives on just such a street—it is even named West Broadway—in Bangor.) Like Castle Rock—another fictional town of King's creation—Derry also seems to have more than its fair share of writers (all also invented by King). For instance, 1990s midlist writer Mort Rainey, author of two novels and a short-story collection, resided there with his wife until their divorce drove him mad. William Denbrough *(IT)*, famous for his fictions about "The Outsiders," also hails from Derry. Finally, there is best-selling author Mike Noonan *(Bag of Bones)*, who, despite a successful career, seemingly abandoned writing in 1998.

Derry seems destined to play an important part in the saga of the Dark Tower. In *IT*, King mentions the Turtle, also called one of the guardians of the Tower in the *Dark Tower* series. The title monster itself, a creature from beyond our reality, may well be the "Beast" who guards the Tower, as described by the magician Walter in *The Gunslinger* (1982).

In *Insomnia*, the author introduces the Crimson King, whose appearances there and in subsequent works implies his status as a pivotal player in the cosmic chess game between order and chaos. The Crimson King tells the main character, Ralph Roberts, that he has been at work in Derry for centuries. It is also revealed that events in the town impact the life and existence of Roland the Gunslinger.

While the connections to the reality of the Dark Tower are fairly obvious, the connections to other worlds and realities are sometimes a bit more subtle. *The Tommyknockers* (1987) is set in Haven, which is just above Derry in King's fictional Maine. In that novel, denizens of Haven see and hear It while traveling in Derry, even though the creature was supposedly destroyed a year before. The *Tommyknockers* connection is significant because it clearly links Derry to the Shop (see section five) and strengthens the connection to the reality of the *Dark Tower*, as Jack Sawyer of *Dark Tower*–related *The Talisman* (1983) makes a cameo appearance within its pages.

Other connections to King's Maine exist. For instance, in *IT*, Beverly Marsh is clearly aware of the infamous exploits of Frank Dodd, the Castle Rock Strangler, as detailed in *The Dead Zone*. It is also clear that *Bag of Bones'* Mike Noonan is familiar with the lives of Castle Rock natives Thad Beaumont and Alan Pangborn, whom readers met in *The Dark Half* (1989). Mike Noonan also owns a home at Dark Score Lake, the summer community where Jessie Burlingame of *Gerald's Game* (1992) was molested by her father.

*Insomnia* and *IT* are also connected in other ways to the prime reality. One example is the picture of Susan Day that hangs in Anna Stephenson's office in *Rose Madder*. Another link from the pages of *Insomnia* is the fact that Atropos, a supernatural (or, perhaps more accurately, supranatural) servant of the Random, has kept Gage Creed's (see *Pet Sematary*) sneaker as a macabre trophy. *IT* is connected to *Misery* in that the latter novel's Paul Sheldon has personal knowledge of Eddie Kaspbrak of *IT*. Another perhaps unintentional connection are the appearances of hotel and motel rooms numbered 217 in *The Shining, Apt Pupil,* and *IT*. A final tie linking the realities is Dick Hallorann's presence in both *The Shining* (in the 1970s) and *IT* (in the 1930s).

Given that the author has spent so much time establishing Derry as one of the battlefields in the war between the Random and the Purpose, between chaos and order, and that such cosmic servants of the Random as the Crimson King and It have been drawn there, it seems virtually guaranteed that readers have not seen Derry for the last time. Stephen King is bound to return there as he moves ever closer to the final battle that so many of his works lead toward.

# 10

## *IT*

---

I N  S I Z E  A N D  S C O P E, *IT* (1986) is a monster of a book. At 1,138
pages, it is easily the lengthiest book King has written to date. Only
the unexpurgated version of his 1978 novel *The Stand* is longer, and
only by a few pages. *IT* constitutes King's definitive examination of
questions about kids and monsters: kids, in that it deals with the rite
of passage from childhood to adulthood, and the mythic power that
childhood holds over our imagination; and monsters, in that It knows
what scares people and uses that against them. The title character is
an amorphous being from beyond the reality we know that is shaped
by our own fears and imaginations. Thus, *IT* is sort of a pop culture
monster mash, with cameos from the Creature from the Black
Lagoon, the Mummy, Dracula, Jaws, the Crawling Eye, Frankenstein,
Rodan, and the Teenage Werewolf, among many others.

There's an intimacy about *IT* that previous King books do not display, perhaps due to the fact that the members of the Losers Club—
focal characters in this book—are contemporaries of their creator, who
was born in 1947. They have experienced the same things King has
lived through. One can imagine them sitting in the same dark movie
theater King frequented in 1957 when the manager stopped the film to
announce that the Russians had just launched Sputnik, an experience
King would describe in *Danse Macabre* (1981). Their coming together
twenty-seven years later probably echoed King's experiences at high
school reunions. The story of a group of friends getting together after

the death of one of their number is not unlike the movie *The Big Chill* (1983), only with monsters added to the mix.

The publication of *IT* marked the advent of a more socially conscious King. At the book's heart, *IT* is an account of child abuse and how isolated and vulnerable children are. *IT* also deals with spousal battery, a theme King would develop further in subsequent writings. In addition, *IT* is a veritable treatise on intolerance and prejudice, dealing with hatred of blacks and gays, and virtually anyone who is different.

Inspired by the classic Norwegian fairy tale "The Three Billy Goats Gruff," *IT* contains some of King's most harrowing turns, including George Denbrough's reluctant descent into his basement and later his death scene. *IT* is also an interesting variation on King's oft-used settings of haunted houses. Here the concept is expanded in that the town itself is permeated by It's sinister influence. Several times throughout the novel, It and Derry—the fictional Maine town where the novel takes place—are spoken of as if they were the same thing. Mike Hanlon, a member of the Losers Club, asks, "Can an entire city be haunted?"

*IT* also represents an interesting technical experiment in time, as King seamlessly melds the events of 1958 with those occurring in 1985.

In the book, King provides a history of Derry, a town he had heretofore mentioned only in passing in stories such as "Mrs. Todd's Shortcut" (collected in 1985's *Skeleton Crew*). In fact the original working title of *IT* was *Derry*. Located to the south of the ill-fated Haven (see *The Tommyknockers*), Derry borders Bangor to the west. It is almost a mirror image of Bangor, containing many similar landmarks. Like the author's hometown, Derry has a series of canals and a unique standpipe/water tower; it, too, boasts an enormous statue of Paul Bunyan, no surprise given the influence of the lumber and paper industry on that region.

*IT* represents the first but not the last time Derry was featured prominently in one of King's books. He has revisited the city several times since, most notably in his 1990 novella, "Secret Window, Secret Garden" (the protagonist of that story, Mort Rainey, owned a house in Derry), in the novels *Insomnia* (1994) and *Bag of Bones* (1998), and in the 1999 short story "The Road Virus Heads North." There is every indication that King will return to the city again. Based on the events related in *Insomnia*, it appears as if the city is a cosmic hot spot, a key location for Roland of the author's *Dark Tower* series. Although King doesn't specifically refer to that saga, *IT* contains many common elements. The Losers could certainly be seen to have formed a ka-tet, similar to that described in the second Dark Tower installment, *The Drawing of the Three* (1987). King also uses circle imagery, images that pop up in the *Dark Tower* books; at one point, Mike Hanlon writes, "If the wheels of the universe are in true, then good always compensates for evil."

There may even be a connection between It and *Insomnia*'s villain, the Crimson King. At one juncture in *IT*, Pennywise the Clown mocks Mike Hanlon, telling him in an *Amos 'n' Andy*–type voice, "I is de Kingfish in Derry, anyhow, and dat's de troof." Perhaps significantly, the Crimson King tells Ralph Roberts in *Insomnia* that he may refer to him as "the Kingfish. You remember the Kingfish from the radio, don't you?" Another connection between the two is that in his trip into hyperreality, Ralph glimpses "deadlights," a concept first mentioned in *IT*.

Links to the Stephen King universe within *IT* are wide and varied. Dick Halloran of *The Shining* spent time in Derry as a cook for the Army Air Corps and was present the night the Black Spot was torched. The Army Air Corps base stood on the spot that serves as Derry's airport today. Referring to Frank Dodd *(The Dead Zone),* Beverly mentions "that crazy cop who killed all those women in Castle Rock, Maine." Voices emanating from a drain tell a frightened Derry resident "Our name is legion," a biblical reference King used before and since in *The Stand* (Tom Cullen speaking about Flagg) and in the 1999 TV miniseries *Storm of the Century* (Linoge is an anagram for Legion). Haven, the setting of *The Tommyknockers,* is mentioned, as is one of its residents, the unfortunate Rebecca Paulson. Henry Bowers is picked up by a "1958 Plymouth Fury," conjuring up images of *Christine* (1983). Henry is a patient at Juniper Hill from 1958 through 1985; King has mentioned the asylum on numerous occasions in other novels (as he did, for example, in 1991's *Needful Things*). Finally, the adult Mike Hanlon lives in Hemingford Home, Nebraska, birthplace of Mother Abagail from *The Stand*.

King also may have been trying to integrate elements of the H. P. Lovecraft mythos into his own universe. Lovecraft fans may recall the author's 1929 tale "The Dunwich Horror," which featured a hideous creature named Yog Sothoth, "an octopus, centipede, spider kind of thing." Like Yog Sothoth, It is a manifestation from beyond and appears to the Losers Club as a giant female spider (recalling the queen bitch from the film *Aliens*). Remember also that William Denbrough went on to create a similar mythos—readers learn in *Bag of Bones* that he writes about "creatures from beyond."

Despite It's apparent death at the end of the novel, characters in *The Tommyknockers*, set a year later than *IT*, see and hear It in visits to Derry, and Ralph Roberts, the hero of *Insomnia*, sees the ethereal deadlights discussed in *IT* on his visit to hyper-reality. This would seem to indicate that It, like Flagg, and the Crimson King, and the Beast who guards the Tower, is still out there, ready to oppose those who do the work of order in the Stephen King universe.

## PRIMARY SUBJECTS

*THE TURTLE.* It and the Turtle exist at "the end of Macroverse." They have existed since the beginning of time, perhaps created by "the final other," the "author of all there was," who dwells in a void beyond the one in which the Turtle resides. Bill Denbrough encounters the Turtle when he is propelled into the Macroverse. The Turtle, who claims to have made the universe, asks Bill not to blame him, as he had a belly-ache that day (yes, our universe was apparently vomited up from a Turtle's belly). The Turtle tells Bill that only the ritual of Chud can defeat It.

*IT (a.k.a. MR. BOB GRAY, PENNYWISE THE CLOWN).* Apparently many centuries old, It, in the form of Pennywise the Clown, bears a chilling resemblance to serial killer John Wayne Gacy, who once entertained children as Pogo the Clown before eventually murdering thirty-three men and boys. The origins of It are shrouded in mystery, though there are a few clues. Richie and Mike have a vision of the coming of It, in which the creature arrives inside a meteor, but this doesn't jibe with Bill's experiences in the Macroverse. According to

Bill, It came from "the outside." When asked to elaborate, he says, "Outside everything," telling his friends that It had always been there.

Indeed, as far as Derry is concerned, It *has* always been there, perhaps waiting eons for the arrival of human inhabitants. From the early 1700s on, It treated Derry as its own private preserve. There are those who believe that It keeps Derry's people as if they were cattle, and those who posit that in some way, It *is* Derry. Speaking with the police after Adrian Mellon's murder, witness Don Hagerty tells of seeing Pennywise on the scene. When asked who it was, Don replies, "It was Derry. It was this town."

After being attacked by her father, Beverly says, "It's everywhere in Derry. It just fills the hollow places." It exists "in a simple cycle of waking to eat and sleeping to dream," emerging from It's home beneath Derry every twenty-seven years or so to feed. In 1958, It is confronted and defeated by a group of seven children calling themselves the Losers Club. Severely wounded, It retreats to its lair to heal and to plan the demise of its enemies. In 1985, It is apparently killed by the Losers Club, now adults. It may still be alive, however.

**THE LOSERS CLUB.** The name given by Richie Tozier to the seven friends (himself, Bill Denbrough, Beverly Marsh, Stan Uris, Ben Hanscom, Mike Hanlon, and Eddie Kaspbrak) who battle It (and Henry Bowers) in the summer of 1958.

**GEORGE DENBROUGH.** Bill's six-year-old brother, George falls victim to It in 1957, (when his arm is ripped out of its socket as he reaches into a sewer to retrieve a paper boat). Bill, who made the boat for his brother, blames himself for George's death.

**WILLIAM (BILL) DENBROUGH.** Seeking to avenge the death of his brother, Bill leads the Losers Club in its battle against It in the summer of 1958. Bill goes on to attend the University of Maine. Pursuing his dream of becoming a writer, Bill sends the manuscript of his first novel, *The Dark*, to Viking Press, mainly because he likes the company logo. Surprisingly, Viking purchases the book, launching Bill's career. His second book, *The Black Rapids,* is filmed as *Pit of the Black*

*Demon;* on the set, he meets actress Audra Phillips, who later becomes his wife.

Like the rest of the Losers Club, Bill receives a call from Mike Hanlon in the summer of 1985, reminding him of the promise they all made to return to Derry should It reappear. At first, Bill can recall only bits and pieces of that summer. Eventually, he regains his memories, as well as the stutter that plagued him in his youth. After It attempts to scare him and the rest of his band away, Bill again leads the others (*sans* Stan Uris and the seriously wounded Mike Hanlon), back into Derry's labyrinthine sewer system to face It. The group triumphs once more, at the cost of Eddie Kaspbrak's life and Audra Denbrough's sanity.

Bill Denbrough is alive and well, but his present whereabouts are unknown. His career is still flourishing.

*AUDRA DENBROUGH.* Bill Denbrough's actress wife, she bears a striking resemblance to Beverly Marsh. Worried about her husband, Audra follows him to Derry, where she is captured by It. Unable to cope with the things she sees in It's deadlights, Audra succumbs to shock. Rescued by the adult Losers, she remains unresponsive and listless even after It's demise. Bill Denbrough has almost reconciled himself to life with the mindless Audra when he spies his beloved bike "Silver" in Mike Hanlon's shed. Carrying Audra on its handlebars, he takes her on a wild ride through downtown Derry. The result is miraculous as the harrowing bicycle trip frees Audra from her mental prison, returning her to normal. Audra is presumed to be alive and well, still living with her husband.

*MIKE HANLON.* Mike differs from most of the Losers in that he has a positive relationship with his parents, especially his father. Being African American, however, he learns the lessons prejudice and hate had to teach him early on. While the other members of the Losers Club leave Derry after It is vanquished, Mike stays. He takes a job as a librarian at the Derry Public Library and begins work on *The Unauthorized History of Derry.* As a result of his research, Mike knows more than anyone else about the evil presence that suffuses the town.

Because Mike stays, he, unlike his friends, never forgets the events of 1958. When Mike notices that It has become active once again, he calls the members of the Losers Club back to Derry. Mike acts as the group's historian, triggering their memories of the summer of 1958. He also points out the group's similarities—they are all very successful, and they are all childless. Although wounded by Henry Bowers, Mike survives his second encounter with It; this time, however, his memory is wiped clean of the events of 1958 and 1985. Mike continues as the librarian in Derry to this day.

*BEN HANSCOM.* Ben has always been a builder—at the age of eleven, he designed the dam the Losers built in the Barrens in the summer of 1958, the dam that also cemented the bonds between the initial members of the Losers Club. Capitalizing on his inherent talent for design, Ben grows up to be a world-famous architect.

Ben survives his second encounter with It; in the process, he becomes romantically involved with Beverly Marsh, the only woman he has ever truly loved. Presumably, Ben returns to Hemingford Home, Nebraska, with Beverly after leaving Derry.

*STAN URIS.* The most reluctant member of the Losers Club, Stan's ultrarational mind was never fully able to accept the terror dwelling in Derry's sewers. When Mike Hanlon calls him twenty-seven years later, his mind snaps. Stan commits suicide in his bathtub, leaving the word It scrawled in his blood on his bathroom wall. It was Stan, however, who forged the bond between the Losers that Mike exploited in 1985. After their first encounter with It, Stan had the group swear a blood oath to return to Derry if It should ever come back.

*BEVERLY ROGAN (née MARSH).* As a child, Beverly was abused by her father; as an adult, she is battered by her husband. Beverly is the only female member of the Losers Club. As tough as any of the others, she bears the group's weapon, a slingshot and silver slugs. During their first encounter with It, Beverly performs another ritual of sorts. By having sex with her male counterparts, she initiates their passage from children into adults.

Due to her second encounter with It and to her budding relationship with Ben Hanscom, Beverly develops confidence she never had before, despite the fact that she grew up to be a world-famous fashion designer. She is presumed alive and well, most likely residing in Hemingford Home.

*TOM ROGAN.* Beverly's abusive husband. Tom forbids her from leaving home after she receives Mike Hanlon's phone call. When she defies him, he attacks her. Fighting back, Beverly fends him off, leaving her surprised husband battered and bruised. It draws Tom to Derry to do It's bidding, using him to kidnap Audra Denbrough. Rogan delivers Audra to It's lair but dies after staring into It's deadlights.

*RICHIE TOZIER.* Always the comedian, young Richie is forever doing impressions. Richie grows up to be a radio personality famous for his repertoire of outrageous characters. During their second encounter with It, Richie enters the Macroverse to bring Bill out.

*EDDIE KASPBRAK.* Dominated by his fearful mother, Eddie develops psychosomatic asthma. Because of his fear of illness, It took the shape of a hideous leper when It confronted Eddie in 1958.

Eddie's aspirator plays an important role in the Losers' battles with It. In their first encounter, each member of the group ritualistically took a shot from the aspirator, further expressing their unity. Eddie, realizing that he too could exploit the nature of It's power, wounds It by spraying It with his aspirator. Eddie suffers a broken arm in both 1958 and 1985. He also guides the group to It both times. Unfortunately, Eddie does not survive his second encounter with It.

*HENRY BOWERS.* As an adult, Ben Hanscom says, "If there has ever been a genuinely evil kid strutting across the skin of the world, Henry Bowers was that kid." A bully who terrorized the Losers in the summer of 1958, Henry has been frustrated in most of his attempts to humiliate and injure the group. He does, however, manage to carve his initials into Ben's stomach and break Eddie's arm. Strangely enough, Henry is indirectly responsible for It's defeat—his constant harassment of those smaller or different from him resulted in the formation of the Losers Club.

Henry, whose hair turned white in 1958 after a personal encounter with It, was blamed for the crimes that occurred that summer. Found insane, he spent the next twenty-seven years as an inmate at Juniper Hill asylum. In 1985, It calls him back to Derry, where he severely wounds Mike Hanlon in the Derry Library. Henry then tries to murder Eddie, who kills him in self-defense.

*THE OTHER.* The otherworldly force that created both It and the Turtle, and also the power behind the formation of the Losers Club.

*THE RITUAL OF CHUD.* The ritual the members of the Losers Club perform to defeat It. As Bill Denbrough explains, it is the only way to subdue a glamour, or taelus, the closest description for It. The taelus sticks its tongue out, its challenger does the same in return, and the opponents bite into each other's tongues and don't let go until one is defeated. The essence of the ritual is that the Losers must look It in the eye to defeat It.

## ADAPTATION

*IT* was adapted as a 1990 television miniseries called *Stephen King's IT.* The production featured Richard Thomas (Bill Denbrough), Harry Anderson (Richie Tozier), Dennis Christopher (Eddie Kaspbrak), Richard Masur (Stan Uris), Annette O'Toole (Beverly Marsh), Tim Reid (Mike Hanlon), and John Ritter (Ben Hanscom). A young Seth Green, later to gain fame playing Oz on *Buffy the Vampire Slayer,* played Richie Tozier as a youth.

Obviously lacking a large budget for special effects (we see the Teenage Werewolf but nothing else), this imaginative production makes effective use of low-tech scares (as when one of the Losers is attacked in the boys' locker room when the shower heads come to life). The suspense mounts until It reveals its true visage to the Losers Club—a very weak special effect—then quickly dissipates, making for an unsatisfying conclusion. Although all the players do a good job, Tim Curry's portrayal of Pennywise the Clown is a standout. Curry is genuinely frightening—his bravura performance has no doubt caused many a nightmare over the years.

# 11

## *Insomnia*

---

COMING ON THE HEELS of *Gerald's Game* (1992) and *Dolores Claiborne* (1993), *Insomnia* (1994) provides further evidence that, following the destruction of Castle Rock in 1991's *Needful Things,* Stephen King had moved on to a new phase in his writing career. The evidence was certainly there: two character-driven novels in a row, with nary a supernatural element in sight, followed by a dark fantasy detailing the adventures of two senior citizens. Had the author made a conscious decision to avoid horror, the genre that had brought him his greatest fame to date?

King had used older characters before in his fiction, but none as elderly as Ralph Roberts and Lois Chasse, and none featured as prominently in a plotline. *Firestarter* (1980), *Pet Sematary* (1983), and *The Shining* (1977) featured Irv Manders, Judson Crandall, and Dick Hallorann, respectively, who served either as father figures to the particular male leads of those novels or as grandfather figures to younger characters. Glen Bateman, a secondary character in *The Stand* (1978), served a similar purpose there, also acting as mentor to the governing body of the Free Zone. King did showcase seniors in more expansive roles in the TV miniseries *Golden Years* (1991), but only briefly. Its protagonist, Harlan Williams, ages backward after he is caught in a blast at a research lab. Of course, *The Stand* also highlights the brittle Mother Abagail, but she exists more as an icon than as a real human being.

*Insomnia*, however, takes two senior citizens and places them at the center of the action. During the novel's slow buildup, readers are told about the perils and mixed blessings of growing old; it isn't until the second half of the narrative that really wild things start to happen.

King zeroes in on the milieu of the elderly with razor-sharp focus. Readers learn the details of Ralph's day-to-day existence, and suffer with him through the loss of his spouse and as his agonizing malady worsens. They see Ralph and the other "old crocks" struggle to live out their final days in dignity, which society and even, in some cases, their own children deny them. For example, prodded by his duplicitous spouse, Lois's son is unnecessarily considering putting her in a rest home.

As Bill McGovern reflects at one point in *Insomnia*, getting old is no job for sissies.

King may have been inspired to tackle the subject herein by Don Robertson's *The Ideal Genuine Man*, a book published by King's own Philtrum Press, which deals with many of the same issues. *Insomnia* is a unique hybrid, at once one of King's more down-to-earth and one of his more "cosmic" novels: down to earth in that it centers on the lives of two senior citizens, who, up until the time the novel begins, have led a quiet, restrained existence; cosmic in its consideration of human fate and destiny, and in its explicit ties to King's *Dark Tower* series, specifically mentioning the Tower of Existence and Roland the gunslinger.

*Insomnia* is similar in a number of ways to King's 1993 short story, "The Ten O'Clock People." There, too, the main character experiences a change in perception due to his attempts to kick his smoking habit. As a result, he can see a race of "batmen" that nonsmokers cannot. *Insomnia* also has ties to several other King novels. The story is set in Derry, the locale of *IT* (1986). King here makes constant references to the events of that novel, like the Great Storm of 1985. Later, he mentions that things that fall into Derry's sewers have a nasty way of popping up again when you least expect them. Mike Hanlon, one of the heroes of *IT*, appears briefly in *Insomnia* in his adult incarnation as chief librarian at the Derry Public Library.

Within *Insomnia*, Ralph escapes the court of the Crimson King and glimpses an unearthly glow of swirling colors, which he instinctively thinks of as "deadlights," a concept also used in *IT.* Lois, meeting TV news personality Connie Chung, tells her she is "her number one fan," perhaps a nod to the catchphrase first introduced in *Misery* (1987). A picture of *Insomnia* character Susan Day is noted in the pages of *Rose Madder* (1995). Atropos, who, in the manner of a serial killer takes souvenirs from his kills, keeps Gage Creed's *(Pet Sematary)* lost sneaker in his lair. Ralph subsequently appears in 1998's *Bag of Bones;* he has a brief conversation with Mike Noonan, who comments that Ralph later died in a car accident.

Most explicit among all of these connections are the links to King's gunslinger books. Clothos and Lachesis tell Ralph and Lois about ka, the great wheel of being. Clothos and Lachesis also label their alliance a ka-tet, a concept introduced in *The Drawing of the Three* (1987). We also learn that Patrick Danville, the young boy in *Insomnia, dreams* about Roland from *The Dark Tower.* After his mother asks him about a picture he has drawn (featuring Roland squaring off against the Red King against the backdrop of the Tower), Patrick tells her that Roland is a king. Finally, after Patrick is saved, the book shifts to a scene where "a man named Roland" turns over in his bedroll and "rests easily once again beneath the alien constellations." Patrick has apparently played a role in combating the cosmic forces working against Roland's quest.

The book can also be seen as another contemplation of Fate and Destiny, topics first explored at great length in *The Dead Zone.* King obviously evokes that subject in *Insomnia's* use of Clothos, Lachesis, and Atropos, the novel's three "little bald doctors," named for the three goddesses of Greek and Roman mythology who were thought to control human destiny. King suggests that we all have roles to play in this life, that we all are part of some cosmic plan.

In mapping out the forces at work in his universe, Stephen King has Clothos and Lachesis explain the four constants of existence—Life, Death, the Random, and the Purpose—and the hierarchy of short timers (normal mortals), long timers (enhanced mortals), and all timers (immortals). They also add that all are part of the same Tower of Existence (to Roland, the Dark Tower). Between the Random and the Purpose—or, to use terms from other King works, the Beast and the Other—a kind of chess game is being played, but still there is mystery aplenty in life. There is a plan, but it can be altered. In *Insomnia*, Atropos, an agent of the Random, tries to do just that, but is frustrated when Ralph and Lois intervene.

More of a dark fantasy than outright supernatural horror, *Insomnia* contains a number of literary references as well: the Bible (Ed Deepneau mentions King Herod in the context of baby killing), J. R. R. Tolkien's epic *The Lord of the Rings* (Ed's wedding ring plays an important part in the narrative, and Bilbo and Frodo Baggins are named), Greek mythology (the little bald doctors may have inspired the legends of Clothos, Lachesis, and Atropos), and Arthurian legend (Ralph is compared to King Arthur and Sir Lancelot several times).

> To promote Insomnia, *King traveled to several independent bookstores across the United States on his Harley-Davidson. The ten-stop tour started in Vermont and ended in California. The trip also provided a great deal of inspiration for* Desperation *and* The Regulators, *both published in 1996.*

With this book, King continues to show a willingness to deal with modern social issues as well. Pro-life versus right-to-choose groups clash in Derry, and the pro-lifers, such as Ed Deepneau, are depicted as madmen. The author also returns to the subject of spousal abuse, a grim topic he deals with in passing in books like *'Salem's Lot* (1975) and *Cujo* (1981), and later explores more graphically in *IT, Gerald's Game,* and *Dolores Claiborne.* King would revisit this subject with a vengeance in his next novel, *Rose Madder.*

## PRIMARY SUBJECTS

*RALPH ROBERTS.* After the tragic death of his wife, seventysomething Ralph begins to suffer from insomnia, waking each night three minutes earlier than the previous night. The insomnia affects many aspects of his existence and causes him to perceive reality in new ways. He begins to see people's auras and can tell when they are about to die, due to the presence of black "death bags" that he perceives hanging over their heads. Ralph's heightened perceptions allow him to observe two tiny, oddly dressed men whom no one else can see. For some reason, he immediately begins to think of them as "the little bald doctors." After he learns their function, Ralph gives them the names Clothos and Lachesis, after the Fates of Greek mythology, who spin and measure the threads of human destiny.

Clothos and Lachesis work to promote the goals of "the Purpose." Another bald doctor opposes them. He is a hideous creature Ralph refers to as Atropos, after the third Fate who severs the human threads of destiny. Atropos serves the Random, and, more directly, a fearsome entity known as the Crimson King. Using Ralph's neighbor Ed Deepneau as a pawn, Atropos sets events in motion that threaten the stability of the universe itself.

Ralph and his friend Lois Chasse have been cursed with insomnia to prepare them to act as human agents of the Purpose. In fact, they have become the "pivot point of great events and vast forces." Ralph and Lois are charged with stopping Ed Deepneau before he destroys the Derry Civic Center. Ed, lost in the throes of madness due to Atropos' manipulations, believes he is attacking Susan Day, a pro-choice advocate who is speaking to a capacity crowd at the Civic Center. In reality, Atropos is using Ed to try to kill a small boy named Patrick Danville, who is attending the event with his mother. Patrick is important to the designs of the Purpose—eighteen years later, he is destined to save two men, one whose existence is also vital to the cause.

Eventually, Ralph squares off against Ed and the master manipulator, the Crimson King. He narrowly defeats them, averting disaster only by a thin margin. Patrick lives, hopefully to fulfill his destiny.

During an encounter with Atropos, the little bald doctor taunts Ralph with a vision of the future in which young Natalie Deepneau, Ed's daughter, is struck and killed by an automobile. Ralph cuts a bargain with the Purpose to save Natalie: once he has fulfilled his own purpose, he will give his life in exchange for hers. As Ralph lies dying in the arms of Lois Chasse, now his wife, Clothos and Lachesis come to guide him to a new plane of existence.

**CAROLYN ROBERTS.** Ralph Roberts's first wife, Carolyn dies from brain cancer. She does, however, remain a presence in his life, as he often "hears" her voice and sees her in his dreams.

**BILL MCGOVERN.** A good friend to Ralph Roberts, Bill is also his tenant. Bill is gay but not openly so. Atropos, who takes souvenirs from his future victims, steals one of Bill's hats and uses it to taunt Ralph. Bill dies after having his "lifeline" cut by Atropos.

**LOIS CHASSE.** Over time, Lois progresses from being Ralph's friend and fellow insomniac to becoming his co-adventurer and his second wife. Lois also sees the special things Ralph sees. She too is chosen by the Purpose to battle the Crimson King. Lois is strong, independent, brave, intelligent, and loving; at once complementing and completing Ralph. Due to the intensity of their supernatural experiences, their mutual admiration quickly deepens into love. Following the conclusion of their adventures, Lois, like Ralph, loses her memory of them. Her memories are reawakened, however, on the day Ralph dies. It is presumed that Lois still resides in Derry.

**ED DEEPNEAU.** A research scientist at Hawking Labs, Ed becomes a pawn of Atropos. Atropos cuts Ed's "string," but Ed doesn't die. Instead, he is driven insane and is programmed by Atropos to mount a kamikaze attack on the Derry Civic Center. Ed dies in the assault on the Civic Center.

**HELEN DEEPNEAU.** Helen's marriage to Ed Deepneau is a nightmare. After a savage beating, she leaves him, fleeing to Woman Care, an organization associated with feminist activist Susan Day. Helen divorces Ed and later adopts a lesbian lifestyle.

**NATALIE DEEPNEAU.** Natalie is Ed and Helen's infant daughter. Ralph sacrifices himself to save her life, thwarting Atropos's plans for vengeance.

**DORRANCE MARSTELLAR.** Though mostly regarded as the town oddball, Ralph learns that "Old Dorr" is privy to the world and thinking of "long timers" like Clothos, Lachesis, and their masters. Old Dorr acts as the long timers' liaison to Ralph and Lois, delivering cryptic messages to them at critical moments and providing guidance to the bewildered duo.

*SUSAN DAY.* A prominent woman's rights activist, her proposed trip to Derry polarizes the pro-life and pro-choice factions there. She is decapitated in the aftermath of Ed Deepneau's attack on the Derry Civic Center, where she is addressing a crowd.

*THE CRIMSON KING.* A mysterious and powerful figure of horrible evil, the Crimson King wants Patrick Danville dead. Raving to Ralph, Ed Deepneau likens the Crimson King to King Herod, going so far as to claim that Herod is merely one of the King's incarnations. Ed states that the Crimson King jumps from body to body and generation to generation, always looking for the Messiah.

During his struggles with Ed, Ralph actually meets the Crimson King in the King's court. The King, apparently plucking memories from Ralph's mind, takes the form of Ralph's mother, then of an enormous red female catfish. Staring intently at the bizarre figure in front of him, Ralph begins to see a shape behind the shape, "a bright man, a red man, with cold eyes and a merciless mouth," an individual who in Ralph's eyes resembles Christ. The King tells Ralph he wants Ed to succeed ("I've worked very hard here in Derry") just before Ralph plunges the sharp point of one of Lois's earrings into the King's bulging eye and escapes.

> *On the striking red-and-white jacket of the Viking hardcover edition of* Insomnia, *King's name is prominently featured in towering white letters, making it clear he should not be characterized as a "crimson" King.*

*THE GREEN MAN.* This mysterious figure appears only briefly in the lives of Ralph Roberts and Lois Chasse, when he returns Lois's earrings, which had been stolen by Atropos. She in turn gives them to Ralph, who later uses them as a weapon in his escape from the court of the Crimson King. Apparently, the Green Man is an enemy of the Crimson King's, but his nature has not been completely revealed as of yet.

*CLOTHOS, LACHESIS, and ATROPOS.* These creatures are mortal but enhanced (long timers) and certainly not human. Ralph Roberts calls them "the three little bald doctors." These otherworldly beings may have been inspired by the Greek myths of the Fates, who weave, measure, and cut the threads of human destiny. Clothos and Lachesis, who describe themselves as "physicians of the last resort," are agents of Death and of the Purpose. Atropos is a rogue, an agent of the Random. Their current whereabouts are unknown.

*PATRICK DANVILLE.* Though only a boy when he comes into contact with Ralph Roberts and Lois Chasse, Patrick is vital to the designs of the Purpose. In the year 2012, Patrick will sacrifice himself to save the lives of two men, one of whom is also key to the Purpose. Atropos is using Ed, who is in the service of the Random, to try to kill Patrick. His death would be disastrous to the Purpose. According to Clothos, Patrick is more important than Adolf Hitler, Winston Churchill, and Augustus Caesar. If he dies, "the Tower of all existence will fall." Fortunately, Ralph and Lois save Patrick from the Crimson King.

# 1 2

## *Bag of Bones*

---

STEPHEN KING created quite a stir in 1997 when word spread through the publishing industry that he was allegedly unhappy with Viking, his New York–based publisher of close to two decades. The press reported that King was rankled by Viking's supposed refusal to meet his asking price for his latest novel. The full story is almost certainly more complex. A resolution was reached when the author signed a three-book deal with Simon & Schuster, entering into a unique partnership with the publisher. Forgoing his usual large advance, King worked out an arrangement that reportedly gave him a higher percentage of the profits at the back end.

The first book King delivered to the publisher's prestigious Scribners imprint was *Bag of Bones*. A marked departure from what the general public had come to expect from "America's best-loved bogeyman," the novel represents yet another step in the author's continuous challenge to himself to elevate the overall quality and emotional scope of his work. Equal parts ghost story, thriller, romance, mystery, and psychological suspense story, *Bag of Bones* demonstrates that King is as adept at evoking heartfelt emotion as he is at sending shivers up readers' spines. Critics who had previously dismissed the popular author as a mere shockmeister, finally upgraded their opinions after experiencing this powerfully told, masterfully crafted roller-coaster of a book. Simply stated, it ranks among the best novels the author has written in his entire career.

A love story with supernatural overtones, *Bag of Bones* consciously evokes Daphne du Maurier's *Rebecca* (1938). King, however, twists the premise of that classic romantic thriller to suit his own purposes. Instead of a wicked woman being mistaken for a good one, *Bag of Bones* features a good woman, Jo Noonan, whose recently revealed secret life causes her husband, bestselling author Mike, to doubt his complete trust of her. There are numerous other overt connections to du Maurier's novel—"I have dreamt again of Manderley" is a familiar refrain throughout—as well as more subtle ties: for example, the character Max Devore evokes *Rebecca's* Maxim de Winter. Other literary connections include Herman Melville's "Bartleby the Scrivener" (1856); the inclusion of Noonan's discussion of this short story earlier in the novel provides a poignancy to his words which close the book. Finally, one of Mike's college professors attributes a particular quote to nineteenth-century British novelist Thomas Hardy: "Compared to the dullest human being actually walking about on the face of the earth and casting his shadow there, the most brilliantly drawn character is nothing but a bag of bones." This quote resonates throughout the novel, and also has a more literal meaning in that a real bag of bones figures in the plot.

*King's office* | BETH GWINN

Besides its central focus as a "haunted love story" (as King himself succinctly describes it), *Bag of Bones* also provides insight on both the writing process and the publishing industry, deftly conveying Mike's (and presumably some of King's) insider views on the interrelationship between business and art. *Bag of Bones* also mentions several of Mike's companions on the bestseller lists, including Tom Clancy, Dean Koontz, Jean Auel, and Mary Higgins Clark. (Interestingly, Noonan never mentions Anne Rice nor, for that matter, himself. Noonan also talks about writing novels and purposely putting them aside for later publication, demanding publication dates influenced not by when the book is done, but by when it will be best positioned to sell out in the marketplace.)

Although it downplays any element of the fantastic at first (Mike lives in Derry, Maine, the setting of *IT* (1986) and *Insomnia* (1994), but has never seen a demonic clown poking his head out of a sewer), *Bag of Bones* is set squarely in the midst of the Stephen King universe. Mike interacts with residents of Derry already familiar to King readers, such as druggist Joe Wyzer and Ralph Roberts. The action later shifts to Dark Score Lake, where Jessie Burlingame (1992's *Gerald's Game*) was sexually molested by her father in 1963. Noonan refers to two writers from the King canon, William Denbrough *(IT)* and Thad Beaumont (1989's *The Dark Half*). Denbrough and his "famous creatures from beyond" are favorites of Jo Noonan's. Thad Beaumont is mentioned in a less pleasant context: after learning that Thad broke up with his wife in *Needful Things* (1991), readers hear from Noonan that the troubled writer has committed suicide. Finally, Mike encounters Norris Ridgewick, formerly of the Castle Rock police (Mike inquires after Alan Pangborn and Polly Chalmers).

*Bag of Bones* marks a milestone of sorts in that beyond its expected bestseller status, the author received extremely favorable reviews worldwide, even from critics who had never read a ghost story—or a Stephen King book—before.

## PRIMARY SUBJECTS

*MIKE NOONAN.* A successful writer who laughingly refers to himself as "V. C. Andrews with a prick," Mike is the author of several bestselling novels, including *Being Two, The Red Shirt Man,* and *All the Way from the Top.* Suffering from severe writer's block after the tragic death of his pregnant wife, Jo, from an aneurysm, Mike resorts to publishing novels he had previously written and then purposely withheld to maintain the illusion that he is still writing new works.

Mike is experiencing strange dreams centering on his vacation home at Dark Score Lake, Maine. Compelled by these dreams and hoping that the change in scenery will calm his anxieties and reignite his creativity, Mike moves back to Dark Score to his lakeside cabin, a large house known to locals as "Sara Laughs." Shortly after arriving, he begins receiving messages from ghostly presences inhabiting his home. These spirits initially make their presence known in harmless ways—wailing in the night, sudden changes in room temperature, and refrigerator magnets that seem to move of their own accord—but their communications soon become more urgent. Mike senses that one of the spirits may be Jo, but there are other angrier and more dangerous presences haunting the environs of Sara Laughs as well.

Mike is troubled by his failure to understand these messages, and by new information he unearths that indicates his beloved Jo may have been having an extramarital affair before she died. He becomes distracted, however, by the plight of Mattie Devore, whom he meets after rescuing her young toddler, Kyra, from a busy local highway. An attractive twenty-year-old widow, Mattie is engaged in a bitter custody battle with her father-in-law, millionaire Max Devore, over Kyra. Sympathetic to her plight and prompted by Jo's spirit messages, Mike offers his help.

Mattie's problems provide a much needed diversion for Mike, who, for the first time since his wife died, actually feels useful. Buoyed by a budding romantic relationship with Mattie, Mike takes the battle directly to Devore, hiring savvy custody lawyer John Storrow to defend Mattie's interests. Max pushes back, first through flunkies like Sheriff George Footman and real estate broker Richard Osgood, and then more directly. Accompanied by his "personal assistant" Rogette Whitmore, Max takes Mike by surprise on the shore of Dark Score Lake, and nearly kills him.

Obviously facing a powerful enemy in Max Devore, Mike has an even more formidable opponent in the vengeful spirit that haunts Sara

Laughs. Following a trail initially blazed by his late wife, Mike learns that Kyra's predicament has its roots in the town's past, specifically in the rape and murder of a vibrant blues singer named Sara Tidwell nearly a century ago. A black woman whose confident, forthright manner offended some of Dark Score's residents, Sara and her son, Kito, were killed by a group of local hooligans led by Max Devore's ancestor Jared. To conceal their crime, the killers stuff the corpses in a burlap bag and bury it near the lake.

Sara takes her revenge on Dark Score from beyond the grave. Instigating the deaths of several children over the course of the next century, she has recently turned to the progeny of her chief tormentor, Jared Devore, seeking the death of Kyra. Knowing she is the root cause of the evil he faces allows Mike to defy Sara's power, which is no mean feat, considering Sara has influenced otherwise loving parents to kill their own children. Mike breaks Sara's hold over the town by uncovering and destroying her remains, which had been laid to rest near the lake. Mike survives his supernatural encounter with the ghost of Sara. When last heard from, he had initiated adoption proceedings to gain custody of Kyra. Shaken to the core by the tragic events, Mike abandons his writing career.

*JO NOONAN (née ARLEN)*. Mike's late wife, Jo died of a brain aneurysm in August 1994 at the age of thirty-four. Adding to the tragedy, Noonan discovers soon thereafter that she was pregnant with their first child. Mike also learns Jo was hiding something from him. Initially, Mike concludes it was an affair. Later, however, he finds out that she had uncovered the secret shame of Dark Score Lake, namely the rape and murder of Sara Tidwell. Jo had gathered these facts in secret, and was presumably waiting for the right moment to reveal them to Mike. Jo's spirit haunts Dark Score Lake, guiding, and aiding Mike in his supernatural fight against Sara Tidwell.

*"SARA LAUGHS"*. The name of the Noonan's summer residence at Dark Score Lake. The cabin is named after blues singer Sara Tidwell, a former resident. Sara was famous for (among other things) her raucous laugh.

*MATTIE DEVORE*. Widow of Lance Devore and mother of Kyra, Mattie becomes involved in a tug-of-war with her father-in-law, Max Devore, over legal custody of Kyra. Although reluctant at first, Mattie accepts Mike's emotional and financial support, promising she will someday pay him back. Despite their age difference (Mike is in his early forties, Mattie is only twenty), she is clearly attracted to him. Mike in turn struggles with his feelings and, eventually professes his love. Tragically, they never consummate their relationship, as George Footman fatally shoots Mattie.

*LANCE DEVORE*. Youngest son of millionaire Max Devore, Lance came to Dark Score Lake in 1994 to survey his father's holdings and instead fell in love with Mattie Stanfield, whom he met at a softball game. Three weeks later they were inseparable and Mattie was pregnant. They were married in September 1994, three months after they met. A little over three years later Lance dies after falling off the roof of their trailer home in the midst of a lightning storm. Lance had been estranged from his father, who disapproved of the marriage (and had in fact offered Mattie a considerable sum to abandon her husband and child). Lance tries to reconcile with his father shortly before his death by sending the old man a picture of his granddaughter. The picture arouses Max's interest in Kyra and prompts him to come to Dark Score Lake a few weeks later.

*KYRA DEVORE*. Daughter of Lance and Mattie Devore, Kyra is a precocious three-year-old who steals Mike Noonan's heart seconds after he "rescues" her from the middle of a busy local highway. Mike develops a strong bond with Kyra, mainly because her name resembles one he and Jo had picked for their unborn child, and because she is the age his child would have been had Jo lived and given birth. Their bond grows stronger as Mike learns that the spirits who haunt Sara Laughs are also speaking to Kyra, and deepens after they share a dream in which they visit Dark Score Lake at the turn of the century. The focus of the custody battle between her mother and grandfather, Kyra is caught in the middle—she loves her mother but also feels affection for her grandfather and her "White Nana," Rogette Whitmore. Kyra is suddenly orphaned when George Footman guns down her mother.

After her mother's death Mike begins proceedings to adopt her legally.

*MAX DEVORE*. Max is the great-grandson of Jared Devore, the man who instigates the attack on Sara Tidwell. Said to be worth some $600 million, eightysomething Max made his money in the advent of the modern computer revolution. Estranged from his son, Lance, Max has cut off all contact with him. After Lance's accidental death, Max returns to his childhood home of Dark Score Lake, currying favor with the locals by spreading his money around. Shortly thereafter, Max seeks custody of his granddaughter, Kyra. Due to the intervention of Mike Noonan, however, these efforts proved unsuccessful. Max dies shortly after he and Rogette Whitmore attack Mike at the lake.

*ROGETTE WHITMORE*. Devore's personal assistant, Rogette is later revealed to be his daughter. Called "White Nana" by her niece, Kyra, Rogette lives for her father's approval, eagerly carrying out his every wish. Although Rogette has been ravaged by cancer (people automatically think of the horrific woman in Edvard Munch's painting *The Scream* when they see her), she seems to have an almost preternatural athletic ability. She demonstrates this skill when she starts hurling rocks at Mike after he tries to escape from Rogette and Max by diving into Dark Score Lake. Rogette's throws are amazingly strong and accurate. One hits Mike in the head, almost causing him to pass out.

After Max's death, Rogette schemes to kill Kyra, sending her father's lackeys to shoot Mattie, Kyra, and their friends. The little girl survives, and Rogette kidnaps Kyra. Kyra again escapes, and Rogette perishes in an attempt to retrieve the little girl.

*GEORGE FOOTMAN*. Castle County Sheriff, George Footman works for Max Devore on the side, threatening Mike in the early stages of the writer's ongoing conflict with the multimillionaire. Footman is the gunman who opens fire on Mattie Devore's trailer, killing her and wounding three of her four guests. Footman is later captured by private investigator George Kennedy and Mike Noonan, and is eventually sent to nearby Shawshank State Prison for his crimes.

*RICHARD OSGOOD.* A local real estate agent who spies on Mattie Devore for her father-in-law, Osgood is driving the car from which George Footman shoots and kills Mattie Devore. Osgood dies horribly when George Kennedy's gunshots ignite the gas tank of the sedan he is driving. Unable to free himself, he is burned alive.

*JOHN STORROW.* The lawyer Mike hires to protect Mattie's interests in her custody battle with Max Devore, Storrow successfully fends off all Max Devore's legal maneuvers. John, who has a crush on Mattie, is wounded in a hail of gunfire during Mattie's victory party to celebrate Max Devore's death.

*SARA TIDWELL.* A provocative turn-of-the-century blues singer, Sara and her family made their home on Dark Score Lake for a time, at least until prejudice brought them all tragedy. Sara makes the fatal mistake of humiliating Jared Devore in front of his cronies, Oren Peebles, Fred Dean, Harry Auster, and George Armbruster. The group strikes back, beating, raping, and finally killing her, but not before she witnesses her son's drowning at the hands of Auster (who, unknown to Mike Noonan, is a distant relative of his). Sara's rage survives her death. Over the ensuing decades, her vengeful spirit is responsible for the deaths of several children at Dark Score Lake, all descendants of the group that took her life. Nearly a hundred years later, Sara sets her murderous sights on Kyra Devore but is ultimately frustrated by the efforts of Mike and Jo Noonan. Her spirit, anchored to Dark Score Lake by her mortal remains, vanishes when Mike destroys her skeleton in a final confrontation.

*THE RED TOPS.* Sara Tidwell's band, consisting of her family and friends. These performers and their families (approximately forty individuals) tried to make their home at Dark Score Lake, settling in what came to be known as Tidwell's Meadow, where they built the home that became known as Sara Laughs. They are described condescendingly in ancient newspaper clippings Mike discovers as Castle County's "Southern Blackbirds" and "rhythmic darkies." Although most members of the white community had no objection to their presence, racism and prejudice eventually rear their ugly heads, resulting in the deaths of Sara and her son, Kito. After that, the locals closed ranks against the survivors, most notably against Sara's brother Reg Tidwell and his family. The Tidwells, et al., abandoned Dark Score after Reg's son, Junior, died of blood poisoning brought on by an injury sustained in a bear trap set on a path he was known to frequent.

## ADAPTATION

A full-length audio version of *Bag of Bones,* read by the author, is available from Simon & Schuster Audio. In many ways, King is the perfect reader for his own novel. Because it is a regional work, the author's natural Maine accent is perfectly suited to the material. Although King is a more successful novelist than Mike, he still has a lot in common with his creation, which lends verisimilitude to his reading. Finally, King is also in tune with what he refers to as the "temperature gradient" of the characters, meaning he knows precisely how much emotion to invest in any given scene. The audio version also includes a substantial interview with the author conducted by the tape's producer, Eve Beglarian, who is reportedly developing an operatic version of King's story "The Man in the Black Suit."

# 13

## Related Tales

---

TWO SHORT STORIES set in or near Derry clearly belong to the same universe as the novels discussed above. "The Road Virus Heads North" is a particularly powerful Derry story. It concerns a writer's unfortunate encounter with a monstrous representative of the Random.

### "AUTOPSY ROOM FOUR"
#### from *Six Stories* (1997)

"Autopsy Room Four," a tale reminiscent of Edgar Allan Poe, details the travails of Howard Cottrell, a golfer rendered unconscious by a snake bite while on Derry Municipal Golf Course. Howard awakens in an autopsy room just as the coroners are preparing to cut him open from stem to stern. Able to see and hear, Howard is still paralyzed by the bite, and watches helplessly as the doctors prepare for their grim task. Fortunately for Howard, the autopsy is interrupted before it does him injury.

Going through his golf bag, paramedics are surprised to find an exotic snake. We won't reveal the ending—King's buildup, leading up to the story's last line, is outright hilarious. Suffice it to say that Howard develops an interesting fetish as a result of his experiences.

## "THE ROAD VIRUS HEADS NORTH"

### (1999)

This tale of the supernatural made its appearance in *999*, a massive anthology edited by Al Sarrantonio and published in 1999. King's contribution is about a figure in a portrait that comes to life, recalling his 1990 novella "The Sun Dog" and his novel *Rose Madder* (1995).

Author Richard Kinnell is on his way back to Derry, Maine, after attending a writer's conference in Boston when he decides to stop at a garage sale in Rosewood. Scanning the items for sale, he is taken with a vivid, framed watercolor. Purchasing the painting despite its bleak subject matter (a picture of a deranged, fanged driver in his Grand Am) and the fact that the artist recently committed suicide, Kinnell puts it in his trunk and proceeds on his journey, stopping at his aunt Trudy's house along the way.

Kinnell shows the picture to his aunt, who is extremely disturbed by it. This bothers him, but not as much as the fact that the picture has changed since he bought it—the figure has moved, if only slightly. The next day, Kinnell tosses the painting into a ditch, only to find it waiting for him when he gets home. The watercolor has changed once again, this time showing a scene of carnage at the Rosewood home where he purchased the painting. Checking the news, Kinnell discovers that the woman who was running the garage sale is dead, brutally murdered by an unknown assailant.

Later, he hears a car outside, and realizes to his horror that the fanged man has come directly to his home.

# SECTION THREE

## The Prime Reality, Part II: Castle Rock

*The Dead Zone*

*Cujo*

*The Dark Half*

*Needful Things*

Related Tales

ING'S EARLY WORK WAS most often set near the small New England mill town of Castle Rock, Maine, which was for many years, without a doubt, the geographical center of the Stephen King universe. Located in southwestern Maine ten miles south of Rumford and about thirty miles west of Augusta, the unusually tragedy-stricken town figures in several short stories (such as "Mrs. Todd's Shortcut," "Nona," "Uncle Otto's Truck," and "It Grows on You"), two novellas ("The Body" and "The Sun Dog"), and four novels. Much more than a mere setting for King's tales of the strange and macabre, the site effectively functioned as a scale model of contemporary American society.

King began experimenting with the idea of the small town as a "social and psychological microcosm" as far back as *Carrie* (1974) and became more ambitious with the concept in *'Salem's Lot* (1975). He did not hit his stride, however, until *The Dead Zone* (1979), his first novel to feature Castle Rock. In this novel, psychic Johnny Smith is asked to lend a hand in tracking down the infamous Castle Rock Strangler. Smith reluctantly agrees, subsequently revealing the killer to be Frank Dodd, a popular local law enforcement officer. Dodd's crimes and subsequent suicide make national headlines, beginning what many locals consider to be nothing less than a curse on the town.

> *King took the name Castle Rock from a favorite novel of his youth, William Golding's 1954 classic* Lord of the Flies. *The name in turn was used by Rob Reiner, director of* Stand by Me, *as the name of his production company.*

Clearly, King knows the town intimately. In the introduction to "The Sun Dog," the author refers to his own wealth of unwritten knowledge about the town, noting examples such as "how Sheriff George Bannerman lost his virginity in the back seat of his dead father's car." As the years passed, the author "became more and more interested in—almost entranced by—the secret life of this town, by the hidden relationships which seemed to come clearer and clearer" to him. Castle Rock had become his town, the way "the mythical town of Isola is Ed McBain's town and the West Virginia village of Glory was Davis Grubb's town."

> *Castle Rock also figures in the fiction of King's wife, Tabitha. One example of this appears in her 1993 novel* One on One, *in which Castle Rock is depicted as a sports rival of Greenspark Academy, the school that two of her main characters attend.*

Unlike the town of Derry, or for that matter *'Salem's Lot,* King has not revealed much of Castle Rock's history before the turn of the twentieth century. In fact, the most ancient history he has related has been in the short stories "The Man in the Black Suit" and "Uncle Otto's Truck." For all practical purposes, the history of Castle Rock as it relates to the Stephen King universe began with the aforementioned *The Dead Zone*. Many residents believe protagonist Frank Dodd's actions cast a spell of evil on the town. Since 1979, Castle Rock has certainly had more than its share of tragedy. In 1981, Joe Camber's 200-pound St. Bernard dog Cujo went rabid and killed several people. In 1989, famous writer Thad Beaumont was attacked by a madman claiming to be George Stark, a man who couldn't possibly exist. Beaumont never fully recovered from the incident, first separating from his wife, then later committing suicide. And in 1990, Reginald "Pop" Merrill, a fixture of Castle Rock's business community, died in a fire of suspicious origin (see "The Sun Dog" as described in the chapter entry on *Four Past Midnight*).

The most disturbing incident, however, has to be the hysteria that gripped the town in the fall of 1991, coincident with the grand opening of the store called Needful Things. Spouses killed each other, neighbor battled neighbor to the death, and rival church congregations fought tooth and nail in the streets. The town was nearly destroyed in the chaos, as several buildings were dynamited by known criminal Ace Merrill.

By 1990, King had decided to "close the book" on Castle Rock. As one can see from the events in *Needful Things*, Castle Rock went out not with a whimper, but with a bang.

> *Like Derry, Castle Rock has spawned more than its share of working authors. Besides the unfortunate Thad Beaumont, the town is also the birthplace of writer Gordon LaChance (an incident from Gordie's childhood is told in the 1982 novella "The Body.")*

Although King had seemingly cut all ties to the town in *Needful Things* (boldly subtitled "The Last Castle Rock Story"), he is still drawn to its familiar environs. For instance, there is the putative epilogue to that book, a short story called "It Grows on You," which appeared in *Nightmares & Dreamscapes* (1993). The town was also mentioned in passing in the 1996 tale "The Man in the Black Suit," and in 1999's *The Girl Who Loved Tom Gordon*. Former townspeople have also appeared in subsequent stories, the most recent example being former Castle Rock deputy Norris Ridgewick's cameo at the conclusion of *Bag of Bones*.

With its constant struggles between good and evil, Castle Rock seems to be a microcosmic version of the cosmic conflict going on in the Stephen King universe as a whole. The town has served as the setting for King's ongoing examination of the struggle between good and evil, shown in the conflicts between Johnny Smith and Frank Dodd, Donna Trenton and Cujo, and Thad Beaumont and George Stark. The battle described in *Needful Things* provides the best example of this theme. Leland Gaunt is the same breed of monster as other evil denizens of King's universe, such as Randall Flagg *(The Stand, The Eyes of the Dragon)*, Andre Linoge *(Storm of the Century)*, Ardelia Lortz ("The library policeman"), and Kurt Barlow *('Salem's Lot)*. The troubles Gaunt causes in the town are a reflection of the battle that rages between the Random and the Purpose mentioned in *Insomnia*.

One could even characterize the human combatants—Alan Pangborn, Polly Chalmers, and Norris Ridgewick—as a ka-tet similar in structure to the one Roland leads. This drives home the point that although evil exists, it is always opposed by good.

Another recurring theme is that evil lingers, as proved by the legacy of Frank Dodd, which King detailed in *Cujo* and has mentioned several times since. Again, however, King points out that the forces of good are just as resilient, and that a champion always arises in a time of need.

On the map of Maine described in *Dolores Claiborne* and *Gerald's Game*, readers can easily see that Castle Rock is part of King's Maine, sitting as it does to the south of towns like Bangor, Derry, and Haven. The reality of the town is supported by the many references King makes to Castle Rock in other books (for instance, Frank Dodd's suicide became national news and was mentioned in passing in *IT*), and his frequent mentions of such landmarks as Shawshank Prison and the mental institution known as Juniper Hill.

Obviously very resilient, the people of Castle Rock have rebuilt their town and continue with their daily lives. Perhaps the conflagration that nearly destroyed the Rock has cleansed the town of evil, allowing its denizens to live out their days in peace. Perhaps though, evil still lingers there, waiting for the proper moment to inflict new horrors on the unsuspecting populace. Perhaps a "thinny" will open up in the middle of town, depositing Roland and his ka-tet in the center.

Only time will tell.

# 14

## The Dead Zone

O F  T H E  D O Z E N S  of character-driven novels that King has published since 1974, *The Dead Zone* remains one of his most powerful, poignant, and emotionally involving. Tragic and terrifying, *The Dead Zone* was King's first novel to demonstrate that the acknowledged master of horror could also move readers to tears. Although not as overtly frightening as such previous bestsellers as *'Salem's Lot* (1975) and *The Shining* (1977), it is no less memorable.

A somber study of one man's strange and sad journey toward his unique destiny, *The Dead Zone* poses the question of whether one man's actions can change the fate of the entire world. The man in question is a New Hampshire high school teacher who goes by the nondescript name of Johnny Smith.

Johnny's bright future is stolen from him when, upon returning from a date with his sweetheart, Sarah Bracknell, he is involved in an automobile accident that renders him comatose for four and a half years. When he finally awakens, he learns from his parents that the world has gone on without him. The most shocking news, however, is that Sarah, with whom he was deeply in love and believed he would marry, has met and wed another man.

Meanwhile, in another part of the country, a sociopath named Greg Stillson has decided to run for political office as a stepping stone toward the presidency of the United States, though by rights he isn't fit to be the town dogcatcher. Shrewd, cruel, and totally amoral,

Stillson wins his first bid for office. Although it will be years before Smith and Stillson eventually meet, their lives are intimately intertwined in ways they can't begin to imagine. Both are outsiders, but one is fated to heal people, the other is destined to destroy the world.

Johnny learns that his traumatic experience has left him with a special gift, a so-called wild talent. He now possesses incredible psychic powers—mainly that of precognition—in which he can see the future of anyone he touches. However, due to what he refers to as "the dead zone" in his brain, Johnny is unable to place geographically where these events occur. Nor can he "see" what his own future will be. Being thought of as a "celebrity psychic" or some kind of sideshow freak is the last thing Johnny wants, but that is his destiny. His past life is over, and his future is a mystery. To further complicate matters, he also has an inoperable brain tumor that is slowly but surely killing him.

*Smith was born in 1947, the same year as the author. Like Johnny, King also was a teacher.*

After a long period of rehabilitation, Johnny reenters the world, trying to use his power to help those who need it most. His experiences, however, prove to be more traumatic than rewarding. The worst is yet to come, though. While attending a political rally for third-party presidential candidate Greg Stillson, Johnny shakes Stillson's hand. Upon contact, Johnny is stunned by a terrifying vision of Stillson as president, about to engage in an unprovoked act of nuclear aggression against the Soviet Union. Horrified, Johnny realizes that this future act will sound the death knell for the entire world.

*In a 1998 interview, King stated that* The Dead Zone *remains one of his two or three favorite novels.* The Dead Zone *was the first book by the author to reach No. 1 on the* New York Times *bestseller list.*

Faced with an incredible moral dilemma, Johnny must decide whether he has the right to intervene and perhaps take the life of someone who—albeit only potentially—may indirectly murder billions. Johnny reluctantly accepts this responsibility, realizing it might cost him his own life.

*The Dead Zone* is remarkable not only for its intimate portrait of Johnny Smith (what better name to subtly represent Everyman?), but also because King for the first time delves into the secrets of Castle Rock. As he had already done with the fictional town of Jerusalem's Lot and would later do with Derry, King would eventually make Castle Rock stand out as vividly as any of his greatest characters. Although its primary focus is on Johnny Smith, *The Dead Zone* also zeroes in on the many secrets concealed by the town's pleasant façade.

King reminds us repeatedly in *The Dead Zone* how little control we ultimately have over our own destinies. Even if we were allowed glimpses into the future, there is little chance that most of us would be able to substantially change our lot in life. It is not the psychic talent that Johnny possesses which makes him special—it is that he has the courage to try to change fate despite the personal cost. As the classic rock 'n' roll song by the Doors goes, "No one here gets out alive." In the Stephen King universe, that is never more eloquently stated than in *The Dead Zone*. King seems to be saying that, unfair though life may be, we must accept the cards fate has dealt us and try to do the best we can. It's a profoundly sad lesson to absorb, to be sure, but a vitally important one.

## PRIMARY SUBJECTS

*JOHNNY SMITH.* Johnny is an ordinary, likable young man whose entire life is changed when he is involved in an automobile accident that leaves him in a coma. Johnny emerges from that coma with the ability to see a person's future merely by touching him or her. Johnny initially does his best to assist all who ask for his help, but ultimately finds his psychic abilities more of a burden than a joy. After shaking the hand of corrupt politician Greg Stillson, Johnny realizes Stillson will someday bring about a nuclear holocaust that will destroy the world. Himself slowly dying of a brain tumor, Johnny devotes the rest of his days to devising a way to eliminate the threat Stillson presents, ultimately concluding he must kill the man. Although he dies in the attempt, Johnny knows that his sacrifice is not in vain—Stillson's cowardly response during Johnny's assassination attempt effectively squashes his political career, thus preventing the disaster Johnny foresaw.

*SARAH BRACKNELL.* Johnny's one true love and fellow English teacher, Sarah is Johnny's date on the night of his automobile accident. Not knowing if he will ever emerge from his coma, Sarah meets and marries Walter Hazlett and bears him two children. Although happy with Hazlett, she still considers Johnny to be the greatest love of her life. She is believed to be still living in Castle Rock.

*FRANK DODD.* A Castle Rock police officer and one of the most respected men in the community, Dodd harbors a terrible secret: he is the serial rapist/killer known as the Castle Rock Strangler. When identified by Johnny Smith, Dodd cheats justice by slitting his own throat after composing a suicide note on the bathroom mirror with his mother's lipstick. The note reads, *"I Confess."*

*SHERIFF GEORGE BANNERMAN.* The likable sheriff of Castle Rock, Bannerman is willing to lend credence to Johnny's paranormal abilities until the psychic accuses his trusted deputy, Frank Dodd, of being the notorious Castle Rock Strangler. Much to his horror, he is proven wrong in his previous evaluation of Dodd. Bannerman remains sheriff until Joe Camber's rabid dog, Cujo, kills him.

*GREG STILLSON.* Stillson is the utterly corrupt, thoroughly demented congressman running for president of the United States. Horribly abused as a child, he spends the rest of his life getting back at the world that he is convinced he is destined to rule. Entering politics late in life, he seems a viable third-party candidate for president. A chance encounter with Johnny Smith changes all that. As they shake hands, Johnny experiences the insanity Stillson is capable of and dedicates his life to stopping him. Seeing no other solution, Johnny attempts to assassinate Stillson at a political rally. He is unsuccessful, and Stillson escapes serious injury. However, in trying to protect himself, Stillson plucks a child from the crowd and uses the infant as a human shield. Although the child is unhurt, Stillson's political career is ended forever.

*DR. SAMUEL WEIZAK.* A Polish refugee of the Nazi concentration camps of World War II, Weizak is the physician who treats Johnny

after he awakens from his coma. Johnny is able to prove his unique
"wild talent" to the doctor when he informs the elderly man that his
mother, long believed to be a victim of the Holocaust, is still alive.
A "small, roly-poly man," he is believed to be still on the staff at the
local hospital, if he has not already retired.

**RICHARD DEES.** Dees is a
brash reporter working for
*Inside View,* a sleazy supermarket tabloid. Dees's newspaper offers Johnny a job as a
celebrity psychic to boost their
circulation.

> *Dees makes another appearance in
> the 1988 short story "The Night
> Flier," which is included in*
> Nightmares & Dreamscapes.

## ADAPTATION

The 103-minute theatrical version of *The Dead Zone,* released in 1983,
remains one of the most faithful and effective adaptations of a
Stephen King work. Although many of the events of the lengthy novel
were modified or compressed, screenwriter Jeffrey Boam does a masterful job of retaining the fragile essence and somber tone of the original book. (Interestingly, at one point executive producer Dino De
Laurentiis asked King himself to take a crack at adapting his own
novel. After the author did so, De Laurentiis rejected the screenplay
as being "involved and convoluted.")

The director chosen for the project was Canadian David
Cronenberg, who up until that point had never directed a movie for
which he had not written the original screenplay. Cronenberg, already
famous for such bizarre shockers as *They Came from Within* (1975), *The
Brood* (1979), and *Videodrome* (1982), did an incredible job of capturing
the Norman Rockwell look of Castle Rock and King's wintry New
England. Reportedly, the author told Cronenberg that some of the
changes Cronenberg and Boam made to his novel improved and
intensified the power of the narrative.

Equally fortunate was the casting, which starred Academy
Award–winning actor Christopher Walken *(The Deer Hunter)* as
Smith. Walken was the best possible choice for playing the lonely and

haunted protagonist. As much as George C. Scott was Patton in the 1970 movie of the same name, so too is Walken the perfect realization of Johnny Smith. He portrays Smith as someone who may truly be one of the "walking wounded," but who knows his innermost moral convictions are still intact.

In supporting roles, the choices in casting were equally appropriate: Brooke Adams as Sarah, Tom Skerritt as Sheriff Bannerman, Herbert Lom as Dr. Weizak, and Colleen Dewhurst as Henrietta Dodd are all tremendous. Martin Sheen, who portrays Greg Stillson, would be one of the few actors—along with Drew Barrymore and Kathy Bates—ever to appear in a second Stephen King film adaptation. He went on to play Captain Hollister, another ruthless, amoral villain, in 1984's *Firestarter.*

*The Dead Zone* is that rare instance in which a superb creative team came together to make the most effective adaptation of a bestselling novel that could be done, while still remaining essentially true to its source material.

# 15

## *Cujo*

---

CREATED IN ROUGHLY the same period during which *The Dead Zone, Firestarter,* and *Roadwork* were written, *Cujo* is in many ways the grimmest but also the most plausible entry of the group. Here, King explores a dramatic situation that does not require people with wild talents or a man intending to blow up a superhighway as its driving force. In fact, *Cujo's* basic premise is deceptively straightforward: King asks, quite simply, "What would happen if a 200-pound St. Bernard went rabid, endangering the inhabitants of a small town in Maine?"

Vic and Donna Trenton have relocated to the small town of Castle Rock, Maine, in an attempt to find a better life for themselves and their four-year-old son, Tad. The Trentons discover, however, that it's hard to exit the fast lane: Vic's New York advertising agency is on the verge of collapse, and he must devote all his time and energy to saving his last big account with the Sharp Cereal Company. Already stressed by the move, Donna feels abandoned by her workaholic husband. More out of boredom than anything else, she drifts into a brief but destructive affair with a local furniture refinisher. Tad, meanwhile, suffers repeated nightmares about a terrible monster lurking in his bedroom closet.

But young Tad needn't concern himself with the imaginary creature that haunts his dreams. After all, there are plenty of monsters to be found in real life—and in broad daylight. The neighbor's friendly

St. Bernard becomes a waking nightmare after it stumbles on a cave filled with rabid bats. Receiving several bites, the huge canine is slowly transformed into a mindless killing machine.

If there's a lesson to be learned in this book, it's that no one is safe, neither family nor friends nor strangers. The Cambers, Cujo's owners, are a case in point. This dysfunctional family is about as far removed from simple, good-natured country folk as you can get. Joe Camber is an abusive, cruel man, who beats his wife, Charity, and their young son, Brett. Their lives don't improve after their beloved family pet embarks on a murderous rampage. Like the Trentons, some of them will live and some will die. What doesn't make sense, however, is why any of them has to die so needlessly and in such an agonizing manner.

> Due to its mainstream sensibility and bleak ending, Cujo at one point was to be published as a Richard Bachman novel.

When Cujo traps Donna and Tad in their subcompact car outside Joe Camber's garage, they must face the beast without any weapons other than their bare hands and their wits. Their ordeal is not one they deserve; at times it seems almost surreal. But the terror is real, and a child will die before this modern tragedy concludes.

> In Cujo, Tad and Donna Trenton are trapped in a Ford Pinto. At one time, Stephen King owned a Ford Pinto.

What is key here is that despite being characterized as a "horror" novel, there is only the faintest trace of the supernatural in Cujo. The "monster in the closet" that terrifies Tad is only a ruse to distract readers from the real danger. In some ways, it would almost be more comforting if a two-headed bogeyman or the ghost of Frank Dodd were lurking in the closet; it would certainly be easier to endure if at the end we could blame it all on the supernatural or paranormal. Instead, King focuses intently on the horrors in everyday life. Rapists and murderers are a fact of life; some even make their homes in quaint, small towns like Castle Rock. A single mistake can trash an entire career. Marriages can be ruined. Spousal abuse and alcoholism can destroy families from within. Misery, unhappiness, and shattered dreams know no age or social barriers. We live in a dangerous world, a world in which even beloved pets can go mad and turn on their masters.

The novel can be seen as a sequel to *The Dead Zone* (1979), in that its opening pages remind us of the tale of psychic Johnny Smith and serial killer Frank Dodd. Johnny, you may recall, used his paranormal talents to assist the Castle Rock police in tracking down the insane police officer, who ultimately escaped justice by committing suicide. In *Cujo*, however, neither the Trentons nor the Cambers have the ability to escape a series of unplanned and undesired events in their lives. Significantly, the Trentons have purchased Frank Dodd's former residence. King hints that the bogeyman in Tad's closet may in fact be the killer's ghost, and later suggests that it might have somehow possessed Cujo.

By invoking the legend of the Castle Rock Strangler, King reminds readers that even though life does go on, so too do the monsters. We needn't be concerned with vampires or werewolves attacking us—the neighborhood wacko will suffice. And if the bogeyman need not be supernatural, it also need not be human. Before becoming rabid, Cujo was one of the most likable dogs in town. It took only an accidental encounter—a minor event in the endless progression of life—to turn the once huggable animal into an insane, vicious beast.

> *Cujo's ghost may appear another time in 1991's* Needful Things. *In that novel, while burying a jar outside Joe Camber's old garage, Polly Chalmers looks up and sees two red eyes peering at her from the dark recesses of the building. Needless to say, she stops what she is doing and flees as quickly as possible.*

Tellingly, King begins the novel with the classic fairy-tale opening, "Once upon a time," as if encouraging readers to put their fears to rest at the very outset, reassuring them that nothing they are about to read is "true." Yet the bitter irony is that there really is nothing present remotely dismissable on the level of a pleasant fable. With the exception of the rare circumstance of a rabid dog on the loose, all the unpleasant, unsavory, and ultimately tragic events presented could happen anywhere.

The author's repeated use of the catchphrase of one of Vic Trenton's ad creations, the Sharp Cereal Professor—"Nope, nothing wrong here"—reveals another facet of the irony that permeates the narrative. Despite reassurances from loved ones and authority figures, there *is* something wrong here. King seems to be warning readers that terror may indeed lurk around the next bend, that life's ugly truths may be revealed to us at any moment. Cujo didn't choose to become rabid. Vic never intended to become so obsessed with work that he ignored his family. Donna never planned on her disastrous affair. Brett Camber isn't consciously growing in the crude and abusive mold of his father. Tad Trenton never should have died in such a violent and senseless manner.

But in the Stephen King universe, fate often throws us a curve. The world is never as safe and peaceful as we wish. Forced to accept the cards that life deals us, we must play the game as best we can. Life isn't fair, King repeatedly reminds us, but whoever promised us that it would be?

> *In 1981, Mysterious Press released a signed, limited edition of 750 copies of the book that sold for $65 each. Two hundred and fifty custom-made guitars, dubbed Cujo Guitars, were manufactured by Taylor Guitars using wood taken from a tree that stood near the film's shooting location. King signed each guitar; the initial price was $3,498.*

## PRIMARY SUBJECTS

*TAD TRENTON.* The four-year-old son of Victor and Donna Trenton, Tad believes that there is a monster in his closet, recalling the classic King short story, "The Bogeyman." Tad learns to fend off his invisible enemy by using a special chant his Dad devises, but can't fend off the terror that's coming his way in the form of Cujo, a rabid St. Bernard. Sadly, Tad and his mother are trapped inside their stalled Ford Pinto by the dog, which seems hell-bent on taking their lives. Suffering from heatstroke and dehydration, young Tad perishes after enduring a terrible two-day ordeal.

*DONNA TRENTON.* A good mother to her son, Tad, Donna is not quite as satisfactory a wife to her husband, Vic. Depressed and lonely, she feels empty whenever her husband or son is not around. She drifts into an affair with Steve Kemp, an affair she quickly comes to regret. Donna is plagued by more mundane problems as well—for instance, her Ford Pinto isn't running well. Taking her car to Joe Camber's garage, Donna becomes involved in the fight of her life when she and Tad are trapped in the stalled vehicle by Camber's rabid St. Bernard, Cujo. Donna and Tad remain prisoners for two days, battling Cujo and the intense heat. Realizing her boy is close to death from dehydration, Donna summons the courage to confront the dog, eventually bludgeoning him to death with a baseball bat. But Donna's heroics prove to be in vain—she's acted too late to save her son and must carry that guilt with her for the rest of her life. Her present whereabouts are unknown.

*VIC TRENTON.* Tad's father and Donna's husband, Vic is a partner in the Ad Worx advertising agency. Vic finds his career in jeopardy when the firm's largest account, the Sharp Cereal Company, almost goes under due to some defective products. Vic loves his wife and son but effectively abandons them as he devotes himself to the fight to save Ad Worx. As a result, he is not present when his family needs him the most. Vic's present whereabouts are unknown.

*STEVE KEMP.* A local furniture refinisher and self-described poet, Steve has a brief affair with Donna Trenton. When she breaks it off, he goes into a violent rage. He breaks into the Trenton house when no one is home and trashes it, leaving a note for Vic cruelly informing him of Donna's extramarital activities. Steve's current whereabouts are unknown.

*JOE CAMBER.* A lifelong Castle Rock resident, Joe operates the local garage. He is also the owner of Cujo. A thin yet surprisingly strong man, he beats his wife and child on a regular basis. Joe is mauled, then killed by Cujo.

*CHARITY CAMBER.* The abused wife of Joe Camber, Charity believes she is doomed to a life of poverty and cruelty. When she wins five thousand dollars in the state lottery, she sees her chance to escape.

Charity tells Joe she's taking their son, Brett, to visit her sister in Connecticut. In reality, she's thinking about abandoning her husband and starting a new life. After Cujo kills Joe, Charity and Brett returned to Castle Rock, but it is not known whether they still reside there.

*BRETT CAMBER.* Joe and Charity Camber's ten-year-old son, Brett considers Cujo his best friend. Despite his fear of his abusive father, Brett exhibits more and more of Joe's worst personality traits with each passing year. After Cujo's death, he is given a new puppy to ease the pain of his loss. It's not clear if he is more upset about losing his father or his former pet.

*SHERIFF GEORGE BANNERMAN.* With Johnny Smith, Bannerman helped end the reign of terror of rapist-killer Frank Dodd (as told in 1979's *The Dead Zone*). Uncharacteristically ignoring proper police procedure in investigating the situation involving Cujo, Bannerman is brutally slain by the rabid dog. As he is being savaged, Bannerman believes for one crazy moment that he sees the evil presence of killer Frank Dodd staring at him through Cujo's eyes.

*FRANK DODD.* Dodd is the Castle Rock police officer responsible for a string of rape-murders several years before Cujo went rabid. His memory still haunts the town; for many, he has taken on the status of a mythical bogeyman.


ADAPTATION

Released in the summer of 1983, the motion picture version of *Cujo* remains one of Stephen King's favorite adaptations. King's first choice to helm the picture was a young director named Lewis Teague, who had already made a few low-budget films *(The Lady in Red, Alligator)* that King greatly enjoyed. Although he did not receive screen credit, King reportedly supplied the initial draft of the screenplay, which was heavily rewritten by the two credited screenwriters, Lauren Currier and Don Carlos Dunaway.

Regardless of who was responsible for the final script, the fact remains that *Cujo* was a relatively simple novel to adapt to the screen, a plus considering King had sold the screen rights to Taft Entertainment, a small, independent firm that couldn't afford a large-scale production or big-name stars. Luckily, there were few locations and a compact cast of characters. In fact, the most challenging aspect of the entire production proved to be making audiences believe that a lovable St. Bernard could become a vicious killer. The filmmakers succeeded on all accounts, and the last half of the ninety-one-minute feature—which primarily consists of an enormous dog attacking two people in a small car—contains some of the most suspenseful and harrowing moments ever put on screen. Dee Wallace (best known as the mother in Steven Spielberg's *E.T.: The Extra-Terrestrial*) is the only name star, and she does a remarkable job of portraying someone who will fight to the death to protect her child. King later stated she should have been nominated for an Academy Award for her stirring performance.

Perhaps the primary reason King liked the production so much is because, like the adaptation of *The Dead Zone,* which was released later that same year, the filmmakers captured the spirit and tone of his original novel, despite one crucial change. Director Teague felt it would be too much of a letdown for the audience to see Tad die, and he wanted to alter King's ending. Realizing that most movies work on a much simpler and often far more direct emotional level than novels do, King agreed. Thus, Tad is spared. This is certainly an unusual instance in which, in their respective mediums, the radically different endings of *Cujo* both work.

# 16

## The Dark Half

I N C O M M O N W I T H *'Salem's Lot* (1975), *The Shining* (1977), *Misery* (1987), and *The Tommyknockers* (1987), *The Dark Half* (1989) features a writer as one of its protagonists. The plot revolves around a permutation of a question King himself had to answer when his Richard Bachman persona was revealed to the world: What if you kill off your pseudonym—and he refuses to stay dead?

To hear him talk, one might think that King regards Bachman as a real person separate and distinct from himself (see the chapters on *Desperation* and *The Regulators* for more on this). As noted in section seven, the author has often stated that "Richard Bachman is Stephen King on a cloudy day." In *The Dark Half*, King plays with this notion, examining it through the lens of his fiction. What if a pseudonym— essentially another part of an author's persona—came to life? How would this being feel if his "creator" had tried to end his existence? King's answer to that question, played out in this novel, is that he'd become enraged, and decide to turn the tables on his soul mate, to kill his creator before he, the creation, fades into nothingness.

Thad Beaumont is a successful novelist, but only under the pseudonym of ultraviolent crime writer George Stark. Tiring of the charade and hoping to devote himself to more serious work, Beaumont decides to publicly reveal his hidden identity and at the same time "kill" him off. The vehicle he chooses is a feature article in *People* magazine, replete with pictures of Beaumont standing over the "grave" of George Stark. Although it's all done in a spirit of harmless fun, something goes seriously awry. Someone begins ruthlessly liquidating people in a manner eerily similar to that of Alexis Machine, a fictional hit man created by George Stark.

Incredibly, fingerprints lifted at the murder scenes seem to indicate that Beaumont is the killer, even though he has an airtight alibi for each night. Although it defies all logic, Beaumont's "dark half," a doppelgänger of sorts, has somehow sprung into being, adopting the identity of Beaumont's cold-blooded alter ego, George Stark. Stark, who writes so well about sadism, cruelty, and death because they are at the core of his essential nature, is now hunting down Thad Beaumont, his wife, and his two infant children. He also seeks out and brutally dispatches anyone remotely related to the *People* article, the one that so glibly "buried" him.

In the end, Beaumont must literally face his dark half in a spectacular confrontation from which only one of them—Beaumont's Dr. Jekyll or Stark's Mr. Hyde—can emerge alive.

Obviously, this novel was inspired by the real-life events in which King's Richard Bachman pseudonym was discovered and made public, ending many years of speculation. Indeed, in a droll author's note at the beginning of the book, King notes, "I'm indebted to the late Richard Bachman for his help and inspiration. This novel could not have been written without him."

The book allows King to comment on the trials and tribulations of being a bestselling author in the twentieth century. Like Ben Mears in *'Salem's Lot* and Paul Sheldon in *Misery,* Thad Beaumont is not struggling to find success in his chosen profession—he is more concerned with how to deal with his considerable fame. Like Sheldon and his romance saga of Misery Chastain, Beaumont is a writer who has attained the good life by giving the public what it wants, not necessarily what he truly desires to write. As he had done so masterfully in *Misery,* King explores the fascinating mechanics of the creative process, most notably the idea that for horror and suspense writers to be truly successful, they must often look into the abyss of their creative dark half, knowing full well the abyss is staring back at *them.*

One might be tempted to conclude that after completing *The Dark Half*, King had said all he had to say about the writing profession. Indeed, at the time of the publication of *Four Past Midnight* (1990), King stated that the novella "Secret Window, Secret Garden" would be his last word on the subject. In 1998, however, he would produce *Bag of Bones*, a novel whose main character is an acclaimed and successful writer. Without a doubt, writing is an endlessly fascinating profession that remains dear to some of the most intriguing inhabitants of the Stephen King universe.

### PRIMARY SUBJECTS

*THAD BEAUMONT.* As a young boy, Thad suffered from unusually severe headaches during which he would hear the ghostly sound of thousands of sparrows in flight. An operation reveals that he has a benign brain tumor caused by a most unusual ailment—an unformed twin. At age eleven, he has the tumor removed and more or less forgets about the entire episode. A gifted scribe, he continues writing all through his adolescence and eventually gets his work published.

Thad's two novels, while well received critically, do not support him financially. He teaches college courses to pay the bills, but his real financial success comes when he creates the pseudonym of "George Stark." It is Stark who writes the grisly crime novels that become international bestsellers, allowing Beaumont and his family to live comfortably.

> *It's quite likely King named Thad Beaumont in honor of the author Charles Beaumont (1929–1967), who is best remembered for writing some of the most chilling episodes of the classic television series* The Twilight Zone.

Thad, who wants to be remembered for his serious work, decides to publicly retire his pseudonym, in effect "killing" Stark. But the Stark persona takes on a life of its own. Enraged, Stark stalks Beaumont, seeking revenge. Facing Stark man to man, Thad emerges the victor, having conquered his dark half. For Beaumont's ultimate fate, please refer to the chapters on *Needful Things* and *Bag of Bones*.

*GEORGE STARK.* The homicidal dark half of Thad Beaumont, Stark is a pseudonym, a fictional alter ego who literally springs to life. Born in New Hampshire, he grew up in Oxford, Mississippi. Also a writer, he composes his fiction in longhand, using a particular brand of pencil (in "stark" contrast to Thad Beaumont, who prefers a typewriter or computer). When Stark is "buried" as part of an elaborate gag for *People* magazine, he rises from his grave and embarks on a blood-drenched journey in his black Toronado to find and slay anyone remotely connected to the creation of that article. His weapon of choice is a straight razor, as he enjoys inflicting pain on his victims. After threatening Thad and his family, Stark is suddenly attacked by thousands of sparrows that carry him away into the night sky. Asked by his wife whether his deadly alter ego is truly dead, Beaumont replies, "The book is closed on George Stark."

*LIZ BEAUMONT.* The loving wife of Thad Beaumont, Liz encourages him to adopt the pseudonym of George Stark. She is equally supportive when Thad decides it is time to go public with his true identity before a man named Fred Clawson exposes the once well-guarded pen name.

*SHERIFF ALAN PANGBORN.* The current sheriff of Castle Rock, Pangborn took over after the previous sheriff, George Bannerman, was done in by a rabid dog. Although never completely swayed by the fantastic idea of a writer's pseudonym coming to life, early on in the investigation Pangborn does become convinced that Thad Beaumont is innocent of the brutal murders that crime scene evidence seems to indicate he committed. Taken prisoner by Stark, the sheriff survives the frightening misadventure. Pangborn's further adventures in the Stephen King universe are chronicled in *Needful Things.*

*FRED CLAWSON.* Clawson is the "creepazoid" (so nicknamed by Thad) who discovered that George Stark is a pseudonym for Thad Beaumont. He intends to reveal the truth to the public, hoping to blackmail Thad in the process. But sometimes a little knowledge is a dangerous thing: Stark goes to Clawson's seedy apartment and mercilessly shreds him with his straight razor.

## ADAPTATION

The motion picture version of *The Dark Half* appeared in 1993, although it had actually been shot and completed a few years earlier (a series of financial problems involving the production company, Orion Pictures, kept the completed film on the shelf). The R-rated picture was adapted and directed by George A. Romero, an outstanding director *(Night of the Living Dead, Martin, Bruiser)* who had been friends with the author for many years. Romero had already helmed *Creepshow* (1982), for which King wrote the screenplay, and had scripted *Creepshow 2* (1987), based on other King stories.

Not surprisingly, Romero's 122-minute adaptation follows the novel quite faithfully, effectively capturing its proper tone and essence. Romero elicits fine performances from an outstanding cast: Timothy Hutton as Thad Beaumont/George Stark, Amy Madigan as Liz Beaumont, and Michael Rooker as Alan Pangborn.

> On the movie poster for The Dark Half, *the character of Thad Beaumont (or is it supposed to be George Stark?) bears an uncanny resemblance to Stephen King.*

*The Dark Half* remains one of the best adaptations of a King work by one of the horror film genre's most influential directors.

# 17

## *Needful Things*

---

**W**ELL KNOWN for his ability to create an atmosphere of intimacy, Stephen King takes it one step further in *Needful Things*. (1991). This novel was his farewell to Castle Rock, the small New England town that served as a backdrop for *The Dead Zone, Cujo,* and the memorable short story, "The Body." The book is the last installment of a loose-knit trilogy begun in *The Dark Half* (in which sheriff Alan Pangborn first appeared) and continued in the short novella "The Sun Dog" (the story of long-time resident "Pop" Merrill's demise). The destruction of the town was reportedly an attempt on King's part to rejuvenate his writing and move on to other things. As he explained, he "wanted to finish things and do it with a bang."

King beckons readers into his world with a punchy prologue, captioned "You've Been Here Before," narrated by an unnamed Castle Rock gossip. The chatty narrator knows a little bit about everything, revealing secrets to an unidentified listener who stands in for the reader. Setting the stage, the narrator drops interesting tidbits about the denizens of Castle Rock and about the new store that's about to open there, a curious operation called Needful Things.

Expertly articulating his thesis of the village as a microcosm of society, King takes us into the hearts and minds of a handful of the townspeople, simultaneously revealing the nobility and evil in each of us. He also explores small-town America in a way he hadn't done since *'Salem's Lot,* detailing the social structure and the unwritten rules of rural life. *Needful Things* is both drama and satire, a critique of American consumerism and greed, and of small-town life in general. King revisits themes from prior books, apparently trying to shake the dust of one style of storytelling off his feet before moving on to a new phase. It is at once one of his more cynical and one of his more hopeful books.

During an unseasonably warm spell in October 1991, a store called Needful Things opens for business in Castle Rock. Eleven-year-old Brian Rusk is the first to meet the proprietor, a tall, kindly but strange old man dressed in an old-fashioned smoking jacket. Introducing himself as Leland Gaunt from Akron, Ohio, the owner cuts the first of many deals he will make with the denizens of Castle Rock. He offers Brian a 1956 Sandy Koufax baseball card worth $100 in return for cash (85 cents) and a seemingly harmless act, a "deed." In Brian's case, it involves splattering a neighbor's clean sheets with mud. The boy agrees. Over the next eight days, several other locals make similar bargains and perform similar deeds.

Only Gaunt knows the ultimate purpose of these deeds. His strategy, honed over centuries, is to sow discontent, then reap a horrible bounty. Each deed unleashes a little of the rage simmering beneath the town's calm façade. The hatred and envy that exist between neighbors, the hatred of one religious group for another, the insecurities people conceal from the light of day—all these are grist for Gaunt's mill. Only Sheriff Alan Pangborn, distracted by the past and by the increasingly violent and bizarre incidents occurring in his jurisdiction, has a prayer of stopping Gaunt before he achieves his goals.

The plot of *Needful Things*—a stranger comes to town, wreaking havoc for his own evil purposes—is certainly not unique. King used it earlier in *'Salem's Lot* (1976), and later in his 1999 teleplay for *Storm of the Century*. The premise comes from a rich tradition in American literature for chronicling events in small towns, from Sherwood Anderson's *Winesburg, Ohio*, to Thornton Wilder's *Our Town*, to Don Robertson's *Paradise Falls*. The horror/suspense genre has similar entries, most notably Ray Bradbury's *Something Wicked This Way Comes*, Charles Beaumont's *The Intruder*, and Richard Matheson's short story "The Distributor." In *Needful Things*, as in *Something Wicked This Way Comes*, Evil, once confronted, flees. This harkens back to *The Stand*, where

Flagg disappears, leaving only a pile of clothes. The comparison doesn't end there, however, because, like Flagg, Gaunt escapes to spread evil in a new locale.

The book showcases King's many strengths. He lovingly populates the novel with vivid, three-dimensional characters, then sends them to their appointments with destiny. The characterizations are brief but effective. As the story hurtles from one situation to another, he never has to reintroduce his characters to remind readers who they are. Of course, he also expertly manipulates his readers' emotions, raising anxiety levels to new heights.

A fascinating character, Gaunt is not unlike Randall Flagg or Andre Linoge (from *Storm of the Century*). He is an evil creature. If he was once human, he is certainly not human now. This self-styled "electrician of the human soul" delights in "cross-wiring" potential victims to achieve maximum chaos. Like Mr. Dark of *Something Wicked This Way Comes*, Gaunt travels the world, feeding off the misery of others. He does this through subtle manipulation and misdirection, exploiting human weakness and greed wherever he finds it.

Gaunt's background is vague. Echoing Bradbury's description of Cooger and Dark's Pandemonium Circus, and his own thumbnail sketch of Randall Flagg in *The Stand*, King tells us:

> He had begun business many years ago—as a wandering peddler on the blind face of a distant land . . . a peddler who usually came at the fall of darkness and was always gone the next morning, leaving bloodshed, horror, and unhappiness behind him. Years later, in Europe, as the plague raged and the deadcarts rolled, he had gone from town to town and country to country in a wagon drawn by a slat-thin white horse with terrible burning eyes and a tongue as black as a killer's heart. He sold his wares from the back of the wagon . . . and was gone before his customers, who paid with small, ragged coins or even in barter, could discover what they had really bought.

Gaunt changes with the times, eventually hawking his wares in a series of storefronts around the world. Where he belongs on the hierarchy of evil beings in the Stephen King universe is unclear, though certainly he would place below Flagg. Yet, they aren't that dissimilar. If they aren't one and the same, all of these villains—Gaunt, Flagg, Linoge, Walter—could be said to be of the same species, brothers in a sense.

No matter how many times they're defeated, these evil creatures return to plague yet another frail, flawed mortal hero, in this case Alan Pangborn. The sheriff exemplifies how tenuous happiness is in the Stephen King universe. In the grand King tradition, he has lost a soul mate (like Ben Mears, Andy McGee, Stu Redman, Ralph Roberts, Mike Noonan, and Roland the gunslinger). In Pangborn's case, his wife and his son die (as do Louis Creed and Donna Trenton) in a car accident. Alan can't fathom why his wife, normally careful about wearing seatbelts, failed to buckle up that fateful day. Haunted by that memory and by the bizarre events he experienced in *The Dark Half,* Alan has tried to move on, focusing on his job as Castle Rock's

> *More interconnections are revealed in* Needful Things *than in almost any other King book, with the possible exception of* The Tommyknockers. *In addition to those mentioned above, there are references to* The Dead Zone, Cujo, The Dark Half, *"The Sun Dog," and more.*

sheriff and in his new relationship with Polly Chalmers. With his vast array of human emotions, Pangborn turns out to be Gaunt's nemesis, not unlike so many before and after him, including many of those named above, as well as Mike Anderson from *Storm of the Century,* which differs from *Needful Things* most particularly in the desires of its villain, and the severity of the secrets hidden by the townspeople.

Interestingly, the hero and villain of the piece don't meet until the final pages of the novel. After shaking off Gaunt's last-ditch attempt to distract him, Pangborn sees through the mask the demonic shopkeeper presents to the public. Echoing the end of *Something Wicked This Way Comes,* Alan uses white magic against Gaunt. First, he opens a "magic" can of snakes that once belonged to his son. Momentarily given life by Gaunt's belief in magic, the snakes attack him, causing him to reveal his true demonic form. Alan then produces a bouquet of paper flowers that generates an intense burst of white light. Finally, he uses his talent at creating hand shadows to invoke the ghosts that haunt the town (the sparrows from *The Dark Half,* and Joe Camber's dog, Cujo).

On a final note, Brian Rusk is an interesting anomaly in the Stephen King universe. Eleven years old, he's still young enough to maintain a child's sense of wonder, a trait that sometimes saves children from severe harm in King's world. Here, however, Brian's naïveté makes him the perfect dupe for Gaunt. By making him complicit in his evil, Gaunt strips Brian of his childhood, thrusting him without warning into the wicked adult world. Unable to cope with his guilt, Brian sees no way out but suicide.


## PRIMARY SUBJECTS

*LELAND GAUNT.* A shadowy figure who turns out to be evil incarnate, Gaunt arrives in Castle Rock to fill the void left by the late "Pop" Merrill, whose novelty store, the Emporium Galorium, burned down a few months earlier. Gaunt's modus operandi is simple: He gives the people what they think they want (Pop called it "selling the worthless to the thoughtless"), secures promises from them to perform some dirty tricks, and sits back to watch the ensuing mayhem. Then, at the crescendo of the hysteria, he sells his customers the weapons they need to efficiently eliminate one another.

Over an eight-day period, Gaunt tightens his grip on the town, exacerbating existing feuds and suspicions between various citizens into violent conflict, even triggering a battle royal between the local Baptist and Catholic congregations. To tie up any loose ends, Gaunt flunkies Buster Keeton and Ace Merrill level the town with several tons of dynamite.

On the verge of achieving his unsavory goal (he's been harvesting the souls of his victims, keeping them in a hyena-hide valise), Gaunt is finally confronted by a formidable opponent in Sheriff Alan Pangborn, a man he has until that time studiously avoided. Pangborn simultaneously exposes Gaunt's true plan and demonic visage, and wrests from his grasp the bag of stolen souls. His plan thwarted, Gaunt flees Castle Rock and settles in Junction City, Iowa, where he opens a new shop called Answered Prayers. It would be foolhardy to presume that he still resides there.

*ALAN PANGBORN.* The sheriff of Castle Rock, Pangborn lost his wife and son in a car accident. His life is haunted by the memory of the incident, and by a series of bizarre events he experienced regarding a writer named Thad Beaumont. Alan tries to move on, losing himself in his work and becoming involved with Polly Chalmers.

Gaunt recognizes Pangborn as someone who could upset his plans. An amateur magician, and thus able to appreciate the power of misdirection, Pangborn is the first to see the connection between the strange events in Castle Rock and Gaunt's store, Needful Things. Through instinct and intuition, Alan manages to access a kind of white magic, with which he drives Gaunt from Castle Rock. Later, he leaves the ruined town in the company of Polly Chalmers and Norris Ridgewick. Pangborn's current whereabouts are unknown.

*POLLY CHALMERS.* Polly, a Castle Rock native, left the town as a young woman when she became pregnant. Too proud and headstrong to accept her parents' assistance, she moves to San Francisco to have her child. There, tragedy strikes—Polly's baby dies in an apartment fire. The pain of this loss affects Polly as much as the pain of the arthritis that turned her hands into misshapen claws. The episode is so shattering that she never tells anyone about it, even her boyfriend, Sheriff Alan Pangborn.

Returning to Castle Rock, Polly eventually opens an establishment called You Sew and Sew, located across the street from Needful Things. Gaunt traps Polly by giving her a locket called an Azka, which relieves her arthritis. In payment, Polly agrees to play a trick on ex-convict Ace Merrill. Performing her errand at the old Camber place, Polly hears growling coming from a barn. Looking in that direction, she sees "two sunken red circles of light peering out at her from the darkness." Afraid Joe Camber's fearsome St. Bernard, Cujo, has risen from the dead, she hurriedly completes her deed and flees.

Her happiness at curing her arthritis blinds her to Gaunt's evil and almost costs her her relationship with Alan. She questions Alan's love after she is manipulated by Gaunt into believing he had made inquiries into her past. Ultimately, Polly escapes from Gaunt's influence by literally embracing her sin, which takes the form of a huge, fanged spider. Her triumph over Gaunt enables her to assist Alan in seeing through the old man's trickery, paving the way for his eventual defeat. Polly leaves town with Alan and Norris Ridgewick. Her current whereabouts are unknown.

*BRIAN RUSK*. Eleven-year-old Brian is the first citizen of Castle Rock to shop at Needful Things. After showing Brian around the store, Gaunt asks Brian what he really wants. The avid baseball card collector responds quickly—he wants a 1956 Sandy Koufax rookie card. Not only does Gaunt have this card, but, strangely enough, it also happens to be autographed to someone named Brian. In exchange, Gaunt takes 85 cents in cash and secures Brian's promise to play a prank on Wilma Jerzcyk. Brian is to throw mud on Wilma's clean sheets that are drying on her clothesline. Later, after Gaunt informs Brian that he's not done paying for the baseball card, the boy hurls rocks with notes tied to them through Wilma's windows, destroying her TV and microwave oven. Consumed by guilt over what he's done, Brian commits suicide with his father's rifle after telling his younger brother, Sean, never to go into Needful Things.

*NETTIE COBB*. Nettie killed her abusive husband after he maliciously broke a piece of her precious carnival glass. She spent the next few years as a resident of Juniper Hill, a local mental institution. Later, sponsored by Polly Chalmers, she attempts to rejoin society. Her efforts are short-circuited by Gaunt's machinations, as he sets her on a collision course with the volatile Wilma Jerzcyk. When Hugh Priest kills her dog with a corkscrew, Nettie assumes Wilma did the deed. Grabbing a meat cleaver, the grief-stricken Nettie attacks the knife-wielding Wilma on a public street.

*WILMA JERZCYK*. Wilma is a hulking battle-ax who lives for a good fight. Primed by Brian Rusk's attacks on her property, she sets out in search of revenge against Nettie Cobb, whom she assumes is responsible. Both women die in the grisly battle that ensues.

*HUGH PRIEST.* In return for a coveted fox's tail, Hugh kills Nettie Cobb's beloved dog, Raider. Hugh eventually squares off against bar owner Henry Beaufort in a gun battle that costs him his life.

*ACE MERRILL.* After doing time in Shawshank prison, Ace is drawn back to Castle Rock to view the burned-out remains of his uncle Pop Merrill's store, the Emporium Galorium. Once there, he is hired by Gaunt as an errand boy. In return for a treasure map ostensibly detailing where Pop buried his considerable fortune, Ace travels to Boston to pick up the weapons that Gaunt later sells to the citizens of Castle Rock. When not running Gaunt's errands, Ace engages in a personal treasure hunt for his uncle's money but discovers nothing of value—only trading stamps and some rolls of World War II steel pennies buried in Crisco tins. In one, he finds a letter planted by Polly Chalmers and supposedly written by Alan Pangborn. In the letter, Pangborn mocks Ace, telling him that he'd already recovered the money in the tin. Fueled by anger and Gaunt's special cocaine, Ace vows to murder Alan, the man who put him in Shawshank for dealing cocaine. Ace is killed by Norris Ridgewick just as he is about to kill Alan.

> *Ace Merrill is one of the bullies in "The Body," which was made into the film* Stand by Me. *Shawshank prison was also the locale of the story "Rita Hayworth and Shawshank Redemption."*

*POP MERRILL.* Ace Merrill's uncle, Pop dies when his store and living quarters, the Emporium Galorium, burns down just prior to Gaunt's arrival.

*NORRIS RIDGEWICK.* Alan Pangborn's deputy, Norris is lured into Gaunt's circle by a fishing rod which brings back pleasant memories of lazy days spent with his father. Later, Norris, on the verge of suicide, suddenly sees through Gaunt's trickery and vows revenge. Although he does not achieve it directly, he does save Alan and Polly from Ace Merrill. Norris leaves town with Alan and Polly.

## ADAPTATION

In the 1993 film adaptation of *Needful Things*, released by Columbia Pictures, Max Von Sydow is well cast as the demonic Gaunt. At once charming and sinister, he embodies the character well. Ed Harris and Bonnie Bedelia are also well cast as Alan Pangborn and Polly Chalmers, but neither is given the chance to fully explore his or her role. The movie cannot take advantage of the leisurely buildup King uses in his novel.

The film also makes subtle changes to certain events, compressing and embellishing them. As a result, all but the major subplots are eliminated. Several of the "needful things" are changed—Brian Rusk's Sandy Koufax card becomes a Mickey Mantle card; Nettie Cobb's carnival glass becomes a Hummel statuette; and Hugh Priest's fox's tail becomes a more convincing varsity football jacket. Ace Merrill is entirely eliminated from the story line. The producers, possibly constrained by a small special-effects budget, even rewrote the ending. Instead of working his magic, Alan is reduced to delivering a Capraesque speech about evil, which Gaunt dismisses with a few pointed quips.

> *King does a masterful job in his full-length reading of the book for the audio version. Especially interesting is the thicker Maine accent he adopts to read the prologue, "You've Been Here Before."*

# 18

# Related Tales

---

KING HAS ALSO used Castle Rock as a backdrop for several
short stories. Here, in no special order, are brief summaries of
those tales.

## "THE BODY"

### from *Different Seasons* (1982)

There are a great many things that Stephen King does well. Some of
them he accomplishes as well as, and arguably better than, anyone else
writing popular fiction today. In "The Body," as in *'Salem's Lot* and *IT*
(1986), King seems to send his imagination back in time to his own
youth. Though only a novella, "The Body" is so steeped in nostalgia
and Americana and thick with emotion, fondness, and primal fear
that it is a fully realized exploration of what it meant to be a boy growing up in Maine in 1960. There are those who have equated King with
Mark Twain. That comparison is never more accurate than here.

"The Body" relates the story of four friends who undertake a
quest—without their parents' knowledge, of course, and in peril of
severe punishment—to see the corpse of a boy who has disappeared,
but whom they discover has been hit by a train. As a coming-of-age-
in-America story, it can rightly be termed a masterpiece.

"I never had any friends later on like I had when I was twelve,"
King, as narrator Gordon LaChance, tells us. "Jesus, does anyone?"

"The Body" also provides a solid foundation for the fictional town of Castle Rock, which would serve as the setting for so many subsequent works. The realism of this tale helps to build a sense of authenticity and history around Castle Rock itself.

In the narrative, the four friends trek through rain and leech-filled ponds and run across a train bridge just ahead of a locomotive, all to find the corpse of Ray Brower. When their goal is reached after a day and a half of hard travel, they feel a sense of proprietorship over the dead boy. However, they are challenged by a gang of local toughs, which includes the older brothers of two of the youths. Though they drive the older boys off, they are eventually beaten soundly for their affront.

*Although the town of Derry was not prominent in King's fictional landscape at the time, it is mentioned in "The Body," as are Jerusalem's Lot and Shawshank penitentiary.*

There are many elements that make this fiction much more than a mere coming-of-age story. Gordie, the main character, is the smart one. He wants to be a writer. Though his best friend, Chris Chambers, is intelligent, he is from a poor family with a reputation for making trouble. The other two, Vern and Teddy, are not very bright and seem destined for a dead-end future.

We learn that Chris later triumphs over the expectations placed on him. He goes to law school and becomes an attorney. Then he dies, senselessly, while trying to break up a fight. We also learn that both Teddy and Vern die senselessly

*"The Body" features many references to Constable Bannerman, who would become Sheriff Bannerman in such later works as* The Dead Zone *(1979) and* Cujo *(1981).*

as well. As the entire story seems to predict, Gordie is the only one who survives and succeeds. Save for Chris, the deaths are revealed with the distance of age and the passage of time, so making them more sad than tragic. We only knew them as the children they were, instead of the men they became. For all the promise and hope we had for Chris Chambers, however, his death is the real tragedy.

## PRIMARY SUBJECTS

***GORDON LaCHANCE.*** Gordie is twelve in 1960, when he and three of his friends go on an adventure to find the corpse of a missing local boy. They find the body, but the experience changes them all, forcing them to grow up in a way that none of them could be prepared for. They drift

> *Gordie LaChance refers to the events of* Cujo *in this story.*

apart afterward, except for Gordie and Chris Chambers. Gordon goes on to become a successful novelist.

***CHRIS CHAMBERS.*** Along with his friends, Chris embarks on a mission to find the corpse. Though he is from a family with a bad reputation, he makes good and eventually becomes an attorney. Sadly, Chris is killed while trying to break up an altercation in a restaurant in Portland, Maine.

***TEDDY DUCHAMP.*** One of the four who set out on a trek to locate a missing local boy, Teddy has never been quite right in the head. He dies in a car accident in late 1971 or early 1972.

***VERN TESSIO.*** Vern overhears his brother telling a friend about the body of Ray Brower, a bit of knowledge that leads to the quest for the missing boy's corpse. Vern dies in a house fire in Lewiston, Maine, in 1966.

***ACE MERRILL.*** A sadistic bully, *Ace* is the leader of the gang of hoods who try to claim the body of Ray Brower after Gordie and his friends find it. He dies many years later when a mysterious man named Leland Gaunt opens a store called Needful Things in Castle Rock.

***RAY BROWER.*** It is never clear whether Ray Brower ran away from home or merely got lost. Either way, he finds himself on the train tracks at the wrong time and is struck and killed. Though a handful of the kids in Castle Rock know where his body is, it is some time before it is finally discovered, thanks to an anonymous tip to the police.

## ADAPTATION

Of the four tales collected in *Different Seasons,* three have been made into films. The first of these, *Stand by Me* (based on "The Body"), was released by Columbia Pictures in 1986. The motion picture adaptation, apparently among King's favorites, was directed by actor-turned-director Rob Reiner *(When Harry Met Sally, The Story of Us)* and featured a plethora of young talent among the cast.

*Star Trek: The Next Generation's* Wil Wheaton portrayed Gordie LaChance (with Richard Dreyfuss playing Gordon as an adult). The late River Phoenix co-starred as tough kid Chris Chambers. Omnipresent 1980s child star Corey Feldman was Teddy Duchamp, and Jerry O'Connell, who would later go on to fame in film *(Scream 2)* and television *(Sliders),* was chubby enough back then to play Vern Tessio. *Stand by Me* also included performances by Kiefer Sutherland as Ace Merrill and John Cusack as Denny LaChance, Gordie's older brother.

Reiner's direction of this coming-of-age story is flawless. Much of King's narrative remains in voice-over by Dreyfuss, and despite moving Castle Rock from Maine to Oregon, there is a universal quality to the representation of the time period here, and a timelessness to the relationships between the kids that makes this picture speak to the entire audience.

*Stand by Me* may be the closest a director has ever come to replicating the texture that King has put down on the page.

## "NONA"

### from *Skeleton Crew* (1985)

A story that recalls Charles Starkweather's murderous rampage in the late 1950s, which inspired such films as Oliver Stone's *Natural Born Killers* (1994), "Nona" tells of a murder spree that concludes in King's fictional town of Castle Rock. Says Nona: "We're going to Castle Rock. It's a small town just south and west of Lewiston-Ashburn." It turns out that the narrator has had a run-in with Castle Rock's most famous juvenile delinquent, Ace Merrill. Ace's presence links the story to the 1982 novella "The Body," as does a mention of the GS&WM railroad trestle.

## PRIMARY SUBJECT

*THE NARRATOR/THE PRISONER.* Nona's narrator is unnamed; we know only that he has just been released from prison. Entering Joe's Good Eats one evening, he meets a woman named Nona. (It is possible that Nona exists only in the mind of the narrator.) After he gets into a fight with one of the patrons, he and Nona leave the diner together, embarking on a long, strange trip to the narrator's hometown of Castle Rock. On the way, he kills a good Samaritan who foolishly picks him up near an offramp, and steals the victim's car. The man also murders a police officer, and two power company employees who are fixing a downed line. The narrator eventually ends up in the crypt of a former girlfriend, where he is found the next day. He is arrested and is presumably spending his days safely locked away in prison again. It is up to the reader to decide whether Nona actually existed or was merely a creation of the narrator's twisted mind.

## "UNCLE OTTO'S TRUCK"

### from *Skeleton Crew* (1985)

Another story of Castle Rock (Billy Dodd, father of Frank Dodd from *The Dead Zone,* is mentioned at one point), this tale is about a haunted truck that despite its decrepitude, drags itself across a field, moving toward the house of the man who once used it as a murder weapon. Like 1985's "Beachworld," this is King in his EC Comics/*Creepshow* frame of mind.

Otto enters into a partnership with George McCutcheon in order to obtain a choice piece of land from the New England Paper Company. Their association makes both men rich, but when they have a falling out, Otto kills George by dropping an old Cresswell truck on him. Otto now spends his days in a house he built across the road. His corpse is found one Wednesday evening by his nephew (Quentin Schenk, the narrator of the story), oil spewing from his mouth, which also contains a 1920s vintage spark plug that almost certainly came from the truck. The coroner's verdict, however, is that Otto committed suicide by swallowing the oil.

## "GRAMMA"

from *Skeleton Crew* (1985)

A tale of a young boy left home alone with his invalid grandmother, this offering, which contains elements King later used in *Dolores Claiborne* (1993), had its roots in the author's childhood. King's sick grandmother lived in their home and nearly drove daughter Ruth crazy with her constant nagging. Apparently, King was home alone with his grandmother the day she died. Again set in Castle Rock, the story features cameos from Henrietta Dodd and Joe Camber, owner of the dog featured in the novel *Cujo* (1981).

The young protagonist of this story, eleven-year-old George, thinks he's a great deal more capable than he really is. Therefore, he is not fazed when his mother asks him to stay alone in the house with his spooky old grandmother. George doesn't know what he's in for, however. Just when it appears Gramma has died, he turns around and discovers she has shambled into the kitchen. It is revealed that Gramma is actually a witch who covets George's youth. It's not clear at the end of the story whether George has been totally possessed by the spirit of the woman or has merely absorbed his grandmother's powers for his own use.

"Gramma" was adapted for television by famed fantasist Harlan Ellison. This 1986 adaptation appeared as part of the anthology series *The New Twilight Zone*.


## "THE SUN DOG"

from *Four Past Midnight* (1990)

Bracketed by 1989's *The Dark Half* and 1991's *Needful Things*, "The Sun Dog" was the second installment of what King has called the Castle Rock trilogy. "The Sun Dog" tells the story of Kevin Delevan and the strange camera he receives on his fifteenth birthday. The Constant Reader hears the names of many of the locals, some of whom are destined to play significant roles in *Needful Things*. Ace Merrill, Norris Ridgewick, Buster Keeton, Alan Pangborn, and Polly Chalmers are all mentioned or make brief cameos.

## PRIMARY SUBJECTS

*KEVIN DELEVAN.* On his fifteenth birthday, Kevin receives a Polaroid 660 instant camera. Something is wrong with the camera, however. No matter what he points it at, it produces pictures of what appear to be a dog in front of a picket fence. Fascinated by the camera, Kevin continues to use it despite the flaw. Laying the pictures out in the order in which he took them, he makes a startling discovery—the dog is moving *closer* to the foreground in every shot. Frightened, he seeks out his dad, who suggests they take the camera to Pop Merrill, a cagey old gent for whom John Delevan has a grudging respect.

Intrigued by the mysterious camera and sensing a quick score, Pop rooks the pair out of their possession. After experimenting with it, Pop tries to unload the camera on one of his customers who he calls the "Mad Hatters" but is unsuccessful. Falling under the camera's spell, he continues to snap shot after shot, bringing the dog closer and closer from that other dimension to this one. Kevin, realizing that Pop has tricked him, confronts the old man just as the last picture is snapped. Fortunately, Kevin has come prepared. Using another Polaroid, he captures the Sun Dog just as it enters this world. The camera then implodes, seemingly ending the threat.

Kevin emerges unscathed, but soon realizes his business with the Sun Dog is not finished. On his sixteenth birthday, he receives a WordStar personal computer. Booting it up, he types, "The quick brown fox jumped over the lazy sleeping dog" and hits the print button. He's shaken to the core by what comes out of the printer: "The dog is loose again, and it is not sleeping. It is not lazy. It's coming for you, Kevin. It's very hungry. And it's very angry."

*JOHN DELEVAN.* Kevin's father, seeking to connect with his troubled son, reveals his secret shame to his offspring. Early on in his marriage, John made and lost an extravagant bet, which threatened the young couple's financial stability. Desperate to hide this from his wife, John borrows money from Pop Merrill to cover the wager. It takes many years of hard work to pay off, given the high rate of interest Pop charges. After relating this story, John convinces Kevin to take the camera to Pop, a man who's seen much in his long and varied life.

*REGINALD MARION (POP) MERRILL.* Pop is a character right out of a Charles Dickens novel, larger than life and twice as cunning. He runs a shop called the Emporium Galorium, and becomes wealthy by making usurious loans and by "selling the worthless to the useless." Pop takes just one look at Kevin's camera and dollar signs instantly spring up in his eyes. Unable to purchase the camera from its owner, Pop quickly conceives and implements a plan to steal it. Pop tries to sell the camera but is unsuccessful.

Unknown to Pop, the camera has been exerting its unnatural influence on him, forcing him to take pictures. Unable to control himself, Pop repeatedly uses the camera until the Sun Dog actually emerges from the last photo. As the Sun Dog draws closer to this reality, the camera grows so hot it eventually bursts into flame. Pop dies in the subsequent fire that guts his store.

*"THE MAD HATTERS".* Pop Merrill's name for a unique group of customers fascinated by the occult. One mad hatter buys a "spirit trumpet" from Pop for $90; another claims to engage in twice-weekly conversations with Adolf Hitler. Pop offers the Polaroid 660 to four mad hatters—Cedric McCarty, the "Pus" Sisters (identical twins Miss Eleusippus Deere and Mrs. Meleusippus Verrill), and Emory Chafe—but is unable to close a sale with any of them.

## "IT GROWS ON YOU"

from *Nightmares & Dreamscapes* (1993)

This tale is an epilogue of sorts to *Needful Things* (1991). It features a handful of elderly survivors of the debacle caused by Leland Gaunt, a demonic evil force who had destroyed most of Castle Rock. Focusing on a strange house that is modified and enlarged whenever someone in town dies, it recalls H. P. Lovecraft's 1929 classic "The Dunwich Horror."

### PRIMARY SUBJECTS

*THE NEWALL HOUSE.* An old house situated out on Town Road No. 3, overlooking the section of Castle Rock known as the Bend. The unpainted house has a look of evil to it that one can sense immediately upon entering.

*JOE NEWALL.* Owner of the Newall House, Joe constantly is adding rooms, then entire wings, to the house, arousing curiosity among the surviving residents of Castle Rock. His life is marred by tragedy: his daughter, born malformed, dies shortly after birth, and his wife, Cora, dies after falling down a flight of stairs.

*GARY PAULSON.* An eighty-four-year-old resident of the Bend, Paulson is an ailing widower who has lost all three of his sons (two in wars, one in a car accident). He suspects some kind of unholy connection exists between the way local people die and the continued construction of the Newall House. When Paulson passes away in his sleep, his friends are not surprised to see a new cupola being added onto a new wing of the Newall House.

*Bridge between Lisbon Falls and Durham* | VINTAGE POSTCARD

## "THE MAN IN THE BLACK SUIT"
from *Six Stories* (1997)

This story of the Devil won both the 1994 World Fantasy Award for best short fiction and the 1996 O. Henry Award for best American short story. A neat tale of innocence confronted by evil, it is perhaps best described as King by way of Ray Bradbury. King has written that the entry comes out of "a long New England tradition of stories which dealt with meeting the devil in the woods . . . he always comes out of the woods—the uncharted regions—to test the human soul."

## PRIMARY SUBJECT

*GARY.* In 1914, fishing off the banks of Castle Stream, young Gary falls asleep and wakes to discover that he is not alone. A sinister man wearing a black suit has entered the glen, a man the boy quickly realizes is not human. The stranger taunts the boy, telling him that his mother is dead, the victim of a bee sting. Terrified because his younger brother, Dan, died the same way a year before, the youngster stands paralyzed. The man approaches, telling Gary he is going to kill him, tear him open, and eat his guts. The threat galvanizes the boy, who takes a fish from his basket and stuffs it into the man's mouth, then runs home. There, he finds his mother alive and well.

Gary is old now and currently resides in a nursing home. He has, however, lived his entire life in fear that the man in the black suit will one day reappear.

# SECTION FOUR

## The Prime Reality, Part III: Jerusalem's Lot and Stephen King's Maine

*Carrie*

*'Salem's Lot*

*Pet Sematary*

*Cycle of the Werewolf*

*Gerald's Game*

*Dolores Claiborne*

*Storm of the Century*

*The Girl Who Loved Tom Gordon*

Related Tales

ITES SUCH AS THOSE THAT we've discussed—the fictional towns of Castle Rock and Derry—represent only a small part of Stephen King's Maine. One must also consider such locales as 'Salem's Lot, Little Tall Island, Dark Score Lake, and other rural Maine communities that have figured so prominently in King's fiction over the years.

The people who inhabit this reality are tough, down-to-earth, stoic types who, given a choice, keep to themselves. They are the people King grew up with, interacted with, went to college with. They are an intriguing mix of good and evil—for every Jud Crandall *(Pet Sematary)*, Mark Petrie *('Salem's Lot)*, Johnny Smith *(The Dead Zone)*, Dolores Claiborne, and Mike Anderson *(Storm of the Century),* there are flawed, troubled, sometimes inhuman types such as Louis Creed, Father Donald Callahan, Frank Dodd, Joe St. George, and Robbie Beals (from the same stories, respectively).

How do these tales of a rural Maine connect to the rest of the prime reality and to the other realities in the Stephen King universe? From one look at the maps in both *Dolores Claiborne,* and *Gerald's Game,* it is obvious that the reality that includes Little Tall Island *(Dolores Claiborne, Storm of the Century),* Dark Score Lake *(Gerald's Game, Bag of Bones),* and Lake Kashwakamak *(Gerald's Game)* is the prime reality, the one that includes Derry, Haven, and Bangor. But other locales figure in his stories as well.

Consider "Rita Hayworth and Shawshank Redemption," set at everyone's favorite penal institution, the oft-mentioned Shawshank prison (in *Needful Things* and *Bag of Bones,* for example). The GS&WM train line, which runs through Castle Rock, also winds through Tarker's Mills, Maine, the setting of *Cycle of the Werewolf.* Louis Creed, the chief protagonist of *Pet Sematary,* lives in Ludlow, near the University of Maine, where he works as the head of health services. Goat Island (from "The Reach") could very well be a sister to Little Tall Island. Finally, *The Girl Who Loved Tom Gordon* is set in Maine, as its heroine wanders the woods in the southern part of the state, hallucinating about her hero, Boston Red Sox pitching sensation Tom Gordon.

> Rachel Creed sees the name Jerusalem's Lot on an ancient road sign, and thinks that it is not a pleasant name. She has no idea of the legends surrounding the accursed town as related in 'Salem's Lot.

Are the characters in these stories aware of the rest of the Stephen King universe? It certainly seems so. In *Pet Sematary,* Jud Crandall makes reference to the events that occurred in *Cujo.*

The University of Maine at Orono, where Louis Creed is employed, is prominently featured in "Hearts in Atlantis" and "Riding the Bullet" (it is also King's alma mater).

In other works, Trisha McFarland of *The Girl Who Loved Tom Gordon* picks up a Castle Rock radio station while listening to her Walkman in the Maine woods. Serial killer Andrew Ray Joubert, who figures in the events described in *Gerald's Game,* is mentioned in passing in *Insomnia.* Perhaps the best example of this cross-pollination is offered by King's novella "The Body". Besides a reference to Derry, Castle Rock Sheriff Bannerman, and a dog named Cujo, the story also mentions 'Salem's Lot and Shawshank prison.

•    •    •

There is one locale we haven't discussed in detail yet, but with ample reason. One of the more important settings in the Stephen King universe, it was effectively reduced to a ghost town over a quarter of a century ago, when it succumbed to a great evil.

Long before the words Castle Rock, Maine, first graced the printed page in *The Dead Zone* (1979), King had created and destroyed another fully realized fictional community. Jerusalem's Lot—'Salem's Lot to the locals—became Maine's answer to Roanoke, North Carolina. England attempted to colonize that now notorious island several times, only to find—first in 1587 with one group, and again with a second in 1590—that the Roanoke colonies had disappeared without a trace.

King has shown an interest in Roanoke, most recently in 1999's TV miniseries *Storm of the Century,* but in the Stephen King universe nothing is so reminiscent of the seemingly cursed Roanoke Island as Jerusalem's Lot. It has been occupied and abandoned several times, and now, after a vampire plague fell upon the town, it is a veritable Flying Dutchman of burned-out homes, stores, and offices. Of the several fictional towns King has created, restructuring the map of Maine to suit his own needs, Jerusalem's Lot was the first. In the novel *'Salem's Lot* (1975) and the short stories "One for the Road" and "Jerusalem's Lot"—both of which appear in the 1978 short-story collection *Night Shift*—King meticulously crafts the birth, life, and awful death of a small American town imbued with evil from its very inception.

In the creation of this town in "Jerusalem's Lot," King has taken a classic horror conceit and made it his own, echoing the works of some of horror's earliest masters, in which a house or even an entire town has been forever tainted by evil. As early as the 1765 publication in England of what is considered the first gothic novel—*The Castle of Otranto* by Horace Walpole which concerned haunting events in a medieval castle—the presence of evil has been a major theme in horror literature. In its use of a mysterious old house that holds dark and unspeakable secrets, "Jerusalem's Lot" seems to be a descendant of Walpole's novel, as well as the Edgar Allan Poe tale "The Fall of the House of Usher" (1839).

The novel 'Salem's Lot, however, with its atmosphere of lurking evil, terror, and the erosion of the natural world, is most reminiscent of the work of H. P. Lovecraft (1890–1937), who is also known to have had quite an influence on King. "The Shadow over Innsmouth" (1936) is just one example of a Lovecraft tale about a cursed village that holds a dark, deadly secret. "The Dunwich Horror" (1929) also features townspeople coming to grips with an evil that lurks among them. Lovecraft had taken the gothic, "old dark house" tale and moved it into the larger setting of an entire town.

In the 1960s, television series such as Rod Serling's *The Twilight Zone* and the classic horror films from England's Hammer Studios contributed to the expansion of the "old dark house" mythos to include an entire town. The work of Richard Matheson, who wrote for *Twilight Zone* in addition to his many novels and short stories, also heavily influenced King. Matheson often demonstrated evil as being present in the most contemporary and mundane surroundings. In other words, a vampire could just as easily be found in a supermarket meat locker in a local supermarket as it could in a musty crypt.

What King has done in the creation of Jerusalem's Lot, and in particular in the novel 'Salem's Lot, is bring that kind of paranoia-inducing fear into a familiar, contemporary setting draped in pop culture. The more familiar elements King introduces into the story, and the more we identify with the characters, the more terrifying the story becomes.

The classic structure of such a story—as shown in the Hammer films *(Horror of Dracula, Curse of Frankenstein)*, in various episodes of *Twilight Zone* and even in the 1981 horror-comedy classic *An American Werewolf in London*—usually went something like this: our protagonists are innocent outsiders who pass through the spooky town in the night and are put off by the odd behavior of its secretive residents, who cower in fear of the evil that lives nearby. While "Jerusalem's Lot" follows that standard structure, 'Salem's Lot and "One for the Road" most certainly do not. The protagonists of these tales are the people who actually live in the town and discover that lurking evil, and who must somehow work as a team to combat and finally destroy it. These people *know* that there are monsters among us, and that they must do something to stop the evil from spreading.

In this deceptively simple manner, with an ancient evil arriving in the average Joe's proverbial backyard, King lays the bedrock for the essential horror tale of the final quarter of the twentieth century. It would have been merely a new take on an age-old conceit, yet before long, virtually dozens of writers—including Dean R. Koontz and Robert R. McCammon—would build entire careers around it during the horror boom of the 1980s.

It is important to note, then, that *'Salem's Lot* was not merely the continuation of a growing trend toward mainstream horror stories, but truly its vital beginning in contemporary literature.

•     •     •

Incorporated in 1765, the town of Jerusalem's Lot was named almost by accident. Jerusalem was the name of a particularly large and nasty pig owned by Charles Belknap Tanner, a local farmer. When Jerusalem escaped her pen, she ran into the nearby woods, prompting Tanner to warn children in the vicinity to stay out of "Jerusalem's lot." Long before that incident, sinister forces had already drawn together in *'Salem's Lot*, establishing a pattern that would leave the town empty and tainted by evil not once, but twice in its history, and eventually lead to its destruction.

Upon examining the text of the short story "Jerusalem's Lot" and the novel *'Salem's Lot*, one can put together a more specific timeline that is haunting in the way in which evil is drawn to the town time after time:

*1710.* A splinter group from the original Puritanical settlers of that region of southern Maine—led by a preacher named James Boon—establishes the town of Jerusalem's Lot. Boon worships a horrid, demonic creature known only as the worm, and leads his followers to do the same. He is a fanatical leader and mates with many of the cult's women.

*1741.* An adjoining hamlet, once called Preacher's Rest and later Preacher's Corners, is founded.

*1765.* Jerusalem's Lot is officially incorporated as a township.

*1782.* Boon's descendants, Robert and Philip Boone (their surname has been inexplicably altered), build a house called Chapelwaite in the Lot, not far from Preacher's Corners. They are unaware at the time that James Boon is their ancestor.

*1789.* On October 27, after Philip has become involved with the cult that still exists in *'Salem's Lot*, Robert follows his brother to the church where James Boon and his cult first worshiped the worm. Whatever happens that night between the Boone brothers, the cult, and the worm, Jerusalem's Lot is completely deserted the next day, with no sign of life at all.

*1850.* Robert's grandson, Charles, moves to Chapelwaite, the family estate, and happens upon documents that reveal part of his family's history. The attitudes of the people of Preacher's Corners cause him to face some of the horrors related to his ancestors. On October 27, Charles faces the worm and the rotted, zombielike form of James Boon, both of which still live beneath the abandoned church.

*1896.* The main street, formerly the Portland Post Road, is renamed Jointner Avenue after a local politician. By now, the evil that has suffused the Lot's history has been all but forgotten, or only whispered about, and the ghost town is settled anew.

*1928.* Hubert Marsten, president of the sizable New England Trucking Company (and secretly a Mafia assassin) retires to 'Salem's Lot with his wife, Birdie.

*1939.* This summer, Marsten inexplicably shoots his wife to death and then hangs himself. It later becomes clear that he had been in touch with a mysterious stranger who was residing in Hitler's Germany. This stranger turns out to be the vampire Kurt Barlow.

***1951.*** On a childhood dare, a young boy named Ben Mears enters the reputedly haunted Marsten House and, in the attic, sees what he believes to be the ghost of Hubie Marsten. It haunts him for the rest of his life.

***1971.*** In October, James Robert Boone, the final descendant of that family, takes up residence in Chapelwaite. Though events seem to indicate that the ancestral home is haunted, there are no subsequent references to the worm, the living corpse of James Boon, or the evil lurking beneath 'Salem's Lot. However, it is also logical to presume that should a Boone ever venture near the spot where the old church had once stood, with the right frame of mind and the right book, that evil would rise again.

***1975.*** On September 5, Ben Mears, who had lived in the Lot as a boy, returns to town only to discover that the Marsten house has been purchased by two mysterious European gentlemen. By mid-fall, the vampire Barlow has killed, transformed, or driven out nearly all of the townspeople. He is finally killed by Ben Mears and Mark Petrie. Ben and Mark destroy as many vampires as they can, then flee the empty township.

***1976 or early 1977.*** Ben Mears and Mark Petrie return to 'Salem's Lot, prompted by newspaper reports of suspicious disappearances that they link to Barlow's remaining vampiric offspring. The two men burn the town to the ground.

***1978.*** On January 10, the Lumley family of New Jersey are taken by the vampires who still hunt the area around the burned-out town. Two men from a neighboring town, Herb Tooklander and his friend Booth, barely escape the same fate.

Though more than two decades have passed as of this writing, the pattern of dark events indicates that something evil still lurks in the remains of 'Salem's Lot.

Located east of Cumberland, some twenty miles north of Portland, Maine, the fictional 'Salem's Lot boasted a population of 1,300 prior to the vampire holocaust that decimated its populace. For the most part, the town was made up of "a lot of old folks, quite a few poor folks, and a lot of young folks who leave the area with their diplomas under their arms, never to return again."

To reach the town, it would be simplest to take Interstate 95 (a.k.a. the Maine Turnpike) to the exit that reads "Route 12, Jerusalem's Lot, Cumberland, Cumberland Center." The offramp from the highway leads down onto Route 12, which, if one were to follow it, would turn into Jointner Avenue. Jointner runs straight through the heart of 'Salem's Lot.

The town itself looks much like the crosshairs in a rifle sight. It is nearly round, with Brock Street and Jointner Avenue intersecting at the center. The northwest corner of town, also called North Jerusalem, consists mainly of heavily wooded hills. On the hill nearest the center of town stood the Marsten house before it burned.

On the west side, where the town borders Cumberland, one might arrive via Burns Road and then turn onto Brooks Road, which passes right by Harmony Hill cemetery. South of there, the poorest of the Lot's residents live in an area called the Bend, which consists mainly of dilapidated trailers and shacks.

Much of the northeast section of town consists of open fields, with the exception of the shimmering Royal River, which once provided a perfect destination for locals who enjoyed fishing now and again.

The southeast section of *'Salem's Lot* is dominated by the Griffen dairy farm, which stretches along both sides of Griffen Road, and by Schoolyard Hill. Electrical towers for Central Maine Power still carry power lines on a straight course from southeast to northwest, cutting through forest and field.

The town itself is governed by town meetings, rather than town council, and 'Salem's Lot had three selectmen, a constable, a town clerk, a school commissioner, and a volunteer fire department. Of course, by 1976 or 1977, when the fire destroyed the town, the volunteer firefighters had either run away, been killed, or been transformed into something terrifying that still hunts by night.

Subsequent to the slaughter of so many of the town's residents and the abandonment of the town, 'Salem's Lot developed a widespread reputation as a local ghost town, not unlike Roanoke Island in North Carolina. Rumors raged like small wildfires about what had happened to cause so many people to disappear or simply up and leave. Some believed a group of young devil worshipers were responsible. Other stories varied widely in plausibility but were all equally mysterious and unpleasant.

Still, over the months that followed, several enterprising people attempted to buy houses or businesses in the Lot only to disappear or flee, just as their predecessors had. Local legends are far more specific as to the probable fate of these individuals. Continued whispers about the undead indicate that the vampire problem may not be over, and those who disappeared may have fallen prey to the creatures. Despite the efforts of Ben Mears and Mark Petrie, who burned the town to the ground, some vampires reportedly still stalk the surrounding communities. These persistent stories keep those in the surrounding towns from going anywhere near Jerusalem's Lot. For the most part.

Since no one has yet to follow up on the saga of the accursed township of Jerusalem's Lot, it must be assumed that those few undead citizens are still there. It appears that Ben Mears and Mark Petrie left the job unfinished. Someday, it may fall to others to complete it. Only time will tell.

Time and blood.

•     •     •

For whatever reason, the battle between good and evil, between the Purpose and the Random, is being fought on many fronts. Without question, the Maine of King's prime reality is perhaps the most common battlefield of all in this war. Whether it be monumental, such as Mike Anderson's struggle with Andre Linoge, or more mundane (but equally horrible), as in Dolores Claiborne's struggle to prevent her husband from molesting their daughter, a great many of these individual battles are almost surely significant in that cosmic struggle.

# 19

## *Carrie*

---

$A$LTHOUGH UNIVERSALLY regarded as King's "first novel," *Carrie* (1974) was not by any means his first attempt at a novel-length work, as the author had been writing novels all through his college years (1966–1970) at the University of Maine. In fact, he began his first Richard Bachman offering, *Rage*, while still in high school.

*Carrie* certainly demonstrates the interests and concerns of someone not far removed from a high school setting, either as student or as instructor. It is a truly heartfelt tale about an outsider, created by someone who clearly understood how cruel teenagers can be. The theme presented here is a common one in the Stephen King universe: an outcast, often with paranormal powers, who is pushed so hard by seemingly "normal" folks that she lashes out against them. It is a subject King would return to in such works as *Firestarter* and *Christine*.

Carrie White lives alone with her domineering mother in the small town of Chamberlain, Maine. She is like most so-called losers in high school—awkward, ridiculed, and almost relieved to be ignored by most of the other students and faculty. Carrie, however, turns out to be a little bit different from the other misfits targeted for harassment by the in-crowd: she discovers she has telekinetic powers at her command. If someone pushes her too hard, she can respond by pushing back a hundred times harder.

Not realizing she's been invited to the school prom as part of an elaborate, cruel prank in which a bucket of pig's blood will be dropped on her, Carrie employs her unnatural talents to convince her posses-sive mother to let her attend. She desperately wants to be accepted by her peers. Ironically, her secret powers make her even more a freak of nature than anyone could have imagined.

To keep the story as real as possible, King structures the narrative as a series of reports, official documents, and eyewitness testimonies so that the extraordinary device of telekinesis can be presented matter-of-factly. If this single paranormal aspect were ignored, *Carrie* could easily be read as a mainstream novel of teenage angst. (King is an acknowledged fan of the thematically conventional *Harrison High* novels written by John Farris in the late 1950s and early 1960s, novels about high school life written by someone who was then only a recent graduate himself.)

For many of us, our first encounters with bigotry, sexism, and narrow-mindedness come while trying to survive high school. King's main concern in *Carrie* seems to be to depict her not as some kind of terri-fying supernatural demon, but as a frightened young woman reacting to the monsters around her in a manner with which most readers would readily, if only secretly, sympathize. All of us have felt like outsiders at one point or another, and certainly some of us would like to strike back at those who taunted us if we only had had the means to do so.

Whereas in other early novels (such as *'Salem's Lot*) King would demonstrate a clear-cut battle between the forces of good against the forces of evil, what is most memorable about this book is that Carrie, certainly the author of evil, remains an innocent until her untimely demise. The monsters in this work are neither vampires, nor serial killers, nor extraterrestrial beings bent on dominating the human race. The monsters here are more mundane but nonetheless horrifying in that they are people we all know. Worse, they might even be us.

*Carrie* was the first of many novels in which the put-upon pro-tagonist is a strong, willful female rather than a male. Although mar-keted by its publisher as a thrilling tale of horror, *Carrie* works just as well as a powerful character study of a dysfunctional family and as a gripping exercise in terror. Carrie White is not the horror—rather, it is what the world does to lost souls like her that is truly unspeakable.

Instead of playing out as a simple tale of gruesome supernatural horror, *Carrie* more accurately involves us on the subliminal level of a classic Grimm's fairy tale, namely Cinderella. Here we have contemporary versions of the cruel stepmother (Margaret White); the fairy godmother who is instrumental in seeing that Cinderella goes to the ball (Susan Snell); the wicked stepsisters (the female students who taunt Carrie); and even a Prince Charming (Tommy Ross) who escorts her to the ball.

Unlike the whitewashed Disney versions of most popular fairy tales, however, there is no happy ending for Carrie. As happens so often in the Stephen King universe, the good perish as frequently and haphazardly as the bad. In "Cinderella," the bad are punished. But, in *Carrie*, the good suffer as well. In the real world, King reminds us, sometimes Cinderella herself doesn't survive the ball.

## PRIMARY SUBJECTS

*CARRIE WHITE.* The only child of Ralph and Margaret White, Carrie grew up a wallflower, destined to be a doormat for the other, more popular students. As fate would have it, Carrie has inherited a rare genetic trait for telekinesis from her late father, a power that manifests shortly after she has her first period. Unfortunately, this happens while Carrie is in the shower at school. Uneducated about menstruation, she panics, believing she is bleeding to death, and exposing herself to even more abuse from those who witnessed her unwarranted hysteria.

> *Carrie White's birthday is September 21, 1963. Interestingly, the author's birthday also falls on September 21.*

Without friends, Carrie has only her demented mother to instruct her in the ways of the world. Unfortunately, Margaret White is an obsessed religious fanatic who is of no help to the teenage girl. Carrie is fatally stabbed by her mother on prom night, but not before the girl lays waste to most of the town and kills many of those who had unwisely wronged her.

*MARGARET WHITE.* Carrie's ultrastrict, super-religious mother, Margaret has spent the majority of her adult life atoning for one night of passion, the result of which was the birth of her only child, Carrie.

Margaret has turned her small home into a sanctuary of religious icons and paintings. She believes sex is evil, even within marriage, and that God has punished her by giving her a sexually maturing daughter as a daily reminder of her unspeakable sin of lust. Her idea of "educating" Carrie about menstruation is to lock her in a closet filled with religious symbols and demand she pray for forgiveness. When Margaret's madness ultimately overwhelms her on the night of the prom, she attempts to kill her daughter with a knife. Wounded, enraged, Carrie uses her telekinetic ability to stop Margaret's heart from beating.

*SUSAN SNELL.* A usually decent sort who nevertheless takes part in ridiculing Carrie in the girls' shower room, Susan later comes to regret her actions and attempts to atone for them by convincing her boyfriend, Tommy Ross, to ask Carrie to the prom. Susan is one of the few survivors of the ensuing night of destruction and death, and even writes a book about the experience, *My Name Is Susan Snell.*

*TOMMY ROSS.* Tommy is Susan Snell's affable boyfriend. Although he agrees to take Carrie to the prom strictly out of respect for his girlfriend's wishes, he gradually comes to like Carrie on her own merits. Attending the dance, he and Carrie are voted prom king and queen. When a falling bucket of pig's blood strikes Tommy and knocks him unconscious, Carrie unleashes her terrible power, turning the high school gym into a killing zone. Tommy ultimately dies in the fire triggered by Carrie's actions.

*CHRIS HARGENSEN.* The classic town slut, Chris is the chief instigator in the hazing Carrie receives in the girls' shower room. Punished for their involvement, Chris and several other girls seek revenge against Carrie, creating an elaborate plan to humiliate her at the prom. Chris's orchestrations ultimately result in Carrie being doused with pig's blood seconds after being voted queen of the prom. Although her plan works like a charm, Chris doesn't reckon on Carrie's rampage. She dies later that night as Carrie, departing the gym, proceeds to lay waste to the town.

**BILLY NOLAN.** Chris Hargensen's sexually driven boyfriend, Billy is every father's worst nightmare. Not very bright, Billy provides the brawn Chris requires to obtain the pig's blood and rig the buckets over the stage. Billy dies alongside Chris when he tries to run Carrie down with his car. Carrie telekinetically deflects the oncoming vehicle, sending it careening into the side of a roadhouse. Billy and Chris are killed in the resulting explosion.

## ADAPTATIONS

*Carrie* was made into a highly successful motion picture in 1976, directed by Brian De Palma from a screenplay by Lawrence D. Cohen. Although the production had a paltry budget of $1.8 million, it was one of the top-grossing films of the year, earning more than $30 million in domestic receipts. The ninety-seven-minute thriller is also notable as the showcase for many young actors who would go on to become major stars, including Amy Irving, William Katt, Nancy Allen, and John Travolta. Sissy Spacek and Piper Laurie, who played Carrie and Margaret White respectively, were both nominated for Academy Awards as best actress and best supporting actress.

Director De Palma and screenwriter Cohen had to restructure the story for the screen, but due to the quality of the young cast and the sincerity with which everyone played his or her part, the R-rated movie remains a truly moving and frightening experience. Unlike so many adaptations of King's works to come, the movie was faithful in spirit to the novel, if not always to the literal translation. For example, budget restrictions did not allow the entire town to be destroyed, but it was not the special effects the filmmakers cared about. It was Carrie who mattered.

> *It is interesting to note that on the first paperback edition of the novel, as part of an unusual marketing plan, Stephen King's name did not appear anywhere on the cover. The same strategy was used for 'Salem's Lot.*

King loved the movie, reportedly attributing his ascension to the best seller lists to the success of the picture and the movie tie-in edition of *Carrie.*

In 1999, *The Rage: Carrie 2* was released. The story shamelessly repeated many of the plot elements of the original: a lonely teenage girl discovers she has telekinetic powers that she uses against her tormenters in high school. The movie starred Emily Bergl in the role of Rachel, and featured the return of Amy Irving as Sue Snell, the sole surviving character from the original film. Directed by Katt Shea and scripted by Rafael Moreu, *The Rage: Carrie 2* died a quick death at the box office. King had no involvement whatsoever with the production.

In contrast to the original movie adaptation, *Carrie: The Musical* was far from successful. Touted as "the biggest flop in Broadway history," the stage musical—budgeted at nearly $8 million—opened on Broadway on May 12, 1988, and closed after a run of only five performances. The best-known actress in the production was Betty Buckley, who coincidentally had portrayed the friendly gym teacher Miss Collins in the first *Carrie*. Here, however, she was cast as Margaret White. An unknown named Linzi Hateley played Carrie.

The New York critics utterly loathed the stage production, and the bad publicity that followed quickly ensured its almost overnight demise. That the theatrical production followed the story line of the blood-soaked and body-strewn movie and book indicates the perhaps insurmountable challenge the naïve producers of a musical version were up against.

# 20

## 'Salem's Lot

---

LONGER THAN *Carrie* (1974), *'Salem's Lot* is still quite succinct in comparison to many of King's later epic novels. As he had done in *Carrie,* the author paints a canvas that is gloriously and unabashedly American, for better or worse, or in this case, both. He weaves a tapestry of small-town life that is startlingly true and familiar and, perhaps most important, safe. Within the sanctuary of this cozy setting, with its colorful characters and nostalgia—reinforced time and again by the memories of the central character—King breeds his horror.

*'Salem's Lot* isn't an epic novel, but it isn't meant to be. Instead, it's a story about a town so far off the map that it could wither and die, and nobody would care. King takes the quintessential Bavarian village from the classic horror films of his own youth and transforms it into a tiny hamlet in Maine, right next door to all the small towns of our collective youthful memories.

This element of the narrative is what made *'Salem's Lot* such a milestone. In several tangible ways, it redefined horror fiction and altered the state of American publishing for years to come. Traditionally, horror previous to *'Salem's Lot* was found in arcane tomes and ancient locales. With this small-town vampire tale, King set off an entire generation's worth of horror stories set in the proverbial backyard of the American reading public.

Strange, perhaps, that King's second book would have that impact, but the reason is quite clear. *Carrie* is more of a precursor to the kind of female-driven thrillers King would write much later in his career. *'Salem's Lot,* by comparison, could not be called anything but a horror novel. It is unashamedly a vampire novel, perhaps the most important such work of this century. What King has done here, in a way others would try to imitate in the ensuing years, is take the traditional horror elements found in ghost stories, monster comic books, and B movies that he had enjoyed as a boy, and transport them to mainstream America.

*King's original title for* 'Salem's Lot *was* Second Coming.

*'Salem's Lot* is also important because it represents the beginning of King's real effort to create a fictional counterpart to his home state of Maine. The town is slipped right into the existing geography of this part of New England, and described in such exhaustive and loving detail that one is almost disappointed to realize it has no real place on the map. With repeated references to surrounding communities and to landmarks like the Androscoggin and Royal rivers (the Royal would also be used later in other tales), he offers a sense of place that would become a touchstone of horror fiction.

'Salem's Lot *is the only novel to which King has ever seriously considered writing a sequel. There are indications, in King's afterword to* Wizard and Glass, *that Father Callahan may cross over into the world of the Dark Tower.*

Moreover, in *'Salem's Lot* King foreshadows themes or elements in later novels. The book appears so early in his career that one must wonder if his reiteration of these elements is intentional. For instance, when Mark Petrie sees the vampiric Ralphie Glick outside his window, he uses a poetic tongue twister to stop himself from falling under Ralphie's hypnotic control. The bit of verse is the same one Bill Denbrough used in his stuttering exercises in *IT.* "He thrusts his fists against the posts and still insists he sees the ghosts." Similarly, when Ben Mears attacks Barlow's resting place in the boarding house, he is filled with a power, the kind "that turns the wheels of the universe," an apparent connection to the themes of *The Dark Tower* series and the overarching conflict of the Stephen King universe. Finally, it is implied that Barlow, the vampire, possesses an ancient book of power covered in human skin. Is it possible this is the same book Randall Flagg reads from in *The Eyes of the Dragon*? It is more than possible that such parallels are not coincidence at all.

In the Stephen King universe, Jerusalem's Lot is the archetypal ghost town, the Flying Dutchman and the Bermuda Triangle rolled into one. The novel introduces the concept that evil begets more evil, that it attracts itself with magnetic force, and can linger long after its perpetrator has gone to his damnation.

Even more to the point, King brings to the forefront the idea that supernatural horror is not necessarily something that can occur only in a Gothic castle in Transylvania (as in Bram Stoker's *Dracula*). The undead can exist in the house just down the street, or in our own attics or basements or our neighbors' backyards. As King shows repeatedly in his novels and short stories, home can be where the horror is.

## PRIMARY SUBJECTS

***JERUSALEM'S LOT.*** If you drive north on Interstate 95 in Maine, you'll cross the Royal River just north of Portland and come to an exit that

*Methodist church next to King's house* | DAVID LOWELL

reads, "Route 12, Jerusalem's Lot, Cumberland, Cumberland Center." As you crest the hill of the off-ramp and look down along Route 12 toward town, you may be able to spot the burned ruins of the enormous manse that once stood sentinel over the town, the old Marsten House.

Before the vampire Kurt Barlow came to town, the Lot was a thriving little New England community. Now it's a ghost town. Or perhaps something worse, given the horrors that occurred there.

Jerusalem's Lot was incorporated in 1765, taking its name from the proprietary behavior of a particularly large pig owned by one Charles Belknap Tanner.

*THE MARSTEN HOUSE.* The residence of the Marstens until Hubert Marsten murdered his wife and took his own life. By the time Ben Mears moves to the Lot as a boy, the Marsten house has become the ultimate haunted mansion. Even the bravest of the local children are afraid to enter the moldy, imposing structure, which sits atop Marsten Hill, almost as though it is watching over the town—albeit more as evil tyrant than vigilant sentinel.

Young Ben enters the house on a dare, and believes he sees the ghost of Hubie Marsten inside. Though the Lot's residents never learn of this connection, it seems the late Marsten had been in frequent correspondence with the vampire, Kurt Barlow, who would later bring his evil to the Lot, inspired by Marsten.

The Marsten house is eventually burned to the ground. However, Ben believes the house itself has somehow retained Marsten's evil, which has acted as a kind of beacon for other horrors. If so, it is possible that the burned-out remains of the house and its very foundation still retain some of that evil essence.

*BEN MEARS.* Born on Long Island, New York, Ben is raised by his aunt Cynthia Stowens in 'Salem's Lot. Haunted by a terrifying experience he had in the Lot as a child, and by the tragic death years later of his wife, Miranda, in a motorcycle accident, Mears returns to 'Salem's Lot to write a new novel. His previous books include *Conway's Daughter, Air Dance,* and *Billy Said Keep Going.*

Ben's memories of the Lot are both fond and melancholy. Though little has changed, the town has certainly forgotten him. He, however, has never forgotten it. He dreams quite regularly of that horrific childhood experience: on a dare, he had entered the spooky Marsten house and come upon a frightening specter of the late owner of the home, a suicidal Mafia hit man named Hubie Marsten. Little does Ben know that Hubie Marsten's evil still lingers, and has drawn another sinister force to the town.

Despite his nostalgia, Ben makes no attempt to contact those few with whom he played as a boy. Instead, he makes new friends in Susan Norton, a younger woman with whom he falls in love; her father, Bill Norton; and an aging teacher named Matthew Burke.

Not long after his return, Ben realizes something is horribly wrong. The vampire Barlow and his manservant, Straker, have been murdering the townspeople or transforming them into vampires, and as an outsider Ben is a prime suspect. Later, he becomes one of the few sees what is happening, and takes action. Along with a local boy named Mark Petrie and a doctor named Jimmy Cody, Ben and those closest to him attempt to permanently rid the town of Barlow and his vampires. They manage to burn down the Marsten house, and kill Barlow, but there are too many vampires. Ben suffers another loss when Susan is transformed into one of the undead.

In the end, Ben and Mark, the only survivors, leave 'Salem's Lot and travel as far away as they are able. Attempting to start a new life, they eventually settle in the small Mexican village of Los Zapatas. Only when they come across a press clipping that indicates the vampires are active again in the Lot do they acknowledge they must return to finish the job.

Together, they go back to the Lot for the last time, and set fire to the entire town. Ben's current whereabouts are unknown.

*SUSAN NORTON.* A young woman who has lived all her life in the Lot and dreams of one day moving to the city, Susan was dating Floyd Tibbits before Ben came into her life. They meet in the park on a sunny September afternoon. Susan is instantly charmed by Ben, partially because she is reading one of his books at the very moment she first spots him.

Susan lives at home with her parents, Bill and Ann. She is a painter who is just beginning to enjoy some success. Sadly, when she investigates Ben's wild claims about the Marsten house, she is captured by

Straker and later turned into a vampire by Barlow. Eventually, Ben is forced to drive a stake through her heart, ending her undead existence. Her soul is now free to make its final journey.

*MATTHEW BURKE.* As an English teacher at Consolidated High School, Matt has earned a great deal of respect from his students, but not many accolades from the school's administration. It is Matt who first realizes what is truly happening in 'Salem's Lot. He encounters a former student, Mike Ryerson, at a bar. Concerned by Ryerson's apparent illness, Matt invites him to stay at his home. During the night, Ryerson is attacked and killed by a vampire. When Ryerson returns as a vampire and approaches Matt, the teacher suffers a massive heart attack. Though the seizure keeps him from the physical struggle, Matt works behind the scenes to help those attempting to thwart Barlow's plans. Sadly, Matt dies of a second heart attack in the hospital, never to learn the fate of his town and his friends.

*MARK PETRIE.* Though he grew up in Kittery, Maine, twelve-year-old Mark has the bad luck to have moved to the Lot with his parents just before the vampires came to town. Tall, but slightly built, and bespectacled, Mark is an intelligent boy who can take care of himself. He is forced to fight the school bully soon after his arrival in the Lot, and makes a fool of him.

Mark also has a fondness for monster movies and Aurora monster model kits. On their way to Mark's house to see these models, Danny and Ralphie Glick are attacked. Danny later appears to Mark as a vampire and attempts to get Mark to invite him inside. Mark, however, uses a plastic cross from his Dracula model to frighten away the vampire.

After being captured by Straker, Mark escapes and kills Straker. Barlow later murders Mark's parents in retribution. Eventually, Mark and Ben Mears terminate Barlow and flee the Lot. They wander the country, eventually settling in a Mexican village called Los Zapatas. When they suspect the vampires are back in Jerusalem's Lot, they return to set fire to the entire town. Mark's current whereabouts are unknown.

*DR. JIMMY CODY.* A local doctor, Cody had been a student of Matt Burke and is Matt's doctor until the old teacher dies. Along with

Ben Mears, Jimmy sits with the corpse of Marjorie Glick, whom they suspect of being a vampire, until she rises from the dead to prove their theory true. She is the first vampire slain by the group. Unfortunately, Cody is killed by one of Barlow's booby traps as he investigates Eva Miller's boarding house, which has become the vampires' stronghold.

*KURT BARLOW.* A horrid, ancient vampire, Barlow thrived in Nazi Germany until he found it necessary to remove himself from that part of the world. He began a correspondence with Hubert Marsten, a Mafia member who resided in 'Salem's Lot and gave Barlow a good deal of information about the town. At one point Straker, Barlow's servant, refers to Marsten as Barlow's "benefactor" in America.

Years pass, and Marsten hangs himself after murdering his wife. Eventually, Barlow determines to come to the United States. 'Salem's Lot is his chosen target, a town where he can "feed" indiscriminately and not be discovered. In a shady real estate deal, he purchases the Marsten house as well as a storefront. There his servant, Straker, opens an antiques shop to cover their true intentions.

When Barlow realizes that some townspeople know who he is, he moves into the basement of Eva Miller's boardinghouse. Here he is eventually killed by Ben Mears and Mark Petrie.

There are those who say Barlow's vampiric offspring continue to roam the area around 'Salem's Lot.

*RICHARD THROCKETT STRAKER.* Straker is Barlow's servant, his human agent. For his master, Straker performs many tasks, from the propitiation of demons to the abduction and murder of children. Striker is preternatually strong. His incredible physical power and enduring youth make it obvious that Straker is not entirely human, thanks to Barlow's influence. However, he is not a vampire. Straker arranges a deal with local real estate agent Larry Crockett to buy the Marsten house and a storefront, where he opens and runs what appears to be an antiques shop.

When Susan Norton and Mark Petrie break into the Marsten house, Straker discovers them. When Mark attempts to escape, Straker tries to kill him and is instead killed by the boy.

*FATHER DONALD CALLAHAN.* The pastor at St. Andrew's Church, Father Callahan is responsible for the spiritual well-being of the town's Catholics. He is an alcoholic, however, and has a great deal of trouble caring for his own soul. Even before the horrible events occur in the Lot, Callahan doubts his faith. When the truth is revealed to him, his faith is restored for a time. Surely, he reasons, the presence of such evil indicates the existence of God as an opposing force.

After Barlow murders Mark Petrie's parents, Callahan saves Mark from the vampire, only to have his faith newly challenged. In the end, his faith is not strong enough, and Barlow takes some of Callahan's blood, enslaving him. In the only act of defiance left to him, Callahan flees 'Salem's Lot forever, leaving his parishioners and the town to suffer in Barlow's evil grasp. His current whereabouts are unknown.

*HUBERT MARSTEN.* An eccentric and evil man, Hubie Marsten was a hit man for the Mafia. He tapes all of his money to the insides of magazines. He corresponded with Barlow the vampire when Barlow still resided in Europe. Later, Marsten murders his wife and then hangs himself in the attic of his old mansion. It is possible that his spirit remains tied to the house, for when young Ben Mears ventures into the house on a dare, he sees a ghastly vision of what might be Hubie Marsten's ghost.

*THE GLICK FAMILY.* Nine-year-old Ralphie Glick is taken by Straker as a sacrifice for Barlow when he and his older brother, Danny, are on their way to Mark Petrie's house. In time, the entire Glick family falls victim to the vampires.

*THE NORTON FAMILY.* Bill and Ann Norton and their daughter, Susan, all become victims of the vampires.

*THE PETRIE FAMILY.* Though their son, Mark, survives the evil that destroys 'Salem's Lot, his parents do not.

*MIKE RYERSON.* A local blue-collar worker and former student of Matt Burke's, Mike is filling in Danny Glick's grave in Harmony Hill cemetery when Danny comes back to life as a vampire. Danny attacks him, and soon Mike is also one of the undead. After his own resurrection, Mike attempts to kill Matt Burke but is unsuccessful.

## ADAPTATIONS

In November 1979, a two-part miniseries based on *'Salem's Lot* aired on CBS. The groundbreaking event featured David Soul *(Starsky and Hutch)* as Ben Mears, respected British actor James Mason *(A Star Is Born)* as Straker, and Bonnie Bedelia (who would later play Bruce Willis's wife in the *Die Hard* series) as Susan Norton. At the time, the miniseries's $4 million was considered an enormous expenditure. Under the able direction of Tobe Hooper, who had previously helmed *The Texas Chainsaw Massacre* (1974) and would later direct *Poltergeist* (1982) and *Lifeforce* (1985), the miniseries turned out to be a highly effective mood piece, though the horror was heavily diluted by network censors.

The miniseries diverged significantly from the book in some aspects of plot. The relocation of Barlow to Eva Miller's boardinghouse late in the novel is changed for the series. There, the final showdown occurs in the Marsten House. But for the most part this was a faithful adaptation by Paul Monash, who previously had produced the 1976 film version of *Carrie*. King was reportedly satisfied with the production—given the restrictions of the medium—though he took issue with the depiction of Barlow as someone who looked more like the ghastly creature from the 1922 silent classic *Nosferatu* than the way he had been portrayed in the novel.

A theatrical version for European distribution was reedited from the miniseries and titled *'Salem's Lot: The Movie.* While it was more graphic in terms of its visual elements, its shorter running time (112 minutes versus the original 210 minutes) left much of the integral character development on the cutting room floor. (Curiously enough, in 1987 writer-director Larry Cohen would be the main creative force behind a direct-to-video sequel authorized by Warner Bros. called *A Return to 'Salem's Lot.* Starring Michael Moriarty and Andrew Duggan, it bore only a passing resemblance to the characters and situations from the original novel. Even so, King was given screen credit as "creative consultant.")

# 21

## *Pet Sematary*

---

A LTHOUGH IT may be argued that such Richard Bachman titles as *Rage* (1977) and *Roadwork* (1981) constitute Stephen King's darkest visions, it must be said that the novel which the writer himself considers his bleakest and most pessimistic is *Pet Sematary* (1983).

Written in the spring of 1979, this book for several years had the reputation of being the "story so horrifying that he was for a time unwilling to finish it" (so states the dust-jacket copy of the hardcover first edition). A further indication of how long King struggled with this work comes from the author's notation on the last page stating that the composition of the novel occurred from February 1979 to December 1982.

What is generally not known is that King actually did complete the novel in the summer of 1979, but found it so grim that he decided not to publish it. Even his wife, Tabitha, whom King has always used as the first reader for all his work, agreed that the story should be put away in a drawer permanently. And so it was. The fact that it was eventually published had far more to do with a dispute involving a past publisher, Doubleday & Co., than it did with a desire to squash the rumor that he had authored a novel he himself found too nasty to have published.

Like so many of his early novels, *Pet Sematary* focuses on the lives of a small family residing in Maine. A young doctor, Louis Creed, moves from Chicago to the small town of Ludlow. His family consists of his lovely wife, Rachel, and two children, five-year-old Ellie and two-year-old Gage. On the surface, life is good: Louis is to be the new head of health services for the University of Maine at nearby Orono. But the comfortable old house in which they live is set near a busy road, one often used by truckers driving their massive eighteen-wheelers. One day Ellie's beloved cat, Church (devolved from Winston Churchill) is run over and killed.

Ellie is grief-stricken, and Louis, who has never been particularly adept at handling matters of religion or faith, is at a loss to comfort her. From an elderly neighbor, Jud Crandall, the doctor learns an incredible secret known only to the locals. Nearby is a "pet sematary" (as it reads on a crude sign misspelled by children) that was once an ancient Indian burial ground and is supposedly haunted by the legendary creature known as the Wendigo. The cemetery's amazing secret is that anything buried there does not stay dead. Louis buries Church there, and incredibly, the cat *does* return—although it is a mean, zombielike incarnation of its former self.

In a situation similar to one expressed in the classic 1902 tale by W. W. Jacobs entitled "The Monkey's Paw," Louis finds himself in the extraordinary circumstance of having the power—through the use of the pet cemetery—to be granted three wishes. His first is to have his daughter's beloved pet returned to her, and it is. It is not normal, it is not friendly, but at least it is *back*.

Then a far greater tragedy occurs—young Gage runs out into the road in front of the house and is struck and killed by a truck. Now it is his parents who cannot be consoled in their overwhelming grief. Rachel's sister had died a lingering death from spinal meningitis when she was young, and Rachel cannot bear the tragic and sudden death of her boy. Too many painful wounds have reopened, and she nearly goes insane. Half mad himself, Louis digs up the body of his dead son from the local cemetery and reburies him in the pet burial ground, hoping against hope that he can bring his son back to life. He doesn't care what price has to be paid for the boy's return; he only knows that he will do anything to make his family whole again. And so his second grisly wish is granted through the unholy power of the Micmac Indian burial ground.

But what returns is his son in appearance only. Gage is actually an undead, soulless monster, cursed with murderous instincts of pure evil.

Using one of his father's scalpels, the boy brutally murders Jud Crandall, then butchers his own mother. Louis is faced with destroying the loathsome creature that was once his son. (Ellie is sent to live with her mother's family in Chicago and is spared the entire ordeal. However, through her psychiclike nightmares, she is aware of the horror befalling the rest of her family.)

Unfortunately, Louis has not learned from his terrible experience. Although he dimly comprehends the unnatural horror that had befallen his son, he believes that if he can bury his recently deceased wife in the pet sematary quickly enough, she will emerge more or less "normal." Louis's third and final wish doesn't come true in quite the way he desires. In the novel's devastating last sentence, his loving wife does return to him after being revived by the supernatural powers of the pet cemetery: "Darling," it says.

*Pet Sematary* shares many themes prevalent in the darkest corners of the Stephen King universe. Chief among them is that no one is truly the master of one's destiny, that anyone and anything we love can be taken away at a moment's notice. The only force we can depend on is the love we share in our families, and even that can be stolen at any point. King has repeatedly stated in interviews that for him, the greatest horror one can experience in life is the sudden and tragic loss of a child.

In the early novels *Carrie* (1974), *Rage* (1977), *The Long Walk* (1979), and especially *Cujo* (1981), teenagers and children die violent and senseless deaths. Yet in each of them, King leaves a faint ray of hope to comfort the reader. However, in *Pet Sematary* there is no sense of a happy ending, even though young Ellie apparently will survive to see another day. The father, mother, and son, are dead—or undead. It is only by mere chance that the daughter is allowed to live, and it's extremely unlikely the remainder of her existence will be a happy or fulfilling one.

The author is also dealing here with questions of faith and religion. As a doctor, Louis believes that he is somehow above the laws of God and nature, and that he can circumvent the natural order of life and death simply because he is well educated and supremely rational. But within the Stephen King universe, death can come at any time to anyone, for any reason. Most important, death can visit any of us—good or bad, young or old, beloved or stranger—for no logical reason whatsoever. Even so, life is not always worth holding on to at any cost.

As Jud Crandall warns an unheeding Louis Creed, "Sometimes, dead is better."

## PRIMARY SUBJECTS

*LOUIS CREED.* Thirty-five-year-old Louis has brought his family to Maine to pursue a medical career and better their lives. A pragmatic man, he holds no strong religious beliefs and looks for the rational explanation behind every mystery. After bringing first his daughter's cat and then his young son back from the dead, he realizes to his everlasting misfortune that there are some mysteries that should never be explored. When he restores his murdered wife to life, it can only be presumed that she in turn destroys him.

*RACHEL CREED.* The loving wife of Louis Creed, Rachel is a devoted mother to her young son and daughter. She has been emotionally scarred since childhood by the death of her sister, Zelda, from spinal meningitis. At age eight, Rachel witnessed her sister's agonizing demise and has never forgotten the horror of that experience. Rachel is later slain at the hands of her own undead son, wielding the bloody scalpel he has stolen from his father's medical bag. Her husband refuses to accept her untimely passing, and brings her back using the supernatural powers of the pet sematary. She returns, however, as a soulless being.

*GAGE CREED.* Two-year-old Gage is killed by a speeding truck and then temporarily laid to rest by his grieving family. Louis Creed digs up his son's corpse and buries him in the pet sematary. Gage returns from the dead as an evil thing who butchers Jud Crandall and later his own mother. Gage is then killed a second time with lethal injections administered by his own father, who has now gone insane.

*ELLIE CREED.* The five-year-old sister of Gage Creed, Ellie escapes the fate of her parents when she is placed in the care of her grandparents in Chicago. Like her father, she is cursed with psychic visions of the dead. Her current whereabouts are unknown.

*VICTOR PASCOW.* A young man who has the misfortune to be fatally hit by a speeding car on the first day that Louis Creed starts work at the university's health center. Before he dies, Victor supernaturally warns Louis about the awful consequences to be reckoned with should he ever use the cursed power of the pet sematary. Ghostly visions of Victor continue to haunt Louis and, later, his daughter, Ellie, but do not prevent further tragedy from befalling the Creed family.

*JUD CRANDALL.* The elderly neighbor who lives closest to the Creed home, Jud becomes fast friends with the Creed family, especially with Louis, who regards Jud as the wise father he had never known. (Louis's father died when the boy was only three.) A native of Maine who enjoys a good beer and a long talk, he reveals to Louis the terrible secret of the pet sematary. After Gage's death, he rightly suspects Louis will try to bring his only son back to life, but his warning goes unheeded. Ultimately, Jud pays for sharing that forbidden knowledge at the murderous hands of the undead Gage.

> *Jud Crandall mentions in passing the story of four people who were savagely killed by a rabid dog. That story was, of course, fully related in* Cujo.

## ADAPTATION

By the time King decided to sell the film rights to *Pet Sematary*, his career had advanced to such a stage that he could demand in his contract that the production be shot in Maine or not be made at all. He also had the power to dictate that only his own screenplay adaptation be used. This was the first of his novels for which he was credited with the screen adaptation. In both cases, his stipulations were carried out, and King had the further pleasure of seeing the motion picture become a moderate success at the box office when it was released in 1989.

Directed by Mary Lambert, who had helmed only one feature previously (*Siesta*, which was not in the horror genre), *Pet Sematary*, being scripted by King, remained faithful to the novel. (King's old friend George Romero was originally slated to direct, but scheduling conflicts forced him to bow out.) Starring Dale Midkiff as Louis Creed and Denise Crosby as Rachel, the most notable bit of casting was Fred Gwynne in the role of Jud. Gwynne delivers a wonderful performance that captures the essence of a Stephen King character better than almost anyone who has come before or since. Unflinchingly gory and shocking, the 102-minute picture is in many ways as dark and bleak as its source material. Unlike the radical change in ending he had allowed in the movie version of *Cujo*, King knew his growing legion of fans could now deal with a totally downbeat ending.

The success of *Pet Sematary* led to a totally unnecessary sequel, *Pet Sematary 2*, released in 1992 and starring Edward Furlong and Anthony Edwards. (A standard clause in the purchasing of motion picture rights for a story or a novel allows the producers to retain the rights to sequels. This explains how, without King's desire or participation, screen sequels—often direct-to-video—were made to *'Salem's Lot*, and to the features based on the stories "Sometimes They Come Back" and "Children of the Corn.") Although *Pet Sematary 2* was also directed by Mary Lambert, there is unfortunately little to recommend it, even for King completists.

> *In the film adaptation, King himself has a cameo as a minister.*

# 22

## Cycle of the Werewolf

O NE OF KING'S quirkier projects, *Cycle of the Werewolf* began
as an idea for a calendar. The concept was to create a story that
would be told in quick bits each month. What better monster for such
a concept than one that appears only once (with a rare exception)
every month—on the night of the full moon.

As the story grew, it soon became too unwieldy for a calendar. The
structure remained, however, and the 113-page book is divided into
twelve chapters, each named for a month. First released in a very limited edition by specialty publisher Land of Enchantment, *Cycle of the
Werewolf* was later rereleased in two different 1985 trade paperback
editions, one of which tied into the published screenplay of the film
version—retitled *Silver Bullet*—and is no longer available.

Despite its brevity, *Cycle of the Werewolf,* is classic King. A werewolf begins to prey on the people of Tarker's Mills, Maine, in January.
Six victims are taken, one a month. In July, the werewolf attempts to
kill Marty Coslaw, a ten-year-old boy who is confined to a wheelchair.
Marty's uncle Al had given him fireworks, and he fires them at the
creature, blasting out one of its eyes and forcing it to flee.

Marty is sent to live with relatives, but when he returns he
searches among the citizens of Tarker's Mills looking for someone
with a damaged eye. It isn't until Halloween night, when he sees the
Reverend Lester Lowe wearing an eye patch, that Marty realizes who
the werewolf actually is. He sends the minister notes, urging him to

turn himself in or kill himself. Unfortunately, Lowe not only has become aware of his dual nature, he also has embraced it.

On New Year's Eve, after Marty has purposely revealed his identity to the minister, he waits in his living room with Uncle Al, who has had a pair of silver bullets made for Marty. Though Al really doesn't believe his nephew's claims about the werewolf, he doesn't dare disbelieve, considering the possible consequences. The wolf inevitably attacks, and despite being confined to a wheelchair, Marty kills it, with Uncle Al and his father as witnesses.

*One-room schoolhouse King attended, Durham* | DAVID LOWELL

Marty is a classic King character, a boy not unlike so many of his others: Mark Petrie in *'Salem's Lot* (1975) and the young cast of *IT* (1986) in particular. King has always written young people with a sureness that reveals how well he must recall or imagine his own youth. But with Marty, Mark Petrie, and the youngsters from *IT* (who even call themselves "the losers"), there is an additional element. They're the odd kids, out of the mainstream, whose usual playground is within their own minds. They also become the only ones among their families (neighbors, teachers) to see that the monster is real and must be stopped. In spite of being "different" from other kids, they find the strength to combat the monster and triumph. Marty is physically disabled, which makes him even more of an outcast and more heroic. It is no coincidence that of the characters in *IT,* Bill Denbrough (who suffers from a severe stutter) is the one who actually does the monster in at the end, triumphing over his impediment. Confined to his wheelchair, Marty faces down a werewolf in his living room, making him perhaps the bravest of all.

## PRIMARY SUBJECTS

*MARTY COSLAW.* Confined to a wheelchair, ten-year-old Marty is the only one of the werewolf's intended victims to survive. When it first attacks Marty in July, he fends it off with fireworks, destroying one of its eyes. When the boy realizes that the werewolf is the Reverend Lester Lowe, he taunts the clergyman into attacking him again. This time, he is ready with silver bullets his uncle has brought him. It is presumed that Marty still resides in Tarker's Mills.

*REVEREND LESTER LOWE.* Minister at the local Baptist church, Lowe is a werewolf. He does not realize his dual nature for some time but eventually discovers and embraces it. When he learns that Marty Coslaw might reveal his secret, he tries again to kill the boy, but Marty shoots him dead with silver bullets.

*AL.* Marty's uncle (his mother's brother), Al doesn't fully believe Marty's claims about Lowe's true nature, but the boy is convincing enough to get Al to have a pair of silver bullets made. Al is present when the werewolf attacks Marty on New Year's Eve and is killed by the boy. It is presumed that Al still lives in Maine and visits his sister's family often.

## ADAPTATION

Perhaps the only movie ever to be made from an idea for a monthly calendar, *Stephen King's Silver Bullet* was released by Paramount Pictures in the fall of 1985. It was the fourth King film project produced by Dino De Laurentiis. Scripted by King and helmed by first-time director Daniel Attias, the $7 million picture is perhaps most notable for its variation on a classic monster theme and its lack of big-name actors. The star, of course, is the werewolf (actually there are a number of variations on the main werewolf), which was created by Italian creature-maker Carlo Rambaldi. His human counterpart was played by the wonderful Everett McGill *(Dune, Twin Peaks)*. King, De Laurentiis, and Attias reportedly never could completely agree on the right "look" for the monster, and so audiences saw a creature that appeared as much as a weredog or werebear as it did a traditional werewolf.

Marty was played by the 1980s kid-movie stalwart Corey Haim *(The Goonies, Lost Boys)* while Gary Busey *(Lethal Weapon, The Buddy Holly Story)* portrayed Marty's uncle, now called Red instead of Al. Although Busey, Academy-Award nominee, is always enjoyable to watch, what is perhaps most extraordinary about the 95-minute feature is how stunningly ordinary it is. There is truly nothing in *Silver Bullet* that anyone with a passing knowledge of werewolf movies hasn't seen before. Had it not been written by the master of horror, it's highly unlikely that such a project would have ever gotten out of the special-effects makeup room.

> Cycle of the Werewolf *is connected to King's other work in perhaps the most natural of ways—by railroad. The GS&WM train line, noted in King's novella "The Body" (1982), apparently runs through both that story's fictional town, Castle Rock, and* Cycle of the Werewolf's *setting, Tarker's Mills.*

# 23

## *Gerald's Game*

---

JUST AS *Needful Things* (1991) marked the end of one phase of Stephen King's career (namely the Castle Rock era), *Gerald's Game* (1992) signaled the beginning of another. Over the course of his next four novels, beginning with *Gerald's Game* and ending with *Rose Madder,* King focused much more intensely on character development. He had already written his end-of-the-world novel, *The Stand* (1978), and published what he considered his ultimate statement on supernatural horror in *IT* (1986). Perhaps he felt it was time to further investigate the two-legged monsters and maniacs who live just down the street or even in the adjoining room.

Although the supernatural remained an important element of his fiction, King shifted to a more realistic style of storytelling reminiscent of *Cujo* (1981) and *Misery* (1987). Like those books, *Gerald's Game* features a single character's struggle for survival against overwhelming odds. The novel is an example of the creative challenges King frequently imposes on himself to keep his creative juices flowing. Here he limits himself to a single character in a single setting to further test his resourcefulness and powers of observation as a writer. It's a tribute to King's talent that he meets these self-imposed challenges so well.

Dedicated to "six good women" (Margaret Spruce Morehouse, Anne Spruce Labree, Catherine Spruce Graves, Tabitha Spruce King, Stephanie Spruce Leonard, and Marcella Spruce) who have had a favorable impact on the author's life in one way or another, *Gerald's*

*Game* signaled the emergence of a more "feminist" King. This may have been in response to critics who asserted that the most convincing females King was capable of creating were either teenagers or small children.

Beginning with *Gerald's Game*, the theme of men as monsters (previously explored briefly in books like *Cujo* and more explicitly in *IT*) emerges again and again in King's work. Gerald Burlingame, the doomed husband of Jessie, is the first in a depressingly long line of loathsome males, child-molesting fathers, and wife beaters King would introduce over the next three to four years.

Originally intended to be one half of a single volume entitled *In the Path of the Eclipse*, *Gerald's Game* is a companion piece to King's next novel, *Dolores Claiborne* (1993). The total eclipse of the sun on July 20, 1963, plays an important part in both novels. During that solar event, twelve-year-old Jessie is molested by her father, while many miles and an entire novel away, Dolores Claiborne slays her abusive husband, Joe St. George. Jessie and Dolores each have visions of the other later that fateful day. Their strange bond persists some thirty years later. On the day her employer, Vera Donovan, passes away, Dolores thinks of Jessie and somehow knows "she's in terrible trouble." The eclipse acts as a powerful metaphor in both novels, expressing the notion of secrets once hidden in the dark eventually emerging into the light of day.

*Gerald's Game*, *Dolores Claiborne*, and *Rose Madder* all showcase women who learn how to take control of their lives. *Gerald's Game* is perhaps the most intense and immediate, relating Jessie's life-and-death struggle to free herself from both physical and mental bonds.

## PRIMARY SUBJECTS

*JESSIE BURLINGAME.* Though she remains reluctant, Jessie participates in yet another of the mild bondage games that her husband finds sexually arousing. Over time, she becomes more and more disturbed by these games, but when Gerald pleads with her, Jessie allows him to handcuff her to the bed in their cabin at Lake Kashwakamak, Maine. Later, having had enough, Jessie demands to be freed. Pretending not to understand, Gerald ignores her pleas. Enraged, Jessie lashes out, kicking him solidly in the chest. The blow triggers a heart attack, and Gerald slumps to the floor, dead. Jessie finds herself alone, almost naked, and handcuffed to the bed, in a cabin on a remote dirt road. Thus begins a twenty-eight-hour ordeal that results in both injury and healing—and changes one woman forever.

The bedroom becomes Jessie's entire world—her major concerns lie in how to reach a glass of water on the shelf behind her and the handcuff keys on the bureau in front of her. Her attempts to free herself become increasingly gruesome, building to the point where she uses her own blood as a lubricant to slip off one of the cuffs.

Wracked by pain and dehydration, Jessie begins to hallucinate. She engages in imaginary conversations with friends and family, and with her mental alter ego, the demure Goodwife Burlingame. What Jessie doesn't realize is that her subconscious is struggling to get her to confront a horrible incident she has spent her whole life trying to forget. Alternating between the rational and the delusional, Jessie eventually uncovers the buried memory of the unfortunate central event of her life: the day of the eclipse, July 20, 1963, when her father molested her. Her father's abuse has ruined her life, perhaps even causing her to make the poor life decisions that have led to her present predicament.

Due to the cabin's utter isolation, it is unlikely someone will find her before she starves to death. Things are complicated by the appearance of Prince the dog, a hungry stray who feasts on Gerald's corpse. Finally, there is "the dead cowboy . . . the specter of love," a hideous creature who shows up at the cabin and simply stares at her. In her delirium, she mistakes the hazy figure for her father, back from the dead. Later, she realizes that the figure is real. Shortly after she frees herself from her bonds, the figure reappears, bent on doing her harm. Summoning all her remaining strength, Jessie escapes and flees in her Mercedes.

Although Jessie achieves closure of sorts regarding her molestation, the experience leaves her traumatized physically and mentally. For months after, she lives as a virtual recluse, shutting herself off from the world. It is only when she reads in the newspaper about the ghoulish Andrew Ray Joubert that she begins to emerge from her self-imposed isolation. Jessie realizes that Joubert is the spectral figure who haunted her during her strange imprisonment. Traveling to the court where Joubert is being tried for various perverted sex crimes, she confronts him; when he laughs at her, she spits in his face. An act of defiance that indicates Jessie may be on the road to a full recovery.

**GERALD BURLINGAME.** A lawyer by profession, Gerald hopes to revitalize his listless marriage by cajoling his wife into participating in bondage games. Jessie goes along out of love and a desire to keep the peace, but is enraged one day when her husband willfully ignores her repeated requests to unlock the handcuffs that chain her to the bed in their remote cabin. Gerald's brutish behavior angers Jessie. She kicks him in the chest, triggering a fatal heart attack. His corpse is later partially consumed by a stray dog. Fortunately for Jessie, Gerald had purchased significant amounts of life insurance—at his death, she receives several large checks, allowing her to live comfortably for the remainder of her life.

**ANDREW RAY JOUBERT.** Joubert, who suffers from acromegaly (a progressive enlargement of the hands, feet, and face that causes his forehead to bulge and his arms to dangle all the way down to his knees), began to indulge his perverted sexual desires by first vandalizing graves, then looting crypts and mausoleums. From these grisly activities, he graduates to taking body parts—noses, arms, feet, hands—and having sex with male corpses. Although the police investigation lasts more than seven years, it is kept very quiet and is not

> *Joubert is later mentioned briefly in* Insomnia *(1994) by a stranger who is involved in a car accident with Ed Deepneau.*

reported in the press until Joubert is apprehended in the act. Searching Joubert's van, the police discover a variety of body parts and cutting tools. On the front seat is a sandwich—a human tongue on Wonder bread, slathered with yellow mustard.

Before his arrest, Joubert comes upon the captive Jessie in the cabin at Lake Kashwakamak. She thinks she is hallucinating, but only when she is free and realizes he is real, does he try to attack her. Later, Jessie appears at his arraignment and spits in his face.

# 24

## *Dolores Claiborne*

---

KING SPENT a great deal of creative time in the 1990s broadening his approach to horror by exploring the psyche and concentrating less on the supernatural in a number of books, including *Gerald's Game* (1992), *Insomnia* (1994), and *Rose Madder* (1995). Primary among these is *Dolores Claiborne* (1993), in which the author created one of his most complex and memorable characters.

Written in the form of a monologue, *Dolores Claiborne* is a well-conceived, marvelously executed work of art, that also functions as a distorted mirror for the events of *Gerald's Game*. The novel explores themes similar to those in *Gerald's Game*, this time from the perspective of an older woman. In both books, a father molests a daughter, but the girl's mother doesn't know, attributing her child's odd behavior to a contrary personality. Eventually, Dolores discovers the problem and takes brutal action to stamp it out. In each case, the molestation has severe consequences some thirty years later. Both women are forced to confront their past, Jessie because of her perilous situation, Dolores because she has been accused of killing her long-time employer, the formidable Vera Donovan.

The relationship between Dolores and Vera echoes situations in King's own past, events about which he wrote in his memorable 1985 short story "Gramma." There, as in *Dolores Claiborne*, an elderly, bedridden woman terrorizes a household. In "Gramma," the title character turns out to be a witch who steals her grandson's soul and takes over his body. In *Dolores Claiborne*, Vera Donovan fills a similar role in a decidedly nonsupernatural manner. (These plot elements may be a reflection of the uneasy relationship between King's mother, Ruth, and his invalid maternal grandmother. Ruth King cared for her mother for many years, enduring her many demands and abusive tongue.)

Readers sympathize with Dolores, both because of the skillful way King builds her characterization and because of the totally unsympathetic way he renders her husband, the sniveling Joe St. George. As in *Gerald's Game*, men are portrayed as the enemy, both for their actions and for their complicity. Dolores's father beats her mother, and Joe St. George beats Dolores. When Joe drains her bank account without her knowledge, Dolores confronts the bank manager who let him do it. His response is a stunning reminder to Dolores that she lives in a male-dominated world. By piling on the injustices done to Dolores, the author deftly switches the expected sympathies on his readers—we quickly move from "Did she do it?" to "Why didn't she do it sooner?"

> *Little Tall Island, where Dolores resides, is a microcosm for her rural state, revealing both its glory and its blemishes. It is also the setting for the 1999 television miniseries* Storm of the Century.

Although this book downplays the horror and the supernatural elements that his readers have come to expect in the majority of his work, there are discomforting glimmers of both in the narrative. One obvious supernatural touch is the strange link between Dolores and Jessie Burlingame (see *Gerald's Game*). King also betrays his lifelong fondness for EC Comics–type touches—Joe's plaintive wails of "Duh-lorrr-iss" issuing from the well bring to mind the mutterings of the assorted reanimated corpses who rise up to torment their killers in those gleefully ghastly comic book stories.

*Dolores Claiborne* is also a remarkable example of King as a regional writer, an aspect previously revealed in shorter works like "Mrs. Todd's Shortcut" (1984), "The Sun Dog" (1990), and the prologue to *Needful Things* (1991). Dolores is clearly a product of her environment, from her practical, pragmatic morality to her thick Maine accent.

## PRIMARY SUBJECTS

*DOLORES CLAIBORNE.* Suspected of murdering Vera Donovan, the ancient, rich, "off-island" woman who employs her first as a maid and then as a caregiver/companion, sixty-six-year-old Dolores insists she is innocent. However, the foul-mouthed, hardheaded, outspoken islander readily admits to the police, by way of explaining more recent events, that she killed her reprobate husband, Joe St. George, some thirty years earlier.

As Dolores tells it, Joe was a mean, ill-tempered, dishonest alcoholic who, after physically abusing her, was likely to brag about it to his low-life friends. One night, Joe hits her in the back with a piece of firewood, hurting her badly. When she is finally able to stand again, Dolores takes swift action, smashing Joe in the side of the head with a cream pitcher, then holding him off with a hatchet.

Dolores promises Joe that if he ever hits her again she will bury the hatchet in his head. Joe, agreeing to end the abuse, finds he is no longer able to perform sexually in bed. Flaunting his behavior, he begins abusing their daughter Selena, first by playing on her sympathies, then by demanding sexual favors. This, together with his mistreatment of their sons, proves too much for Dolores, who decides to leave Joe and move to the mainland with her children. But, when she goes to the bank to withdraw the money she has been saving to send the children to college, she discovers that Joe has secretly transferred the funds to his own account. Later, the frustrated Dolores breaks down in front of her employer, Vera Donovan, who, trying to comfort her, tells her that sometimes an accident can be a woman's best friend. She cites herself as an example, pointing out that she inherited her husband's estate when he passed away. Vera gives Dolores the impression that Vera may have been instrumental in her spouse's demise.

Inspired by Vera's example and desperate to save herself and her children from further abuse, Dolores devises a plan to dispatch her husband. On July 20, 1963, the day a total eclipse of the sun darkens the skies, Dolores gets Joe drunk, then tricks him into running over the rotted wood covering of an abandoned well she's discovered near their home. He falls through the flimsy covering, later attempts to emerge wounded but alive, and is killed by Dolores.

The widowed Dolores raises her children and sends them out into the world. She continues working for Vera Donovan, evolving from maid to primary caregiver. Over the years, Vera deteriorates mentally and physically and lives in irrational fear of the "dust bunnies" under her bed, afraid they will kill her. One morning she becomes so frightened that she flees her bedroom and in a panic throws herself down a staircase. Near death, she pleads with Dolores to kill her. Dolores reluctantly agrees but is saved from performing this grisly duty when Vera expires on her own. The police, however, suspect foul play. At the police station, Dolores reveals her involvement in Joe's death.

Eventually cleared of a possible wrongful death in the demise of Vera Donovan, it is presumed that Dolores Claiborne still resides on Little Tall Island.

*VERA DONOVAN.* Vera is a wealthy widow who employs Dolores Claiborne as a maid and then as caregiver for more than thirty years. During that time, in a strange way, Vera and Dolores become best friends. The two women share a mutual understanding and respect, accepting abuse from each other they simply would not tolerate from anyone else. Vera, who very likely murdered her own abusive husband, gives Dolores the idea to kill Joe St. George. Vera becomes mentally unstable in her later years. One day she flees her bedroom in abject terror and throws herself down a flight of stairs, an irrational act that causes her death.

*JOE ST. GEORGE.* Joe is a chronically unemployed, drunken coward, a despicable man who sees nothing wrong with physically, sexually, and emotionally abusing his wife and children. A classic ne'er-do-well, he is manipulated by his wife, Dolores Claiborne, into falling into an abandoned well. Although injured, he climbs out, only to have Dolores push him back down. He dies when struck by a large rock Dolores shoves down the well.

*SELENA ST. GEORGE.* Dolores's daughter and eldest child, Selena is another victim of Joe St. George, who abuses her mentally and sexually. Selena only escapes further mistreatment because her mother kills

Joe. Selena grows up to be a successful but troubled journalist in New York City. It is presumed that she still resides there.

*DR. JOHN McAULIFFE.* The medical examiner who investigates Joe St. George's death, McAuliffe suspects that something is amiss. He questions Dolores about her activities on the day Joe died but is unable to shake her story. McAuliffe reluctantly renders a finding of "death by misadventure" regarding Joe's demise.

*LITTLE TALL ISLAND.* A tiny island off the coast of central Maine, Little Tall is the home of Dolores Claiborne and Vera Donovan. The community is close-knit, inbred and ingrown, like those of other small Maine towns.

## ADAPTATION

Released in 1995, the R-rated film version of *Dolores Claiborne* starred Kathy Bates in the title role and was directed by Taylor Hackford. Bates won an Oscar for her portrayal of another King character, the demented Annie Wilkes, in *Misery*. The movie also starred Jennifer Jason Leigh as Selena St. George and Christopher Plummer as John McAuliffe.

*The actress Frances Sternhagen who appeared in such film and television projects as* Misery *(1990) and* Golden Years *(1991), is the reader on the* Dolores Claiborne *audiobook, and gives a truly memorable performance.*

The 131-minute feature is a compelling yet strange reflection of the book—Tony Gilroy's screenplay focuses far more on Selena and McAuliffe than does King's novel. Selena, who lives in New York City, returns to Little Tall Island after Dolores is accused of murdering Vera Donovan. The estranged daughter has repressed the memories of her father's abuse, but these soon resurface due to her mother's current situation.

McAuliffe, convinced Dolores escaped justice thirty earlier, seeks vengeance. In the movie, Dolores does not confess to Joe's murder; the viewer learns the facts via a series of flashbacks. McAuliffe brings

Dolores up on charges, but Selena is able to convince the presiding magistrate of her mother's innocence.

Kathy Bates brings Dolores to life, dominating the screen when allowed. Some key scenes from the novel—Vera's death, the night Dolores stands up to Joe, the day Dolores learns her spouse stole her savings, and Selena's recounting of Joe's molestation—are faithfully and powerfully rendered. Jennifer Jason Leigh gives yet another outstanding performance as an emotionally scarred survivor of a dysfunctional childhood. The script, however, focuses entirely too much on Selena and McAuliffe, diminishing the intense, powerful title character that readers came to know so intimately in King's book. The fact that Dolores, an outspoken, proud woman if there ever was one, does not speak in her own defense at her hearing is a perfect example of the movie's conceptual flaws.

# 25

## *Storm of the Century*

---

**W**IDELY PROMOTED as Stephen King's first "novel for television," *Storm of the Century* (1999) was broadcast by ABC television during the February 1999 sweeps period, and its massive teleplay was simultaneously published in trade paperback by Pocket Books. In a lengthy introduction to the trade edition, King relates the genesis of the story and provides fascinating background notes to the production. Tim Daly, star of the TV series *Wings*, has the lead role of Mike Anderson, while Debra Farentino plays his wife, Molly. Casey Siemaszko plays Mike's able deputy, Alton "Hatch" Hatcher, and Jeffrey DeMunn (who also appears in the feature film version of *The Green Mile*, released later that same year) adds a lot of color as Robbie Beals. In the pivotal role of Linoge is Colm Feore.

As he had done so often in recent productions, King handpicked the director for the $35 million, six-hour miniseries that aired over three nights. He was Craig R. Baxley, a relatively unknown filmmaker of such exploitation movies as *The Twilight Man* (1996) and *I Come in Peace* (1990), starring Dolph Lundgren. As with *Golden Years* (1991), *Sleepwalkers* (1992), and others, this miniseries must be considered as much a part of the Stephen King universe as any work of prose. Indeed, it is a vital part and a worthy addition to the canon of King's work.

*Storm of the Century* is a disturbing tale of community, almost perverse in the pleasure it takes in depicting a group of people who come together to make an impossible decision. It also plays on a subject that became very familiar and dear to King in the 1990s: secrecy.

In his introduction to the published teleplay, King discusses the milieu of the narrative by drawing comparisons and contrasts between the self-sufficiency and isolation of small-town people in general, and island people in particular. There are similarities, of course. King grew up in a small town in Maine, so when he created 'Salem's Lot, Castle Rock, and Derry, he knew what he was writing about.

But when he devised Little Tall Island, the setting for this story and for *Dolores Claiborne* (1993), he admits he was writing as "an outsider." You'd never know it. What King has observed here is that, as insular and familial as small towns can be, they are positively cosmopolitan in comparison to island communities. The people of Little Tall Island are, as a group, descended from half a dozen families who first settled there. In one sense or another, they are nearly all family to one another.

Like a family, they keep one another's secrets, no matter how great, and extend this silence with the mainland world as well. Just as many families do not discuss the

> *In* Storm of the Century, *Robbie Beals makes specific reference to* Dolores Claiborne *and the secrets the islanders have kept about her for years. This is another link solidifying the Stephen King universe.*

dark truths they have kept hidden, the entire community of Little Tall Island keeps its own counsel. They may know that one of their number, Peter Godsoe, imports marijuana, but they will never speak of it. They may be aware of who has slept with whom and which local deaths might not have been accidental, but they won't share that knowledge. Even in the company of others who also know the truth, such grave matters are not discussed—like the secret of Dolores Claiborne, some years previous to the events of *Storm of the Century,* and what really happened to those who "disappeared" in the storm.

An interesting parallel can be drawn between this chronicle and another King creation, *Needful Things* (1991), which was billed as "the last Castle Rock story." Comparing the two illustrates what King is expressing about island communities. Like *Storm, Needful Things* relates the account of a community with horrible secrets, and an evil stranger who comes to town and uses his intimate knowledge of those guarded secrets to tear the town apart. At the center of the plotline is the town's top lawman. While the structure of the two narratives may seem quite similar at first, the differences set *Storm of the Century* apart as not merely its own entity, but as one with a far more insidious nature.

In *Needful Things*, as in *'Salem's Lot* (1975), and on a much larger scale, *The Stand* (1978), there is a crisis that shatters the society, pitting residents against one another. The island village self-destructs until someone with the necessary moral strength makes a stand against the evil that has poisoned the populace, and wins. Good triumphs over evil and, particularly, over chaos.

But in *Storm of the Century*, the island community is not splintered. It is too tightly woven to be torn asunder so simply. Instead, the neighborhood is drawn together to face the crisis and make a terrible decision: face probable death at the hands of a profoundly evil creature, or willingly hand over one of their children to that same demonic force. Any parent worthy of the job knows the only real decision.

When an entire town, whose lives are in jeopardy, must decide, how can they be expected to choose the safety of someone else's child over their own? Apparently we can't, for the people of Little Tall Island vote, in a relatively orderly and traditional fashion, to give the demonic sorcerer Andre Linoge one of their children. The chosen one? The son of our hero, Mike Anderson, the island's constable. Linoge takes little Ralphie Anderson away to corrupt and raise as his own and transform into a being just like Linoge himself, and the town breathes a sigh of relief that it is done. Except for Mike and Molly Anderson, whose lives are destroyed by what their community has decided.

But just like the rest of the people on Little Tall Island, they keep the secret.

## PRIMARY SUBJECTS

*MIKE ANDERSON.* The constable of Little Tall Island and the owner of Anderson's General Store, Mike has lived on the island all his life. When Andre Linoge comes to town and murders Martha Clarendon,

Mike and his deputy, Alton "Hatch" Hatcher, arrest him. Anderson is also one of the first to suspect that Linoge is not precisely human.

Once Linoge has suitably terrified the town, caused the murder of several of its inhabitants, and stolen the minds of its children, it quickly becomes apparent that the monstrous being regards Mike as his main opposition. Finally, when Linoge presents the locals with his ultimatum—give up one of their children willingly to become what he is in order to save all their lives—Mike is the sole opposing voice.

> *King has a cameo in* Storm of the Century, *appearing on Martha Clarendon's television set while Andre Linoge awaits arrest.*

The fact that Molly Anderson, Mike's wife, is willing to make a deal with Linoge at the possible expense of their son, Ralphie, destroys the marriage in an instant. In due course, the worst happens, and Ralphie is chosen. Linoge takes the boy away, and when Mike tries to stop him, the townspeople prevent him from doing so in order to save themselves.

Mike leaves Molly and Little Tall Island forever. He takes to the road for a while and ends up in San Francisco, where he goes back to school and eventually becomes a federal marshal. On the streets of San Francisco, he sees Linoge and Ralphie. Years have passed. His son is now a teenager and doesn't recognize his father. When Mike approaches, Ralphie hisses, revealing fangs just like Linoge's. He has become something horrendous, something evil. Linoge has won. However, Mike Anderson isn't a quitter. Now that he has seen Ralphie again, he knows his son is out there and that Linoge still lives. There is always the possibility that Mike will try to track them down.

*ANDRE LINOGE.* "I've lived a long time—thousands of years—but I'm not a god, nor am I one of the immortals." Those are the words of Andre Linoge when he finally identifies himself and his desires to the people of Little Tall Island.

What he is, however, is not much clearer than that. It seems likely that he is related to creatures such as Randall Flagg of *The Stand* (1978), the *Dark Tower* series (1982–present), and *The Eyes of the Dragon* (1987). Linoge has a great many extraordinary abilities: to see the truth in the darkest corners of people's thoughts, to control minds, to whisk people away to another dimension, to move objects with his mind, to change his appearance and mingle with the shadows. That is only a sampling of Linoge's talents.

Powerful as he is, Linoge will die eventually. Ever since his mortality became apparent to him, he has attempted to find a human child he can teach and make his own, a youngster he can mold to become what he is. At least once before, on Roanoke Island, North Carolina, in 1587, Linoge attempted to force a community of humans to provide him the heir he requires. It didn't work then, and in retaliation he destroyed the entire population.

It should be noted that the word "Croatoan," which may be the name of an ancient city or something completely different, is associated with Linoge's visits to any given place.

*RALPH (RALPHIE) ANDERSON.* The son of Mike and Molly Anderson, Ralphie seems, from the very beginning, to attract the attention of Linoge. When Ralphie is chosen to be handed over to the stranger, it does not seem an accident or whim. Years later, when he encounters his father again, Ralphie does not seem to recognize Mike. By then, Ralph has already begun his transformation into a being like Andre Linoge.

*MOLLY ANDERSON.* The town's day care provider, Molly is the wife of Mike Anderson and the mother of Ralph. When the question is put to her, rather than standing with her husband in defiance of Linoge, Molly agrees with the townspeople to risk a single child's life to save them all. After Ralph is taken away by Linoge and Mike leaves her, Molly goes into therapy and eventually marries Hatch. It is believed Molly still lives on Little Tall.

*ROBBIE BEALS.* The town manager, Robbie clashes with Mike Anderson over the initial treatment of the situation with Linoge. Despised by his wife, Sandra, and father to bratty Don Beals, Robbie is not a likable man. He is tormented by Linoge's knowledge that when Robbie's mother was ailing, he put her in a disgusting rest home, and he was with a prostitute on the mainland when she died.

According to Linoge, Robbie's mother has become a cannibal now that she's in hell, and she plans to eat him when he arrives down there. This will happen over and over again, because that's what hell is about: repetition.

Sandra Beals drowns herself seven years after the storm, though she leaves the word "Croatoan" written on the boat she has taken out into the water. Apparently, she was still haunted by Linoge or at least his memory.

It is presumed that Robbie and his son Don still live on Little Tall.

*MARTHA CLARENDON.* An innocent old woman, Martha is Linoge's first victim on Little Tall. He clubs her to death with his silver wolfshead cane. Her body is found by Davey Hopewell.

*CAT WITHERS.* An employee at Anderson's General Store, Cat is impregnated by Billy Soames and doesn't tell a soul, even Billy (because she knows he is cheating on her). Instead, she has an abortion on the mainland. Cat is eventually mesmerized by Linoge and his wolfshead cane and is driven to beat Billy to death with the cane.

It is presumed that Cat still lives on Little Tall.

> *Though no mention of it is made in dialogue, the published teleplay of* Storm of the Century *notes in passing that at one point Cat Withers reads to a group of children from* The Little Puppy, *a book that the author notes was "a great favorite of Danny Torrance's, once upon a time." Danny Torrance, of course, is the little boy in* The Shining *(1977).*

*ALTON (HATCH) HATCHER.* Mike Anderson's deputy, Hatch and his wife, Melinda, have a daughter, Pippa, who is in Molly Anderson's day care. (Melinda works at Anderson's.) A year after the storm, Melinda dies of a heart attack, and eventually Hatch marries Molly Anderson. It is presumed that Hatch, Molly, and Pippa still live on Little Tall.

*LITTLE TALL ISLAND.* Located just across from Machias on the coast of Maine, Little Tall Island is nevertheless a world away. The people there are descended from its original settlers, and the community knows how to keep its secrets.

*THE WOLFSHEAD CANE.* Linoge's cane seems to be either the source of his power or a significant outlet for it. The stick appears and disappears at will and mesmerizes humans, and the wolfshead both moves and hisses.

*ROANOKE (1587).* In 1587 the entire population of Roanoke Island, North Carolina, disappeared. Their fate is a mystery, but according to Andre Linoge, he forced them all to take their own lives after they refused to provide him with an appropriate heir.

*MACHIAS.* A mainland town just across the water from Little Tall Island.

# 26

## *The Girl Who Loved Tom Gordon*

---

"THE WORLD HAD TEETH and it could bite you with them anytime it wanted. Trisha McFarland discovered this when she was nine years old." So begins *The Girl Who Loved Tom Gordon*, a novel that, despite its relatively average size, manages to touch on many of King's favorite themes: spirituality, baseball, children in jeopardy, and the uneasy feeling that something bad is always lurking just over the horizon.

The book came as a total surprise to everyone—his fans, his publisher, and even the author himself. (In a note to reviewers accompanying promotional copies of this novel, King wrote, "If books were babies, I'd call *The Girl Who Loved Tom Gordon* the result of an unplanned pregnancy.") King's idea, conceived during a baseball game at Boston's Fenway Park, was to write a variation on "Hansel and Gretel," only without Hansel. The end result was a modern fairy tale divided into nine "innings" rather than chapters, a thoughtful reflection on the nature of God with echoes of Jack London's classic story "To Light a Fire" thrown in for good measure.

King has been writing about God—the possibility of God, and the ramifications of his existence—for over two decades now, in books as diverse as *The Stand* (1978) and *Desperation* (1996). Lost in the woods, young Trisha McFarland, the central character in *The Girl Who Loved Tom Gordon*, finds herself contemplating this subject as well; praying, she reflects on a conversation she had with her father a month before. During that talk, she asked him if he believed in God. Her bemused dad said he didn't have faith in a God that marks the death "of every bird in Australia or every bug in India." But he does believe there has to be *something;* he refers to this "insensate force for the good" as the "Subaudible," reflecting his belief in a benevolent deity who doesn't necessarily involve himself in humanity's day-to-day activities.

*At 224 pages in the hardcover edition,* The Girl Who Loved Tom Gordon *is, after* Carrie, King's *shortest novel published to date.*

The author walks a fine line between these two concepts, never quite committing to either one. This being a Stephen King novel, however, there is a countervailing force, a malevolent entity that Trisha comes to think of as "the God of the Lost." This god feeds on her fear, waiting for the proper moment to strike.

Utterly realistic, this *bildungsroman,* or coming-of-age fiction, nevertheless contains numerous references to the Stephen King universe. For example, listening to her Walkman, Trisha picks up radio station WCAS in Castle Rock, a town she remembers passing through once on her way to the Appalachian Trail. The town has apparently recovered from the massive wounds Leland Gaunt inflicted on it.

*Actress Anne Heche narrates an unabridged audio version of* The Girl Who Loved Tom Gordon.

In delivering the local news, the announcer mentions that folks in the Rock are up in arms over a bar that is featuring topless dancers, and that Castle Rock Speedway is supposed to reopen on the Fourth of July.

## PRIMARY SUBJECTS

**TRISHA McFARLAND.** Nine years old but "big for her age," Trisha finds herself in an uncomfortable position after her parents' divorce. Although favoring her father, Trisha is placed in her mother's custody along with her older brother, Pete. Life with her mother is OK, but Trisha feels that her whiny brother gets all the attention. Coerced into participating in a six-mile hike (part of her mother's forced program of family togetherness), Trisha wanders off the trail to relieve herself and to escape her mother and brother's constant bickering. Mistakenly believing that she is only a few yards from the trail, Trisha loses her bearings. But because she keeps moving, she quickly places herself beyond the reach of even the most diligent search party.

Trisha spends nine days wandering in the forest, searching for a way out. She proves quite resourceful, able to survive thanks to bits and pieces of forest lore she has managed to store up over her young life. Desperate for food and nearly dehydrated, Trisha begins to hallucinate, imagining that she is being accompanied by her hero, Boston Red Sox relief pitcher Tom Gordon. At first merely a silent, reassuring presence, Gordon eventually begins to talk with her, revealing his philosophy on being a good closer in the game. Trisha takes this advice to heart; it proves invaluable when she is forced to confront the God of the Lost, a malevolent presence that has been stalking her since she entered the forest.

Trisha survives her ordeal. When last seen, she is recuperating from pneumonia in a hospital bed.

*TOM GORDON*. Lost in the woods, Trisha imagines that her favorite Boston Red Sox player, relief pitcher Tom Gordon, is with her. Tom's presence keeps her sane; his advice helps her stay alive. Tom tells Trisha that, like a relief pitcher, it's God's nature to come on in the bottom of the ninth. He also advises her that the secret of being a good closer is establishing who is better—you can let your opponent beat you, but you must not beat yourself. These are the thoughts that cascade through Trisha's mind when the God of the Lost confronts her near the end of her journey. The God, having taken the form of a bear, looms over the girl, ready to maul her. Trisha faces the deadly animal, hitting it between the eyes with her Walkman, delivering a pitch her hero would surely appreciate.

(It should be noted for non-sports fans that professional baseball player Tom Gordon, #36, is a real person. In 1998, he saved forty-four games for King's beloved Red Sox. Gordon is famous for what one character in *The Girl Who Loved Tom Gordon* refers to as "that pointin' thing"—after each successful save, he points briefly to the sky, acknowledging God's presence. )

*LARRY McFARLAND.* Trisha's dad is a folksy man given to saying things like "I believe it's beer o'clock." Larry and his daughter are quite close, bonding during the many happy hours they spend together watching and discussing the Boston Red Sox. Larry introduces Trisha to the idea of the "Subaudible." Although Larry takes comfort in his wife's bed during their ordeal, it seems apparent that they will not reconcile.

*QUILLA ANDERSON.* Trisha's mother, Quilla does the best she can as a single parent of two children. Forced to minister to her whiny son, Pete, Quilla virtually ignores her daughter, Trisha. This benign neglect contributes to Trisha's exasperation with her mother and brother, which leads her to abandon the trail and become lost in the Maine woods.

*THE SUBAUDIBLE.* Larry McFarland's name for the force "that keeps drunken teenagers—most drunken teenagers—from crashing their cars when they're coming home from the senior prom or their first big rock concert. That keeps most planes from crashing even when something goes wrong." Larry believes that the very fact that no country has used a nuclear weapon on living people since 1945 suggests *something* must be looking out for the human race. He calls that something the Subaudible.

*THE THREE ROBED FIGURES.* Trisha hallucinates about this trio, who represent the various gods Trisha has been thinking about during her trek. Two of them are in white garb, one wears black. The first, who resembles Mr. Bork, Trisha's science teacher at Sanford Elementary School, is clothed in white. He tells Trisha he represents the god of Tom Gordon, the "one he points up to when he gets the save." He also informs her that Tom's god can't help, being busy with other things. "As a rule he doesn't intervene in human affairs, anyway, although I must admit he is a sports fan. Not necessarily a Red Sox fan, however."

The second figure is also outfitted in white. He resembles Trisha's father, Larry McFarland. When Trisha asks him if he comes from the Subaudible, he tells her he *is* the Subaudible. Stating he is "quite weak," the figure tells her he, too, cannot help her. The third figure, draped in black, lifts its claws to its hood, pushing it back to reveal a misshapen head made of wasps. "I come from the thing in the woods," he tells her. "I come from the God of the Lost. It has been watching you. It has been waiting for you. It is your miracle, and you are its."

*THE GOD OF THE WOODS.* Also known as the God of the Lost. Shortly into her odyssey, Trisha realizes she is not entirely alone— something subhuman, purely evil, is stalking her, waiting for an opportunity to strike. Trisha knows instinctively that it can take her anytime it wants, but is merely waiting for her to "ripen." The God of the Woods confronts Trisha at the end of the novel, taking the form of a bear.

*TRAVIS HERRICK.* A poacher, Travis is hunting for an out-of-season deer when he comes upon a little girl facing off against a bear. The youngster is Trisha, the bear is the God of the Lost. Herrick shoots the bear's ear off seconds before Trisha throws her Walkman and hits him in the head. Shaken, the bear lumbers off into the woods. Instead of receiving a fine, Travis becomes a hero, having a float dedicated to him in Grafton Notch's 1998 Fourth of July parade.

# 27

# Related Tales

---

**M**ANY OF THE FOLLOWING have strong direct connections to section four of the Primary Reality. While *Night Shift*'s initial offering, "Jerusalem's Lot," is a prequel to the novel *'Salem's Lot* (1975), "One for the Road" is the novel's coda. Other stories pick up specific characters and places encountered in the novels.

## "JERUSALEM'S LOT"
### from *Night Shift* (1974)

A Lovecraftian-style tale that introduces a dark prehistory for the novel *'Salem's Lot*. The story is valuable for its fleshing out of the southern Maine setting, a location vital to the Stephen King universe. It concerns the resurgence of an old horror thought to have been vanquished, and the connection that malignant presence seems to have to one family in particular.

### PRIMARY SUBJECTS

*CHARLES BOONE*. In 1850, Charles had inherited his family home—called Chapelwaite—which was located in or around Jerusalem's Lot. He moved there with his companion, Calvin McCann, and later discovered a horrible evil dwelling beneath the town. Apparently it had initially been called there by a cult led by his ancestor, James Boon.

*JAMES BOON.* An ancestor of Charles Boone, James is said to have founded Jerusalem's Lot in 1765. This is in contradiction to another local belief among the townspeople, which sets forth that the town was founded by a farmer named Charles Belknap Tanner. James Boon was apparently a religious leader who worshiped old, dark powers, until those forces claimed him.

*JAMES ROBERT BOONE.* The last survivor of the Boone family line. In 1971, he moves into Chapelwaite, and the horrors Charles Boone confronted twelve decades earlier begin to resurface. The fate of James Robert Boone is unknown.

*CALVIN McCANN.* Charles Boone's friend and companion, who is killed by the worm.

*THE WORM.* An ancient, demonic creature, the Worm was apparently worshiped by James Boon and his followers in the eighteenth century. Later, when its existence is threatened by Charles Boone and Calvin McCann, it rises again to attack them, killing McCann in the process.

*DEMON DWELLINGS (by DeGoudge).* A book of horrid, arcane knowledge used by James Boon in the religious guidance offered to the cult that sprang up around him in Jerusalem's Lot.

*MYSTERIES OF THE WORM.* Another book of terrible magic and ritual, used in connection with worship of the demonic worm. Only five copies were known to exist as of 1850, and one of those was burned by Charles Boone.

## "GRAVEYARD SHIFT"
### from *Night Shift* (1974)

A particularly gruesome narrative, "Graveyard Shift" concerns a drifter named Hall who has come to work at a mill in Gates Falls, Maine. Over the Fourth of July holiday, he agrees to help with a cleanup that is many years overdue. During the job, he and the cleanup crew encounter giant, mutated rat-creatures in a sub-sub-basement.

## PRIMARY SUBJECTS

*HALL.* A worker at the mill, Hall despises Warwick, the foreman. This hatred causes him to insist—almost in the form of a challenge—that the two men descend into the sub-sub-basement and clean the rats out. Hall is devoured by the monster rodents.

*WARWICK.* The mill's tyrannical foreman, Warwick is consumed by the huge, blind queen of the rats.

*HARRY WISCONSKY.* One of Hall's co-workers, Harry has the misfortune to join Hall and Warwick on their descent into the hellish basement, but turns and runs, saving his own life. Harry Wisconsky's current whereabouts are unknown.

## "ONE FOR THE ROAD"

from *Night Shift* (1974)

The story establishes a legend that will surround the town for generations. During a blizzard in Maine, a pair of old-timers try to save a family from the vampires that still haunt *'Salem's Lot.*

## PRIMARY SUBJECTS

*BOOTH.* During the blizzard, Booth is at Tookey's, his favorite watering hole, when a tourist from New York stumbles in, covered with frostbite. Booth learns that the man had gotten his car stuck while trying to take the unplowed road through 'Salem's Lot—and left his wife and daughter in the car while he went for help. Booth is more fearful of marauding vampires than of the idea that the tourist's wife and daughter might freeze to death. He and Tookey and the tourist head out to try to rescue them, only to find that they have already been turned into vampires. He is almost the victim of the little girl, but Tookey saves him. Booth's current whereabouts are unknown.

*HERB TOOKLANDER.* The owner of Tookey's, Herb closes for the night to set out to save the tourist family. During the course of events, he has a heart attack but manages to save Booth by throwing a Bible at the little girl vampire. Herb dies two years later, peacefully, during the night.

*GERARD LUMLEY.* A tourist from New York who foolishly tries to drive on an unplowed stretch of highway in the middle of a blizzard. The car becomes snowbound and, while he goes for help, his family is turned into vampires. Later, when he returns with help, Lumley is either killed or turned into a vampire.

*FRANCIE LUMLEY.* Lumley's wife who becomes a vampire.

*JANEY LUMLEY.* Lumley's daughter, who is also turned into a vampire, and would have fed off Booth if Tookey didn't stop her.

## "RITA HAYWORTH AND SHAWSHANK REDEMPTION"

from *Different Seasons* (1982)

Though the novella is narrated in the first person by a convict named Red, this wonderful tale is the story of Andy Dufresne. Falsely accused and later convicted of the murder of his wife and her lover, Andy is a banker and lawyer who puts his education to work for him behind bars at Maine's Shawshank prison. But that education would be nothing without the single-mindedness with which he goes about arranging his escape—over the course of many, many years—digging a hole in the wall of his cell and hiding it behind a succession of posters that begins with one featuring Rita Hayworth. Andy succeeds in breaking out of the prison. Later, when his fellow inmate Red is paroled, he sets off to join his friend.

King's representation of life inside a prison is extremely convincing. It does not feel like the typical genre story. There is a kind of monotony here against which the colorful story of Andy Dufresne is all the more fascinating. To anyone who doubted that King had the ability to write mainstream fiction, this first novella in *Different Seasons* erased all such concerns. Of course, King would return to a prison setting much later with the incredibly successful serialized novel, *The Green Mile* (1996).

One is tempted, upon examining this novella, to study King's other nonhorror, nonfantasy work for parallels. "Rita Hayworth . . ." is, after all, a story about triumph over adversity. A man is wrongly imprisoned and even those who know the truth conspire to keep him down. Yet he works tirelessly over an almost inhuman span of time, on a scale that would drive most people insane, until he finally achieves his freedom.

With that as the story's outline, however, it isn't King's mainstream work that most echoes this tale. Rather, it is *The Eyes of the Dragon*. Strangely enough, that fantasy novel, written for his daughter, rife with castles and wizards and dragons and kings, has a fundamental structure quite similar to "Rita Hayworth . . ." There, also, a person wrongly accused of murder takes years and years to achieve his escape, right in front of his captors.

## PRIMARY SUBJECTS

*ANDY DUFRESNE.* Wrongly imprisoned for the murder of his wife and her boyfriend, banker Andy Dufresne spends a large part of his life in prison, planning his escape. Though he finds a way to prove his innocence, his efforts are met with resistance. Not only does Andy manage to manipulate the prison system so that he can have his own cell, but under the noses of his captors, he tunnels out of his confinement and finds

> *It is quite possible that Peter Stephens, the assumed name Andy Dufresne uses in "Rita Hayworth and Shawshank Redemption," is a combination of the names of the author and his good friend, novelist Peter Straub.*

freedom. He now lives in Zihuatanejo, Mexico, under the assumed name Peter Stephens.

*LINDA DUFRESNE.* Andy's late wife. She is murdered by a man named Elwood Blatch, and Andy is imprisoned falsely for the crime.

*GLENN QUENTIN.* A golf pro who was Linda Dufresne's lover, Quentin is murdered by Elwood Blatch. Andy is wrongly convicted of the homicide.

*RED.* An inmate at Shawshank, Red is serving a life sentence for the murder of his wife, a neighbor woman, and the neighbor's infant. He had only meant to do away with his spouse and he has never denied that, though he grieves for the other deaths he caused. In prison, Red is the one who can get things for other inmates, making him a prime black marketeer. Red becomes friendly with Andy Dufresne in prison, and supplies him with the things he needs to escape—though Red doesn't realize Andy's purpose until after Andy breaks out.

Red is paroled from Shawshank in 1976. The next year he breaks his parole and follows Andy to Zihuatanejo, Mexico. It is presumed that both are alive and well and still living there today.

*ELWOOD BLATCH.* He kills Andy Dufresne's wife and her boyfriend. Though he eventually goes to prison on other charges, Blatch is never charged with the murders for which Andy did time.

## ADAPTATION

*The Shawshank Redemption*, minus "Rita Hayworth and," was adapted and directed by Frank Darabont (who would also adapt and direct 1999's *The Green Mile*). Made by Castle Rock Entertainment (no small irony there, as the company was formed by Rob Reiner—who also directed *Stand by Me*—and named it after King's fictional town). The prison drama starred Morgan Freeman as Red and Tim Robbins as Andy Dufresne. Released in 1994 by Columbia Pictures, it received seven Oscar nominations, including best picture, best actor (Freeman), and best screenplay adaptation.

> *Darabont, writer-director of the films* The Shawshank Redemption *and* The Green Mile, *had done an earlier King adaptation as well—a student film of King's short story "The Woman in the Room," for which King granted permission.*

While *Shawshank* is a slow-moving feature, reflecting the passage of time in prison, it is also a triumphant one. Though not a box-office success, it has nevertheless gained in reputation over time, and some consider it among the best American movies ever made. Its popularity on video and DVD, as noted in magazines such as *Entertainment Weekly* and online at such Web sites as Reel.com, is testament to its popularity.

## "MRS. TODD'S SHORTCUT"
### from *Skeleton Crew* (1985)

A trip through King's version of Maine, this tale tells of a cosmic road trip that begins in Castle Rock, winds its way through towns like Haven and Derry, and ends in King's own hometown of Bangor. In his note on this story, King reveals that his wife, always seeking the shortest distance between two points on her local treks, is the inspiration for Mrs. Todd.

### PRIMARY SUBJECTS

*OPHELIA TODD.* The first wife of Worth Todd, Ophelia was obsessed with finding the quickest route to her destination. Ophelia disappeared in 1973.

*HOMER BUCKLAND.* Employed as a caretaker by the Todd family, Homer tells the story of Mrs. Todd's shortcut to Dave Owens. Driving to Bangor with Ophelia Todd in her Mercedes, he travels through a hole in reality and visits a surreal landscape.

## "THE REACH"
### from *Skeleton Crew* (1985)

One of King's most poignant tales, it was originally published as "Do the Dead Sing?" in *Yankee* magazine in 1981. Stella Flanders is the oldest resident of Goat Island. Well into her nineties, she has never been off the island. When she begins seeing specters from her past, however, she knows it is time for her to leave. One cold January night, Stella rises from her sickbed and sets out to cross the Reach (the name the locals have given to the water between the island and the mainland), which is frozen for the first time in over forty years. Stella's spirit is reunited with her husband and friends; her frozen corpse is found later on the mainland, seated in a natural chair of rock.

## "SECRET WINDOW, SECRET GARDEN"

### from *Four Past Midnight* (1990)

"Secret Window, Secret Garden" is another of King's metafictions, a disturbing morality play that stands proudly next to other works of this nature, such as *Misery* (1987) and *The Dark Half* (1989). Written between drafts of *The Dark Half*, the narrative is King's effort to convey the powerful hold fiction can have over a writer. King calls this his "last story about writers and writing and the strange no-man's land which exists between what's real and what's make believe." If that is indeed the case, he goes out with a bang, delivering a roundhouse punch of a story about how the sins of the past can catch up with you when you least expect it.

### PRIMARY SUBJECT

*MORT RAINEY.* In *Bag of Bones* (1998), author Mike Noonan says, "A writer is a man who has taught his mind to misbehave." Mort Rainey, author of *The Delacourte Family, The Organ Grinder's Boy,* and the short-story collection *Everybody Drops the Dime* can attest to that—his mind misbehaves in a manner that ultimately proves fatal. One day, a stranger appears at his door, clutching a manuscript titled "Secret Window, Secret Garden." The man, who introduces himself as John Shooter, tells Rainey, "You stole my story. You stole my story and something's got to be done about it."

At first skeptical of Shooter's claim, Rainey later realizes the story is a dead ringer for one he published many years earlier called "Sowing Season." The stories, each about a man who murders his wife and buries her in a garden, are eerily similar in terms of grammar and syntax.

Shooter doesn't go away, even when Rainey claims Shooter's story was written after his own. Shooter wants tangible evidence, in the form of the magazine where the story was first published. Rainey promises to show him his file copy, which is stored at his ex-wife's house in Derry. Before he can retrieve it, however, his house burns down under mysterious circumstances. An increasingly frantic Rainey requests a copy from the publisher, but the issue arrives sans his story—someone has removed it with a razor.

Rainey tells his story to various people on the lake, but anyone who can confirm his encounters with Shooter is later found dead. Under extreme pressure, Rainey's mental state deteriorates; he has a flashback to an incident in his past, a time when he, in a moment of desperation, claimed another writer's story as his own, one he renamed "Sowing Season." It turns out that Rainey has carried the guilt of this crime with him ever since. Wanting to punish himself, he convinces himself of Shooter's existence when it was actually *Rainey* who burned his own house down, mutilated the magazine, and murdered the people who threatened to expose his charade.

Driven insane by this realization, Rainey surrenders control to his John Shooter personality, allowing it to take over for good. He attacks his ex-wife, Carolyn. Before he can seriously harm her, he is shot and killed.

## "SUFFER THE LITTLE CHILDREN"

from *Nightmares & Dreamscapes* (1993)

King calls this a "ghastly sick-joke with no redeeming social merit whatever." He adds, "I like that in a story." Reminiscent of the early, more sinister work of Ray Bradbury, in the theme of all children being natural born monsters or some form of aliens, "Suffer the Children" is an effective chiller.

### PRIMARY SUBJECT

*MISS SIDLEY.* Veteran grade-school teacher Miss Sidley sees something out of the corner of her eye one morning that shakes her—the face of one of her students seems to change for a moment into something monstrous. That student, Robert, adds to her disquiet, telling her that "there's quite a few of us." Miss Sidley becomes more and more paranoid, increasingly certain her class is full of monsters hiding behind human masks. Taking matters into her own hands, Miss Sidley invites Robert to accompany her to the mimeograph room, where she kills him. She eliminates eleven more students before she is stopped. There is no trial. Miss Sidley is committed to the asylum known as Juniper Hill, located in Augusta, Maine, where she eventually kills herself.

*Stephen King—"Teen Anger"* | SUSANNE MOSS

## "THE NIGHT FLIER"

from *Nightmares & Dreamscapes* (1993)

This modern vampire tale originally appeared in the popular 1988 anthology *Prime Evil: New Stories by the Masters of Modern Horror,* edited by noted King scholar and biographer Douglas E. Winter. Among its other qualities, the story is notable for bringing back to the limelight reporter Richard Dees, who was first seen in *The Dead Zone* (1979).

### PRIMARY SUBJECTS

*THE NIGHT FLIER.* A vampire pilot who travels from airport to airport in his Cessna Skymaster in search of prey, the Night Flier sleeps in the plane's cargo hold, and is more amused than annoyed with his pursuer, Richard Dees. Instead of ripping Dees's throat out, he lets him go with a warning to keep his distance. The Night Flier has a wry sense of humor, using the name of Dwight Renfield to identify himself to various airport officials. (Horror aficionados know this is a play on the name Dwight Frye; a character actor, Frye appeared in a handful of classic horror movies, among them Tod Browning's 1931 production of *Dracula,* where he played the part of Renfield.)

*RICHARD DEES.* A reporter and photographer who once hounded Johnny Smith for his unusual life story as detailed in *The Dead Zone.* Pursuing the facts of the Night Flier killings for the tabloid newspaper, *Inside View,* Dees picks up on the mysterious Dwight Renfield's trail, eventually meeting the vampire face-to-face in an airport men's room. The completely terrified Dees escapes with his life, but is not allowed to keep the photos he took of the Night Flier in action.

## "POPSY"

from *Nightmares & Dreamscapes* (1993)

Another contemporary vampire tale, written in much the same vein as "The Night Flier."

## PRIMARY SUBJECTS

*SHERIDAN.* A gambler who has fallen on hard times, Sheridan kidnaps small children and sells them to an unsavory character named "the Turk." One day, he makes the mistake of snatching a small child whose grandfather turns out to be a vampire. The grandparent eventually catches up with Sheridan, beats him, and then feeds him to his grandson.

*POPSY.* The boy's grandfather, Popsy happens to be a vampire. In his commentary on the story, King asks, "Is this little boy's grandfather the same creature that demands Richard Dees open his camera and expose his film at the end of "The Night Flier"? You know, I rather think he is."

# "THE RAINY SEASON"
### from *Nightmares & Dreamscapes* (1993)

The second "peculiar town" story in this collection, this one recalls Shirley Jackson's 1948 classic tale of ritual sacrifice, "The Lottery," a story that is a personal favorite of King's. It's never explained why deadly frogs rain from the sky every seven years on the rural Maine hamlet of Willow; what matters is that somebody—anybody—has to be sacrificed to make it stop.

## PRIMARY SUBJECTS

*ELISE and JOHN GRAHAM.* A vacationing couple visiting the small Maine town of Willow on the eve of what the locals call the rainy season, Elise and John ignore the warnings to beware of an imminent rain of toads falling from the sky. They are both eaten alive when they encounter the hideous fallout, which hits Willow every seven years on June 17. The only way the bizarre rain of razor-toothed toads can be stopped is to sacrifice two outsiders to appease whatever dark gods have cursed this otherwise idyllic town. The snobbish Grahams serve that purpose well.

## "RIDING THE BULLET"

### (2000)

This short story, available only on-line as of this writing, created quite a stir when King published it early in the year 2000. Web sites offering the tale were inundated with requests; it is estimated that more than 400,000 customers downloaded it.

This story of college student Alan Parker's unfortunate encounter with the supernatural echoes such tales as "Mrs. Todd's Shortcut" and "The Road Virus Heads North" in that it is essentially a travelogue through King's Maine. Informed that his mother has just suffered a stroke, the carless Parker decides to hitchhike from the University of Maine at Orono to his hometown in Lewiston, some 120 miles south. Along the way, he is picked up by one George Staub, who Parker knows died in a car accident almost three decades prior. Staub, whose body is apparently held together by stitches, tells the frightened Parker that he must choose between his life and his mother's. Panicked, Parker chooses his own and is released. Mrs. Parker lives for a few years longer before succumbing, but Alan remains tortured by his cowardice.

Describing his ordeal early in the story, Parker says something many denizens of the Stephen King universe might agree with: "The way I looked at the world changed that night, changed quite a lot. I came to understand that there are things underneath, you see— underneath—and no book can explain what they are. I think that sometimes it's best to just forget those things are there. If you can, that is."

# SECTION FIVE

## The Prime Reality, Part IV:
## Tales of the Shop

*Firestarter*

*The Tommyknockers*

*Stephen King's Golden Years*

"The Langoliers"

 FAMILIAR THEME BY NOW, particularly in the post–*X-Files* generation, is the idea that within the American government there exists a covert organization dedicated to the study of the paranormal. In the Stephen King universe, that organization is known only as the Shop.

As noted in the chapters that follow, the Shop investigates such phenomena, but it also *instigates*. As in *Firestarter*, it has been known to fund experiments in the paranormal. Further, like all ominous, covert groups (mostly fictional, we hope), it is willing to go to any lengths, including assassination, to achieve its goals and keep its secrets.

The tales surrounding or tangentially touching upon the Shop clearly exist within the prime reality of the Stephen King universe. One must only read *The Tommyknockers*, which includes Shop agents as supporting characters, to know that. For in that novel, there are connections to a great many other King works set in the prime reality.

> *In* The Tommyknockers *(1987), the shop dispatches agents to investigate the odd happenings in Haven, Maine.*

Though the Shop does not play an obvious role in the cosmic struggle between the Purpose and the Random, it is logical that the Shop may have served either side unwittingly over the years. Two observations can be made. First, though operating in the prime reality, the Shop seems to share certain facets with the "low men in yellow coats" from Roland's reality ("Hearts in Atlantis"). Second, if there are thinnies between the prime reality and any of the others, the Shop is almost certainly aware of them.

# 28

## *Firestarter*

---

ONSIDERING ITS protagonist—a young girl with terrifying
paranormal powers—*Firestarter* (1980) is an interesting counter-
point to *Carrie* (1974). Whereas the latter is a tale of great tragedy and
loss, *Firestarter* is an uplifting if relentless thriller. In part, it is the
account of two innocent college students, Andy McGee and Vicky
Tomlinson, who take part in a secret government experiment intended
to jump-start paranormal abilities in test subjects. In the case of Andy
and Vicky, the experiment succeeds—and more successfully than anyone could have ever imagined. Partially as a result of this shared experience, they fall in love, marry, and have a daughter. This girl, Charlie,
is the central character of *Firestarter*. In fact, the title takes its name
from her ability to start fires simply with her mind. And pyrokinesis
is only one of Charlie's amazing paranormal abilities.

The novel is a masterwork of paranoia that preceded TV's *The
X-Files* (1993–) by well over a decade. Yet, pyrokinesis is exactly the
type of case Scully and Mulder would get involved with, though
hopefully they would not be as merciless as the government agents
from the Shop. Andy and Vicky participate in an experiment run by
the Department of Scientific Intelligence, which portrays itself as a
benevolent research organization. In reality, however, it is the Shop,
which does whatever it takes—including parascientific research—to
create fantastic new weapons for America's arsenal. (The Shop would
receive mention in later works by King, but none of the principal

characters of *Firestarter* has made subsequent appearances in these works.)

*Carrie* is also the chronicle of a young woman born with paranormal abilities, but the two novels could not be more different. Whereas Carrie is subject to emotional and physical abuse by her mother, Charlie is purely a victim of circumstance and the greed of ruthless adults. Her dad loves her more than life itself and ultimately proves it. Carrie is finally destroyed by her "wild talent," but Charlie is tempered by it, like steel in the forge. She emerges more powerful—and wiser—in the wake of her tragedy. The evil that King presents is not Charlie's fantastic talent, but the fact that government agents would purposely use human beings in immoral experiments simply to develop secret weapons. The killers here are people in the U.S. government, whose salaries the public pays unknowingly.

*Firestarter* is among a handful of King's novels that, like *'Salem's Lot* (1975), absolutely demands a sequel. At the book's end, after Charlie walks into the offices of *Rolling Stone* magazine to tell a reporter all that has happened to her thus far in her amazing life, the story of Charlie McGee can hardly be considered over. *Firestarter* proves to be a book about hope and affirmation, not destruction and loss. Whereas *Carrie* concerns itself mostly with the despair and tragic life of its central female character, the

> Firestarter *was one of the first King novels to be issued as a signed, limited edition. It appeared in 1980 from Phantasia Press in an edition of 725 copies at $35 each. Even more "fireproof" was a tiny run of only 26 copies that were specially bound in asbestos cloth.*

heroine of *Firestarter* is just that—heroic, and a survivor against incredible odds. Charlie overcomes the gravest injustices and immoral actions a nation can heap on one of its own citizens, and manages to triumph over that adversity.

Lest we forget, however, those still working for the Shop remain deeply concerned that a girl with Charlie's power might one day, as she matures, gain the awesome power to split the world itself in two with merely a concentrated thought. And Charlie and others just like her are still out there in the Stephen King universe.

## PRIMARY SUBJECTS

*CHARLIE McGEE.* From birth, Charlene "Charlie" Roberta McGee has shown herself to be gifted—or cursed—with a number of remarkable psychic abilities. These have included limited telekinesis, a kind of instinctive clairvoyance, and most powerful of all, pyrokinesis.

As college students, Charlie's parents, Andy McGee and Vicky Tomlinson McGee, were experimented upon by the Shop. While most of the subjects in that test died or committed suicide, Andy and Vicky both gained certain psychic abilities and later married.

Not long after Charlie's birth, the infant begins to set fires with her mind. Her crib and other areas need to be fireproofed, and Andy and Vicky have to fire-train her, in a manner similar to the way in which other parents potty-train their children. Charlie's memory of the burning of her beloved teddy bear stays with her to this day. Her father tells her that starting fires is a very bad thing. So Charlie, even as a very small girl, determines never to do it again.

Then her mother is murdered by the Shop, and its agents set out on a horrible quest to bring in Andy and Charlie for scrutiny. Eventually they succeed. Under the direction of Cap Hollister, and with the influence of the assassin known as John Rainbird, Charlie is convinced not only to light fires again, but to practice doing so, to learn to better control her power.

When her father reveals to her the depth of the Shop's deceptions and their intention to kill them both when she outlives her usefulness, Charlie uses her power to burn the Shop compound to the ground.

Charlie McGee's current whereabouts are unknown.

*ANDY McGEE.* In 1969, desperate for money, Andy participates in an experiment held on his college campus. The testing, conducted by Dr. Joseph Wanless for the Shop, involves a drug known as Lot Six. Lot Six is supposed to draw out of the dormant parts of the human brain certain paranormal abilities that would otherwise never manifest themselves. In Andy, it is something he calls "the push." By concentrating, Andy can suggest very strongly to someone to do a particular thing, and that person will comply instantly. He can also convince people that they are seeing something they are not.

Eventually, Andy marries Vicky Tomlinson, who was also part of the Lot Six experiment, and together they have a child, Charlie.

Over time, Andy's "push" ability diminishes. He begins to suspect that using the power causes him minor brain damage each time, and that the ill effects are growing worse. He tries not to use his power anymore, but is forced to employ it quite frequently. Meanwhile, Vicky is murdered by the Shop, and Andy and Charlie go on the run.

After their eventual capture, Andy spends months in a drug-induced haze. However, after that time, he is able to recover the "push" ability and uses it to arrange for his and Charlie's escape. During their flight, Andy goes up against the assassin John Rainbird and is killed.

*VICKY TOMLINSON McGEE.* As a young woman, Vicky was sexually assaulted. It is only through the special telepathic bond that she and Andy McGee share during the Lot Six experiment that she is able to overcome the fears of intimacy that had been with her since that assault.

She and Andy marry, and Vicky later gives birth to Charlie. For many years, Vicky has a low-grade telekinetic ability that seems to come and go. Her use of it is instinctive, and sometimes she doesn't even realize she is employing it. Apparently, the limited scope of her gift makes her expendable. When the Shop determines to take Charlie and Andy into custody, Vicky is tortured and murdered.

> *Pay close attention while watching the movie version of* Firestarter. *She isn't onscreen long, but in the role of the doomed Vicky McGee, is Heather Locklear, whose TV credits include* Spin City, Melrose Place, Dynasty, *and* T. J. Hooker.

*JOHN RAINBIRD.* A Native American assassin for the Shop, Rainbird is obsessed with death. He enjoys looking into the eyes of the people whose lives he claims, trying to determine what happens to their life force when they die, and searching for some sign of passage to another world.

Rainbird is assigned the execution of Dr. Joseph Wanless, the scientist behind the Lot Six experiment. He is also responsible for the capture of Andy and Charlie McGee. Later, Rainbird uses his knowledge of the Shop's operations and the personal life of its director, Captain Hollister, to force Cap into allowing him certain "freedoms" with young Charlie.

The assassin poses as an orderly at the Shop installation where Charlie is a prisoner and cleans her rooms every day for months. One night, during a blackout, he finally gains the girl's confidence by fabricating a story about his Vietnam War service, playing on the sympathy she feels for him because of the horrible scars on his face, and the loss of one of his eyes.

It is Rainbird who convinces Charlie to start setting fires again and cooperate with the Shop. Rainbird also gets everything the Shop wants from her. He does all of this in return for a guarantee from Cap Hollister that when it comes time for Charlie to be executed, the job will be his. She is, in Rainbird's estimation, an extraordinary and powerful young girl. As such, he wants to watch her eyes while he slowly kills her.

When he discovers that Andy McGee has regained his "pushing" power, Rainbird foils Andy's escape plan and kills him, only to be burned to death by Charlie.

*CAPTAIN JAMES HOLLISTER*. As director of the Department of Scientific Intelligence, Cap Hollister is in charge of all operations relating to the fallout from the late 1960s Lot Six experiments. These include the pursuit, capture, and experimentation on Charlie and Andy McGee. Hollister also orders John Rainbird to execute Dr. Wanless. In addition, he arranges for Rainbird to work with Charlie and is later psychically co-opted by Andy McGee into helping Andy and Charlie escape. In the ensuing chaos, he is burned to death by Charlie.

*DR. JOSEPH WANLESS*. The scientist who supervises the trial experiments with a chemical compound called Lot Six, Wanless later has a stroke and advocates executing participants in that experiment, including Charlie McGee, the offspring of two of those participants. When Cap Hollister decides that Wanless has become a nuisance and a potential danger to him politically, he orders John Rainbird to execute the doctor.

*THE SHOP.* Also known as the Department of Scientific Intelligence, the Shop is a Longmont, Virginia–based agency of the American government that participates in what are generally referred to as black ops. Loosely defined, these are operations not officially sanctioned by the U.S. Congress, and their budgets are blacked out or buried within those of other operations. The Shop's specialty is researching scientific avenues for potential use in warfare.

*LOT SIX.* A chemical compound created by the Shop, that forces latent paranormal powers to manifest in certain test subjects, and causes madness in others.

*DR. PATRICK HOCKSTETTER.* Hockstetter is the scientist in charge of testing Charlie McGee while she is held captive by the Shop. Hockstetter apparently survives the conflagration that destroys the Shop compound in Virginia. His current whereabouts are unknown.

*ORVILLE JAMIESON.* Also known as O. J. or Juice, Jamieson is a Shop agent. He is one of the few to survive the fire that Charlie McGee visits upon the Longmont compound. His current whereabouts are unknown.

*IRV and NORMA MANDERS.* On the run from the Shop, Andy and Charlie McGee are hitchhiking when they are picked up by a farmer named Irv Manders. He and his wife, Norma, show the McGees every hospitality, right up until several carloads of Shop agents come looking for the fugitives. Irv tries to protect his guests and his property with a shotgun—enraged that an American citizen's rights could be so heinously violated—and is shot for his trouble.

In the ensuing battle, Charlie lets her power loose on a large scale for the first time, and the Manders house is burned to the ground. Irv later recovers from his gunshot wound.

After the destruction of the Shop compound, Charlie finds her way back to Irv and Norma on her own. They lovingly help her recover from the horrors she has been through, and set her on the path to bring to light the truth about the Shop, as her father would have wanted.

It is assumed that Irv and Norma Manders still live on the Bailings Road in Hastings Glen, New York.

*TASHMORE POND.* The Vermont retreat where Granther McGee, Andy's grandfather, used to take him and his family when he was a boy. This cabin in the woods is also where Andy and Charlie hide out from the Shop for an entire winter. Unfortunately, it is also where they are captured by John Rainbird and other Shop agents.

## ADAPTATION

In October 1984, just in time for Halloween, Universal Pictures released the film version of *Firestarter*. Though faithfully adapted by screenwriter Stanley Mann, it was, in a curious and detrimental way, *too* faithful. Due mainly to the fact that each scene is put together with little texture or characterization but rather with an eye to expediency—in order, possibly, to fit in all of the novel—the resulting film comes off flat and lifeless. Every major character and scene from the original novel is in the film—but King himself would later comment that the whole of the movie was somehow less than the sum of its parts.

This might well be the fault of director Mark L. Lester, whose only real claim to fame was the cult favorite *Class of 1984* (1982). His other films include such "classics" as *Truck Stop Women* (1974), *Bobbie Jo and the Outlaw* (1976), and the early Arnold Schwarzenegger vehicle, *Commando* (1986). Clearly Lester knew how to blow things up and set people on fire, but whenever it came to drawing more than rudimentary performances from his powerhouse cast, the director seemed out of his element.

The film benefits greatly from its lead actor, David Keith *(An Officer and a Gentleman)*, as Andy McGee, and the presence of Martin Sheen as Cap Hollister. (Sheen had appeared in the film version of *The Dead Zone*.) Drew Barrymore, the only real choice in 1984 to play the title role, was widely considered the finest young natural actress working in Hollywood at the time. King later saw that she was cast in another film, *Cat's Eye*. Unfortunately, like so many others in the cast, Barrymore delivers a rather flat performance, though her undeniable charm is apparent.

Art Carney and Louise Fletcher, two of the most well-respected character actors in Hollywood, have small yet worthy roles as Irv and Norma Manders, and their presence lends substance and humanity to the screen project. Ironically, however, the opposite is true of the presence of another Academy Award–winning actor, George C. Scott. A legendary talent, Scott does only an adequate job in portraying the terrifying Native American assassin John Rainbird. No matter how much Scott glowers, no matter what makeup effects are used to make his face appear scarred, he simply is *not* Rainbird. In one of the few times in his career, he's just an actor cashing a paycheck.

Still, on a $15 million budget, *Firestarter* is competently executed and fast-paced. It must be applauded for its faithfulness to the original novel, a move rarely taken by any Hollywood production of a best-selling book.

# 29

## The Tommyknockers

I N   H I S   B I T T E R S W E E T  look at science run amok, *The Tommy-knockers* (1987) King shows how unchecked technological change for its own sake is not necessarily progress. Here, the author examines the ramifications of "dumb evolution," looking at a community so enraptured by what it *can* do that it never stops to wonder if it is doing what it *should*. This book is extremely relevant to our times, in which new technology becomes obsolete almost immediately after it is introduced. Like the Tommyknockers, the town's nickname for a race of highly advanced aliens, we love our gadgets—even if we have no idea how they work, or if they ultimately cause more harm than good.

Stories like "The Word Processor of the Gods" aside, King has always evidenced a healthy mistrust of technology and science. Examples abound in his fiction: Captain Tripps, the superflu that kills most of the world's population in *The Stand* (1978), was most likely created as part of a secret military project. Likewise, "The Mist" may have had its origins in the military's fabled Arrowhead Project. In *Firestarter* (1980), the Shop meddles with human DNA, producing mutants using the experimental chemical solution code-named Lot Six. Then there's machinery that is in itself dangerous. Who could forget "The Mangler," which featured the evil Model-6 Speed Ironer and Folder, or the malign vehicles depicted in "Trucks" and *Christine* (1983)? King even casts a wary eye on the scientific method; in *'Salem's Lot* (1975), rationalism allows the vampire epidemic to spread through an entire town.

The adults in *The Tommyknockers* also convey the fears King must have felt as a child growing up during the Cold War. As a product of the 1950s, King evinces both a healthy fear of radiation from the Bomb and the loss of individuality so feared by Americans threatened by Communism. Whatever emanates from the uncovered Tommy-knocker ship, its effects mimic radiation poisoning. The Tommy-knockers' takeover of Haven, Maine, brings to mind classic cinematic parables of paranoia such as *Invasion of the Body Snatchers* (1956) and *Invaders from Mars* (1953).

Purposely reminiscent of H. P. Lovecraft's classic 1927 tale "The Colour Out of Space," *The Tommyknockers* also contains several explicit connections to the rest of the Stephen King universe. Desperate to reveal the strange doings in Haven, local Ev Hillman speaks with David Bright, a journalist who reported on the events chronicled in *The Dead Zone* (1979). In Derry attending to the needs of his comatose grandson, Ev hears chuckling sounds emanating from a sewer. While passing through Derry, another Haven resident thinks he sees a clown "grinning up at him from an open sewer manhole" on Wentworth Street. As *The Tommyknockers* is clearly set in 1986, this would indicate that the main evil known simply as It, a.k.a. Pennywise the Clown from *IT* (1986), may still be alive at the time of the events occurring in Haven.

Besides *IT, The Tommyknockers* also has ties to *The Talisman* (1984). Emerging from an alcoholic blackout, Jim Gardener awakens on Arcadia Beach. There he meets a strange, sad youth. Gardener speaks with the boy and learns he lives in a nearby hotel, the Alhambra, and that he is an orphan, his mother having died in a car crash. Although the young man doesn't mention his name, it is clear that he is Jack Sawyer, the young hero of *The Talisman*. Furthermore, the surviving Haven Tommyknockers are brought to a government installation in Virginia. In an obvious reference to the events detailed in *Firestarter*, King tells readers, "This installation, which had once been burned to the ground by a child, was the Shop." Finally, King indirectly references himself, as when Ev Hillman briefly thinks about smutty books "like that fellow up in Bangor wrote."

## PRIMARY SUBJECTS

*ROBERTA (BOBBI) ANDERSON.* Walking in the woods one day, Bobbi trips over a piece of metal partially buried in the earth. Curious, she tries to dig it out, only to realize that it is part of something much bigger. For reasons she cannot yet fathom, she feels compelled to free the object from its earthen tomb. Forgoing her writing (Bobbi is a bestselling author of several westerns), she works on her dig day and night. Although she doesn't know it yet, Bobbi has fallen under the influence of the Tommyknockers, a race of highly advanced intergalactic gypsies. Her contact with the ship yields varied results. On the positive side, she is able to improve her water heater's efficiency several times over, modify her tractor (the gearshift now has a setting that reads "UP,") and invent a typewriter that reads her subconscious so she can write in her sleep. On the negative side, she seems to be suffering the effects of long-term radiation poisoning: Bobbi's general health deteriorates, and her teeth begin to fall out.

The first to start "becoming" (a process by which human beings are transformed into Tommyknockers), Bobbi becomes the de facto leader of the townsfolk in Haven who fall under the Tommyknockers' influence. Although she's quickly shedding her humanity, Bobbi does retain some human traits—her love for Jim Gardener, for instance. Despite repeated demands from her compatriots that she dispose of Jim, Bobbi keeps him alive. This proves to be a bad mistake. Shortly after they explore the alien vehicle for the first time together, Gardener suddenly turns on his former lover. Their brief scuffle in Bobbie's kitchen ends in her accidental death.

*PETER.* Bobbi's aged beagle, Peter is invigorated by his exposure to the Tommyknocker ship. As she slowly loses her humanity, Bobbi coldly turns the animal into a sort of living battery. Keeping him in the shed adjacent to her home, the former pet is later joined there by Ev Hillman and Anne Anderson.

*JIM GARDENER.* Bobbi's friend and lover, Jim is a poet and an alcoholic. He is not with Bobbi when she first finds the spaceship carrying the Tommyknockers—he's traveling New England as part of a caravan of poets. At one of these parties, Jim gets drunk in spectacular fashion: enraged by the statements of a proponent of nuclear power, antinuclear activist Jim delivers a spirited lecture, then proceeds to completely disrupt the party.

Jim continues his drinking binge, waking up several days later on a beach in New Hampshire. Frightened by his relapse, he returns home to beg Bobbi's forgiveness. Seeing the woman for the first time in weeks, Gardener is frightened by her unhealthy appearance and odd behavior. After agreeing to help with her excavation project, Jim spends the next few weeks digging during the day and drinking himself into a stupor at night. Although Jim is not immune to the effects of the Tommyknocker ship, his "becoming" is hindered by the presence of a metal plate in his skull, a souvenir of a youthful ski accident. The plate also keeps the telepathic Tommyknockers in town from reading his thoughts.

Although he helps Bobbi, Jim certainly doesn't condone her bizarre behavior. Discovering that Bobbi has turned Peter, Ev Hillman, and her sister, Anne, into human batteries, he decides he must stop her. After exploring the Tommyknocker ship for the first time, Jim decides to act and attempts to shoot Bobbi. The gun misfires, and they scuffle. Bobbi is fatally electrocuted when a radio falls into a puddle of liquid she's standing in.

Jim then enters the Tommyknocker ship for a second time, assuming control of its simplistic navigation system. At his command, the ship rises from the woods and takes off into space. The effort proves fatal. When last we see Jim, he lies dying on the transparent floor of the ship's control room in a widening pool of his own blood.

*RUTH McCAUSLAND.* Haven's no-nonsense police chief, Ruth is the heart and conscience of the town. When the Tommyknockers begin taking over various residents, Ruth resists becoming mentally enslaved. The rest of the town, however, do not agree with her and as a result cruelly shun her. Realizing she won't be able to resist the Tommyknockers much longer, Ruth sacrifices herself in an attempt to warn the outside world by blowing up the clock tower in hopes of attracting the attention of neighboring townships. The sacrifice is in vain, as the Tommyknockers produce a convincing hologram of the tower that manages to fool the eyes of the investigating Maine state troopers.

*HILLY BROWN*. Under the influence of the Tommyknockers, aspiring magician Hilly invents a device that actually makes things disappear. Unfortunately, ten-year-old Hilly uses his younger brother David as a "volunteer." Hilly sends David to the world of Altair-4 but can't bring him back. Sick with guilt, Hilly worries himself into a coma. He escapes the influence of the Tommyknockers when his grandfather takes him to the hospital in Derry.

*DAVID BROWN*. Hilly's younger brother, David is whisked to a world the Tommyknockers refer to as Altair-4. David spends several uncomfortable days there but survives the experience, due to the combined efforts of his grandfather and Jim Gardener. David was last seen alive and well in the Derry hospital.

*EV HILLMAN*. If Ruth McCausland is the heart and conscience of Haven, Ev Hillman could be thought of as its memory. Realizing early on that something is very wrong in Haven, Ev spirits his remaining grandson, Hilly Brown, out of town before anything else can happen to him. While in Derry, Ev tries to sound the alarm. His tale is too wild for the local newspapers to publish, but he does convince Derry police officer Butch Dugan to investigate. Unfortunately, Ev and Butch are captured while searching the woods near Bobbi Anderson's home. Butch is programmed by the Tommyknockers to commit suicide while Ev is taken to Bobbi's shed and used as a human battery.

*BIG INJUN WOODS*. Also known as Burning Woods, this piece of land borders Bobbi Anderson's property. The site of many an odd occurrence over the years, it is also the resting place of the Tommyknocker ship.

*THE SHOP*. When this secret government agency, first introduced in *Firestarter*, learns of the strange goings-on in the town, it descends on Haven only hours after Jim Gardener has piloted the Tommyknocker craft into deep space. The Shop studies the devices left behind by the Tommyknockers and also examines Haven's survivors, all well on their way to becoming Tommyknockers themselves. How much the Shop is able to learn is not known—all survivors die within two months.

*THE TOMMYKNOCKERS.* As King states in a prefatory note to the book, *Webster's Unabridged* states that Tommyknockers are either tunneling ogres, or ghosts that haunt deserted mines or caves. The author received his original inspiration from a verse he had heard as a child:

> *Late last night and the night before,*
> *Tommyknockers, Tommyknockers,*
> *knocking at the door.*
> *I want to go out, don't know if I can,*
> *'cause I'm so afraid*
> *of the Tommyknocker man.*

Instead of ogres or ghosts, in King's novel the Tommyknockers are the alien inhabitants of the ship Bobbi Anderson finds buried in the earth. Judging by its depth, the enormous craft has been there for centuries. When Jim boards the vehicle, he notes that its occupants have six-fingered hands, taloned feet, and what looks like a dog's head on top of a large frame. Described as "interstellar gypsies with no king," this belligerent race (they were apparently fighting among themselves when their ship crashed) has created technology that they themselves don't fully understand.

Besides the aliens themselves, the citizens of Haven are in the process of "becoming" Tommyknockers. Toward the end of the novel, King begins to refer to both groups by that name. The fantastic process by which humans become Tommyknockers is never made clear, but it has something to do with repeated exposure to the Tommyknocker ship and to treatments given to Havenites within the confines of Bobbi Anderson's shed. The process is long and slow, and requires a change in atmosphere—the newly minted Tommyknockers create a bubble over Haven, filling it with rarified Tommyknocker air. Outsiders entering Haven become ill; Haven residents who leave the town risk death.

### ADAPTATION

*Stephen King's The Tommyknockers,* a four-hour ABC-TV miniseries, adapted by Lawrence D. Cohen and directed by John Power, premiered in May 1993. Starring Jimmy Smits *(L.A. Law)* and Marg Helgenberger *(China Beach, CSI: Crime Scene Investigation)* as Jim Gardener and Bobbi Anderson, the miniseries also features *Creepshow* alumnus E. G. Marshall as Ev Hillman and former adult-film star Traci Lords as Nancy Voss. The production was shot entirely in New Zealand, even though the story is set in Maine. The well-produced miniseries remains fairly faithful to the novel, but differs noticeably by providing a happier ending for Bobbi (here she survives and reverts back to human form, her body and movements conveying none of the trauma of "becoming" a Tommyknocker).

Other changes were made, but most add to rather than detract from the overall narrative. Examples include an eerie scene in which Ruth McCausland (Joanna Cassidy) is attacked by her doll collection, and a scene in which Rebecca Paulson (Allyce Beasley) is informed of her husband's extramarital escapades by a chatty television game show host. The special effects are uniformly excellent—the producers obviously took the effort to make the Tommyknockers look right. Cohen, who wrote the screenplay for *Carrie* (1976) and co-wrote the telepay for the miniseries *IT* (1990), clearly has a strong affinity for the work of Stephen King.

# 30

## *Stephen King's Golden Years*

---

WITHOUT A DOUBT, *Stephen King's Golden Years* (1991) is a singular oddity in the Stephen King canon. It aired in 1991 as a summer replacement series on CBS and lasted for seven one-hour episodes, ending in a cliffhanger.

The hope at the time was that the network would pick up the series, which would then continue where the original segments left off. When that did not happen, the series' producers released a videotape version of *Golden Years* that brought the story to a still-somewhat-mysterious conclusion. To do so, however, they changed several scenes leading up to the ending. This book focuses on the televised version of *Golden Years*, with the exception of the changes made and new additions included in the videotape release.

The series starred Keith Szarabajka as Harlan Williams, with Frances Sternhagen *(Misery)* as his wife, Gina. Others in the cast included Felicity Huffman as Terry Spann and Ed Lauter as General Louis Crewes. The seven episodes boasted a variety of directors, most notably Michael Gornick, who directed the feature *Creepshow 2* in 1987.

The main character is Harlan Williams, an elderly janitor working at a top-secret military installation, where agricultural testing supposedly takes place. But no one actually believes that, given the high-voltage electric fence that surrounds the Falco Plains facility. In truth, the bizarre Dr. Richard Todhunter (Bill Raymond) is doing research on cellular regeneration. His negligence leads to an accidental explosion. Caught in the explosion, Harlan is exposed to an experimental energy form called K-R3, which causes him to grow younger.

One of the federal agents sent to investigate the accident, Jude Andrews (R. D. Call), turns out to be working for the insidious covert government agency called the Shop. The installation's security director, Terry Spann, had once been employed by the Shop as well. Appalled by Jude's depravity, she quit and came to work at Falco Plains. Learning Jude is searching for Harlan, Terry

> *Of the seven episodes that were completed for* Golden Years, *King wrote the first five. The last two were penned by Josef Anderson based on King's outlines.*

realizes the old man will suffer a horrible fate unless she saves him. She finds an ally in the facility's director, General Crewes.

*Old Durham town hall*
DAVID LOWELL

The Shop first appeared in the Stephen King universe as the antagonists in *Firestarter*. Not only does the sinister organization perform assassinations and any other nasty little job that no other government agency would, but it also has been involved in the kind of experimentation that Todhunter was conducting. It is only natural, then, for the Shop to take an interest in Harlan.

Jude has his orders: bring Williams in as a test subject, no matter what. If that means he has to murder Harlan's wife, Gina, it isn't something he's going to lose any sleep over. In fact, Jude is so cold-blooded, he is considered to be the best assassin the Shop has ever had—better, even, than the legendary John Rainbird of *Firestarter*, (1980). The Shop also plays a role in both *The Tommyknockers* (1987) and "The Langoliers," a novella from *Four Past Midnight* (1990).

*Golden Years* is yet another work in which King delves into the concept of a government experiment gone horribly wrong, a theme repeated in *Firestarter*, *The Stand* (1978), "The Mist" (collected in *Skeleton Crew*, 1985), and various other King short stories. The theme of aging—in this case, the defiance of age—is also a major part of this television excursion. Earlier in his career, King had touched on this subject primarily in short stories such as "The Reach," and subsequently it became a

> *King has a cameo in the fourth episode as a bus driver.*

major theme in both *The Green Mile* (1996) and *Insomnia* (1994).

*Golden Years* is also quite notable for its inconclusive ending. It had been previously implied that Harlan's power is growing exponentially, in a fashion greatly similar to the Shop's predictions about Charlie McGee's potential power level in *Firestarter*. Harlan can cause earthquakes, speed up time, and make mechanical things go haywire. In the end, he creates a force field of energy that protects himself and his wife, Gina, from Jude's attack. Then both Harlan and Gina disappear.

But to where? It is implied that Harlan is able to teleport, and that he regresses himself and Gina backward in age to before their births, effectively erasing their existence, but that hardly seems in character for Harlan.

So what happened to Harlan and Gina Williams? Time will tell.

## PRIMARY SUBJECTS

*HARLAN WILLIAMS*. A janitor at the Falco Plains military research installation, Harlan is caught in an accidental explosion and exposed to an experimental form of energy that causes him to begin regressing in age. As a result, he is pursued both by the military and by the insidious government agency known as the Shop. During the final confrontation with Jude Andrews, a Shop agent, Harlan disappears in a flash of green energy. His fate and whereabouts are unknown.

*TERRY SPANN*. A former Shop agent, Terry is director of security at Falco Plains and enters into a relationship with the commanding officer of the facility, General Louis Crewes. The relationship suffers when she chooses to protect Harlan Williams from Jude Andrews, her former partner from the Shop. To save Harlan, Terry kills Andrews, but by then Crewes has come around to her way of thinking, and the two depart together. Her current whereabouts are unknown.

*GINA WILLIAMS*. The wife of Harlan Williams, Gina is the first to notice that he is growing younger. Her life is put in jeopardy when Jude Andrews threatens to kill her if Harlan doesn't turn himself in. In the end, she disappears with her husband in a flash of green energy. Her fate and whereabouts are unknown.

> *In the original televised version of* Golden Years, *Gina Williams dies. However, in the videotape version, she is alive thanks to the miracle of editing.*

*FRANCESCA WILLIAMS*. The blind daughter of Harlan and Gina Williams, Francesca, who lives in Chicago, does her best to keep her parents out of danger. First, she takes them to a kind of hippie commune where she once lived, hoping they will be safe there. Later, she visits a friend who creates false identities for her parents, hoping to aid them in starting a new life. While she is gone, her parents have their final confrontation with Jude Andrews and then disappear. It is presumed that Francesca still resides in Chicago.

**DR. RICHARD TODHUNTER.** A scientist at Falco Plains, the mentally unbalanced Todhunter is doing research into cellular regeneration for the U.S. government. During an experiment, a malfunction occurs, but Todhunter ignores the warnings of his staff and an explosion follows. He lies his way out of trouble, and it is presumed that he is still conducting research at Falco Plains.

**GENERAL LOUIS CREWES.** Crewes is the commanding officer in charge of the military research installation at Falco Plains at the time of the incident that changes Harlan Williams. At first he obeys orders to put Harlan under surveillance, but when he discovers that the Shop is involved, he teams up with Terry Spann, with whom he is romantically involved, to protect Harlan. After Terry murders Jude Andrews, Crewes goes off with her. His current whereabouts are unknown.

**JUDE ANDREWS.** Andrews is an agent for the Shop, a covert government agency. He is reputed to be the best assassin the Shop has ever employed. He is assigned to bring Harlan Williams in for study, but is eventually killed by his former partner, Terry Spann.

**CAPTAIN TRIPS.** A resident at the commune where Francesca Williams takes her parents, the man called Captain Trips is actually a Shop infiltrator. He tells the Shop where to find the Williamses and is later killed by Shop agent Jude Andrews.

> Captain Trips is not only the name of the Shop informant in Golden Years, *but it is also the nickname of the horrible virus in* The Stand.

# 31

## "The Langoliers"

---

SUBMITTED FOR YOUR APPROVAL: Captain Brian Engle, a pilot with American Pride Airlines. Captain Engle is a sturdy soul, but he's just been shaken to the core by an inflight pressurization problem that almost caused the explosive decompression of the aircraft he was piloting. He managed to land that craft safely in Los Angeles and is now walking toward the terminal, where he'll receive tragic news about his ex-wife. Forgoing rest, Engle will board American Pride flight 29, a flight that is heading toward a date with destiny. Although scheduled to land in Boston, flight 29 will be forced to make a detour that will take it directly into the heart of . . . the Twilight Zone."

While "The Langoliers" (from 1990's *Four Past Midnight*) was never an installment of *The Twilight Zone*, it certainly feels like a lost episode of that classic TV show. Dedicated to "Joe, another white-knuckle flier," this story had its origins in a bizarre image that flashed through King's mind of a woman pressing her hand over a crack in the wall of a commercial jetliner. The plot is simple: ten passengers taking a flight from Los Angeles to Boston wake up in midflight to find the crew and the majority of their cabinmates gone (one other passenger is present but asleep). Luckily, one of their number can pilot the craft. Unable to contact anyone on the ground (no one responds to his calls, and major cities are blacked out), Captain Brian Engle makes an executive decision to land at Bangor International Airport. There the group discovers they are the only beings in the immediate vicinity. Nothing feels right to them; even the air smells different. Then they hear sounds in the distance, crunching sounds, as if someone is literally chewing up the landscape. Before the day is through, these unlucky souls discover where all our yesterdays go.

This unique tale of time travel contains several links to the Stephen King universe. Debating what has occurred, one passenger mentions similar events in history, mainly the disappearances of the entire crew of the *Mary Celeste* and of the colonists on Roanoke Island, North Carolina, two events that have fascinated King for years. The same passenger wonders if he and his fellow travelers may be guinea pigs in an experiment conducted by a top-secret outfit like the Shop, a ruthless black-ops government agency first introduced in *Firestarter*. Most of the action of the story takes place at Bangor International Airport, located in King's hometown in Maine.

## PRIMARY SUBJECTS

*THE LANGOLIERS*. According to Craig Toomey's father, the Langoliers are horrid monsters who prey on lazy, time-wasting children. The passengers of flight 29 adopt Toomey's name for the creatures he's convinced are coming to destroy them. They are described as black balls that contract and then expand again: "They shimmered and twitched and wavered like faces made of glowing swamp gas. The eyes were only rudimentary indentations, but the mouths were huge: semicircular caves lined with gnashing, whirring teeth." The Langoliers use those teeth to literally chew up the scenery of the world. They are reality's scavengers, consumers of yesterday.

*CAPTAIN BRIAN ENGLE*. Engle is proof that bad luck does come in threes. As the tale begins, Engle has just safely landed a plane that almost underwent an explosive decompression. Arriving at the airport, he is informed that his ex-wife has been killed in a fire. Last, and most important to the story, he boards American Pride flight 29 for the trip back to Boston to deal with his wife's remains. Exhausted, Engle falls asleep the minute he sits in his seat. Awakened by Dinah Bellman's screams, he realizes the crew and most of his fellow passengers are no longer aboard. After breaking down the door to the cockpit with the help of Nick Hopewell, Engle assumes control of the plane and, indirectly, of the remaining passengers. Engle survives the incredible appearance of the Langoliers—he's among those who wink back into existence before the eyes of a startled little girl at the end of their journey.

*DINAH BELLMAN.* A blind girl with paranormal powers (she can see through others' eye, and communicate with them telepathically across great distances), Dinah is on flight 29 with her aunt Vicky, traveling to Boston to have an operation that may restore her sight. The first to stir after the plane literally crosses over into yesterday, she awakens the remaining passengers with her frightened screams. Dinah demonstrates her powers when she views the other passengers through Craig Toomey's eyes (he sees them as monsters). Frightened by this vision, she clings to Laurel Stephenson for the rest of the ordeal. Despite being stabbed by the paranoid Toomey, the little girl plays an important part in the group's eventual escape, mentally luring the near-dead Toomey to reveal himself to the ravenous Langoliers. The creatures then veer toward him, giving those on the plane valuable time to take off. Mortally injured, Dinah passes away before the aircraft safely crosses back across the border between yesterday and today.

*ALBERT KLAUSNER.* An exceedingly bright young man, Albert, along with Robert Jenkins, represents the brains of the beleaguered group. It is Albert who realizes that, coming from the future, they and their craft are far more real than their present surroundings at Bangor Airport. Applying his theory, the group refuels their plane with the flat (other-dimensional) mixture contained in the fuel tanks at the airport. Once inside flight 29's tanks, the fuel becomes more real, allowing them to take off at the approach of the Langoliers. Albert also survives the Langoliers. He is presumed alive and well, perhaps pursuing a romantic relationship with Bethany Sims.

*LAUREL STEPHENSON.* A schoolteacher, Laurel is making the flight to Massachusetts to meet with a man she knows only through letters. During her adventures in the world of the Langoliers, she and Nick

Hopewell fall in love. Before Nick sacrifices himself to save the rest of the group, he asks Laurel to pass a message on to his estranged father. She agrees.

*NICK HOPEWELL.* An operative of the British government, Nick describes himself as Her Majesty's mechanic. On his way to Boston to assassinate the paramour of an outspoken supporter of the IRA, Nick instead becomes involved in the adventure of a lifetime. He becomes the *de facto* leader of the group once Captain Engle lands the plane. His sure manner and quick thinking make him a good leader; his no-nonsense attitude keeps human time bomb Craig Toomey in line long enough for Engle to touch down safely. Attempting to return home the way they came, the group realizes that they need to be asleep to cross the barrier safely. Even though he knows it could mean his death, Nick volunteers to remain awake and see the craft safely through the temporary portal. Nick is gone when his fellow passengers emerge from their brief sleep and is presumed dead.

*DON GAFFNEY.* Don takes charge of Craig Toomey after Nick quells his initial outburst (Nick grabs Toomey by the nose, threatening to break it if he doesn't back off). Toomey later kills Don with a letter opener.

*CRAIG TOOMEY.* In introducing this character, King references certain fish that live on the ocean floor and thrive despite the tremendous pressure. Bring these fish up to the surface, however, and they explode: "Craig Toomey had been raised in his own dark trench, had lived in his own atmosphere of high pressure." Raised by a domineering father and castrating mother, Toomey has grown into a paranoid, insecure, type A adult. An employee of Desert Sun Banking Corporation, the self-destructive Toomey has made a disastrous investment, costing the company millions.

Waking up onboard the nearly empty plane, Toomey begins his final descent into madness. Utterly panicked, he starts bullying his fellow passengers until Nick Hopewell forcibly convinces him to back off. His paranoia reaches epic proportions, and he attacks the group at the Bangor Airport. First, he shoots Albert Klausner point-blank in the chest, but the bullet, subject to the laws of this reality, is not propelled with enough force to hurt the boy. He later stabs Dinah Bellman with a letter opener, giving her the wound that eventually kills her. He uses the same weapon to dispatch Don Gaffney shortly thereafter.

Toomey then tries again to kill Albert, but fails, taking a heavy beating in the process. Albert leaves him at the airport, but a dying Dinah rouses Toomey telepathically, forcing him to walk out to the airfield. Once there, he is attacked and devoured by the Langoliers.

**ROBERT JENKINS.** Introducing himself to Albert Klausner (who eventually comes to play Dr. Watson to Jenkins's Sherlock Holmes), Jenkins says, "I write mysteries for a living. Deduction is my bread and butter, you might say." Jenkins is thrilled by the intellectual challenge his predicament provides—his theories are usually right on the money, helping the others to remain calm and survive in their strange new environs. Jenkins saves the day when he realizes he and his fellow passengers must be asleep to safely cross the divide. Jenkins is presumably alive and well, still writing mystery novels.

**BETHANY SIMS.** Bethany's mom is sending her to visit her aunt Shawna, who would most likely have placed her alcoholic niece in a rehab center to dry out. Bethany forms a romantic bond with Albert Klausner, who becomes her knight in shining armor. She is presumably alive and well, perhaps pursuing a romantic relationship with Albert.

**RUDY WARWICK.** Also known as "the bald man," Rudy's main preoccupation is eating. At the Bangor Airport, he finds to his horror that the food is tasteless and inedible. One of the six people who survive the journey to the land of the Langoliers, Rudy is presumed to be alive and well.

## ADAPTATION

*Stephen King's The Langoliers* was made into a four-hour miniseries in 1995. Directed by Tom Holland (who also helmed the lackluster feature version of *Thinner* a year later), this ABC-TV production is faithful to its source material but comes off as an overly long episode of *The Twilight Zone*. The acting is competent though surprisingly wooden for the most part. There are bright spots: David Morse (who later appeared in the film version of *The Green Mile*) and Dean Stockwell turn in convincing performances as Captain Engle and Bob Jenkins, and Bronson Pinchot is downright brilliant as Toomey. Like the 1990 miniseries version of *IT*, however, *The Langoliers* is diminished by cheap special effects. All the carefully wrought tension evaporates when the Langoliers—strange hybrids of a Pac-Man and the Tasmanian Devil cartoon character—finally appear.

Look closely for Stephen King's cameo as Tom Holby, senior vice president of Desert Sun Banking. The author appears in a fantasy sequence that occurs near the end of the show.

# SECTION SIX

## Other Prime Reality Tales

*The Shining*

*Night Shift*

*Creepshow*

*Different Seasons*

*Christine*

*Skeleton Crew*

*Cat's Eye*

*Misery*

*Four Past Midnight*

*Sleepwalkers*

*Nightmares & Dreamscapes*

*Rose Madder*

*The Green Mile*

*Six Stories*

Uncollected Stories

T HE PRIME REALITY CAN BE seen as the backbone of the Stephen King universe, or perhaps the main stage on which most of King's fictional dramas are played out. Some elements of the prime reality tales cannot be clearly assigned to any of the other sections of the prime reality discussed in this book. That is why the bulk of King's shorter fiction is addressed in this section.

As pointed out in the introduction to *The Dark Tower* section, King himself only recently came to understand that Roland's world indeed contains all the others of the author's making. What remains to be seen is just *how* all the worlds are connected. Some connections are obvious while others are not, and only King can create the connective tissue that pulls all the parts into a cohesive whole. Perhaps readers will see this develop in the remaining volumes of the *Dark Tower* series. To venture forth, it seems reasonable to tie all of the material in this section to the rest of the prime reality. We can logically presume that this material is thus connected to the realities of *The Dark Tower*, *The Stand*, and the works of Richard Bachman.

That said, some of the works within this section may be examined in more detail. Some connections are explicit, some are a little more tenuous but valid nonetheless. Some are not readily apparent but someday might be made clear.

.     .     .

The first entry deals with *The Shining*, about a boy with a wild talent. It must be evident at this point that King's universe contains numerous examples of people with similar talents, such as those in *Carrie*, *The Dead Zone*, *Firestarter*, and in another book described in this section, *The Green Mile*.

A more explicit connection lies in one of *The Shining*'s main characters, Dick Hallorann, who briefly lived in Derry during his military service. Dick is instrumental in helping young Danny Torrance defeat the evil that permeates the Overlook Hotel, an evil reminiscent of that which saturates another famous King edifice, the Marsten house in *'Salem's Lot*. Dick and Danny's battle could very well be another, although lesser, skirmish in the eternal war between good and evil, which is the overarching theme and plot in the Stephen King universe. This case could also be made for the events detailed in *The Green Mile*, which features the miracle worker John Coffey—surely a soldier for good in what King perceives as the never-ending war between the Random and the Purpose.

There are also connections to be found in *Rose Madder*. The title character of that novel visits a world within a painting. Because a resident of that world makes references to the city of Lud, we strongly suspect that the world in the painting is Roland's. This is neither the first nor the last time that realities have spilled from one into another, as demonstrated by Randall Flagg's reality hopping or by Roland's brief foray into the world of *The Stand*, chronicled in *The Dark Tower IV: Wizard and Glass*.

Further connections within the prime reality itself spring from Paul Sheldon, bestselling author and protagonist of the novel *Misery*. Sheldon's books are mentioned in both *Rose Madder* and *Desperation*. Since *Rose Madder* is connected to the reality of the *Dark Tower*, by virtue of Paul Sheldon, so is *Misery*. A similar argument can be made to connect the prime reality to the reality of King's pseudonymous Richard Bachman novels. The prime reality's *Desperation* (covered in section seven) chronicles events that parallel goings-on in the Bachman reality novel *The Regulators*. There is also an explicit connection between Paul Sheldon and Eddie Kaspbrak from *IT*, mentioned in *Misery*.

*King playing with the Rock Bottom Remainders* | SUSANNE MOSS

This reality also contains most of King's shorter work, which tends to be more eclectic and quirky than his novels. Thus, we consider King's numerous short-story collections in this section (though some stories have been assigned to their proper realities where applicable). *Night Shift*, for instance, features two stories, "Jerusalem's Lot" and "One for the Road," which can be taken respectively as prologue and epilogue to the novel *'Salem's Lot*. *Skeleton Crew, Nightmares & Dreamscapes*, and *Six Stories* contain several stories set in the town of Jerusalem's Lot. (*Nightmares & Dreamscapes* also features "The Night Flier," a story starring Richard Dees, who figures prominently in *The Dead Zone*.)

*Six Stories* contains "Blind Willie," a precursor to a story that appeared in *Hearts in Atlantis*, linking that volume to the reality of the Dark Tower via *Hearts'* novella "Low Men in Yellow Coats." It also contains "Autopsy Room Four," which takes place in Derry. Finally, *Four Past Midnight* has references to the Shop (in a casual comment from one of the passengers in "The Langoliers"), Castle Rock (where "The Sun Dog" is set) and Derry (the unfortunate soul in "Secret Window, Secret Garden" used to live there). There is also a link between *Four Past Midnight* and *Needful Things*, as readers are informed at the end of the latter that Leland Gaunt has set up shop in the Junction City, Iowa, building that once housed the insurance office of Sam Peebles (from "The Library Policeman").

With all the connections that exist between the books, and King's own declaration that his works are connected, it seems evident that the cosmic war for the fate of the multiverse, the battle between the Random and the Purpose, will go on. One can hypothesize that though certain stories seem distantly removed from that cosmic struggle, all of the works are connected. The battle goes on, and nowhere on a more individual level than the prime reality of the Stephen King universe, this parallel dimension where the author has spent the lion's share of his time and energy.

# 32

# *The Shining*

---

MOST READERS rightly judged *'Salem's Lot* (1975) to be one of the finest contemporary treatments of the vampire legend. Stephen King once again hit the bull's-eye only two years later with *The Shining* (1977). Many critics regard it as one of the greatest contemporary ghost stories in the history of the genre. Yet even if the supernatural element were removed—and this is where King's often overlooked strengths as a mainstream writer quickly become evident—the story would be no less powerful or tragic . . . and no less terrifying.

On the surface, *The Shining* concerns the old Overlook Hotel situated high in the Colorado Rockies. The massive resort has had a violent history and is rumored to be haunted by a sinister presence. Because the severe winters make the only road to the summit inaccessible, the hotel is closed for several months out of the year. A caretaker is hired annually to maintain the facility until it reopens in the spring. The caretaker's family is required to stay at the Overlook as well, and the solitude in the high mountains can sometimes make a person go off the deep end. Call it extreme cabin fever, if you will.

The family newly hired for the winter is the Torrances: Jack, his wife, Wendy, and their son, five-year-old Danny. Jack, currently between careers, is appointed to the caretaker's job by a sympathetic friend. None of them has any interest in legends of the supernatural or ghosts. Unfortunately, this small family is already haunted by emotional and psychological problems that make them perfect potential victims for whatever diabolism is hovering about the Overlook.

Jack has been fired from his teaching position at Stovington Preparatory Academy, but he believes the months of isolation will aid him in writing what he hopes will be a Pulitzer Prize–winning play. Always supportive, Wendy is well aware that her husband is deeply troubled. He has such monumental doubts about himself as a man, a husband, and a father that he drinks to excess. When he does so, he loses control of his inner rages and becomes both verbally and physically abusive toward his wife and son. But since no alcohol is kept in the Overlook during the winter off-season, Wendy is convinced Jack can find the peace of mind both to write and to become close once again to her and their troubled youngster.

Little Danny has his own nearly overwhelming concerns. He has disturbing visions that cannot be rationally explained. The child has an amazing psychic gift that the Overlook's friendly cook, Dick Hallorann, calls "the shining." The elderly Hallorann admits he has never seen anyone with such a powerful grasp of the power at such a young age. Even though the shining allows Danny to glimpse the future, it's a dark gift. The grisly sights he witnesses are often episodes of the utmost violence and horror, and the boy realizes his own family is not going to be spared.

On top of everything, a powerful, evil presence is waiting patiently for those who overstay their welcome at the Overlook. It craves young Danny most of all so it can harness his tremendous psychic powers. Yet the presence realizes that because the boy's father is so weak at heart, it will possess Jack instead more swiftly to destroy this already highly fragile family unit.

The accelerating destruction of the family is of the greatest concern to King in *The Shining*. Indeed, in much of the Stephen King universe, families are often shown as being broken or dysfunctional in some manner. In *Carrie* (1974) and *'Salem's Lot* (1975), the young people are often portrayed as growing up without caring parents, or if they have a mother or father, they are perhaps better off without them. Monsters can come in many forms and guises—they can sometimes be the people we are supposed to love.

Throughout *The Shining,* King depicts young Danny as being in as much danger from his own mentally unbalanced father as from his recurring supernatural visions. By making the horrors of child abuse, alcoholism, mental illness, and spousal abuse so terribly plausible, the author is able to take the reader to the point of accepting *anything* that happens to the Torrances. And if bad things can befall good people like them, why couldn't they occur to any one of us?

In its ability to induce palpable fear in the reader, *The Shining* may be King's masterpiece of horror to date. Many critics feel it is truly one of the most frightening novels ever published. Anyone who reads of Danny's awful encounter with the dead woman in Room 217 will never forget it. As King has stated in interviews, "I create people you care about—and then I turn the monsters loose."

*The Shining* is unusual in its geographical placement in the Stephen King universe because it is *not* set in Maine. (Though if King had not chosen to base the Overlook on a real hotel in Colorado he once visited, the resort most certainly could have been situated somewhere in rural northern New England.) Because so much of the action takes place within a single isolated setting, it does not really matter in what state the novel is set. In future works, King does not stray very far afield from the geographical locations in Maine that he knows so well.

On the other hand, this would not be the last time that King's protagonist would be a writer. (Ben Mears of *'Salem's Lot* was a moderately successful author.) In such future works as *Misery* (1987), *The Dark Half* (1987), and *Bag of Bones* (1998), the main character would also be an author, although each would be far more successful than the doomed Jack Torrance. Again, the unique trials and tribulations of a working writer are subjects King is highly qualified to explore.

## PRIMARY SUBJECTS

*DANNY TORRANCE.* A shy five-year-old, Danny is gifted—or cursed—with the precognitive power called "the shining." Like his parents, he is trapped for the winter in the Overlook Hotel and stalked by an unseen evil presence. When the hotel explodes, killing his possessed father in the process, Danny escapes with his mother and the hotel cook. He is last seen recovering from his terrifying ordeal at a lodge in western Maine.

*TONY.* Danny's imaginary friend, Tony warns Danny when something bad is going to happen. In times of stress, he often murmurs the dire word "redrum." (Spell it backward.)

*JACK TORRANCE.* Failed teacher, recovering drunk, unsuccessful writer, desperate husband, and occasionally abusive husband and father, Jack see the caretaker's job at the Overlook as his last chance to straighten out his life and prove his worth to himself, his wife, and their son. Regrettably, the loathsome presence of the Overlook knows Jack will make a perfect vessel through which it can obtain the raw psychic power that exists in his son. Jack tries to fight off the demons within and around him but ultimately is taken over by the horrific presence. After trying to kill Wendy, Danny, and Dick Hallorann, Jack dies in the explosion that destroys the Hotel.

*WENDY TORRANCE.* Jack's submissive wife and Danny's overly protective mother. She must do battle against the growing madness of her husband and the horrors of the Overlook. In the end she survives with her son, but loses her husband to the demons who possessed him and the Overlook.

*DICK HALLORANN.* Head cook of the Overlook, Hallorann also possesses the psychic ability known as "the shining," and instructs Danny on how to use the power and what its limitations are. A tall, retirement age African-American, he rescues Danny and his mother Wendy from the Overlook when the boy "calls" to him using his psychic powers. Hallorann survives being attacked by a possessed

*The original title of the novel was* The Shine. *King changed it to prevent it from being misconstrued as a racial slur.*

Jack Torrance and later, the destruction of the cursed hotel. He eventually becomes a cook at the Red Arrow Lodge in Maine.

*DELBERT GRADY.* A previous caretaker of the Overlook. The specters in the hotel eventually drove Grady mad, and he murdered his two young daughters with an ax and did in his wife with a shotgun. After blowing his brains out with the same weapon, he becomes a ghost and permanent guest at the Overlook.

*MRS. MASSEY.* A sixty-year-old guest of the Overlook who killed herself when her seventeen-year-old lover deserted her. Her lonely, lustful spirit haunts room 217, waiting in the bathtub for her beau to return.

*THE OVERLOOK HOTEL.* A massive structure with 110 rooms, situated high in the Colorado mountains. Constructed between 1907 and 1909, the Overlook is one of the most beautiful resort hotels ever built; it was also the most evil. When Jack Torrance fails to properly maintain the boilers, the entire facility explodes and goes up in flames. It is unclear if the evil presence, which existed in every room, board, and nail of the hotel, was destroyed in the resulting devastation.

## ADAPTATIONS

In 1980, legendary filmmaker Stanley Kubrick brought to the screen what many believed was a powerful and extremely visual interpretation of *The Shining*. Although King was at first flattered that the great director would choose to adapt this novel, the author was ultimately dissatisfied with the final result. For one thing, Kubrick rejected the screenplay offered by King, and adapted it himself with another screenwriter.

Although the production boasted impressive performances from Jack Nicholson, Shelley Duvall, Scatman Crothers, and newcomer Danny Lloyd as young Danny Torrance, it was evident that Kubrick's ideas on how to portray cinematic horror were clearly not the same as King's. Kubrick also had no hesitation about changing characterizations or crucial elements of the novel to better suit his own needs as a visual stylist, such as the totally unwarranted plot twist of slaying Dick Hallorann. King also believed that Nicholson never portrayed Torrance other than as a man already half-insane when we first see him, thus giving the audience an unpleasant character few could remotely care about.

King has often stated that the R-rated film reminded him of a big, expensive-looking car that had no engine to make it go. The author also holds that the director was to some degree "above" making a genre horror movie—that it would somehow be beneath his talents if he truly tried to frighten the audience. The pace of the movie also didn't help. Originally at 146 minutes, the filmmaker cut it by four minutes for general release. In spite of King's increasing fame over the years that followed, the movie would forever be known—for good reasons and bad—as "Stanley Kubrick's *The Shining.*"

> *The novel version of* The Shining *was originally constructed in the form of a five-act play. To keep the novel from becoming too long, King dropped both the prologue and the epilogue. However, a reworked version of "Before the Play" appeared in the April 26, 1997, issue of* TV Guide *that featured articles on the television production of* The Shining.

King became less and less a fan of the 1980 motion picture and never had any hesitation in letting his feelings be known to the public. In 1996, King convinced ABC that the novel's author was the best judge of who should write and produce a definitive version of this modern classic of horror. King worked with one of his favorite directors, Mick Garris, to create a six-hour miniseries that initially aired in three parts (April 27, April 28, and May 1, 1997). King firmly believed that the television miniseries format—which had worked so well with *The Stand* (1994)—was the best way to present his vision of *The Shining.*

By this point, in the late 1990s, King had far more clout than when Kubrick had first optioned the film rights to *The Shining.* ABC had reportedly offered him a blank check to act as executive producer of his next miniseries (ultimately budgeted at about $23 million) and the choice of any of his works to adapt. King had always wanted to remake *The Shining,* but to do so, he had to strike a bargain with Stanley Kubrick in which King would no longer publicly comment on or criticize Kubrick's film version.

Yet even King took liberties in adapting his story to the miniseries format, and to a noticeable degree focused strongly on Jack Torrance's drinking problem as an integral part of the plotline. Rather than use well-known movie stars like Jack Nicholson, King purposely chose lesser-known actors, tapping Steven Weber (from the series *Wings*) to play Jack and Rebecca De Mornay to play Wendy. Under the capable direction of Garris (who had also helmed *Sleepwalkers* and *The Stand*), there finally came to be a version that will forever be known— for both good reasons and bad—as "Stephen King's *The Shining*."

*Stephen King has a cameo role in the television miniseries portraying a ghostly bandleader. The name of his orchestra? The Gage Creed Band.*

# 33

## *Night Shift*

---

AFTER ONLY THREE NOVELS in print under his own name, King published his first volume of short stories. Most of the tales in *Night Shift* (1978) first appeared in various men's magazines during the early to mid-1970s, a time when publications such as *Penthouse*, *Cavalier*, and *Gallery* were a booming market for horror fiction. The two exceptions include "One for the Road," a coda of sorts to *'Salem's Lot* (1975), which ran in *Maine* magazine, and "I Know What You Need," which was first published in *Cosmopolitan*.

Within this collection is some of King's earliest work. Some of the material predates *Carrie* (1974) significantly. In addition, a good number of the stories have a familiar flavor to them reminiscent of the kinds of classic science fiction and horror that King weaned himself on. The first entry, "Jerusalem's Lot," is a traditional horror tale in the mold of genre grandmaster H. P. Lovecraft, author of such bizarre short classics as "The Dunwich Horror" and "The Shadow over Innsmouth." Rising beyond the nod—or even homage—to Lovecraft, King's own voice, familiar and confident, is clear. Throughout the rest of the volume, King establishes without question that his is the only voice in this book. Each of these stories is spun from the webbing of his unmistakable imagination.

> Night Shift *is the only book by* King *that carries no dedication.*

It's as simple as the first line of his foreword to *Night Shift*. "Let's talk, you and I," the author says seductively. "Let's talk about fear."

And he does—magnificently.

## "I AM THE DOORWAY"

A former astronaut is afflicted with a terrible curse: an alien intelligence has infiltrated his body and begins to take it over. Using his body, it murders those who might threaten it.

### PRIMARY SUBJECTS

*ARTHUR*. An astronaut who, while on a mission code-named Project: Zeus—whose purpose is to find intelligent life in outer space—is infected or infiltrated by an alien presence that begins to grow in his body. First, it manifests as golden eyes on his fingers and palms. After Arthur burns them off, the eyes grow on his chest, attempting to control his every action. Arthur's fate is unknown, though he was last seen to be contemplating suicide.

*RICHARD*. A friend of Arthur's, who is murdered by the creature inhabiting Arthur's body when the alien decides Richard might jeopardize its presence on Earth.

*LEDERER*. An astronaut whose failed mission leaves him trapped in a spaceship that will orbit the sun until he dies.

## "THE MANGLER"

A horrifying series of accidents at an industrial laundry leads a police officer to realize that an incredible set of coincidences has allowed a powerful demon to possess a laundry ironer and folder.

### PRIMARY SUBJECTS

*JOHN HUNTON*. As a police officer, his investigation of the death of Adelle leads Hunton to consider the possibility of the laundry machine's demonic possession. When he and his friend Mark Jackson attempt to exorcise the demon, the giant laundry machine roars to life and attacks them. It is not known if Hunton survived his final confrontation with the Mangler.

*MARK JACKSON.* Partially due to Mark Jackson's influence, John Hunton begins to consider demonic possession as a possible explanation for the deaths at Blue Ribbon Laundry. Jackson's research allows them to confirm that suspicion. It is not known if Jackson survived his final confrontation with the Mangler.

*SHERRY OUELETTE.* Due to the fact that she is a virgin, Sherry's blood is a vital ingredient in the purely unintentional ritual that invests a demonic spirit into the Mangler.

*BLUE RIBBON LAUNDRY.* The industrial laundry, in an unnamed American city, where the Mangler comes to life.

*THE POSSESSED REFRIGERATOR.* A safety inspector tells Hunton the tale of a refrigerator that had been moved to a dump, only to prey on anything that came near it, including birds and a young boy whose parents believed he knew better than to crawl inside a discarded refrigerator.

*THE MANGLER.* A Hadley-Watson model 6 speed ironer and dryer, it became known as "the Mangler" due to several accidents that took place involving the machine. Eventually, it becomes possessed by a demon and later, to protect itself, literally comes to life, tears its way out of the Blue Ribbon Laundry, and pursues those who would destroy it. It is not known if the Mangler survived the final confrontation with its enemies.

## "THE BOGEYMAN"

Over the course of several years, Lester Billings's three children die mysteriously in their cribs. Lester reveals to his new psychiatrist, Dr. Harper, that in hindsight the behavior of his children just prior to their deaths has led him to the conclusion that they were murdered by a creature called the Bogeyman, who turns out to be Harper.

### PRIMARY SUBJECTS

*LESTER BILLINGS*. All three of Lester's children supposedly died at the hands of the Bogeyman.

*DR. HARPER*. Lester's psychiatrist. It is unclear, but it seems either that the Bogeyman murdered the real Harper and disguised itself as the psychiatrist in order to continue terrorizing Billings, or that Harper has always been the Bogeyman.

*THE BOGEYMAN*. A legendary monster who supposedly lurks in closets, attacking children when they are made vulnerable by their parents' disbelief in such mythical creatures.

## "GRAY MATTER"

A group of older men hanging out at a package store called Henry's Nite-Owl are surprised one night by a visit from Timmy Grenadine. The boy claims that a bacteria-infected beer has transformed his father into a gelatinous monster who eats dead, putrefying animals and perhaps even worse. The men investigate the boy's story.

### PRIMARY SUBJECTS

*RICHIE GRENADINE*. Richie's unemployment leads him to drink more heavily than usual. One day, a "skunked" beer containing a kind of bacterium or virus, infects him, and he begins to change into something monstrous—a huge, gelatinous creature with a hunger for flesh, living or dead. The result of his confrontation with Henry Parmalee is unknown.

*TIMMY GRENADINE*. Timmy, Richie's son, who tells Henry Parmalee and the other regulars at the Nite-Owl what has been happening to his father. His current whereabouts are unknown.

*HENRY PARMALEE.* Owner of the Nite-Owl, Parmalee is horrified by Timmy Grenadine's story and convinced to go out in a snowstorm to check it out. Though he is armed with a gun, the outcome of his battle with Richie Grenadine remains unknown.

## "BATTLEGROUND"

A hit man assassinates the owner of a toy company, only to have the victim's mother send him a box of toy soldiers that are somehow—perhaps through supernatural means—alive and determined to murder him.

### PRIMARY SUBJECTS

*JOHN RENSHAW.* Renshaw is a professional assassin in the employ of a syndicate of organized crime figures. His career is cut short when the mother of his most recent target decides to retaliate. Renshaw is murdered by the living toy soldiers sent by Mrs. Morris.

*HANS MORRIS.* Owner of the Morris Toy Company, Morris is assassinated by John Renshaw.

*MRS. MORRIS.* Hans Morris's mother, she sends living toys to take revenge upon her son's killer.

*TOY SOLDIERS.* While the soldiers' sentience is never explained, it seems there are two possibilities. Either they are tiny, finely manufactured, artificially intelligent, robots, or they are invested with supernatural life and intelligence.

## "SOMETIMES THEY COME BACK"

A high school English teacher is terrified to discover that the teenagers who murdered his brother when they were kids all later died violently. They have now returned as demonic yet incarnate spirits to dispose of him.

## PRIMARY SUBJECTS

*JIM NORMAN*. In 1957, when Jim was nine and his older brother, Wayne, was twelve, they were assaulted by a group of older bullies. Wayne Norman was murdered as he screamed at Jim to flee. Decades later Jim, now a schoolteacher, suffers from recurring nightmares. After he begins teaching at Davis High, some of his students die mysteriously, and the new students who fill their vacant seats turn out to be the demonic spirits of the boys who killed his brother years earlier. He is forced to call uon the spirit of his deceased sibling to defend him once again. Jim Norman's current whereabouts are unknown.

*WAYNE NORMAN*. Jim's older brother, Wayne was murdered at the age of twelve.

*VINNIE COREY, DAVID GARCIA, and BOBBY LAWSON*. Three teenage thugs who murdered Wayne Norman in 1957. Later, they each died a violent death, and eventually return as spirits to torment and attempt to kill Jim Norman. Their spirits are destroyed or returned to their rightful resting place.

*RAISING DEMONS*. The book used by Jim Norman to find the spell that he uses to raise the spirit of his brother, Wayne.

## "STRAWBERRY SPRING"

A man tells the story of a series of murders that took place on the campus of New Sharon Teachers' College, located in an unnamed American city, while he was a student there. He then relates a series of recent murders that seem to be the work of the same killer, whom the authorities dub Springheel Jack.

## PRIMARY SUBJECT

*SPRINGHEEL JACK*. A vicious serial murderer who turns out to be the narrator of this chilling tale. His current whereabouts are unknown.

## "THE LAWNMOWER MAN"

A man reluctant to mow his own lawn hires a lawn care service and gets more than he bargains for when a mysterious, barely human figure with a sentient lawnmower arrives to do the job.

### PRIMARY SUBJECTS

*HAROLD PARKETTE.* Not wanting to mow his own lawn, Harold hires the lawnmower man. Eventually, the lawnmower man orders his supernaturally intelligent mower to kill Harold, and the lawnmower mulches him.

*THE LAWNMOWER MAN.* A cloven-hoofed worshiper of the god Pan, the lawnmower man follows his mower around in the nude and eats all the grass clippings. He later murders Harold Parkette for being an unbeliever and threatening to call the police.

---

*The powers of Ed Hamner in "I Know What You Need" are similar to those of the main character in a classic* Twilight Zone *episode that might have inspired King to write this story. Its title? "What You Need."*

## "I KNOW WHAT YOU NEED"

A young woman discovers that the man she has been dating has been obsessed with her since childhood and has used voodoo to force her to fall in love with him.

### PRIMARY SUBJECTS

*LIZ HOGAN.* Liz is a college student whose boyfriend, Ed Hamner, has been magically manipulating her and has also committed murder. She manages to break free of him, but is left with a great deal of self-doubt. Her current whereabouts are unknown.

*ED HAMNER.* Since boyhood, Ed has had special mental powers that allow him to read the minds and needs of those around him, and simply to know things otherwise impossible for him to know. Not only does he cause the deaths of his own parents, but he also is responsible for the death of Liz Hogan's previous boyfriend. His current whereabouts are unknown.

## "CHILDREN OF THE CORN"

A young couple on a cross-country trip come upon a town whose children have slaughtered all the adults at the behest of a demonic presence that lives in the cornfields of Gatlin, Nebraska.

### PRIMARY SUBJECTS

**BURT ROBESON.** When a dead boy is thrown in front of his car on a Nebraska highway, Burt insists that he and his wife go to the nearest town. There, they are captured by the children of the corn and sacrificed to their dark god.

*At the opening of the film version of* Children of the Corn, *the main characters are driving along a deserted road in Nebraska. On their dashboard is a paperback copy of* Night Shift.

**VICKY ROBESON.** When the Robesons run over a dead boy on the highway, Vicky wants to backtrack to the last major town they had passed through, and leave the body there. Burt insists they go on. Like her husband, Vicky is crucified by the children of the corn and offered up as a sacrifice.

**HE WHO WALKS BEHIND THE ROWS.** The demonic presence worshiped by the children of the corn. It is presumed that he *still* walks behind the rows.

## "THE LAST RUNG ON THE LADDER"

Upon discovering that his sister, Kitty, has killed herself, Larry recalls the childhood day when he saved his sister's life. Now he feels a great deal of guilt for not having been there for her in the end.

## "THE MAN WHO LOVED FLOWERS"

A serial murderer who uses a hammer as his weapon of choice buys flowers for a long-lost love and confuses his victims with his old flame. He presents the flowers to his victim before he strikes. It is presumed he is still at large.

## "THE WOMAN IN THE ROOM"

A man assists in the suicide of his disease-ravaged mother at the Central Maine Hospital in Lewiston.

> *"The Woman in the Room" was likely influenced and certainly informed by King's own deeply personal and traumatic experience: his mother's death from cancer.*

*Note:* Discussions of several remaining stories from *Night Shift* can be found elsewhere in this book. "Jerusalem's Lot," "Graveyard Shift," and "One for the Road" are discussed in section four. "The Ledge" and "Quitters, Inc." are covered in section seven. "Night Surf" is addressed in section one. For the story "Trucks," see p. 443.

### ADAPTATIONS

*Night Shift* has the distinction of having spawned more film and television projects than any other King collection to date.

In 1983, Granite Entertainment produced a direct-to-video release containing two short films based on "The Bogeyman" and "The Woman in the Room." Entitled *Stephen King's Night Shift Collection*, it is perhaps most notable for the fact that the latter tale was adapted and directed by Frank Darabont, who would go on to adapt and direct both *The Shawshank Redemption* (1994) and *The Green Mile* (1999).

The following year, actor Peter Horton *(Thirtysomething)* and *Terminator* star Linda Hamilton appeared in the screen version of *Children of the Corn*, which has spawned countless (and increasingly only vaguely related) sequels.

The 1985 feature film *Cat's Eye*, directed by Lewis Teague, incorporated two tales from this collection. "Quitters, Inc." starred James Woods and Alan King, while "The Ledge" featured *Airplane* actor Robert Hays. (See p. 327 for a discussion of this film, which was scripted by King.)

Released in 1987, *Maximum Overdrive* was at that point the only movie written and directed by King, who adapted the screenplay from his short story "Trucks." The R-rated thriller featured Emilio Estevez, Pat Hingle (*Batman's* Commissioner Gordon) and Yeardley Smith (the voice of Lisa Simpson on *The Simpsons*) and is not to be confused with the 1997 cable television version of *Trucks*, which headlined Timothy Busfield *(The West Wing)*.

> *"The Lawnmower Man" was adapted by King and Walt Simonson in 1981 for the black-and-white Marvel Comics maga-*zine Bizarre Adventures. *Save for the stories in* Creepshow, *which was published in a comics version as a tie-in with the film's 1982 release, "Lawnmower Man" stands with "Popsy"—adapted for Innovation Comics' horror anthol-*ogy Masques—*as the only such adaptation of King's work.*

Paramount Pictures released *Stephen King's "Graveyard Shift"* in 1990. It was based on the wild story of the same name and starring popular character actor Brad Dourif.

The year 1991 brought the made-for-television version of *Sometimes They Come Back*, starring Tim Matheson and Brooke Adams. The release led to several direct-to-video sequels.

Lest we forget, 1992's *The Lawnmower Man* was named after—and purported to be based on—King's short story of the same name. However, the sci-fi thriller shared so little with the original story that King successfully sued to have his name removed from the project, which didn't stop the producers from making a sequel, even without an official King connection to exploit.

# 34

## *Creepshow*

---

NEITHER A NOVEL nor a short story collection the two incarnations of *Creepshow* (1982) are as a motion picture and as a graphic novel.

The film version consists of five stories, plus a sort of prologue and epilogue featuring a character called the Creep, whose resemblance to *Tales from the Crypt's* Cryptkeeper only solidifies the relationship the stories have to such classic 1950s horror anthology comics as *Tales from the Crypt* and *Vault of Horror.* Thus it is only fitting that the published version of *Creepshow* was presented in comic-book form. Released shortly after the film opened, it featured art by legendary horror comics master Berni Wrightson (who later provided the illustrations for *Cycle of the Werewolf*).

Two of the stories in the film have their origins in text form. "The Lonesome Death of Jordy Verrill" began life in the mid-1970s as a short story published in a pair of men's magazines, *Cavalier* and *Nugget,* both of which were repositories for many early King stories. "The Crate" first appeared in *Gallery* magazine. Both have the kind of structure and twist ending that were typical of the comics King read and loved as a young man.

*Creepshow* was conceived as a kind of "living" version of those horror anthology comics. In addition to creating the Creep, King added three brand-new stories to the script: "Father's Day," "Something to Tide You Over," and "They're Creeping Up on You." King also altered the two previously published stories used in the picture. Most notably, and particularly for our purposes, King moved Jordy Verrill's small town from New Hampshire to Maine, only several miles away from Castle Rock, a major component of the King universe.

It is these revised versions that we discuss in this chapter. Since the *Creepshow* screenplay was written by King, we consider the film's script to be the official continuity.

## "THE LONESOME DEATH OF JORDY VERRILL"

In this story (a.k.a. "Weeds") a slow-witted farmer discovers a meteor on his property. He believes, at first, that he will be able to sell it for a great deal of money. However, when he attempts to retrieve it from the hole it made on his farm, he burns himself. Worse, the meteor infects him with a spore or virus of some kind that causes green weeds to grow wildly over everything, including his own flesh.

### PRIMARY SUBJECTS

*JORDY VERRILL.* Jordy is the doomed and none-too bright farmer. He has what he calls "Verrill luck," which is all bad. After being infected by the "meteor shit," Jordy commits suicide by blowing off his head with a shotgun.

*THE METEOR SHIT.* Whatever it is that comes out of the meteor continues growing all over Jordy Verrill's farm, five miles from Castle Rock. If this is the same Castle Rock seen in other stories, and not some alternate dimension, we must presume that the spread of the infection was somehow interrupted. However, the manner of that interruption and its permanence are unknown at this time.

## "FATHER'S DAY"

A cruel old man, murdered by his much-beleaguered daughter, returns from the grave seven years later to take vengeance upon her and the rest of his cold-hearted family.

## PRIMARY SUBJECTS

*BEDELIA GRANTHAM.* After caring for her ungrateful father, Nathan, for thirty years, Bedelia is finally driven over the edge when Nathan arranges the murder of her fiancé. On Father's Day, Bedelia crushes her father's skull with a glass ashtray. Each subsequent year, she returns on that day to dine with her family and visit her father's grave. Seven years after she killed him, Nathan returns from the grave to kill his daughter and the rest of the family.

*NATHAN GRANTHAM.* A sadistic old man, Nathan is murdered by his daughter after arranging the "accidental" death of her fiancé. He comes back from the grave seven years later to kill her as well as numerous other family members. The current status of the resurrected corpse that was Nathan Grantham is unknown.

*PETER YARBRO.* An unfortunate man, Peter makes the mistake of becoming engaged to Bedelia Grantham. Unwilling to be separated from the daughter he treats as a slave, Bedelia's father, Nathan, has Peter murdered.

## "THE CRATE"

In June 1834, an explorer named Julia Carpenter sends a large crate from the Arctic to Horlicks University. Misplaced, the crate remains under a stairwell in Amberson Hall for more than a century and a half until it is discovered by a janitor. The janitor informs Professor Dexter Stanley, who hurries to Amberson Hall to open the crate. Inside, he and the janitor find a vicious monster who promptly eats the janitor and later a student.

## PRIMARY SUBJECTS

*HENRY NORTHRUP.* A much put-upon professor, Northrup learns of the monster in a crate from his colleague Dexter Stanley. He then leads his shrewish wife into a trap and she is devoured by the beast. Northrup's current whereabouts are unknown.

*WILMA NORTHRUP.* Wilma insists on being called Billie, right up until the time her husband—whom she has tormented and sneered at for years—traps her with the evil thing in the crate. Billie is consumed by the creature.

*PROFESSOR DEXTER STANLEY.* Stanley is the one who actually opens the crate containing the monster, an action that immediately results in the deaths of two people. Distraught, he tells Henry Northrup about it. Henry drugs him, proceeds to have the monster devour his wife, and traps the monster back in the crate. Later, Northrup and Stanley make a pact of mutual silence. His current whereabouts are unknown.

*THE MONSTER IN THE CRATE.* After this evil creature kills three people, Henry Northrup manages to chain it again in the crate. The box is then dumped into Ryder's Quarry. However, Henry does not do a very good job. It seems likely that the monster has escaped, but its current whereabouts are unknown.

## "SOMETHING TO TIDE YOU OVER"

In a homicidal rage, Richard Vickers murders his wife and her lover by burying them up to their necks at the beach, and then letting the tide do them in. When he returns to find the bodies, they appear to have been swept out to sea. They show up, however, as undead creatures ready to dispatch him the way he disposed of them.

### PRIMARY SUBJECTS

*HARRY WENTWORTH.* Harry is murdered by the enraged husband of his lover, Becky Vickers. After their deaths, the lovers return from their watery grave to take vengeance.

*BECKY VICKERS.* Killed for her infidelity, Becky comes back from the dead to get even with her husband.

*RICHARD VICKERS.* After eliminating his cheating wife and her lover by burying them up to their necks on the beach and waiting for the tide to come in, Richard is killed in the same manner by his resurrected victims.

## "THEY'RE CREEPING UP ON YOU"

A fabulously rich recluse, Upson Pratt is a soulless businessman who destroys lives without remorse. He is also obsessed with his environment, keeping his home perfectly white, very neat, and almost completely sterile. When an army of cockroaches shows up in force during a blackout, it drives him over the edge.

### PRIMARY SUBJECT

*UPSON PRATT.* Obsessed with hygiene, Pratt particularly hates insects, especially cockroaches, which begin to proliferate in his seemingly sterile apartment. Perhaps it is some kind of cosmic payback for the life of cruelty Pratt has led, as thousands of cockroaches enter his body and take up residence in his hollowed-out corpse.

### ADAPTATIONS

In October 1982, Warner Bros. released *Creepshow,* written by King and directed by horror veteran (and personal friend) George A. Romero. The producer was Richard Rubinstein, whose Laurel Entertainment would later produce *Tales from the Darkside.* The film's special effects were created by another horror vet, Tom Savini.

*Savini also appears as a garbage man in a cameo at the end of this movie.*

The five stories in the picture are bookended by a brief framing sequence in which a young boy is seen reading *Creepshow* the comic book, only to have it taken away by his mother.

The 120-minute film features an array of stellar talent in brief appearances. "Father's Day" stars Viveca Lindfors as Aunt Bedelia and Ed Harris in the small role of Hank Blaine. "Something to Tide You

Over" showcases Leslie Nielsen as Richard Vickers and Ted Danson as Harry Wentworth. "The Crate" has Hal Holbrook as Harry Northrup, Adrienne Barbeau as Billie Northrup, and Fritz Weaver as Dexter Stanley. Finally, "They're Creeping Up on You" features veteran actor E. G. Marshall as Upson Pratt. King himself appears as the title character in "The Lonesome Death of Jordy Verrill."

While the R-rated release was by no means a blockbuster at the box office, it did well enough to spawn a sequel in 1987. The aptly titled *Creepshow 2* (1987) was written (but not directed) by Romero and was based on stories by King. However, only "The Raft" is based on a published King story. The other two installments, "Old Chief Wood'nhead" and "The Hitchhiker" are apparently stories initially developed by King and later scripted by Romero.

Plans for *Creepshow 3* never reached the production stage.

> *The boy, Billy, in* Creepshow *is played by Joe King, son of the author.*

> *In* Creepshow 2, *King has a cameo as a truck driver, and his longtime assistant, Shirley Sonderegger, plays Mrs. Cavenaugh.*

# 35

## *Different Seasons*

---

O F  T H E  F O U R novellas in *Different Seasons* (1982), a collection
that marked another turning point in Stephen King's career,
three are specifically *not* horror stories, though one, *Apt Pupil,* is certainly disturbingly horrific. Given that the author had been crowned
the "king" of horror and was expected to write nothing else, producing such mainstream work—and in novella form—was indeed a risk.
Fortunately, it was a gamble that was eagerly embraced by the public.
Though novellas are generally considered by publishers to be difficult
to market in book form, they are the perfect length for development
into dramas for the screen.

In some ways, the entries included here are the best loved of
King's writing to date. That might at first seem hard to accept. Fans
love *The Stand* (1978) and *The Shining* (1977), among others. But the
films *The Shawshank Redemption* (1994), *Apt Pupil* (1998), and *Stand by
Me* (1986) all originated from this material, with *Shawshank* and *Stand
by Me* receiving Oscar nominations. *Different Seasons* has reached one
of the broadest audiences and received perhaps the best response of all
of King's works.

### "APT PUPIL"

Without a doubt, *Apt Pupil* is the dark heart of this remarkable collection and among the grimmest pieces King has ever written. Just as

304

he has subverted so many long-accepted conventions of Americana over the years, here King takes a small-town conceit and relationship worthy of Norman Rockwell and inverts it, turning the innocence of that *Saturday Evening Post* image into a perversely insightful study of evil.

*Apt Pupil* is the story of Todd Bowden, a practical, above-average student with a sense of humor and natural athletic ability. He's every parent's dream child, except for the fact that he has a weird, unwholesome fascination for all things related to Nazi Germany and the Holocaust. When Todd recognizes an old man on the bus as the former commander of a Nazi death camp who is living in hiding in rural California (where the novella is set), Todd's response is not at all that of a normal teen.

He doesn't confide in his friends. He doesn't tell his parents. He doesn't inform the police. Instead, he is thrilled by his discovery. Todd uses his extensive knowledge to blackmail the Nazi, Kurt Dussander, into sharing with him the horrible stories of his past, down to the last nasty detail. Like a hideous Peeping Tom, Todd gets a rush from all of this morbid activity.

Meanwhile, his optimistic, conventional parents see only the Norman Rockwell side of things. From their point of view, Todd is a good kid, spending time reading to an elderly man who is losing his sight. What could be more a part of the American myth? Meanwhile, when Todd's promising academic career starts falling apart, he dares not tell his parents, and proceeds to confide in and rely on Dussander.

What begins as a strange obsession and a blackmail scheme begins to evolve. Spurred on by the evil nature of what they share, Todd and Dussander each turn to murder and eventually trap each other in a web of lies. Because of their shared guilt, neither can inform on the other. In the end, Dussander has a heart attack and is later recognized by a man who had been incarcerated at the death camp where the Nazi was commandant. After the truth hits the news, Todd is visited by Ed French, the school counselor whom Dussander helped him deceive. Todd kills the counselor before retreating to a tree above a nearby highway, where he fires upon cars passing below for hours before police sharpshooters take him down.

Like *Rage* (1977), one of the half dozen novels King wrote under the Richard Bachman pseudonym, *Apt Pupil* showcases harrowing behavior by a high school student. In today's climate, when the Columbine tragedy and other events involving teens and guns have become all too common in real life, we have become greatly sensitized. *Apt Pupil* is far more complex than the acts of violence described therein, yet it is easy to let the violence overshadow the story and themes King is trying to tell. There is rage in many young people. But what causes them to turn to violence and murder? There is no single answer.

In the case of *Apt Pupil,* it seems clear that Todd Bowden is genuinely a bad seed, a mind ripe for twisting. Evil may lurk within him the way it lingers in the Marsten house in *'Salem's Lot* (1975) or in the Overlook Hotel in *The Shining.*

*In* Apt Pupil, *Ed French attends a conference and stays in room 217 at a Holiday Inn. That's the number of the room in which the ghost of an old woman tries to kill Danny Torrance at the Overlook Hotel in* The Shining.

Bowden is evil, not merely misguided or misunderstood, as it appears he may be at the outset. It is unusual in a King book for a mere human being to be so unrepentantly sinister, but that is attributable to the exploratory nature of this narrative.

## PRIMARY SUBJECTS

*TODD BOWDEN.* A California high school student, Todd discovers that Nazi death camp commander Kurt Dussander is living in the boy's hometown under an assumed name. Obsessed with the Holocaust, Todd blackmails Dussander into sharing his horrifying memories, and the two enter into a symbiotic relationship that leads them each to commit murder. After Dussander's death, Todd takes a rifle up into a tree overlooking the highway and fires at cars passing below. He is killed by police sharpshooters.

*ARTHUR DENKER (a.k.a. KURT DUSSANDER).* Under his Denker alias, Dussander has created a new life for himself in America after having spent years as a death camp commander in Nazi Germany.

When Todd discovers his true identity, Dussander must confront a past he has tried to escape. In doing so, he finds himself compelled to commit more atrocities. After suffering a heart attack, he is hospitalized and shares a room with a survivor of the camp, who recognizes him and turns him in. Dussander commits suicide in the hospital.

> *Kurt Dussander has made quite a bit of money from a stock portfolio set up for him by Andy Dufresne, whom we met in "Rita Hayworth and Shawshank Redemption."*

*EDWARD FRENCH.* As Todd Bowden's guidance counselor, French is taken in by a ruse conceived by Todd and Dussander: when Todd's grades start to fall, Dussander pretends to be the boy's grandfather and speaks to French on Todd's behalf. When Dussander dies, French realizes the deception and would have revealed the truth if Todd had not murdered him first.

*MORRIS HEISEL.* A survivor of the Nazi death camps, Heisel recognizes his one-time tormentor, Dussander, when he sees him in the hospital. Heisel's current whereabouts are unknown.

## "THE BREATHING METHOD"

It is appropriate that "The Breathing Method" is dedicated to Peter Straub and his wife, since the fundamental conceit owes so much to Straub. Like the Chowder Society in Straub's masterpiece *Ghost Story* (1979), King introduces a men's club dedicated to the telling of tales. On the wall is a plaque that reads: IT IS THE TALE, NOT HE WHO TELLS IT.

King has put his own imprint on this premise. On the shelves of the club are volumes of masterful prose and poetry by writers the narrator has never heard of, published by houses that don't exist. The building itself, an old brownstone, seems to have endless rooms in which people become lost forever. The butler, the *de facto* host of the club, is named Stephens, perhaps after King himself.

Are those rooms pathways to other dimensions? Perhaps. Is each door a "thinny," introduced in the *Dark Tower* series (1982–)? That seems likely. Suffice to say it could be a setting for a great many of King's tales.

King introduces the reader to a man named David Adley, who has achieved moderate success in his firm but knows he will rise no further. When his boss invites him to an exclusive men's club, Adley thinks it may be a step up. On that count, he is disappointed. However, Adley is drawn into the enigmatic group of men who gather at the club to tell stories around the fire. Though

> *"The Man Who Would Not Shake Hands" from* Skeleton Crew *takes place in the same brownstone.*

a "weird tale" is always told at Christmas, the stories are usually not sinister or even supernatural.

The one exception is the tale related by Dr. Emlyn McCarron: the narrative of Sandra Stansfield and the breathing method. It is worth noting that thus far this is the one piece in this collection that has not been filmed. Nor is it likely to be, given the hideousness of the conclusion, in which a woman who has been decapitated continues to breathe for many minutes in order to give birth to her child.

It seems likely that King will revisit the club in the future. As Stevens says, "there are always more tales."

## PRIMARY SUBJECTS

*DAVID ADLEY.* Adley is a middle-management drone. He becomes a member of the club after being invited by a senior partner at his firm. It is presumed that he still holds the same position at the company.

*EMLYN McCARRON.* McCarron is a doctor and a member of the club. One night, he relates his experiences with Sandra Stansfield, a young single woman who had become pregnant, and to whom he had taught "the breathing method," a practice much maligned in its time, but which McCarron heartily endorses. Though retired, it is presumed that McCarron is still a member of the club.

*SANDRA STANSFIELD.* A young single woman, Stansfield becomes pregnant by a man who deserts her, and she seeks Dr. Emlyn

McCarron's help. When she is about to deliver, she jumps into a taxi and rushes to the hospital. The cab is involved in an accident, and Sandra is decapitated. Somehow, she continues to breathe through her severed windpipe for the duration of time it takes McCarron to safely deliver her child, and then she dies.

*STEVENS.* The butler at the club. It is presumed that he still holds that position; he may, in fact, hold it forever.

*Note:* The remaining two novellas in *Different Seasons*, and their film adaptations, are discussed in other chapters: For "The Body," see section three. For "Rita Hayworth and Shawshank Redemption," see section four.

*Outside King's high school* | DAVID LOWELL

### ADAPTATIONS

Of the four tales collected in *Different Seasons*, three have been made into feature films. The first of these, *Stand by Me* (based on "The Body"), was released by Columbia Pictures in 1986. *The Shawshank*

*Redemption* was adapted and directed by Frank Darabont, who would later bring *The Green Mile* to the screen in 1999.

If *Stand by Me* is about hope and *The Shawshank Redemption* is about the triumph of the spirit, then *Apt Pupil* is the antithesis of both. A TriStar picture starring Ian McKellen as Kurt Dussander and Brad Renfro as Todd Bowden, this 1998 drama was directed by Bryan Singer *(The Usual Suspects, X-Men).* Though there are a number of major differences between the text and the screen adaptation (primarily in the number of murders committed by each character), the essence of the novella remains the same. A notable exception is the ending. Rather than send Todd up into a tree to shoot at passing cars until he himself is shot down, director Singer shows Todd mentally intimidating the one man who can reveal his secret, threatening to destroy him with rumor and innuendo. As depicted onscreen, Todd is much more consciously evil than in the book. This switch, while making the ending less brutal, achieves the impossible: it makes the ending even darker.

> *Before the 1998 screen version, an earlier adaptation of* Apt Pupil *was planned and even began filming with* NYPD Blue's *Rick Schroder as Todd Bowden, and* Excalibur's *Nicol Williamson as Dussander. The film was abandoned when financing fell through.*

The critical success of these three films has contributed to the growing perception of *Different Seasons* as a seminal work in King's career.

# 36

## *Christine*

A S  WE  ALL  KNOW, the classic love-affair formula is boy meets girl, boy gets girl, boy loses girl. But in today's popular culture, we have seen a common variation on that theme: boy sees car, boy buys car, boy falls in love with car, and both live happily ever after to a rock 'n' roll soundtrack. Oddly enough, in the mythology of twentieth-century America, men can rely far more on their automobiles than they can on true love with a living, breathing human being.

In *Christine* (1983), King takes that bizarre notion and twists it into the heights of perversity. It is a novel of obsession and hauntings, of teenage lust and high school angst. If this story line were pitched in Hollywood, it would be *Carrie* meets *The Shining* . . . with cars.

Cars are everywhere in the book. To nearly all the characters—save for its protagonist and narrator, Dennis Guilder—cars are vitally important. It's a wonder that the plotline is set in the Pittsburgh suburb of Libertyville, instead of somewhere outside of Detroit. King grew up in New England in the late 1950s and early 1960s, when a flashy car was everything to a teenage boy. It still is today, though other things have since become almost as crucial. So it's no surprise that the status symbol coveted by all the males in the story—teenagers and adults alike—is a fine automobile.

The exception is Dennis Guilder, who is sufficiently mature to look askance at this kind of posturing. Unfortunately, his best friend, Arnie Cunningham, not only partakes of this, but also embraces it.

Arnie becomes a contorted funhouse-mirror image of what the average American male's obsession with cars looks like to someone who doesn't share that passion.

But, it really isn't Arnie's fault. He's a lonely, pimply-faced kid lusting after the smart, pretty girl in school whom he thinks barely notices him. His best friend is Dennis, a handsome jock to whom Arnie is just the sad sidekick.

Until Arnie meets Christine, a 1958 red Plymouth Fury. In reality, she's a pile of junk, but she calls out to him, seduces him. He can see in her a vision of what she should be, and buys her in order to restore that beauty. Arnie believes that he also has that beauty and specialness within himself, and he sees restoring Christine as a way to bring it out.

Christine isn't your average automobile. She's possessed by the corrupt spirit of her first owner, Roland LeBay. He's a vicious man, and he plays Arnie wonderfully, manipulating him until his insecurities have made him so desperate and cruel that he almost becomes evil himself. Fortunately, Arnie is eventually redeemed. Sadly, it comes too late.

Perhaps more than any other of King's works, *Christine* is also a paean to rock music. As a musician and radio station owner himself, there's no doubt that music is important to the author. Here, King puts music in perspective as part of the high school experience. Each segment of the narrative begins with a quote from a classic rock song. More than that, when Christine (or, more accurately, the ghost of LeBay) goes out on the prowl to punish those who've wronged Arnie, the music pouring from the car's speakers is the music of the period in which the auto was built.

The theme of evil possession is also present in King's masterpiece of a haunting, *The Shining* (1977). Like the malevolent auto in *Christine*, the Overlook Hotel (and the Marsten house of 1975's *'Salem's Lot*) is not only inhabited by the spirits of the damned, but in a real, tangible way, it is also possessed by a greater, more distinct evil. In *Christine*, this presence is never truly elaborated on. (In *The Shining*, however, the evil is actually seen rising in the firecloud above the exploding hotel.)

*Christine, Salem's Lot,* and *The Shining* present their malignancy as a collaboration between seemingly ancient, preternatural evil and simple human cruelty and corruption. The lingering malignance is created, in all three novels, by that collaboration of ethereal malevolence, human weakness, and, interestingly, the creations of humanity: a car, a house, a hotel. This combination recurs frequently within King's work, where events conspire to make an object the focus of both mortal and immortal evil. Further, the human weakness on display plays itself out in the form of obsession: Arnie Cunningham's fixation on Christine; Jack Torrance's mania involving the hotel, his job, and the play he's trying to write; Ben Mears's preoccupation with the Marsten house. (In the latter case, Ben turns his obsession into positive action, rather than descending into insanity as do Arnie and Jack.)

Yet another similarity is that each of these characters' obsessions reflects the warped passion of a predecessor. Arnie takes the place of Roland LeBay. Jack takes the place of Delbert Grady, former caretaker of the hotel, who murdered his entire family with an ax. Both of them still exist as ghosts within their respective man-made hosts. In 'Salem's Lot, things are different. Ben Mears does not replace Hubie Marsten, the obsessed, evil man who killed his wife and himself in his home. Rather, he sets himself against Marsten's heinous legacy.

*Christine* also focuses on the horrors of high school. Arnie is a loser on the same scale as the title character in *Carrie* and suffers many of the same kinds of injustices from his peers. Like Carrie's callous tormentors, *Christine's* Buddy Repperton and his cronies represent the worst that high school has to offer. The cruelty of the teens seems to bring in the form of the inescapable horrors that occur at the climaxes of both books. With its mix of pop culture and King's special brand of evil, *Christine* is a classic American ghost story.

## PRIMARY SUBJECTS

*ARNIE CUNNINGHAM.* A senior at Libertyville High School, Arnie is the quintessential sidekick. He speaks softly and minds his own business, as he tries to avoid getting picked on by his peers and hopes to live long enough to survive high school. He loves Leigh Cabot, but he doesn't have the courage to ask her out until he buys Christine, a red 1958 Plymouth Fury. Arnie's new car changes him in more ways than one. At first, he seems more confident. He dates Leigh for a bit. The car has given Arnie the boost he needs to feel good about himself. Or so it seems.

But Christine has wrought other changes in Arnie. His appearance changes. His pimply face clears up, and he carries himself differently. His best friend, Dennis Guilder, takes note of this and finds over time that he really doesn't like the new Arnie, and eventually neither does Leigh.

Arnie literally is not himself. He has been manipulated and at times possessed by the malignant ghost of Roland LeBay, the first owner of Christine. In the end, Arnie sees what he has done to his life and how much he has hurt the people he loves the most. He wrests control of himself from LeBay one final time and attempts to save his mother's life. It is a failed attempt, and both Arnie and his mother are killed.

*CHRISTINE.* A 1958 Plymouth Fury, Christine was built on the assembly line in Detroit, and she was born bad. There was something evil about her from the beginning, a supernatural force that reaches out to hurt those it comes into contact with. Christine's first owner was Roland LeBay, an Army veteran. LeBay was a cruel man who prized his car more than anything. Upon his death—shortly after selling Christine to Arnie Cunningham—his spirit merges with the car, combining his cruelty with Christine's already considerable evil.

Arnie is tainted by Christine's evil and LeBay's presence as well. After local toughs led by Buddy Repperton vandalize Christine, the car sets out on its own at night, hunting them down and killing them. Eventually, in an effort to put an end to the evil, Arnie's friends, Dennis Guilder and Leigh Cabot, use an enormous sewage truck to crush Christine into scrap. Later, she is destroyed in a compactor at a junkyard.

That may not be the end. Out in California, a kid named Sandy Galton, who had helped the bullies vandalize Christine, is struck and killed by a car. Dennis Guilder wonders if the murderer is Christine, and fears she still might be coming for him.

*DENNIS GUILDER.* The most valuable player on the football team at Libertyville High, Dennis isn't the average jock. His relationship with Arnie Cunningham proves that. Dennis is handsome, athletic, and outgoing, whereas Arnie is none of those things. Yet they have been friends since grade school. Dennis is Arnie's protector and tries to be his voice of reason when things in Arnie's life get out of control. Despite their outward differences, both are intelligent young men, and their friendship means more than the prejudices of high school or the cruelties of teenage life.

Things have always been easier for Dennis than for Arnie. Both are enamored of the same girl, Leigh Cabot, but Arnie doesn't believe he stands a chance if Dennis is his competition. When Arnie begins to change thanks to Christine's influence, he finds the courage to ask Leigh out, and she says yes.

Over time, however, both Leigh and Dennis have to deal with the further changes in Arnie and the way his obsession with Christine has twisted him. As a result, the two of them are drawn together and eventually fall in love. Together, Dennis and Leigh destroy Christine—or at least believe they have.

Presently, Dennis Guilder remains in Libertyville, where he is a high school teacher. He still fears that one day Christine may return to unleash vengeance upon him.

**ROLAND LeBAY.** Born and raised in Libertyville, Pennsylvania, LeBay was a misanthrope all his life. A cruel individual, he was a sociopath who despised other people. But he understood cars. In the Army, he was a mechanic known for his ability to fix anything. When he bought Christine in 1958, it was a match made in hell. The car was evil, and LeBay's natural hatred of people fed the auto, just as it fed him.

Some twenty years later, LeBay sells Christine to a local teenager named Arnie Cunningham. Shortly thereafter, he dies, at least physically. His spirit, however, merges with Christine, and together the two of them change and possess Arnie. In the end, when Christine is destroyed, LeBay's spirit flees the vehicle. He tries to fully possess Arnie himself, but Arnie fights him. The struggle takes place in a speeding car, resulting in an accident that takes Arnie's life and that of his mother, Regina.

It is presumed that without a host, Roland LeBay's spirit has gone to its final reward, or final punishment as the case may be.

*LEIGH (CABOT) ACKERMAN.* A senior at Libertyville High, Leigh has the misfortune to become the girlfriend of Arnie Cunningham and the object of Roland LeBay's obsession. Leigh cares for Arnie a great deal, but soon comes to realize that his fixation on his car is unhealthy. Along with Arnie's best friend, Dennis Guilder, Leigh realizes something supernatural is at work. With Dennis, she aids in the destruction of Christine.

For a time afterward, Leigh and Dennis remain a couple. Eventually, however, they split and Leigh marries another. She settles in Taos, New Mexico, where she still lives with her husband and their twin girls.

*WILL DARNELL.* The owner of Darnell's Garage, where Arnie Cunningham restores and garages Christine, Darnell is a common criminal. He uses his operation to smuggle drugs, among other things, inside cars. When Arnie is arrested, Darnell lets him take the fall. In vengeance, Christine kills Darnell.

*BUDDY REPPERTON.* The most notorious member of Arnie's class at Libertyville High, Buddy is the leader of a group of students who frequently abuse Arnie. When Arnie begins to change and grow more confident—and less fearful of Buddy—Repperton and his friends vandalize Christine. For that act, Christine forces Buddy's car off the road, and Buddy and several of his friends die in the ensuing crash.

*SANDY GALTON.* Though Sandy doesn't participate in the assault on Christine, he is the one who tells Buddy where the car can be found, and lets them into the airport parking lot where the attack occurs. Although Sandy appears to have escaped Christine's vengeance, it is later reported that he has been struck and killed by a hit-and-run driver in California. Dennis Guilder believes Christine has somehow returned and is responsible for Sandy Galton's death.

*VERONICA and RITA LeBAY.* The wife and young daughter of Roland LeBay, both die while inside Christine. Rita chokes to death. Veronica's death appears to be suicide, but Dennis Guilder believes Christine murdered her.

## ADAPTATION

Just in time for Christmas in 1983, Columbia Pictures released the motion picture version of *Christine*. Despite the marquee value of the Stephen King name, the film was marketed as "John Carpenter's Christine." Carpenter, director of *Halloween* (1978), *The Fog* (1980) and *Escape From New York* (1981) among other films, clearly had his own box-office appeal, but the billing seemed awkward nevertheless.

Produced by Carpenter's longtime collaborators Richard Kobritz, and adapted to the screen by Bill Phillips, the 111-minute movie remained relatively faithful to the original novel. Keith Gordon, who would later become a director himself, plays the doomed Arnie Cunningham, and John Stockwell is Dennis Guilder.

*Alexandra Paul, who plays Leigh Cabot in the film, went on to co-star in the most-watched television series in the world, Baywatch, in the 1990s. Kelly Preston plays the relatively minor role of Roseanne, a girl Dennis Guilder briefly dates. In an odd confluence of events, the novel describes Dennis and Roseanne going to see the movie Grease (1978), which stars John Travolta, who is married in real life to Kelly Preston. Travolta played Billy Nolan in Carrie (1976).*

The film version met with mediocre reviews and unimpressive box office, but continues to survive in the eternity of video.

# 37

## *Skeleton Crew*

---

SEVEN YEARS AFTER the publication of *Night Shift*, in 1985, Stephen King released a second short-story collection titled *Skeleton Crew*. He penned both an introduction and a chapter of story notes for the volume, both of which give readers valuable insight into the mind of the author. As King states in his introduction, the tales span a long period in his life. The oldest, "The Reaper's Image," was created shortly after he graduated high school in 1966. The newest, "The Ballad of the Flexible Bullet," was composed in 1983.

The volume's contents reflect King's change in fortune since his first collection, especially in the markets now available to him. The majority of the entries in *Night Shift* had first appeared in slick men's magazines like *Cavalier, Penthouse,* and *Gallery*. Some of the stories featured in *Skeleton Crew* were first published in men's magazines as well, but in more reputable and better-paying publications such as *Playboy*. An examination of the book's copyright page reveals King's growing influence on the horror genre: several of the stories had also appeared in Kirby McCauley's landmark *Dark Forces: New Stories of Suspense and Supernatural Horror,* (1980), *Rod Serling's The Twilight Zone Magazine,* the revived *Weird Tales,* and assorted volumes of Charles L. Grant's critically acclaimed *Shadows* anthologies from the early 1980s.

The collection, which features twenty stories and two poems, contains an epigram that reads, "Do you love?" Variations of the phrase show up three times in the collection, first in "Nona" (the title character poses the question to the narrator as he stands over the corpse of an ex-girlfriend), then in "The Raft" (Randy somewhat absurdly asks the oil slick creature the same question), and finally, most poignantly in "The Reach" (as the narrator inquires, "Do the dead sing? Do they love?").

> *A signed, limited edition of* Skeleton Crew *was published by Scream/Press in 1985. It reportedly sold out before the trade edition was published.*

## "HERE THERE BE TYGERS"

A chilling short story, this piece is all the more effective because King never explains how a tiger came to be in the boys' bathroom at the Acorn Street Grammar School.

### PRIMARY SUBJECTS

*CHARLES.* A third-grader who first encounters the tiger in the boys' restroom but manages to escape back to his homeroom.

*KENNY GRIFFIN.* A third-grader who is eaten by the tiger in the boys' restroom after being instructed by Miss Bird to check on Charles.

*MISS BIRD.* Charles's third-grade teacher scoffs at his assertion that there is a deadly tiger in the boys' restroom. Entering the restroom, she, too, is presumably killed by the tiger.

## "THE MONKEY"

This story takes a commonplace object—a toy—and turns it into something utterly terrifying. In this narrative, the object of terror is a mechanical wind-up monkey, the kind that clashes a pair of cymbals together. (King has told similar stories since, namely "Chattery Teeth," which appears in *Nightmares & Dreamscapes,* and "Chinga," a teleplay he co-wrote for *The X-Files* in the late 1990s. The first features a set of novelty windup teeth; the latter showcases a possessed doll.)

Hal Shelbourne was abandoned by his father at a young age. Searching through his father's effects one day, Hal discovers a mechanical monkey. He winds it up, and watches the cymbals clash. Shortly thereafter, the family babysitter, Beulah, is accidentally killed in a shootout. Then, in rapid succession, Hal loses the family dog, his best friend, and tragically his mother. Each time, the monkey's clashing cymbals preceded the death. Fearful of the toy, Hal throws it down a well. The toy resurfaces years later, scaring Hal out of his wits. Knowing its presence threatens the well-being of his family, Hal ties it down with weights and throws it into Crystal Lake, presumably destroying it forever. Unfortunately, it is reported that hundreds of fish died in the lake soon thereafter.

## "CAIN ROSE UP"

Originally published in the spring 1968 issue of *Ubris* (the literary magazine of the University of Maine at Orono), "Cain Rose Up" was inspired in part by Charles Whitman's killing spree at the University of Texas at Austin. In 1966, Whitman, a student, shot at people from the university's 300-foot tower. He killed fourteen and injured dozens more in about 90 minutes before he was shot and killed by Austin police. This type of story soon became a subgenre; Harlan Ellison's "Thrillkill" and others cover similar terrain. Sadly, acts of violence similar to those in these stories have become a fact of life in modern-day America.

Shortly after finals, Curt Garrish starts shooting people from his dorm room window. His motivation for doing so is never explained.

## "THE RAFT"

A tragic coming-of-age story, one in which all the principals succumb to the hypnotic callings of a carnivorous oil slick that makes its home in a Pennsylvania lake. King originally submitted this story to *Adam,* a men's magazine that published horror fiction at the time. The tale—then titled "The Float"—was accepted, and King was duly paid. Because it was *Adam's* policy to pay on publication, King assumes the story was published, even though the magazine folded soon thereafter and he never saw the story in print. Rewritten years later, its first official publication was in yet another men's magazine, *Gallery.*

### PRIMARY SUBJECT

*RANDY.* The narrator of the events that occur on the raft, Randy usually acquiesces to the whims of his best friend, Deke. When Deke suggests they commemorate the end of summer by taking a dip in an isolated Pennsylvania lake, Randy reluctantly agrees. The two pals take their girlfriends, Rachel and Laverne, with them. Diving into the lake, they swim out to a floating raft, where they are cornered by a sentient oil slick. Rachel, who makes the mistake of trying to touch it, is consumed when the creature surges onto her arm and pulls her in. Deke is next, literally pulled through a crack in the boards that make up the raft. After Laverne is taken, Randy is left with only the creature for company. He is slowly hypnotized by the colors that swirl in the living oil slick. Presumably, he succumbs and is consumed by the creature.

Adapted by writer-driector George A. Romero, "The Raft" was the most effective segment in the film *Creepshow 2* (1987), and starred Daniel Beer, Jeremy Green, Page Hannah, and Paul Satterfield.

## "WORD PROCESSOR OF THE GODS"

This story came about because of King's fascination one day with the Delete button on his keyboard.

English teacher Richard Hagstrom has always wondered how his sister-in-law, Belinda, could have married such a worthless, abusive drunk as his brother, Roger. Further, he marvels at how such a disjointed union could have produced such a wonderful child as his beloved nephew, Jonathan. Married to the shrewish Lina, and father to the loathsome Seth, Richard wonders why fate has screwed things up for him. Richard is heartbroken when Jon and Belinda are killed in an automobile accident caused by his drunken brother. All he has left of them are his memories and the homemade word processor Jon built for him before his death.

Richard is aghast to discover that the Delete and Execute buttons on his keyboard actually work in the most literal sense. Experimenting with a portrait, Richard makes it disappear, then brings it back merely by typing a phrase on his keyboard. Realizing the machine's potential, he next deletes his repulsive son and wife. He then types "I AM A MAN WHO LIVES ALONE EXCEPT FOR MY WIFE, BELINDA, AND MY SON, JONATHAN," and hits Execute. Although the machine is destroyed in the process, it still manages to alter reality, providing Richard with a new and much happier home life.

This story was adapted by Michael McDowell (who would later co-write the screenplay for 1996's feature version of *Thinner*) and appeared in 1985 as an episode of *Tales from the Darkside*, a television series produced by George A. Romero and Richard Rubinstein.

## "THE MAN WHO WOULD NOT SHAKE HANDS"

This tale is narrated by George Gregson, a member of a poker club that meets at a brownstone located at 249B East 34th Street, New York City, a locale King readers will recognize from the novella "The Breathing Method" in 1982's *Different Seasons*. Gregson relates the curious events that took place in the club in 1919.

### PRIMARY SUBJECTS

*HENRY BROWER*. Brower is the man referred to in the title of the story. An Indian holy man who blames Brower for the death of his son puts a curse on Brower that makes him cause the death of anyone he touches. As a result, Brower must shun all human contact. Playing poker one night at the club, he wins a round, upon which one of his opponents, Jason Davidson, grabs his hand and shakes it. Brower pulls away and flees into the night. Following Brower, George Gregson confronts him and hears his story. When Gregson laughs, Brower demonstrates his power, killing a nearby dog merely by touching its paw. Gregson remains unconvinced until Davidson dies suddenly. Brower commits suicide, apparently by grasping one of his hands with the other.

*STEVENS.* Stevens, or someone who very much resembled Stevens (he claims it was his grandfather), has worked as a butler at 249B for as long as anyone can remember. Stevens has the uncanny ability to choose the club member who is most in need of relating a tale.

## "THE REAPER'S IMAGE"

This story has the distinction of being King's second professional sale after "The Glass Floor." It originally appeared in the spring 1969 issue of *Startling Mystery Stories.*

### PRIMARY SUBJECTS

*THE DeIVER LOOKING GLASS.* An enchanted mirror displayed in the Samuel Claggert Memorial Museum, this mirror was designed by John DeIver, "an English craftsman of Norman descent who made mirrors in . . . the Elizabethan period of England's history." His mirrors are collector's items because of their fine craftsmanship and because DeIver used a "form of crystal that has a mildly magnifying and distorting effect upon the eye of the beholder." Over the centuries, many have looked into the mirror and seen the image of the Grim Reaper in the upper left-hand corner of the glass. All those who have done so, including a judge named Crater, then vanished off the face of the earth.

*MR. CARLIN.* The current guardian of the DeIver glass and curator of the Claggert Museum, Carlin explains the strange history of the mirror to the curious Mr. Spangler.

*JOHNSON SPANGLER.* Spangler visits the Claggert Museum for the express purpose of studying the DeIver glass, only to become its latest victim.

## "SURVIVOR TYPE"

As King explains it, he got to thinking about cannibalism one day, wondering if a person could eat himself. This particularly unpleasant account, reminiscent of King in his Richard Bachman (or George Stark) storytelling mode, was the result.

Surgeon turned drug dealer Richard Pine finds himself stranded on a desert island with only meager supplies (including two kilos of heroin) to sustain him. Pine survives a month or so on these provisions and on the birds he can catch and eat, but soon must resort to his only remaining food source—himself. Using the heroin as an anesthetic, he amputates, then eats his right foot, then his left, then his right leg to the knee, then . . . well, you get the picture.

## "MORNING DELIVERIES (MILKMAN #1)" & "BIG WHEELS, A TALE OF THE LAUNDRY GAME (MILKMAN #2)"

These tales were plucked from King's abandoned novel, *The Milkman*. They are interesting mostly because they seem to be his first attempt at developing ideas that eventually appeared in *Needful Things* (1991).

In "Morning Deliveries," readers join milkman Spike Milligan as he makes his predawn rounds. In addition to dairy products, however, Spike delivers such items as spiders, deadly nightshade, and bottles of acid gel to his customers.

The second chapter follows the misadventures of two drunken laundry workers, Johnny "Rocky" Rockwell and Leo Edwards, as they visit a gas station to obtain an inspection sticker. We learn that Rocky is being cuckolded by Spike Milligan. Leo has worse problems, however: he has a gaping hole in his back, caused by water dripping from a hole in the laundry's roof.

## "THE BALLAD OF THE FLEXIBLE BULLET"

A story about storytellers, "The Ballad of the Flexible Bullet" is one of King's earliest examinations of the relationship between madness and writing.

*King in 1998* | BETH GWINN

## PRIMARY SUBJECTS

**HENRY WILSON.** The narrator of the tale, Wilson tells how he fell under the spell of Reg Thorpe, a writer who believes a tiny creature called a *fornit* lives in his typewriter and acts as his muse. At first, Wilson goes along with Thorpe's mad ideas out of respect. But as they continue to exchange letters, he catches Thorpe's madness, validating the writer's obsession and paranoia. Wilson has since regained his sanity, but still wonders just how crazy Thorpe really was.

*REG THORPE.* The author of *Underworld Figures* and the story that Henry Wilson championed, "The Ballad of the Flexible Bullet," Reg kills himself after shooting his wife, Jane, their housekeeper, Gertrude, and Gertrude's son, Jimmy. Reg goes off the deep end when he discovers Jimmy shooting Reg's fornit, Rackne, with "death rays" from a toy ray gun.

*THE FORNITS—RACKNE and BELLIS.* Rackne is Reg Thorpe's fornit, a tiny, elflike creature who lives inside his typewriter. Reg believes Rackne is the true creative force behind his writing and becomes enraged when he learns his housekeeper's son has been torturing the creature. The discovery comes too late, however—Jimmy zaps Rackne with a toy ray gun, exploding the creature's body. Bellis is Henry Wilson's fornit. Whether these creatures exist only in Reg's twisted imagination is a matter for debate. True, his typewriter is found drenched in blood, but the blood is type O—Reg's blood type.

## "PARANOID: A CHANT" & "FOR OWEN"

*Skeleton Crew* also contains two poems. The first, entitled "Paranoid: A Chant," takes readers inside the mind of a man both mad and completely paranoid. In the second, "For Owen," a father walks his son to school. Though King has published millions of words in an impressive variety of mediums and formats, he has for reasons unknown published only a handful of poems.

*Note:* "Mrs. Todd's Shortcut" and "The Reach" are discussed in section four. "The Jaunt," "The Mist," and "Beachworld" are covered in section eight. "The Wedding Gig" is discussed in section seven.

# 38

## *Cat's Eye*

---

T**HE FILM** *Cat's Eye* (1985) was produced during an extraordinarily prolific period in King's career, when there seemed to be almost as many movies being made from his novels as there were books being published. In a two-year period, no less than six motion pictures were produced based on his works: *Cujo* (1983), *The Dead Zone* (1983), *Christine* (1983), *Children of the Corn* (1984), *Firestarter* (1984), and *Silver Bullet* (1985).

Perhaps most noteworthy about the relatively minor *Cat's Eye* is that it was only the second original screenplay of his to be produced, and that the author intentionally made fun of several established elements of the still-burgeoning Stephen King universe. The movie is also significant in that King was not responsible for its genesis. Veteran producer Dino De Laurentiis, who would eventually be involved with a half dozen movies based on the author's work, held the screen rights to several of the remaining short stories from *Night Shift* (1978). (King had already adapted some of the stories from this collection for his first produced screenplay, *Creepshow*, in 1983.) De Laurentiis had been so impressed with Drew Barrymore's work in the yet-to-be-released *Firestarter* that he flew to Bangor, Maine, to convince King to write a script that not only would be based on those unused stories from *Night Shift*, but also would feature Barrymore in each episode.

Intrigued by the challenge, King readily agreed, but with a hidden agenda: he would have as much fun amusing his audience as he would frightening them. He also agreed to work within the restrictions of a PG-13 rating. Most horror films receive an R rating. King also sought to conceal the fact that the movie, like *Creepshow*, would be an anthology of unrelated stories. In theory, a cat was to be the connecting link between the tales, each of which takes place in a different part of the United States.

Based on two previously published stories, "Quitter's, Inc." and "The Ledge," and a new one called "The General," *Cat's Eye* is unquestionably and overtly an anthology film. It shares much in spirit with the adaptations used in *Creepshow* in that King purposely attempted to combine humor and horror, gore and guffaws. To a large degree, the 93-minute feature succeeds on that intended middle ground, especially considering the PG-13 rating and the mainstream audience for which it was intended.

What is not widely known, however, is that the prologue to the film's "wraparound" story was shot, but later removed following test screenings. Consequently, when the picture was finally released, audiences were confused by the story line. Who was the anonymous cat? Why was the ghostly vision of a little girl speaking to it as if it might be a former pet? What was the cat traveling across America in search of?

In King's original screenplay, the narrative opens with the funeral of a little girl who has died in her sleep for reasons never clearly explained. Her mother, insane with grief, believes that somehow the girl's pet cat had "stolen her life's breath" (as was believed in ancient times by some European cultures). Going berserk, she attempts to kill the cat with an Uzi. The cat escapes, and the ghost of the little girl urges the feline to find the supernatural creature that actually stole her life—a hideous troll that lived in the walls of her bedroom.

> *Country-western singer Ray Stevens sings the original theme song "Cat's Eye" over the movie's end credits.*

Studio executives at MGM were concerned that audiences wouldn't respond favorably to a film that opened with the funeral of a child, or a cat being put in such extreme peril. So the prologue was deleted, leaving audiences wondering why Drew Barrymore (who plays multiple roles) would first appear as a ghost, and why this ordinary cat was wandering in and out of the different plotlines. (Of course, the fact that the film was promoted as "the latest Stephen King thriller" should have tipped off viewers that they weren't going to see anything mainstream.)

If we disregard the crippled wraparound story, what remains is entertaining enough, albeit not particularly memorable or distinctive. *Cat's Eye* is perhaps important only as an affectionate sendup of what was already recognizably the Stephen King universe. Besides the considerable novelty and suspense inherent in the stories themselves, King demonstrates from the outset (with the full cooperation of director Lewis Teague, who had previously directed *Cujo*) that the world's best-selling horror author was not above poking fun at himself. Consider the film's amusing cross-references to other King works:

- Early on, an obviously rabid St. Bernard chases the cat. *(Cujo)*

- The cat is nearly run over by a red 1958 Plymouth Fury. *(Christine)*

- Morrison complains, "I don't know who writes this crap!" while watching a horror movie starring Christopher Walken and Herbert Lom on television. (The film is *The Dead Zone*.)

- Morrison's daughter attends a private school appropriately called Saint Stephen's School for the Exceptional.

- Amanda's mother reads *Pet Sematary* in bed.

Unlike *Creepshow*, in which the stories were relatively obscure, the two stories adapted for *Cat's Eye* are familiar to longtime King readers from their appearance in *Night Shift*. Therefore, we consider "Quitters, Inc." and "The Ledge" to be part of the Stephen King universe continuity. They are covered in section seven. Only "The General," written for the film, is dealt with here.

## "THE GENERAL"

This segment follows the trail of the film's apparently indestructible cat (who made fleeting appearances in the previous two episodes) to the home of another little girl, Amanda, who lives in Wilmington, North Carolina. There the cat, now named "the General," battles a deadly troll who intends to steal the life-force of Amanda while she sleeps. Naturally, her unsuspecting father (James Naughton) and mother (Candy Clark) have no idea of the mortal danger their daughter is in after they go to bed. They mistakenly believe that the General is the cause of their daughter's vivid nightmares.

Ultimately, good triumphs over evil in this tale, as both the youngster and the cat (which has no doubt used up almost all of its nine lives) survive the final attack of the horrid little monster. To keep the bizarre incident a secret, Amanda sweetly blackmails her still perplexed parents into letting the General join their family.

> *The film's prop department made a bed for "The General" sequence that was later cited in* The Guinness Book of World Records *as the world's largest bed.*

### PRIMARY SUBJECTS

*AMANDA.* A precocious little girl, Amanda suffers from bad dreams about a tiny monster coming into her room late at night and trying to steal her life-force through her breath. Of course, Amanda is correct in her wild belief that it is more than just a bad dream, even if she can't convince her understandably skeptical parents. Fortunately, she is able to convey her fears to the stray cat she calls the General, and this brave feline is instrumental in the destruction of the deadly troll.

*HUGH.* Hugh, Amanda's sympathetic dad, doesn't truly believe her story of a monster hiding inside the walls of her room, but fortunately he does share her love of cats. He sides with Amanda every time her mother tries to convince them that the General is the monster in the child's nightmares.

*SALLY ANN.* Sally Ann, Amanda's less-than-sympathetic mom, does not believe monsters are lurking in her daughter's closet or under her bed, much less inside the walls. Worse still, she is definitely not a cat lover. At one point she captures the General and brings him to an animal shelter to be put to sleep. Once she realizes that the animal somehow saved her only child's life, she relents.

*THE TROLL IN THE WALL.* This nameless creature invades the home of Amanda and her parents. True to legend, the little monster comes out only at night and scampers close to the face of the sleeping Amanda. Then it tries to suck out the youngster's life-force by magically stealing the breath from her body. Even armed with a tiny dagger, it does not survive a battle to the death with the General.

# 39

## *Misery*

---

ALTHOUGH STEPHEN KING would make writers the protagonists of some of his most intriguing novels *(The Tommyknockers,
The Dark Half, Bag of Bones)*, it is *Misery* (1987) that remains his most
memorable examination of those who practice that profession. Who
is better qualified to write a story about a best-selling author stalked
by an insane fan than a best-selling author who in real life has been
stalked by an insane fan?

Paul Sheldon is a popular novelist with an unusual dilemma. He
owes his success to a single character, one who has in many ways taken
over his entire career: Misery Chastain, star of a series of historical
romances, has made Sheldon a household name and a minor celebrity.
Sheldon wants to write more than popular genre fiction; he wants to
produce a literary novel that will keep his name alive long after he has
passed on. To serve that end, he writes *Fast Cars*, a novel about his
rough-and-tumble life growing up on the mean streets of the big city.
The second step in his carefully conceived plan is to publish *Misery's
Child*, in which Misery dies during childbirth. By doing so, Paul hopes
to free himself from the literary shackles with which success has bur-
dened him.

But fate is not going to allow Sheldon to change gears so quickly
and painlessly. When the novelist leaves the small resort hotel in the
Colorado Rockies where he has finished *Fast Cars*, he finds himself
caught in a sudden blizzard. Sheldon loses control of his car and

crashes, but his life is saved by a mysterious stranger who takes him to her secluded farm. The new woman in his life is Annie Wilkes, and fortunately for Sheldon, she just happens to be a former nurse. She also happens to be his "number one fan." She owns every Paul Sheldon book—and every Misery Chastain novel—that has been published. She has even named her pet pig Misery.

As the days pass, Sheldon comes to realize that his hostess is not altogether sane. Unfortunately, there is not much he can do about this unsettling realization. He is her prisoner, and he has a multitude of injuries, including a dislocated pelvis and two broken legs. He's not only completely bedridden and totally at her mercy, but she has also hooked him on a potent brand of painkillers.

It turns out Annie Wilkes is a female Dr. Jekyll and Mr. Hyde. Her mood swings are abrupt and unpredictable; she is sweet and solicitous one moment, furious and violent the next. Sheldon later learns that her anger has found unfortunate outlets in the past. It seems that many of Annie's charges have died over the years under mysterious circumstances. Somewhat brazenly, Annie has kept a scrapbook detailing these incidents.

Annie is dismayed to discover that his new novel is *not* the latest chapter in the Misery saga. Possessed of a peculiar temperament that includes a strong revulsion to obscenities, Annie is further shocked when she reads Sheldon's new novel. How could the beloved creator of Misery Chastain be the writer of such utter filth? Convinced he has been delivered to her by the hand of God, Annie demands that he burn his only copy of *Fast Cars*. If he does not, he will suffer the consequences personally.

But Paul's suffering does not end even after he reluctantly complies with his captor's wishes. Annie, who can afford only paperbacks and has thus not yet heard of Misery's "retirement," becomes enraged when she learns her precious heroine dies at the end of *Misery's Child*, which she only recently purchased. Threatening further psychological and physical torture, Annie buys Sheldon a used typewriter and several reams of typing paper and instructs him to write a new Misery novel, to be titled *Misery's Return*. And the Lord have mercy on Paul Sheldon's slowly healing legs if he doesn't deliver a book that meets her expectations.

Trapped, addicted to painkillers, and totally cut off from the rest of the world, Paul employs his creative as well as his physical powers to stay alive. Plotting his escape, Paul takes perverse pleasure in devising the best Misery novel ever. He is literally writing as if his life depended on it.

*Misery* fits well into the Stephen King universe in that it deals with several themes that appear repeatedly in other works, most predominantly the idea that life is not fair and that accidents control our lives, not our will or desires. Although Annie Wilkes is a sadistic monster, she is also a tragic figure who, on one level, realizes she is ill. Annie has accepted that she is destined to lead a miserable existence filled with loneliness and despair. Although life has treated her poorly, she finds solace in reading the Misery saga. To have her favorite writer kill off her beloved Misery is a blow she can barely stand.

*In the original paperback edition of* Misery, *a second, interior cover is actually a lavishly rendered version of* Misery's Return, *in which the bold hero is holding Misery lovingly in his arms. The distinctive face on that dashing hero belongs to none other than Stephen King!*

Paul Sheldon, meanwhile, has found great success writing in a genre he really doesn't respect and secretly wishes he could escape. But if he doesn't create the ultimate Misery novel for Annie, he will never live to write anything else. It's an ironic situation in which Sheldon has to appease a fan before he can be allowed to please himself. It is a situation to which King surely can relate, as he has been asked by critics repeatedly throughout his career when he was going to abandon the "scary stuff" and write something "serious" and "literary." To his credit, King has always been proud to be a horror writer, but he has also never wished to be typecast as someone who can perform successfully only in that genre.

*Due to its realistic themes and dark ending, King originally intended* Misery *to be published as a Richard Bachman novel.*

Yet the fame, fortune, and acclaim King has received as "the world's most popular horror writer" has been a double-edged sword.

For a time, he must have wondered if the only way he would be accepted by his legions of fans would be in the role of literary bogey-man. (Part of the reason he created the alter ego of Richard Bachman was to publish novels—with the exception of 1984's *Thinner*—that were clearly not in the horror genre.) In *Misery,* King was addressing several issues that only a celebrated writer would have to deal with: fame, fortune—and the occasional deranged fan.

*Misery* is also a gripping psychological study in which former nurse Annie Wilkes is not the only monster Paul Sheldon must com-bat. The novelist has his share of inner demons and personality quirks. He is not quite "all there" either, at least in the sense that he almost exclusively defines himself by what he does for a living—writing, cre-ating characters out of whole cloth, then living in their imaginary worlds until the story or novel is done.

*Misery* was clearly inspired by events in King's own life. He has been stalked by obsessive fans, and his home was once invaded by someone claiming to have a bomb. In 1980, he reportedly signed one of his books for a stranger who literally did call himself King's "num-ber one fan." That lost soul was Mark Chapman, who would later earn his place in history by shooting and killing John Lennon shortly thereafter.

*Signing at Betts Bookstore* | BETH GWINN

Once asked what he thought about being a world-famous writer, King curtly replied, "Being famous sucks."

## PRIMARY SUBJECTS

*PAUL SHELDON.* A successful novelist with few friends or acquaintances outside the publishing industry, Paul has reached the top of the bestseller lists with a series of historical romances starring the plucky heroine Misery Chastain. Feeling stifled by such genre work, Sheldon decides to free himself of the character by killing her off in the latest saga, *Misery's Child.*

> *A Mrs. Kaspbrak was a neighbor of Paul Sheldon's family when he was a child. This may mean that Sheldon may have known Eddie Kaspbrak, a character who appears in* IT *(1986).*

While trapped at Annie Wilkes's farm near Sidewinder, Colorado, he writes his best Misery novel while desperately trying to find a means of escape. When his captor purposely cripples—hobbles is the old slave term—Sheldon by first mutilating his foot and then one of his hands, the writer realizes it is only a matter of time before she will kill him.

Surviving the ordeal by killing the woman in a brutal fight, he suffers the irony of becoming a better writer for enduring the horrible experience by publishing the Misery novel he wrote for Annie Wilkes. Of course, he also finds himself more typecast and potentially vulnerable to the next number one fan he might encounter one day. Paul Sheldon currently resides somewhere in New York City.

*ANNIE WILKES.* A large, unattractive woman in her mid-forties, Annie is also hopelessly insane. After she kidnaps Paul Sheldon, he discovers that her homicidal tendencies have been with her since she was a teenager, when she apparently set fire to the home of the three children she had been babysitting. Keeping a scrapbook called Memory Lane, she fills it with various accounts of the people she has known and the places where she has been employed as a nurse. Unfortunately, almost every account ends with a sudden and violent death. All are dismissed by the local authorities as tragic accidents.

The deceased include her own father, a roommate at nursing school, and dozens of patients at the various hospitals where she has been employed.

Having become an avid reader to pass the lonely hours, Annie has read all eight of Paul Sheldon's novels, but had reread his four Misery titles dozens of times. In her madness, she sees herself as Sheldon's lover, mentor, and creative inspiration. As she swings back and forth between sanity and insanity, she displays a venomous temper that can quickly work itself up into a murderous rage. When she realizes Sheldon is trying to escape, she cripples him to prevent him from ever walking again. In a final fight with the tortured author, she is finally killed.

## ADAPTATION

The 107-minute movie version of *Misery* was released in 1990 and has the distinction of being the first adaptation of a Stephen King novel to win an Academy Award. The Oscar went to actress Kathy Bates, who did a masterful job of playing the Jekyll/Hyde character of Annie Wilkes. James Caan, best known for his tough-guy roles in such films as *The Godfather* (1972) and *The Killer Elite* (1975), turned in an equally strong performance in the role of Paul Sheldon.

The R-rated picture was directed by Rob Reiner, who had already done a superior job in 1986 with *Stand by Me* (based on the novella "The Body" from 1982's *Different Seasons*). The author was reportedly extremely pleased with the way the second screen production with Reiner turned out, as he had been with *Stand by Me*. (In a 1999 article for *Entertainment Weekly*, the author listed *Misery* as one of his ten personal favorite screen adaptations.)

What is most interesting is how Academy Award–winning screenwriter William Goldman *(Butch Cassidy and the Sundance Kid, All the President's Men)* deftly modified the novel to bring it to the big screen. Except for the last few pages in which Sheldon is seen back in New York trying to get a new novel under way, virtually all of King's story takes place inside the home of Annie Wilkes. In many ways, the novel is set up like a two-character play on a single claustrophobic set. Goldman purposely "opened up" the story by creating the characters of Sheriff Buster (Richard Farnsworth) and his deputy-wife Virginia (Frances Sternhagen), who spend much of their screen time searching for the missing novelist. He also opened and closed the story by having Sheldon meet with high-powered literary agent Marcia Sindell (Lauren Bacall).

In addition, Goldman toned down some of the extreme physical tortures that Annie Wilkes puts Sheldon through, most notably the scene in which she breaks his ankles so he can't walk. (In the novel, Annie practically shears off Sheldon's foot with an axe and then cauterizes the gaping wound with a blowtorch.)

Goldman also has Sheldon destroying his only copy of *Misery's Return* in his climactic fight with Annie Wilkes. Therefore, when he returns to New York to recuperate, he spends his time writing the mainstream literary novel he had always hoped to write. Finally, he is freed of the "curse" of Misery and can realize his career goal of being a serious novelist. In King's novel, however, Sheldon does *not* destroy the only copy of the manuscript. Ironically, when *Misery's Return* is published, it makes him richer and more famous than ever before.

# 40

## Four Past Midnight

I T'S INEVITABLE that *Four Past Midnight* be compared to *Different Seasons* (1982). Like the prior collection, *Four Past Midnight* gathers four of Stephen King's longer, novella-length works together. But unlike *Different Seasons,* which contains three more or less mainstream stories, *Four Past Midnight* features four terrifying journeys into the fantastic and the truly horrific.

*Note:* "Secret Window, Secret Garden" is discussed in section four. For "The Sun Dog," see section three. "The Langoliers" is discussed in section five.

### "THE LIBRARY POLICEMAN"

In a prefatory note, King reveals that "The Library Policeman" had its genesis in an exchange he had one morning with his son, Owen. The boy needed a book to read for school; his father quite naturally suggested a visit to the library. Owen was reluctant to do so, because he feared the library police, maniacal enforcers who actually came to patrons' houses if they fail to return their loaned-out books on time. This story delighted King, who had heard similar tales in his youth. Crafting a story around the idea, the author realized the library police were mere stand-ins for other, darker fears. Thus, "The Library Policeman" developed into a tale about childhood trauma and secret shame.

Like "The Sun Dog," this novella is about growing up. In "The Sun Dog," Kevin becomes an adult in a moment of stress and terror. Sam Peebles, the protagonist of "The Library Policeman," differs from Kevin, however, in that his own traumatic moment actually retards his growth into a mature adult, keeping him from trusting those around him. Like "Secret Window, Secret Garden," it's also a tale about repressed memory. This was a hotly debated topic at the beginning of the 1990s, when real-life horror stories about unspeakable memories began resurfacing in individuals decades after the alleged incidents, producing a psychiatric cottage industry in so-called repressed memories. In this story at least, King seems to be saying we should extend to these children the benefit of the doubt.

*The Rock Bottom Remainders relaxing* | SUSANNE MOSS

## PRIMARY SUBJECTS

*SAM PEEBLES.* Everything, Sam Peebles later decides, is the fault of "the god damned acrobat." The acrobat, who is scheduled to perform at a rotary club meeting, breaks his neck, leaving a hole in the schedule. Strong-armed by a friend, real estate agent Sam Peebles agrees to fill in as a guest speaker. After finishing the draft for his speech, he shows it to his secretary, Naomi Higgins, who suggests he punch it up with quotes and sends him to the library. There he meets an odd librarian, Ardelia Lortz, who recommends *Best Loved Poems of the American People* and *The Speakers Companion*. A grateful Sam checks the books out. As he leaves, Miss Lortz admonishes him to return the books on time—after all, she wouldn't want to be forced to send the library policeman after him.

His speech is a rousing success. Basking in the glow, Sam forgets all about the library books. After receiving threatening calls from Ardelia, he searches for the books, and to his dismay determines they must have accidentally been tossed out with the recycling. He goes to the library to make amends and is surprised when he enters—it's the same place, but with a more modern feel. Inquiring about Ardelia, Sam is informed that nobody by that name is employed there.

Doing some research, Sam realizes he has had an encounter with a ghost, the spirit of a vicious woman who committed a handful of murders several years earlier. Ardelia also has a powerful ally; she sends the library policeman to terrorize Sam.

Ardelia is actually a creature who feeds on fear. Sam realizes that the only way to combat her is by confronting his childhood fears, and he eventually defeats Ardelia.

*NAOMI HIGGINS.* Sam's part-time secretary, Naomi sets the events of the story in motion by suggesting Sam visit the library. Naomi later provides Sam with much-needed background information on Ardelia Lortz, data that allows Sam to eventually uncover the truth.

*ARDELIA LORTZ.* The librarian who, sensing Sam's vulnerability, appears to him many years after she supposedly died. Ardelia is a shape-shifter; like a cicada, she emerges every few years to gorge on human fear. Although she may take human form, her true self is disgustingly horrific. Her most prominent feature is a huge, funnel-shaped proboscis that can suck the fear out of a person through their tear ducts. Ardelia manufactures fear by telling horrid versions of classic fairy tales to her children's story hour group. Mesmerizing the children, she then feeds on their traumatized emotions.

Ardelia is nearly slain after Sam, in a symbolic rejection of his childhood fears, sticks a wad of red licorice in her snout. She survives the encounter, however, and attaches herself in embryonic form to Naomi's neck. Sam realizes what has happened and finally destroys the parasite for good. Ardelia Lortz is quite durable, however, and may yet haunt the Stephen King universe.

*(DIRTY) DAVE DUNCAN.* Ardelia's lover and accomplice in the 1950s, Dave turned to drink after she "killed" herself. Dave is homeless and makes a living off of other people's recyclables. Perhaps still under the influence of his old girlfriend, Dave accidentally takes Sam's library books to the recycling center along with his old newspapers, prompting Ardelia to terrorize Sam. Dave gives Sam insight into Ardelia's true nature before dying at the hands of the loathsome "Ardelia thing."

*THE LIBRARY POLICEMAN.* The being that came to life in the form of the molester who abused Sam as a child. Also, the imaginary character featured in a sinister wall poster created for Ardelia Lortz by Dave Duncan. Using Sam's fear, Ardelia gives the library policeman life and sends him after Sam.

*JUNCTION CITY, IOWA.* The small Iowa town where Sam Peebles meets Ardelia Lortz and the library policeman. According to the epilogue of *Needful Things* (1991), Sam and Naomi Higgins marry and leave Junction City soon after the events recorded in "The Library Policeman." Readers also learn that Leland Gaunt, the evil being of *Needful Things* and other King stories, now occupies Sam's old office.

# 41

## *Sleepwalkers*

---

ALTHOUGH IT IS NOT by any means the first Stephen King screenplay (*Creepshow*, *Cat's Eye*, *Silver Bullet*, *Maximum Overdrive*, and *Pet Sematary* preceded it), 1992's *Sleepwalkers* was his first truly *original* screenplay, that is, one not based on a previously published short story or novel. It was also the first feature film in which the best-selling author would work with a talented young director named Mick Garris, whom King would later select to direct the television miniseries adaptations of *The Stand* (1994) and *The Shining* (1997).

With *Sleepwalkers*, King chose to work with some of his favorite supernatural themes and monsters: werewolves, vampires, and in particular, cats. (*Cat's Eye* [1985] featured a feline in all three story lines, and 1989's *Pet Sematary* revolved to a large degree around the unholy resurrection of a family cat named Church.) Even though *Sleepwalkers* may not be the most memorable movie ever to deal with the topic of shape-shifters, the R-rated feature makes for a scary and fast-moving 91-minute thriller.

The narrative is essentially a twisted love triangle, an outrageous blending of the supernatural with the forbidden erotic. Charles Brady (Brian Krause) appears to be a handsome high school student who has just moved to a quiet, small town in Indiana with his beloved mother, Mary (Alice Krige), from yet another quiet, small town in Ohio. In truth, Charles is an ancient and apparently immortal shape-shifter—a "sleepwalker"—who can instantly change from human to animal form when angered, and render himself and other objects invisible, at least briefly. Except for his mother, he is also apparently the last of his species, one that survives by way of a unique process. Charles is the food gatherer who feeds both himself and his mother. But Charles doesn't eat food—rather, he feeds on the life force of virgin girls, transmitting what he doesn't need to his mother through sexual intercourse.

King takes great pains to show that these two creatures are only human in appearance. Whenever they look into a mirror, their true identities as hideous demonic entities are revealed. Apparently, even demons have emotions, as Charles develops genuine feelings for his next intended victim, a beautiful student named Tanya (Madchen Amick).

This leads to a twisted love triangle. Though he is drawn to Tanya, Charles knows he must kill her if his mother is to survive. Although this premise would have made for a fascinating story line in its own right, King fails to go any further down that particular course. Rather, after Charles and Tanya go to a local cemetery to obtain gravestone rubbings, his barely controllable animalistic tendencies take over. He attempts to date rape the girl, and in doing so reveals his true nature to her.

*King has a cameo appearance as a cemetery caretaker who complains to anyone within earshot, "You can't blame this one on me!" Popular horror film directors Tobe Hooper and Clive Barker (as forensic technicians), as well as Joe Dante and John Landis (as lab assistants) also appear in cameos.*

When a deputy sheriff, who just happens to have his pet cat with him, arrives on the scene, the feline instinctively attacks Charles after he kills the deputy. Even though the sleepwalkers appear to be part feline themselves, they are mortal enemies with all cats—the only creatures that can do them harm. Grievously wounded, Charles manages to return home and collapse in Mary's arms. Now it's up to his enraged mother to return to town and kidnap an already traumatized Tanya so her now bedridden son can finish the job he started in the cemetery. If he is unable to do so soon, he will die from his wounds, and Mary, in turn, will die of starvation.

As dozens of cats begin to gather outside her house, Mary kidnaps Tanya and drags her home. The police, however, also arrive ready to avenge their fallen comrade. Before this night of incredible horror is over, nearly everyone involved is either injured or killed, including the two mysterious sleepwalkers.

*Cemetery, Durham* | DAVID LOWELL

In *Sleepwalkers*, women play the pivotal roles: one is the heroine, another the main villain. With the exception of Charles, all the other men are either arrogant fools or inherently weak. The most developed and vital figures clearly are Tanya and Mary. Even Tanya's mother is shown, in her brief time on screen, to be a more complex and stronger character than her husband. King clearly enjoyed creating a new species of supernatural monsters whose incestual sexual habits are their most shocking and memorable characteristic. The early scene of the erotically charged Mary being playfully "seduced" by the young man who is her son strikes an unsettling chord in viewers.

Unfortunately, the author raises too many unresolved questions in his intriguing if not fully developed premise. Why does he call them sleepwalkers? Why have we never heard of this species of shape-shifter before? Why are there apparently only two of them left in the world? Why can't the female of the species take the life force herself from young virgin males? Why are they so afraid of cats when they have such immense power? And how did these beings develop the incredible ability to temporarily render themselves and huge objects invisible (such as moving automobiles!).

## PRIMARY SUBJECTS

*CHARLES BRADY.* One of the last two surviving members of a species of shape-shifters called sleepwalkers, Charles appears to be an extremely charming young man in his late teens. In reality, he is actually a creature who feeds on the life force of virgin girls, and who can make himself (and other objects) temporarily invisible. Although humans cannot perceive his true visage, his reflection in a mirror shows a loathsome creature, a horrid blend of human, reptilian, and feline features. Apparently immortal, his kind greatly fears cats, which inexplicably have the power to destroy them. After being attacked by a cat, Charles ultimately dies from his wounds, even though his mother tries valiantly to save him.

*MARY BRADY.* The lovely mother of Charles Brady, Mary is also an immortal shape-shifter. She too needs to feed on the life force of virgin girls. It is up to her son to suck the life force from "nice girls" he meets in school so that he can in turn feed his mother by having sexual intercourse with her. After the death of her beloved Charles, Mary is destroyed by the latest "nice girl" whom she had hoped Charles would bring home for dinner . . . as the main course.

*TANYA ROBERTSON.* Tanya is the pretty high school student who finds herself attracted to the new kid in school after hearing him read a self-composed fantasy tale entitled "Sleepwalkers" in class. From the way she speaks and carries herself, it appears she is still a virgin, and Charles set his sights on making her his next meal. After Charles attacks her in a cemetery in his animalistic state, Tanya quickly realizes that no one will believe the wild story she has to tell. Returning home, she is kidnapped by Mary and dragged to the Brady house. Escaping her captor, Tanya employs all her resources to combat the two supernatural creatures. With the assistance of a large pack of cats that have surrounded the Brady home, Tanya kills both sleepwalkers and escapes. Her current whereabouts are unknown.

*DEPUTY SHERIFF SIMPSON.* Deputy Simpson has the unfortunate assignment of being on the lookout for speeders when Charles Brady's vehicle roars past his patrol car on the main road out of town. Pursuing Charles, Deputy Simpson tracks him down at the local cemetery. There he encounters a hysterical Tanya, who tries to warn him that something inhuman is after her. While trying to protect her, Simpson is mauled, stabbed, and finally shot and killed by a raging animalistic Charles. However, his pet cat, Clovis, fearlessly attacks this ancient enemy and gravely wounds the shape-shifter.

> *Although the plot of* Sleepwalkers *is set in Travis, Indiana, at one point Sheriff Ira calls the police station dispatcher to ask for more police backup from the township of Castle Rock. Although this is not the same Castle Rock in Maine that King visits elsewhere, the reference to his fictional town is an amusing in-joke.*

*SHERIFF IRA.* The local sheriff, Ira doesn't understand what is going on in his peaceful community, but he knows his job is to protect the innocent—no matter what the price. After repeatedly wounding Mary Brady, he is slain by her when she impales him on a picket fence.

# 42

## *Nightmares & Dreamscapes*

---

I T ' S   A   M E A S U R E   of King's extraordinarily rich imagination that he found it difficult to compress his ideas into short works of fiction. In the introduction to 1985's *Skeleton Crew*, Stephen King wrote:

> Writing short stories hasn't gotten easier for me over the years; it's gotten harder. The time to do them has shrunk, for one thing. They keep wanting to bloat, for another (I have a real problem with bloat—I write like fat ladies diet), and it seems harder to find the voice for these tales. . . . The thing to do is keep trying, I think. It's better to keep kissing and get your face slapped a few times than it is to give up altogether.

King did indeed keep trying. The sheer size (816 pages in the hardcover version) of *Nightmares & Dreamscapes* (1993) is a testament to that effort. In the introduction, a slightly more militant King again discusses how hard it is for him to write short stories:

> These days it seems that everything wants to be a novel, and every novel wants to be approximately four thousand pages long. A fair number of critics have mentioned this, and usually not favorably. In reviews of every long novel I have ever written, from *The Stand* to *Needful Things*, I have been accused of overwriting. In some cases the criticisms have

merit; in others they are just the ill-tempered yappings of men and women who have accepted the literary anorexia of the last thirty years with a puzzling (to me at least) lack of discussion and dissent.

Perhaps for the reasons stated above, his short fiction output has dwindled since then, but he continues to work in the form as the mood strikes him. Evidence of this is found most recently in 1997's *Six Stories*, which features the multiple award–winning tale "The Man in the Black Suit." (See p. 170, as well as the section on his most recent uncollected stories [pp. 376–380].)

Although *The Stephen King Universe* is primarily concerned with King's fiction, it should be noted that *Nightmares & Dreamscapes* also contains an excellent nonfiction work titled "Head Down." This essay/memoir chronicles the triumphs and travails of the Bangor West All-Star Little League Team as it battled for the Maine State Championship in 1989. Baseball fan King characterizes "Head Down" as "the opportunity of a lifetime," stating that his editor, Chip McGrath of *The New Yorker*, "coaxed the best nonfiction writing of my life out of me."

*Nightmares & Dreamscapes* also contains a poem about Ebbet's Field and the Brooklyn Dodgers, titled "Brooklyn August." A departure from his usual oeuvre, the piece has since been reprinted several times in various baseball-related anthologies.

*Note:* Several stories in *Nightmares & Dreamscapes* are discussed elsewhere in this book. "It Grows on You" is found in section three, "Suffer the Little Children," "The Night Flier," "Popsy," and "The Rainy Season" are discussed in section four. "The End of the Whole Mess," "Home Delivery," and "The Doctor's Case" are covered in section eight. For discussions of "The Fifth Quarter," "My Pretty Pony," and "Dolan's Cadillac," see section seven.

## "CHATTERY TEETH"

A bizarre tale that recalls an early King tale, "The Monkey," particularly because it features a cheap novelty toy in a major role.

## PRIMARY SUBJECTS

*BILL HOGAN.* Hogan, a traveling salesman, purchases a set of windup chattery teeth at a diner. The false teeth, which seem to have a life of their own, come to his rescue by attacking and killing a psychopathic hitchhiker who threatens Hogan. Hogan thinks he saw the teeth dragging the hitchhiker's body into the desert but now believes he was delirious. Returning to the diner a year later, Hogan finds that the proprietor has a package for him—a paper bag containing the supernaturally endowed chattery teeth. Struck dumb, Hogan takes the teeth back, concluding they would be a nice gift for his son in case someone tries to attack him.

*BRYAN ADAMS.* The young, longhaired drifter who accepts a ride from Hogan. Although Adams appears harmless, he pulls a knife during the course of their trip and threatens to kill the salesman. After a fight in the van in which it appears that Adams is going to carry out his threat, the supernatural chattery teeth viciously bite and tear the drifter to death.

*Shop in Auburn that appears in "Chattery Teeth"* | DAVID LOWELL

## "DEDICATION"

King has often stated that he isn't afraid to gross his readers out if that is what it takes to make an effective story. This tale most definitely shows his courage.

Martha Rosewall, an African American, has worked as a maid at Le Palais, one of New York's finest hotels, for decades. She tells how her contact with a famous resident of the hotel drastically altered her life. Pregnant by her shiftless husband Johnny, Martha is stunned when a neighborhood *bruja* woman (a witch) tells her she must find the child's "natural father." A name immediately springs to Martha's mind as to who would make a better father: A man who resides at the hotel where she works, a Caucasian writer named Peter Jeffries. While cleaning Jeffries's bedroom each morning, Martha, under the influence of a spell cast by the witch, swallows the deposits Jeffries leaves on his sheets after masturbating each night.

As far as Martha is concerned, the spell works. Her son, Peter Rosewall, grows up to be an author. His first novel, about the ravages of war, was called *Blaze of Glory*, echoing the title of his "natural" father's first book, *Blaze of Heaven* (also a war novel).

## "THE MOVING FINGER"

The question not answered in this surrealistic story is this: If there is one gigantic finger waiting to attack us, where are the others? And what about that killer thumb? In his notes, King states that "my favorite sort of short story has always been the kind where things happen just because they happen."

One day, mild-mannered accountant Howard Mitla discovers a finger poking up out of his bathroom sink drain. The only one who can see it, Howard tries to rid himself of the pest by pouring Drano on it, then by attacking it with a pair of electric hedge clippers (the mangled finger grows to a length of over seven feet before disappearing). Howard is later found by police who have been summoned by angry neighbors. He is all alone in the corner of the blood-splattered bathroom, mumbling incoherently.

## "SNEAKERS"

Another entry whose main action takes place in a bathroom, "Sneakers" revolves around a haunted toilet stall. John Tell, the narrator of this strange tale, relates his experiences as a record producer. Visiting a men's room at a recording studio, he notices a pair of sneakers poking out from under a stall door. Unremarkable in and of themselves, the sneakers are surrounded by dozens of dead flies. He dismisses the strange sight and leaves. Subsequent visits over the next few days reveal that the sneakers haven't budged—the only thing that has changed is the increasing number of dead flies. Tell steels himself and opens the door, confronting the specter inside the stall. The spirit, finally able to tell his story, gratefully abandons the stall. Clearly, for King, there may be mystery or even evil behind literally any door—even the door of a toilet stall.

## "YOU KNOW THEY GOT A HELL OF A BAND"

This is one of two stories in *Nightmares & Dreamscapes*—the other is "The Rainy Season"—that deal with what Stephen King terms "a peculiar little town." "You Know They Got a Hell of a Band" is also reminiscent of "Children of the Corn," an early story collected in *Night Shift* (1978). It would make a terrific episode for any revival of *The Twilight Zone.*

Lost on the back roads of Oregon, Mary and Clark Willingham end up in a small town named Rock and Roll Heaven. The doomed couple quickly realize that the residents don't merely look like various deceased rock stars (Jim Morrison, Janis Joplin, Otis Redding, Rick Nelson, and of course Elvis Presley), but they are in fact the real thing. Because performers require an audience, people who wander into town are never permitted to leave—for here the cliché "rock and roll will never die" is taken literally.

## "SORRY, RIGHT NUMBER"

This is an original half-hour teleplay originally written for Steven Spielberg's TV series *Amazing Stories* (1985–1987), but it eventually was produced as an installment of George Romero and Richard

Rubinstein's syndicated series *Tales from the Darkside* (1984–1988). It is a rare example of a published teleplay. (King has also published the scripts for 1985's *Silver Bullet* and his 1999 "novel for television" *Storm of the Century*.)

One evening, Katie Wiederman receives a phone call from a hysterical woman with an oddly familiar voice. Cut off before she can identify the caller, Katie's attention is diverted shortly thereafter by the sudden death of her husband. Years later, she accidentally dials her old number and hears the events of that fateful night played out on the other end of the line. Distraught, she attempts to warn her past self of the impeding disaster, but can utter only meaningless phrases. Katie finally realizes why the voice sounded so familiar—it was her own.

## "THE TEN O'CLOCK PEOPLE"

A group of smokers is inexplicably able to see the true face of a race of aliens who, planning to take over the world, have infiltrated positions of power all over the globe. This story reads as an homage to classic science fiction television shows like *The Invaders* (1966–1967), or to paranoia films like John Carpenter's *They Live* (1988). It can also be seen as a dry run for concepts King later used in *Insomnia* (1994). An ex-smoker himself, King in late 1999 would release an audio-only book entitled *Blood and Smoke,* containing three tales in which smokers or smoking was a central element to the plot.

### PRIMARY SUBJECTS

***BRANDON PEARSON.*** While taking his ten o'clock cigarette break, bank employee Brandon is stunned to see a hideous bat creature dressed in an expensive suit walking toward him. He is about to scream when he is pulled away by an associate, Duke Rhinemann, before he can attract attention to himself. Duke explains to Brandon why he can see the usually masked aliens (something to do with his many attempts to quit smoking) and the bat people's motivations (like most aliens, they want to take over the world). Brandon becomes involved in the anti-bat resistance movement, spending the rest of his days combating the monstrous creatures.

***DUKE RHINEMANN.*** Duke, who works in computer services, is the first to realize that Brandon Pearson also has the ability to see the otherwise invisible alien bat creatures. He introduces Brandon to other smokers who are combating the aliens, convincing him to join their cause to save the human race.

## "CROUCH END"

This is a contemporary "Cthulhu Mythos" story (a story set in the elder-gods-from-space mythology created by author H. P. Lovecraft in the early twentieth century). It was inspired by events that occurred when King and his wife, Tabitha, became lost in London while on their way to visit author Peter Straub in 1977. Straub, of course, would later collaborate with King on the epic novel *The Talisman* (1984), and in 1999 both authors began work on a then-untitled sequel. "Crouch End"

*Tabitha King*
PHOTOGRAPHER
UNKNOWN

originally appeared in the 1980 anthology edited by Ramsey Campbell, *New Tales of the Cthulhu Mythos,* a collection of original stories inspired by the writings of horror legend H. P. Lovecraft (1890–1937).

Like the unfortunate couples in "The Rainy Season" and "You Know They Got a Hell of a Band," Doris and Lonnie Freeman are American tourists who are destined take a side trip straight to hell after getting lost searching for a friend's home. That side trip leads them into London's creepy Crouch End, where loathsome Lovecraftian demons—like the Goat with a Thousand Young—lie in wait for fresh victims.

## "THE HOUSE ON MAPLE STREET"

This story once again demonstrates the profound influence of the author Ray Bradbury on King, from the last name and ages of its heroes to the subject matter of the tale itself. It appears for the first time in *Nightmares & Dreamscapes,* and King states in his notes that it was actually inspired by an illustration from Chris Van Allsburg's wonderfully strange 1984 picture book, *The Mysteries of Harris Burdick.*

The Bradbury children discover that their residence hides the contours of a spaceship, a craft that is counting down to takeoff. Able to pinpoint the launch, they lure their evil stepfather into the house just as it lifts off into space.

## "UMNEY'S LAST CASE"

First appearing in *Nightmares & Dreamscapes,* "Umney's Last Case" was later reissued as a Penguin Single, an elite group of paperback specials published by Penguin Books in 1995 for the publisher's sixtieth anniversary. A Raymond Chandler/Ross McDonald pastiche, "Umney's" is yet another of King's journeys into the mind of a writer, this time exploring the relationship between an author and a character he has created. In his notes, King states that this tale is a personal favorite.

### PRIMARY SUBJECTS

*CLYDE UMNEY.* In 1938, private investigator Clyde Umney is faced with a serious dilemma. In the course of a single day, his entire world comes crashing down around him. His problems, he learns, are caused by a visitor to his office named Samuel D. Landry. Landry not only looks like an older version of himself, but he also claims to have created Umney and the entire world he inhabits in a series of gritty, violent novels such as *Scarlet Town*—which was first published in 1977! Landry informs Umney he has grown tired of his unsatisfying and complicated life in the 1990s and wants to change realities with him. Before Umney can stop him, Landry accomplishes the deed, trapping Umney in the real world of today. The hard-boiled detective does his best to cope, even teaching himself to be a writer, living for the day when he can turn the tables on Landry.

*SAMUEL D. LANDRY.* A successful writer of crime and private eye novels, Landry finds the fictional Depression-era Los Angeles he has created to be more vibrant and real to him than the world he is actually inhabiting in 1994. He possesses a futuristic device that allows him to switch realities with one of his favorite characters, a hard-boiled shamus named Clyde Umney. In spite of Umney's stunned disbelief that the author has created his entire world, Landry is able to usurp Umney's place in the 1930s. Here Landry can make all his childhood dreams of being a private eye literally come true.


## "THE BEGGAR AND THE DIAMOND"

Included almost as an afterthought, this is King's retelling of a Hindu parable told to him by a man named Surrendra Pate. King westernizes the tale by substituting God and his angel Uriel for Lord Shiva and his wife, Parvati.

Ramu begins to curse his lot in life after he trips over something in the road. Ironically, it is a huge diamond God has sent down at the insistence of the angel Uriel to provide Ramu with enough money to live out the rest of his days in comfort. Ramu's anger quickly dissipates. Counting his blessings, he picks himself up and walks away, eventually to find a sturdy stick God has left in his path, a gift that will prove far more useful to him than any diamond.

# 43

## *Rose Madder*

---

IN RETROSPECT, it seems as if King had been building toward *Rose Madder* (1995) his whole career. The theme of spousal and child abuse, touched on in early novels like *'Salem's Lot* (1975), *The Shining* (1977), and *Cujo* (1981), later emerged more prominently in *IT* (1986). The notion of men as the enemy became more explicit in *Gerald's Game* (1992). In that book, the insensitive Gerald Burlingame was only the first in a depressingly long line of abusive males King would introduce to readers over the course of his next four novels. Readers were disgusted and horrified as Jessie Burlingame was sexually molested by her father. In *Dolores Claiborne*, they saw another child abuser, the loathsome Joe St. George, strike his wife with a piece of firewood. King also pursued this track in *Insomnia* (1994), when the increasingly erratic Ed Deepneau beats his wife, Natalie, putting an end to their marriage.

To date, however, *Rose Madder* stands as King's most unflinching look at spousal abuse. It is the account of Rose Daniels and her monstrous husband, Norman, King's scariest psychopath since Greg Stillson of *The Dead Zone* (1979). Norman is not satisfied with merely hitting his wife or degrading her verbally. He takes abuse to a new level, burning Rose and sodomizing her with foreign objects. He's also what psychologists call a biter, and Rose bears the scars of his strange pathology.

The brutal realities of *Rose Madder* are balanced by a fantasy element, a subplot involving a world accessed through an otherwise unremarkable portrait Rose discovers in a pawn shop. This world seems to be the same one inhabited by Roland the gunslinger. An inhabitant of this world, alternately known as Wendy Yarrow and Dorcas, tells Rosie: "I've seen wars . . . heads by the hundreds poked onto poles along the streets of the City of Lud. I've seen wise leaders assassinated and fools put in their places."

Dorcas speaks of Lud, a city that appears in King's *Dark Tower* saga, and the reference to the assassination of wise leaders and fools being put in their places could be a veiled reference to events within *The Eyes of the Dragon* (1987). Both Wendy and Rose Madder also mention "ka," a concept familiar to readers of *The Dark Tower*.

More so than in other works, King spends time in *Rose Madder* referencing classic works of fantasy and mythology. Lewis Carroll's *Through the Looking Glass* (1872) is mentioned as Rose enters the world of the painting. In naming the bull in the temple Erinyes, the author evokes Greek mythology. In having Rose pass through a maze in the temple, he recalls the legend of the Minotaur.

> *The character Cynthia Smith of* Rose Madder *also appears in* Desperation. *An alternate-universe version of the same character also appears in* The Regulators, *published that same year.*

## PRIMARY SUBJECTS

***ROSE McCLENDON DANIELS.*** Rose leads a miserable existence with her savagely abusive husband, Norman. After one particularly brutal beating, a distraught Rose miscarries the baby she's come to think of as Caroline. Rose remains with her police detective husband for nine more years, and the constant beatings take a physical and mental toll. One day, as she is making her bed, a single drop of blood falls from her nose, landing on a pillow. Seeing the blood triggers an uncharacteristic response in the usually docile Rose. Acting almost on instinct, she drops everything and flees the home that had been her prison for nearly fourteen years.

Rose decides she will not go by the name Rose Daniels any longer, and reinvents herself as Rosie McClendon, the hopeful young woman she was before she met Norman.

The newly minted Rosie travels to Liberty City, a town some 800 miles west, and ends up at Daughters and Sisters, a shelter for battered women. There, she meets Anna Stevenson, the shelter's strong-willed founder, who finds Rosie an apartment and a position as a maid at a local hotel. Needing cash, Rosie visits Liberty City Loan and Pawn to hock her wedding ring. The owner, Bill Steiner, informs her that the stone is only zirconium, not a diamond as Norman had led her to believe. Rosie is shaken but not surprised—it is just one more slap in the face from the deceitful Norman.

Entering that store changes her life. Bill Steiner falls in love with Rosie. Overhearing her voice, Robbie Lefferts, a producer of audio-books who is in the shop at the time, is convinced she would be perfect as a reader and later offers her a job. Finally, while browsing through the store, Rosie comes across an oil painting in a wooden frame. The painting is a portrait of a blond woman in a rose madder toga standing on a hill, her back to the viewer, facing the ruins of what appears to be a Greek temple. Written on the back of the painting are the words *Rose Madder*.

Titillated by the connection to her given name, Rosie is seized by a desire to own the artwork. Even though it isn't a very good painting, the image portrayed on the canvas speaks to her on an almost primal level. Bartering her ring, Rosie acquires the painting and leaves. Rosie hangs the painting on a wall in her apartment, and it blends in as if it belongs there. Rosie starts hearing things that are alien to her urban environment, such as the sounds of crickets chirping and wind blowing through grass. At times, the vista in the painting seems to expand. Sometimes Rosie believes items are actually moving within that vista. The painting comes to exert an influence on her daily life. Rosie dyes her hair blond and has it done in the style of the woman in the portrait.

One evening, Rosie awakens to find the painting covering the entire wall. Strangely unafraid, she enters the world of the painting and encounters a woman she recognizes as Wendy Yarrow, another victim of her husband's rage. Wendy serves as Rosie's guide, introducing her to the woman in the toga, whose name is Rose Madder. Rose is an imperfect double of Rosie; her skin is mottled, her voice harsh, her state of mind near madness.

At her request, Rosie retrieves Rose's baby from a temple guarded by the blind bull Erinyes. When Rosie returns with the infant, Wendy tells her about the importance of forgetting the past and of getting on with her life. After expressing her disdain for men, Rose promises Rosie she will repay her act of kindness. Rosie returns to the real world with three seeds from the tree of forgetfulness and Rose's golden armlet as keepsakes.

Rose makes good on her promise when Norman, who has almost telepathic abilities, tracks Rosie across the country, leaving a trail of corpses in his wake. Finding her apartment, Norman follows her into Rose Madder's world. Mistaking Rose for his wife, Norman attacks her and is killed. Rosie marries Bill Steiner and gives birth to a child whom she names Pamela Gertrude, after her friends Pam Haverford and Gert Kinshaw.

Rosie, Bill, and Pamela Gertrude Steiner are alive and well, presumably still living in Liberty City.

*ROSE MADDER.* Rosie's mad doppelgänger, Rose inhabits the world of the painting Rosie finds in the pawnshop. Although Rose's features are the same as Rosie's, she is radically different; in fact, she can be viewed as the embodiment of all the rage Rosie suppresses. This fury has driven her mad and has even disfigured her. As recompense for the favor Rosie does for her, Rose draws Norman into the world of the painting, confronts him, and eventually kills him.

After killing Norman, Rose leaves her station in front of Erinyes' temple, presumably to travel in the world of the portrait. Rose is accompanied by her infant daughter and Dorcas. Their present whereabouts are unknown.

*NORMAN DANIELS.* When she was fifteen, Rosie McClendon met Norman Daniels at a varsity basketball game. Norman woos, wins, and finally weds young Rosie, marrying her after her graduation, then proceeds to make her life a living hell. Over the course of their fourteen-year union, the police detective beats Rosie regularly. In 1985, he beats her so severely that she miscarries. Norman's temper is always quick to flare—besides beating his wife, he also brutalizes suspects. In 1985,

Norman and his partner accidentally beat an innocent young woman named Wendy Yarrow to death.

After Rosie leaves him, Norman becomes even more volatile, killing a hooker who resembles her, then embarking on a murderous rampage in search of his spouse. Utilizing his uncanny ability to get into the minds of those he is tracking (he calls it trolling), Norman traces Rosie to Liberty City, where his murder spree continues, targeting many of Rosie's friends and protectors.

Norman impulsively steals a mask of Ferdinand the bull. (This is no doubt a likeness of the character in the children's book *The Story of Ferdinand*, created by Munro Leaf and illustrated by Robert Lawson.) The mask begins to talk to Norman in the voice of his deceased, abusive father. Perhaps reflecting a latent telepathic ability of Norman's, the mask provides information about Rosie, eventually leading him to her apartment. There, after donning the mask, Norman follows Rosie into the painting, where he in effect becomes the embodiment of Erinyes, the bull god of the temple. Still wearing the mask that has somehow grafted itself to his face, Norman meets his fate at the hands of the vengeful Rose Madder.

**ERINYES.** In Greek mythology, the Erinyes, or Furies, punished sinners. Known as "those who walk in darkness," they had snakes for hair and wept tears of blood. *Erinyes* comes from the Greek word meaning "hunting down" or "persecuting." Thus it is fitting that a skilled tracker like Norman, whose only real emotion seems to be anger, became Erinyes in the world of the painting.

In the painting, Erinyes is the blind, one-eyed bull inhabiting the temple. Rosie braves that temple and its dangers to save Rose Madder's child. Just as Rosie and Rose are linked, so are Erinyes and Norman. They connect when Norman finds the Ferdinand the bull mask in the real world. The mask guides Norman to Rosie's apartment, where Norman follows Rosie into the artwork. There, he dons the mask and in effect becomes Erinyes.

**WENDY YARROW.** A young woman who falls victim to Norman Daniel's anger in the real world, Wendy is seemingly reincarnated in the world of the painting as Dorcas, Rose's companion. Dorcas acts as Rosie's mentor in the strange world of the artwork, telling her what she must do there, and giving her the tools and the information she needs to survive. She later lectures Rosie on the importance of forgetting the past. At present, she is wandering the world of the painting with Rose Madder.

**BILL STEINER.** Owner of Liberty City Pawn and Loan, he meets Rosie when she comes in to pawn her wedding ring. It falls to Bill to tell her that the diamond in the ring is not real, and thus worth only a small amount. Smitten with Rosie, Bill asks her out, becoming the first man Rosie has ever had a romantic relationship with besides Norman. Norman's polar opposite, Bill helps Rosie in her transformation from submissive victim to confident adult. After Norman's death, Bill and Rosie marry and have a child, Pamela Gertrude.

**DAUGHTERS AND SISTERS.** A shelter for battered women, Daughters and Sisters became Rosie's home for a short time following her escape from Norman.

**ANNA STEVENSON.** The formidable administrator of Daughters and Sisters, Anna reminds Rosie of Beatrice Arthur, the acerbic actress who played Maude on the sitcom of the same name. Anna takes Rosie under her wing, enabling her to start a new life under the name of Rosie McClendon. Anna is later slaughtered by the rampaging Norman.

*Rosie McClendon and Anna Stevenson are fans of Paul Sheldon, the fictional author who is the main character of King's novel* Misery *(1987).*

**ROBBIE LEFFERTS.** A producer of books on tape, Robbie hires Rosie to read hard-boiled mysteries penned by women writing under male pseudonyms. The first book Rosie narrates is *The Manta Ray*, written by Christina Bell under the name of Richard Racine. Robbie is lucky in that he never meets Norman Daniels. He presumably still makes his home in Liberty City.

# 44

## *The Green Mile*

MANY READERS were surprised—particularly longtime follow-ers of Stephen King—when *The Green Mile* was originally pub-lished. He had recently written several books about women in jeopardy, and for the most part they had not been well received. The last thing anyone would have expected from the author at the time was a serial novel about prison guards and inmates on death row in 1932, published in six, thin, monthly installments.

It was an idea and a book that seemed to fit more comfortably with some of the works he had produced much earlier in his career. And yet, as written, it is obviously a story only the middle-aged King could cre-ate with the degree of subtlety that is present in the narrative.

Serial novels are a dead publishing format. Until that point the medium hadn't been successful in decades, and it hadn't been done by a pop culture icon since Charles Dickens wrote in serial form during the nineteenth-century in England. But in March 1996, the first part of *The Green Mile*, "The Two Dead Girls," appeared and was an immediate critical and popular success. The idea of such a series of cliffhangers from the undisputed master of horror (though this is hardly a horror story) appealed to a vast number of readers. Anyone who had ever read King, and probably a great many who never had, picked up the first part and were hooked.

It wasn't just the promotional gimmick that did it. A gimmick is, after all, effective only once. The truth of the matter was that *The*

*Green Mile* was King's best writing in years, which was interesting, considering the author plainly admitted to not having had the ending fully fleshed out even as the first installments were being published.

The story is a deceptively simple one. Paul Edgecombe is the senior guard working on E Block at Cold Mountain prison in the southern United States in 1932. E Block is, for all intents and purposes, death row. A new prisoner, John Coffey, is brought into E Block and changes the lives of everyone with whom he comes into contact. A simpleton with a supernatural healing gift, Coffey is set to be executed for a crime he didn't commit. The interaction between the guards and the inmates make for a chilling and tragic plot and a wonderful morality play. The fact that it is bookended by the story of the 104-year-old Edgecombe looking back on the events adds texture that is surprising in a book as short (when compared to most of King's works) as this. On the other hand, since the long-term effects of exposure to John Coffey are really what the book is about—along with mortality and the fragility of the human condition, both physical and emotional—the book could not have worked successfully without that framing sequence.

King had already successfully written a "prison novel" (or novella), "Rita Hayworth and Shawshank Redemption." It appeared in 1982 in the collection *Different Seasons*. More dauntingly, by the time King was working on *The Green Mile*, the novella had been made into an extraordinarily good film (faithful to the original), *The Shawshank Redemption* (1994).

The author had proven he could write about the atmosphere of prison life. These two stories, however, are very different. They share a central character who is apparently innocent of the crimes for which he has been imprisoned, but there is little similarity beyond that. *Shawshank* is about the prison experience and finding a way to triumph over a system that has malfunctioned and destroyed an individual's life. It is about escape. There are moments in *The Green Mile* when it seems about to turn into a caper yarn. It never does.

*The Green Mile* is about a tragedy caused by a malfunction in the system (here, of course, the system is not only prison but society as a whole, since racism is one of the keys to Coffey's wrongful imprisonment). It is not about beating the system: it is about changing it from within. The story focuses on what the characters around John Coffey learn from the wrongs he has suffered, and the benevolence with which he faces them. Finally, more than anything, *The Green Mile* is about transcendence, both for John Coffey and for the other characters involved in the narrative.

Also unlike *Shawshank*, *The Green Mile* surprised readers by including a supernatural element. Though its presentation is subtle throughout the story, it is there nevertheless. John Coffey is empathic. His healing touch isn't merely the alleged God-given gift of a faith healer. It is a real, tangible thing. Coffey pulls the pain and suffering and disease of others into himself, feels the agony, and then expels it in a horrid, visible form, not unlike the demon rising from the ruins of the Overlook Hotel in *The Shining* (1977).

The second unnaturalistic element is Mr. Jingles, the mouse. Mr. Jingles is no ordinary rodent even before Coffey gets his hands on him. It may be possible that a mouse is just a mouse, but it's clear that King doesn't think so. Neither does Paul Edgecombe.

This brings us to a third element of the supernatural in the novel, something even more subtle than the others. As Coffey's execution approaches, Paul—and, we are led to believe, the other characters in the story—can feel the almost electrical current running through the air. The weather changes, the air itself is altered, as if some preternatural force is disturbed by what is about to occur. But there is no *deus ex machina*, as Paul and the readers might have hoped for. If some cosmic force has empowered John Coffey or is bothered by the notion of his execution, it does nothing to save him.

But in Paul Edgecombe, and in Mr. Jingles, the "magic" legacy of John Coffey lives on for a very long time.

## PRIMARY SUBJECTS

*PAUL EDGECOMBE.* As the senior guard on E Block at Cold Mountain penitentiary, Paul has a job no one would envy (save perhaps for the sadistic Percy Wetmore). E Block is where prisoners are sent after they are sentenced to die on Old Sparky, Cold Mountain's electric chair, and Paul is frequently required to strap the convicts into the chair.

During that period in 1932, when John Coffey is on E Block, Paul has one of the strangest and most tragic experiences of his life. Coffey has been convicted of murdering two young girls, but from the moment he is brought into the prison, Paul believes there is something just a little different about John Coffey.

Over time, experiencing at first hand Coffey's ability to heal and realizing the large black man is fairly simple-minded, Paul begins to believe Coffey is innocent of the murders. He sets out to prove that, but racial issues prevent anyone from reopening the case, even though Paul believes he has the actual killer, Billy Wharton, right there on E Block.

Eventually, Coffey is executed. None of the other guards will give the order to throw the switch, and Paul is forced to do it himself. Not long thereafter, Paul retires, never to participate in another execution. Coffey's legacy does not die with him. The influence of his healing power remains in Paul's life, as well as in the "life" of the mouse, Mr. Jingles. Paul experiences flashes of telepathy, an ability that eventually fades. He remains perfectly healthy all his life, up to his present age of 104.

In 1956, Paul and his wife, Janice, are in a horrible bus accident, from which only four people walk away. Janice dies, but Paul emerges without a scratch. At Georgia Pines, he begins to write the story of John Coffey and the events at Cold Mountain. He meets a woman named Elaine Connelly, who becomes his companion. He gives her the account to read. Though Elaine finds the story—particularly Paul's advanced age—difficult to swallow, she becomes a believer when Paul shows her the "pet" he has been keeping: Mr. Jingles. The mouse has survived all that time, just like Paul, thanks to John Coffey's lasting power.

Eventually, though, Mr. Jingles expires. Elaine passes on as well. For his part, Paul continues on in good health at Georgia Pines.

*JOHN COFFEY.* A black migrant worker, John Coffey was born with something extra. He has a special empathy with people and the ability to heal others, to take their pain into himself for a time and then release it into the ether. Fate is not kind to John Coffey, however. While traveling through the woods, he comes upon the bodies of two young white girls who have just been murdered. Coffey does his best to revive the victims, to heal them, but he cannot. When the bodies are found, Coffey is crying over them, blood on his hands.

Simple-minded, Coffey does not have the wits or the will to defend himself and is convicted of the crime and sentenced to death. While on E Block awaiting execution, he meets and heals senior guard Paul Edgecombe as well as others. Edgecombe and several other guards try to help Coffey, but to no avail.

Much to Edgecombe's dismay, Coffey seems almost relieved to face his execution. His empathy—feeling the pain of those around him constantly—has become an almost unbearable burden. Coffey is executed on November 20, 1932, for crimes he did not commit.

*EDUARD DELACROIX.* Delacroix lands on E Block after he rapes a girl and sets a fire to cover up the crime, taking the lives of six more people. While in prison, the skittish inmate keeps mostly to himself, making friends only with Mr. Jingles, a mouse who becomes his pet. The guards on E Block have some questions, mostly in jest, as to who is the owner and who the pet. Delacroix claims that Mr. Jingles speaks to him, whispers in his ear, and it seems the tricks the inmate "trains" the mouse to do might not have required very much training at all.

It is Delacroix's ill fortune that sadistic guard Percy Wetmore takes an instant dislike to him. Percy brutalizes Delacroix and, when preparing him for execution, purposely does not properly wet the sponges that go into the helmet of the electric chair. As a result, Delacroix is not so much electrocuted as he is burned alive in the chair.

*MR. JINGLES.* The guards on E Block originally call this mouse Steamboat Willie, after the famous Mickey Mouse cartoon. However, the mysterious rodent, who always seems a bit more intelligent than any mouse ought to be, eventually becomes the pet of inmate Eduard Delacroix. Delacroix claims that Mr. Jingles speaks to him and has told him his "real" name. To hurt Delacroix, sadistic guard Percy Wetmore kills Mr. Jingles, but the mouse is revived and healed by John Coffey.

Coffey uses enough of his power to infuse Mr. Jingles with a miraculous life span (just as Coffey does with Paul Edgecombe). Mr. Jingles later shows up, almost as if he'd been searching the man out, on the step of Edgecombe's Georgia retirement home. It seems an unlikely coincidence, and one can only assume that there is, indeed, more to the mouse than meets the eye. Whether that comes from Coffey's power, or, as seems to be indicated, was always inherent in Mr. Jingles, remains a mystery.

Mr. Jingles dies in the care of Paul Edgecombe at Georgia Pines.

*BILLY (THE KID) WHARTON.* A nineteen-year-old serial killer, Wharton fancies himself a modern-day Billy the Kid. Upon his arrival at E Block, he tries to kill a guard named Dean Stanton. It becomes obvious to the jailers that Wharton is likely responsible for the murders of the two little girls for which John Coffey is facing execution, but they can do nothing about it.

Coffey, on the other hand, can. After healing the wife of the warden, Coffey holds on to her pain and sickness until he returns to the prison. He then sends all that dark pain into Percy Wetmore, a sadistic guard whom he hates, and somehow manipulates Percy into turning that pain on Wharton, whom Wetmore shoots six times. Billy the Kid never makes it to Old Sparky.

*PERCY WETMORE.* A born sadist, Percy Wetmore won his job on E Block by virtue of being the governor's nephew. That connection also allows him to make a great deal of trouble for Paul Edgecombe and the other keepers on E Block. He brutalizes inmates, both physically and emotionally, and purposely interferes in Eduard Delacroix's execution so the man will not be electrocuted but instead burned to death by the electricity. After that event, he is intimidated into requesting a transfer to Briar Ridge Mental Hospital.

Eventually, after Percy murders an inmate (though his will is not entirely his own at the time), he is sent to Briar Ridge as a patient, and dies there in 1965.

*BRUTUS HOWELL.* A tall, imposing guard on E Block along with Paul Edgecombe, Brutus believes in John Coffey's innocence and participates in the trek with Coffey that leads to the healing of the warden's wife. His nickname is "Brutal," perhaps more because he is physically intimidating than because of any actual brutality he engages in. Brutus dies in 1957 of a heart attack.

*HAL MOORES.* Warden of Cold Mountain penitentiary, Hal is reluctant to see John Coffey executed after Coffey heals his wife's brain tumor. However, he is helpless to stop the execution. Warden Moores later dies of a stroke.

*MELINDA MOORES.* The wife of Cold Mountain's warden, Hal Moores, Melinda is dying of an inoperable brain tumor before she is miraculously healed by John Coffey. She dies of a heart attack in 1943.

*JANICE EDGECOMBE.* Paul's wife, Janice keeps after him to find a way to prove John Coffey's innocence or to help him escape. She dies in a bus accident in 1956.

*ELAINE CONNELLY.* A resident of Georgia Pines retirement home, Elaine becomes Paul Edgecombe's companion in his (very) old age. Though both Paul and Elaine are tormented by a sadistic orderly (not unlike Paul's old co-worker Percy Wetmore) named Brad Dolan, Elaine manages to intimidate Dolan somewhat with her connections at the Georgia state house.

Elaine dies of a heart attack three months after reading Paul's story about John Coffey and Cold Mountain.

## ADAPTATION

King's groundbreaking serial novel was adapted for the big screen in 1999 by writer-director Frank Darabont, who had previously performed the same miracle with *The Shawshank Redemption.*

The Green Mile features one of Hollywood's favorite leading men, Tom Hanks, as Paul Edgecombe, but also sports a marvelous supporting cast. Michael Clarke Duncan *(Armageddon)* manages the challenging role of John Coffey with

> *Director Frank Darabont has joked that, after his first two films, he's firmly established himself as the major force in a sub-sub-subgenre: lengthy period prison dramas based on the works of Stephen King. However, the auteur has also been working for quite some time on an adaptation of King's novella "The Mist."*

quiet dignity and aplomb. James Cromwell *(L.A. Confidential)* is a perfect Warden Moores, and Bonnie Hunt *(Jumanji)* portrays Janice Edgecombe with a twinkle in her eye and a confidence not often found in such roles. Chameleon-like actor Michael Jeter achieves great pathos as Delacroix, and Doug Hutchison and Sam Rockwell are gloriously evil in their respective roles as Percy Wetmore and Billy Wharton. Barry Pepper and Jeffrey DeMunn are equally adept as Paul's fellow prison guards Dean Stanton and Harry Terwilliger. Perhaps the film's best performance, however, can be attributed to character actor David Morse *(The Rock)*, who gives prison guard Brutus Howell amazing range and texture of emotion.

> *Jeffrey DeMunn, who portrays Harry in the film version of* The Green Mile, *appears in King's 1999 television miniseries* Storm of the Century *as Robbie Beals.*

Darabont's adaptation is extremely faithful to King's original text. The only major deviation concerns the wraparound story that the author included mainly as a necessity of the serial publishing format. The film opens and closes with the elderly Paul Edgecombe and Elaine Connelly, and includes Mr. Jingles—all of the elements pertinent to the themes of the narrative—but the Percy Wetmore–like orderly, Brad Dolan, has been excised completely.

> *Veteran character actor Harry Dean Stanton appears in the film as inmate trustee Toot Toot, and two of the guards on E block are named "Harry" and "Dean Stanton." The actor is also featured in the film version of* Christine. *It is highly doubtful that this is a coincidence.*

*The Green Mile* received four Academy Award nominations, including best picture and best supporting actor (Michael Clark Duncan).

# 45

## *Six Stories*

---

PUBLISHED BY King's own Philtrum Press, the signed, limited edition of 1,100 copies of *Six Stories* became an instant collector's item, quickly appreciating from its original sales price of $85. Designed by Michael Alpert, this handsome trade paperback features two previously unpublished works, "L. T.'s Theory of Pets" and "Autopsy Room Four." The other four stories—"Lunch at the Gotham Café," "The Luckey Quarter," "Blind Willie," and "The Man in the Black Suit"—were previously published in the anthology *Dark Love* (1995).

*Six Stories* (1997) is comparable to the novella collection *Different Seasons* (1982), in that the stories don't quite fit within the normal King mode. However, the author's very distinctive voice and astounding storytelling ability make this a memorable collection. More odd than horrific, these tales highlight King's extraordinary ability to create believable, three-dimensional characters to which readers can relate and sympathize.

*Note:* "The Man in the Black Suit" is discussed in section three. "Autopsy Room Four" is discussed in section two.

### "LUNCH AT THE GOTHAM CAFÉ"

First and foremost, this is a tale about smoking, a companion piece to King classics like "Quitters, Inc." and "The Ten O'Clock People." It is also a story about perceptions: Steven's and Diane's differing viewpoints about the state of their marriage, Steven's change in outlook after giving up cigarettes, and the maitre d's warped concept of reality.

## PRIMARY SUBJECTS

*STEVEN DAVIS.* Steven returns home one evening to discover that his wife, Diane, has abandoned him. Painfully aware that his marriage is obviously troubled, Steven is nevertheless stunned by this development. He sleepwalks through the next few weeks, clinging to the hope that he and his wife might reconcile. During this troubled time, he manages to give up cigarettes, which can be viewed as either as an act of penance or as Steven's attempt to gain control over at least one aspect of his life. His hopes for reconciliation are dashed by a call from his wife's attorney, requesting a luncheon meeting at Manhattan's Gotham Café to discuss the terms of their divorce. Steven reluctantly attends despite feelings of disorientation (primarily due to nicotine withdrawal) and the fact that his lawyer isn't available to accompany him.

*In 1999, "Lunch at the Gotham Café" was released as an audiobook along with two other smoking-related tales. The package was entitled* Blood and Smoke.

Arriving at the restaurant, Steven is greeted by a high-strung maitre d' who, while showing the patron to his table, keeps muttering about Steven's umbrella, which he apparently mistakes for a small dog. The conference, which quickly turns bitter, is interrupted by the maitre d', who attacks and kills Diane's lawyer, Humboldt, with a huge butcher knife. He then turns to Steven, who flees with Diane to the kitchen. The maitre d' follows, ranting, and kills the chef. Steven manages to subdue the maitre d', who is taken away on a stretcher, still raving. Steven Davis is presumably alive and well, at large in the Stephen King universe.

*DIANE DAVIS.* It is obvious that Diane feels her husband, Steven, has greatly wronged her. Even after Steven saves her from the maitre d', Diane still hates her spouse. Diane Davis is presumably alive and well, at large in the Stephen King universe.

**WILLIAM HUMBOLDT.** Diane's divorce attorney, this tough customer is eliminated by the Gotham Cafe's mad maitre d'. Humboldt's last word is "boot."

**GUY (THE MAITRE D' FROM HELL).** Little is known about the madman who is maitre d' at the Gotham Café. His first name is Guy. Apparently in the grip of potent hallucinations, Guy stabs William Humboldt in the head, then guts a co-worker in the kitchen. Steven Davis manages to disable him before he can kill again. When last seen, Guy is being taken away on a stretcher by paramedics. He is presumably still alive, but certainly not well. His whereabouts are unknown, but one would hope he is incarcerated in a place where he can do no further harm.

## "L. T.'S THEORY OF PETS"

"L. T.'s Theory of Pets" also deals with a broken marriage, this time between dog lover Lulu DeWitt, and cat lover L. T. DeWitt. Lulu abruptly leaves her husband and is never heard from again. Some folks think she has been slaughtered by the serial killer known as the Axe Man. Others think L. T. may have had something to do with it. L. T.'s devotion to Lulu and his sadness at his abandonment is poignant, almost pitiful, but never maudlin. King keeps this sad, gently humorous tale on track without making L. T. the object of ridicule he is to his peers. This story of pet ownership and failed marriages is either sad or macabre depending on your thoughts about L. T.'s possible involvement in his wife's death.

What *is* L. T.'s theory of pets? Simply this: "If your dog and cat are getting along better than you and your wife, you better expect to come home some night and find a Dear John note on your refrigerator door."

### PRIMARY SUBJECTS

**L. T. DeWITT.** L. T., an employee of the W. S. Epperton Processed Meats Plant of Ames, Iowa, is happy to tell his tale of woe to anyone who will listen. The breakup of his marriage began shortly after his wife, Lulubelle, buys him a dog, a Jack Russell terrier that he names Frank. Instead of being man's best friend, however, Frank takes to Lulu in a big way. Lulu responds to his affections, and the two form a deep bond that makes L. T. jealous. Hoping to drive a wedge between the two, L. T. buys Lulu a kitten. Since turnabout is fair play, the kitten, named Lucy, develops a crush on L. T.

Shaky to begin with, the DeWitts' marriage is further strained by the presence of the jealous pets. One day L. T. returns home to discover a Dear John letter on his refrigerator door—Lu has left, taking Frank with her. L. T. respects her request for privacy and never attempts to follow her. He remains at the meat-packing plant, trotting out his sad story every time a new recruit comes to work at the factory. L. T. DeWitt still resides in Ames, Iowa.

*LULUBELLE DeWITT.* Lulu, wife of L. T. DeWitt, disappears for good the day she leaves L. T. Her car is found splattered with animal blood, which turns out to belong to her dog, Frank. Police discover Frank's body near the scene, but Lulu remains missing. Some suspect she is the sixth victim of the serial killer known to authorities as The Axe Man.

## "THE LUCKEY QUARTER"

"The Luckey Quarter" unravels the account of Darlene Pullman, a woman who lives off the tips she earns as a maid at the seedy Rancher's Hotel. One morning, Darlene finds a quarter in the gratuity envelope she left in room 322. The tip is accompanied by a note that reads, "This is a Luckey quarter! It's true! Luckey you!" A practical woman, Darlene is nevertheless taken with the possibility that the coin may indeed be a good-luck piece, as demonstrated by a gripping fantasy sequence in which she beats the odds at a local casino. Darlene ultimately realizes she is already blessed with outrageous luck, and gives the quarter to her son.

## "BLIND WILLIE"

"Blind Willie," the most intriguing story in this collection, follows mild-mannered businessman Bill Teale on his commute to work in

New York City. Bill arrives at his office, then proceeds to another room in the same building, where he changes clothes, becoming Willie Teale. He departs, only to switch outfits again in a posh Manhattan hotel. Willie then goes to his real place of employment— Fifth Avenue, just outside of St. Patrick's Cathedral, where he earns a living as Blind Willie, Vietnam vet and panhandler. Despite its unique take on the phenomenon of street people, this narrative has a lot to say about the plight of the homeless.

An altered and expanded version of this story is incorporated into 1999's *Hearts in Atlantis*.

# 46

# Uncollected Stories

---

A SCATTERING OF RECENTLY published tales that have not yet been gathered into a formal collection are the following, written in the last few years of the 1990's.

## "EVERYTHING'S EVENTUAL"

This story, about a young man gifted with a paranormal "wild talent" (King labels him a "tranny"), appeared in the October/November 1997 issue of *The Magazine of Fantasy and Science Fiction*. It represents the author's most recent return to the science fiction genre and continues his fascination with otherwise ordinary individuals possessing incredible psychic abilities.

*According to sources close to King, the character Dinky is a Breaker, just like Ted Brautigan in* Hearts in Atlantis.

Dinky Earnshaw, the teenage narrator, tells of his ability to kill people merely by writing them letters, a talent he discovered when he dispatched a neighborhood dog simply by etching arcane symbols on an adjacent sidewalk. Dinky lives a pampered existence, his every need seen to by TransCorp, a private enterprise whose goals seem to parallel those of the secret research unit known as the Shop. All Dinky has to do is write letters to people the corporation designates as targets. At first compliant, Dinky comes to loathe his job. Eventually he turns on his handler, the mysterious Mr. Sharpton, after receiving a message from a fellow tranny that causes him to question what he is doing.

## "THAT FEELING, YOU CAN ONLY SAY WHAT IT IS IN FRENCH"

First appearing in the June 22, 1999, summer fiction issue of *The New Yorker*, this is a tale concerning marriage and *déjà vu*. King does a great job depicting how good and bad memories bind a couple together, and conveys feelings of *déjà vu* to his readers by repeating sequences from different angles throughout the story.

Embarking on a second honeymoon with her husband Bill to celebrate their silver anniversary, Carol Shelton reflects on their life together during the flight. On the way to their honeymoon hideaway, Carol experiences vague feelings that she's been in this situation before. At times she's able to predict exactly what's around the bend, but just as often, her guesses are inexact or outright wrong. Throughout, she wonders where she heard the name Floyd before and why she associates it with disaster. Floyd, she finally discovers, is the pilot of the plane she and her husband are on.

Readers are left to wonder if some of the terrifying visions she's had throughout the story are about to occur, or whether they are merely flights of fancy.

## "IN THE DEATH ROOM"

Part of the audiobook *Blood and Smoke*, a 1999 collection of three stories in which the act of smoking cigarettes is a central element, "In the Death Room" finds King dealing with horror of the most realistic sort. (The other two stories in the audiobook are "Lunch at the Gotham Café," collected in 1997's *Six Stories*, and "1408.") A contemporary tale set in an unnamed South American country, it asks: What would you do if you were in an interrogation room with four strangers who intended to torture you to death?

Fletcher, a New York reporter traveling abroad, finds himself in just such a dilemma. He is locked in a basement room of the Ministry of Information after being kidnapped off the streets in broad daylight. Fletcher is suspected of conspiring with a revolutionary group of insurgents to overthrow the current fascist regime He is introduced to the four other people in the room: first the guard Ramon, then Escabar, chief minister of information, who is an experienced torturer. The other two people are an unnamed woman in her sixties whose hairstyle reminds the reporter of the title character of the classic horror film *Bride of Frankenstein,* and a small bespectacled man named Hinds. Hinds is in charge of an electrical generator specially designed to do one thing—inflict incredible pain on anyone it touches with the tip of its specially designed steel rod.

Fletcher figures he has a "one or two chance in thirty" of surviving the interrogation if he tells what he believes his captors want to hear. He soon realizes it doesn't matter whether he lies or tells the truth; he probably will not leave the aptly named death room alive. His only chance for escape is if he finally accepts the Marlboro cigarette repeatedly offered as a token of humanity by the inhumane Escabar.

Against incredible odds, Fletcher not only kills all his captors, but also manages to escape out of the country altogether. When he finally returns to New York months later, looking like the survivor of a concentration camp, the first thing he does is treat himself to a single cigarette he purchases on Forty-third Street.

## PRIMARY SUBJECTS

*FLETCHER.* A reporter for the *New York Times,* Fletcher realizes the only chance of his escaping the torture room is by somehow employing the sole cigarette he is offered by his captors. After being subjected to indescribable pain by a specially designed torture machine, he realizes he will be killed unless he manages to slay his captors instead. When he is offered a lit cigarette, he plunges the burning tip into the eye of the guard Ramon. Taking the guard's gun, he successfully shoots Ramon, Escabar, and the "Bride of Frankenstein." Believing the punishment should fit the crime, he forces the chief torturer, Hinds, to subject himself to the pain of his own machine. Fletcher eventually escapes from the violent, fascist country with his life.

*ESCABAR*. A fat, greasy man, Escabar is not only minister of information in this small nation, he is also one of the chief torturers. He dies when Fletcher shoots him in a scuffle in the Death Room.

*"THE BRIDE OF FRANKENSTEIN."* This regal-looking woman, who does not speak with any Spanish accent, is in her sixties. Due to her dark black hair, with streaks of white running through it, Fletcher thinks of her as "the Bride of Frankenstein." She dies when she is shot by Fletcher.

*HINDS*. A small man who is bald and wears glasses, Hinds is the torture technician. It is his sadistic task to operate a machine he has apparently devised which sends an electrical current through prisoners via the tip of a steel rod. The pain the device induces can be deadly—he almost kills Fletcher while using only one-quarter of the machine's potential charge. After Fletcher dispatches his three other captors, he ensures that Hinds dies the most horrible death of all: Fletcher tricks him into putting the steel tip into his mouth, then turns the dial on full power and flips the switch.

*RAMON*. An obese prison guard (he is even fatter than Escabar) who is there to silently watch over the torture proceedings. Ramon dies when, after having a lit cigarette jammed into his eye, he is shot with his own gun by the desperate reporter.

## "1408"

This is the second of three tales read by the author in the audiobooks *Blood and Smoke*, and it is truly one of King's creepiest. Until the story appears in a collection, it is a most satisfying experience to hear the author read "1408" dramatically, guiding the unwary listener into this maelstrom of supernatural horror.

This story concerns Mike Enslin, author of "true" ghost stories, who spends the night in a haunted hotel room in New York City, where he goes through a harrowing experience while trying to quit smoking. "1408" is the number of the most haunted hotel room in the world, located in an otherwise ordinary establishment somewhere off Fifth Avenue. Skeptic Enslin has demanded to spend the night in that room, even though the hotel manager is extremely reluctant. He tells Mike that the room is truly haunted and thirty people have mysteriously died or disappeared there since the hotel opened in 1910. That is precisely why Mike insists on having the room for the night. The manager knows exactly what Mike does for a living. Mike Enslin is the author of three *New York Times* bestsellers: *Ten Nights in Ten Haunted Houses, Ten Nights in Ten Haunted Graveyards,* and *Ten Nights in Ten Haunted Castles.* His current work-in-progress is no doubt going to be published as *Ten Nights in Ten Haunted Hotels.* The brash writer is finally allowed into the room, which he truly believes cannot be haunted. In spite of his chosen subject matter, the author has never seen a real ghost, nor does he believe in their existence. But the incredible supernatural events that occur in room 1408 change Mike's views on the subject of haunts and evil spirits forever.

## PRIMARY SUBJECTS

*MIKE ENSLIN.* A cynical writer of "true" ghost stories, Mike writes these books because he knows he can make a good living from them, not because he believes in the supernatural. After spending only seventy minutes in room 1408, Mike nearly loses his life after being assaulted by the evil presence in that hotel room. Completely shattered by the experience, he gives up his writing career completely and lives in constant fear of being assaulted again by those dark forces.

*MR. OWEN.* A short, round man, Mr. Owen tries to talk Mike out of staying in the room. He tells the author the room's grim history, but it is not enough to dissuade the writer. After Mike reminds the hotel manager that he cannot, by state and federal law, prevent him from renting any specific room that is not occupied, Mr. Owen reluctantly allows the writer to have 1408. It is presumed Mr. Owen is still working at the hotel in spite of the legacy of room 1408.

*RUFUS DEARBORN.* The sewing machine salesman who saves Mike's life by dousing him with the contents of an ice bucket after he observes the author making a mad dash from room 1408 with his upper torso ablaze.

# SECTION SEVEN

## The World of Richard Bachman

*Rage*

*The Long Walk*

*Roadwork*

*The Running Man*

*Thinner*

*Desperation*

*The Regulators*

Related Tales

ICHARD BACHMAN—JUST who was, or is, he?

Is it true that he was really a New Hampshire dairy farmer who wrote novels of science fiction and psychological terror whenever he wasn't tending to his cows? Or was he the pseudonym of the world's most popular contemporary author, Stephen King?

As the world now knows, Richard Bachman was indeed a pen name for King, one he still might be using to this day if the literary deception had not been discovered in the spring of 1985. Questions still remain, however. Just *why* did the author create him in the first place? How do the Bachman titles, whether written before or after disclosure, relate to the rest of the known Stephen King universe?

Early in his career, King faced a dilemma that plagues many best-selling authors. Traditionally, publishers prefer that a highly successful writer release only *one* novel or short-story collection each calendar year. This preference is based on the logic that the publisher is then better able to promote sales (first in hardcover and later in paperback) of the individual title throughout that time period. In theory, if the author wanted to publish more than one title a year, he would have to do it under a pseudonym, as the supposedly literate public would not be capable of reading more than one new book per annum from the same author.

King has since completely shattered that unwritten rule of publishing. A look at his career chronology will show that in certain years the author introduced three or four new books, *all* of which were successful.

King also had another dilemma. By the time of the publication of his third novel, *The Shining*, in 1977, he was already universally recognized—and marketed—as a best-selling writer of horror. But the prolific author had other books that he wanted to see in print—works that would not belong to a specific genre (or were not as readily marketable) as new titles from "the undisputed master of modern horror." These include some of his earliest efforts, such as *Getting It On* (a.k.a. *Rage*) and *The Long Walk*, both written before *Carrie*, which saw print in 1974, as well as such later mainstream works as *Roadwork* and another overtly science fiction tale, *The Running Man*. Besides the understandable urge to publish what he had written, King, as an admitted brand-name author, was curious as to whether he could repeat his success strictly on literary, rather than marketing and advertising, terms.

In 1977, King asked his editor at New American Library (NAL), Elaine Koster, if she would consider publishing *Rage* as a paperback original. More important, he asked if she would agree to publish it under the name of an author other than Stephen King. Koster agreed, and *Rage* was published in 1977 with King's secret closely guarded.

According to Douglas E. Winter's *Stephen King: The Art of Darkness* (1984) King's first choice for a pen name was that of his maternal grandfather, Guy Pillsbury. NAL, fearing that someone might trace the family lineage, called the author and requested another pseudonym.

Reportedly, King was listening to the rock 'n' roll band Bachman-Turner-Overdrive at the time of the publisher's call. On his desk at that moment was a novel by Richard Stark (a pseudonym for novelist Donald E. Westlake). Seizing on these disparate elements for inspiration, King opted to use the name Richard Bachman.

Each of the Bachman novels provides clues to readers as to the true identity of its author (for people in the know, the dedications alone were a dead giveaway). With the publication of each Bachman title, King had to repeatedly deny rumors that surfaced in the horror-fiction community that he was, in fact, Richard Bachman. Although he was able to successfully deny the speculations with the first four titles (all of which were published as mass-market paperback originals with little or no fanfare or acclaim), his denials became less and less plausible with the 1984 release of *Thinner*. Not only was this novel clearly a tale of the supernatural, it was written precisely in the style which the best-selling author's millions of fans could readily recognize as being "brand-name Stephen King." The book's in-jokes (as when one of the characters notes "You were starting to sound a little like a Stephen King novel.") further indicated that the author himself was going to let the cat out of the bag sooner rather than later. It did not help the deception any that NAL, for the first time, brought out this latest Richard Bachman novel in a hardcover edition and heavily promoted it. Hundreds of advance copies were given away at the American Booksellers Association convention that year.

For some time, specialty book dealers such as Robert Weinberg and L. W. Currey had been stating in their catalogs that the Richard Bachman entries could have been written only by King, openly selling these titles to their customers as "Stephen King writing as Richard Bachman." Despite this, the general public was not yet aware just how many "unknown" King novels were actually in print.

The truth was finally publicly revealed in spring of 1985 when a Washington D.C. bookstore clerk named Steve Brown went to the Library of Congress to examine the copyright forms that had been issued for the Bachman novels. Unfortunately for King, someone at NAL had inadvertently identified him as the author of *Rage* on those documents, rather than the registered pseudonym of Richard Bachman. (Because the publisher files these forms, it's highly unlikely

King ever saw them.) In short order it was revealed to the world that King and Bachman were indeed one and the same.

Even though Bachman was now for all intents and purposes dead—the author would state in later interviews how "Dickie" had died early of "cancer of the pseudonym"—that wasn't to be the case for long. In the Stephen King universe, just because you kill someone, that doesn't always mean they stay dead. Writing under a pseudonym obviously appealed to King, as demonstrated by his comments in various forums. His bitterness at Bachman's apparent demise was evident, likely inspiring his fictional treatment of the subject in *The Dark Half* (1989). As is so aptly stated in the author's note at the beginning of that novel: "I'm indebted to the late Richard Bachman for his help and inspiration. This novel could not have been written without him."

As King explained in his introduction to the second edition (1996) of *The Bachman Books*, he had learned that Donald E. Westlake had written his exceedingly grim and violent Richard Stark novels on what he termed his "rainy days." On "sunny days" he authored books as Westlake. This was how King felt as Bachman: "Bachman—a fictional creation who became more real with each published book which bore his byline—was a rainy-day sort of guy if there ever was one."

When he began to write *The Regulators* (1996), King decided it was time to bring Bachman back from the dead. He revealed that Bachman had conveniently "left" a stack of unpublished manuscripts in his home that had been unearthed by his widow, Claudia Inez Eschelman. This information, related in a second edition of the omnibus collection *The Bachman Books*, published as a trade paperback in 1996 to coincide with the publication of *The Regulators*, strongly suggests that *The Regulators* is only the first of many "unpublished" works of Richard Bachman. As King states, "I have to wonder if there are any other good manuscripts, at or near completion, in that box found by the former Mrs. Bachman in the cellar of their New Hampshire farmhouse. Sometimes I wonder about that *a lot.*"

Other indications of how King has come to perceive his alter ego can be found in the subtle differences among the various omnibus collections of Bachman's novels. The first, published in 1985, was called *The Bachman Books: Four Early Novels by Stephen King.* The title of the original introduction, "Why I Was Bachman," is openly confessional.

The latest edition, released in 1996, was called *The Bachman Books: Four Early Novels by Richard Bachman*. Note the change in title. The new introduction for this edition—the only place King is mentioned in the entire book—is titled "The Importance of Being Bachman." Bachman was now, with the publication of *The Regulators*, still a vital part of the imagination of Stephen King.

Clearly, the early Bachman titles *(Rage, The Long Walk, Roadwork, The Running Man)* were never meant to be identified as books by Stephen King. They do, however, contain certain elements that link them to the Stephen King universe. Most of these elements are subtle—for instance, *Rage* and *The Long Walk* are set in Maine, and *Roadwork* mentions the Blue Ribbon Laundry chain, which is in the short story "The Mangler." (A supporting character in that story is identified as hailing from Portland, Maine, as well).

What is perhaps most intriguing about *The Running Man*— particularly since the town in question would not become a significant part of the prime reality of the Stephen King universe for some years—is that a large part of the story's action takes place at a regional airport in a small Maine town called Derry. This may indicate a nightmare future for the Derry of Bachman's mirror-image reality.

Although Bangor, Maine, features prominently in *Thinner,* and King is also mentioned by name, that book's major connections to the Stephen King universe lie in the use of "trademark" characters and themes, most notably in the fact that it is clearly a horror novel rather than science fiction or suspense. Those connections may have indeed become more explicit: King has stated that *Misery,* with its numerous ties to the Stephen King universe, was originally slated to be the next Bachman book.

It was only with the publication of the "mirrored" volumes of *Desperation* (by King) and *The Regulators* (by Bachman), both released in 1996 after his pseudonym had became almost as well known as his own name, that the author consciously chose to incorporate the Bachman books into the Stephen King universe. In these two novels there are heroes and villains fighting a cosmic battle of good versus evil. The references are infrequent (Ellen Carver in *Desperation* is a fan of Paul Sheldon's Misery novels) and the connecting characters minor (Cynthia Smith from *Rose Madder* appears in *Desperation*), but

King at last allows the world of Richard Bachman to interact with his other parallel realities.

As far as King is concerned, Bachman is indeed alive and well, lurking in the darkest recesses of the author's imagination, waiting for the next rainy day. But as far as the relationship between the world of Richard Bachman and the rest of the Stephen King universe is concerned, there are parallels to be drawn other than the coincidences noted above. However, in order to do so, one must examine *Desperation* and its mirror image, *The Regulators*. Both books feature Tak, a powerful being from beyond our familiar reality. Tak is described as an "outsider," a word used to describe the evil force in King's *Bag of Bones*. Indeed, the two creatures—along with *It* from the novel of that same name—seem to have a great deal in common.

In both books, King has returned to the cosmic battle between chaos and order, or the Random and the Purpose, on a microcosmic level. Clearly, though, the connection between the Bachman corner of the Stephen King universe and its other facets is strongest and clearest in these two works.

# 47

## *Rage*

---

ALTHOUGH TECHNICALLY the third novel King published, *Rage* (1977) was the first issued under the author's pseudonym of Richard Bachman. It has since been learned that *Rage* was in fact the very first novel-length work ever completed by King. Begun in 1966 while still in high school, King would not complete the manuscript until 1971 when he was in college. Prior to the book's publication, King updated the story by inserting mentions of best-selling books and popular movies of the mid-1970s.

Regardless of when it was originally written, *Rage* remains one of King's darkest, most pessimistic and, unfortunately, most chillingly plausible works. As to where it fits within the Stephen King universe, one must first take into account that by the time he had first reached the hardcover bestseller lists with *The Shining* in 1977, King was already firmly established in the public's mind as a writer of supernatural horror. This was to be expected, given the horrific content of *Carrie*, *'Salem's Lot*, and *The Shining*, not to mention the numerous short stories he had penned. It would not be long before reviewers would crown him as the king of modern horror or king of the bogeymen.

But King knew—even if his readers would not for several years—that he was capable of writing vital and important works of suspense outside the horror genre as well. He also knew that, due to his incredible early success, he had enough leverage to rescue his earliest works from the traditional writer's "trunk" where they had been languishing and publish them, albeit under a pen name and only as mass market paperback originals. By creating Richard Bachman, the author believed he could best serve his desire to see *all* of his early fiction published, and, even more liberating, break free of readers' expecta-tions. Not only would King get to see his early novels in print, but he also would gain the freedom to create new works on any topic and in any style he cared to experiment with, and no one but Bachman fans would be impressed or upset with the published results.

> *The original title for the novel was Getting It On.*

"The morning I got it on was nice" is how *Rage*, this ticking time bomb of a novel, begins. The young man planning to "get it on" (a pop-ular phrase of the 1960s, originally meaning to get something accom-plished no matter what the consequences) is Charlie Decker. An average student, Charlie outwardly appears no different from the oth-ers in his class, except for the fact that he's taken to carrying a handgun to school. Before this "nice" day is over, people will be ter-rorized and humiliated. Some will be shot. Some will die.

Charlie is a classic trou-bled youth, a teenager who has big problems with authority, problems that manifested themselves a few months ear-lier when he attacked a teacher with a wrench. Shortly after a troubling encounter with his overbearing father, something inside Charlie snaps. He sets fire to his school locker, then proceeds to shoot two teachers. Holding his classmates hostage, Charlie forces his terrified peers to examine where each of them belongs in this world, in a chilling game of trying to decide who is worthy to live through this ordeal and who is not.

> *Charlie's father admires the crime novels of Richard Stark. That name is a pseudonym of one of King's favorite writers, Donald E. Westlake. King, of course, published* Rage *under a pseudonym. Later in his career, King would write* The Dark Half *(1989), in which the main character, author Thad Beaumont, uses "George Stark" as a pseudonym.*

Although Charlie is unflinchingly portrayed at all times as an unrepentant killer, King still manages to evoke sympathy for him. The reader often finds himself or herself thinking, *You know, I might have done the same thing if I had walked a mile in his shoes.* Even as Charlie is taken away into custody, we are left with the unsettling impression that there are a lot more young people like him just waiting for something to set them off, something that will for no apparent reason trigger a murderous urge to "get it on." As recent tragic events in schools across the country have shown, there are troubled students who have in fact forsaken everything to unleash their murderous rage against their teachers and peers.

Not surprisingly, this novel bears a number of striking similarities to *Carrie,* also about a troubled high school student (although not published until 1977, *Rage* actually was written several years before *Carrie*). Like Carrie White, Charlie Decker is someone who doesn't fit in with any established clique or group. The only way he thinks he can resolve his personal conflicts is to lash out against others in a violent and deadly manner. Both novels deal with young individuals trying to survive in what for them is a harsh and brutal environment: high school. The major difference between the two works is that *Carrie* is basically science fiction, featuring a young woman with a so-called wild talent. *Rage*'s premise is all too believable, although in one sense it almost falls into the category of science fiction in that the novel predicted—decades before it would occur in reality—the scenario of young, fresh-faced killers stalking the classroom.

In terms of its place in the Stephen King universe, *Rage* is indeed a contemporary horror novel. It deals with strictly plausible horrors, which the author would later explore in *Cujo* (1981), *Gerald's Game* (1992), *Misery* (1987) and "Apt Pupil." The latter, originally published in the 1982 collection *Different Seasons,* is especially significant. In that novella, King again explores the idea that sometimes the best place for true evil to fester and grow is within a high school student.

From the very beginning of his career, King has always reminded readers that perhaps the greatest horror in life is that sometimes good people die unexpectedly. Just as unfairly, sometimes bad and evil people go on living. He is also telling us, of course, that the scariest monsters in this world are not vampires or zombies, but the one we may encounter staring back at us from a mirror.

*King in campus protest* | YEARBOOK PHOTO

Because of the belief that many young people may have been inspired by *Rage* to carry out their own violent acts in school, King has reportedly decided to allow the book to go out of print. In the introduction to the second edition of *The Bachman Books* (1996), King relates the many sleepless nights he has spent wrestling with the idea that something he has written, however remotely, may have been part of what he terms "a triggering mechanism" to later acts of violence. The author himself does realize *Rage* is about the consequences of extreme anger, and it is obvious on every page that the book was written by someone who was also inwardly frustrated and resentful at the world. King can barely recall what kind of person he was at the time he wrote *Rage,* which may be another reason why he is reluctantly but willingly letting it go.

## PRIMARY SUBJECTS

*CHARLIE DECKER.* A lonely misfit, Charlie is a young man who resents most adults and authority figures, especially his brutish father. After various altercations with his father, his teachers, and the school principal, Charlie can no longer contain his growing feelings of resentment and rage. Shortly after he is expelled from Placerville High School, Charlie retrieves a gun from his locker and proceeds to shoot two teachers, taking a class of his peers hostage in the process. After he is captured, Charlie is judged unfit to stand trial by reason of insanity and sent to the Augusta State Hospital in Augusta, Maine.

*TED JONES.* One of the most popular boys in school, Ted is one of the students Charlie holds hostage. Publicly humiliated during the course of a violent "encounter session" instigated by Charlie, Ted has a nervous breakdown. He is eventually committed to a mental institution, where it is presumed he still resides.

*CAPTAIN FRANK PHILBRICK.* The man in charge of the Maine State Police unit who respond to the hostage crisis, it is his task to try and talk Charlie Decker into surrendering without further violence. He also gives the order to a sharpshooter to try and kill Charlie.

*DANIEL MALVERN.* A member of the Maine State Police, he is considered the state's best sharpshooter. He fires one shot at Charlie using a Mauser rifle with a telescopic lens. The bullet hits Charlie directly in the area of the heart, but the young man is spared a fatal injury when the bullet is deflected by a padlock he had placed in his shirt pocket earlier in the day.

# 48

## *The Long Walk*

---

ONE OF THE EARLY Bachman books (along with *Rage,* *Roadwork,* and *The Running Man*), *The Long Walk* (1979) is the second novel-length work ever completed by King. Written in 1966 during his freshman year at the University of Maine at Orono, it was also one of his earliest attempts at what could be termed a work of science fiction rather than the horror novels and short stories on which his initial fame would rest. (Interestingly, King himself considers *Carrie* (1974), *The Dead Zone* (1979), and *Firestarter* (1980) to be more in line with what he calls science fiction, as he believes these explorations of fantastic paranormal talents were but variations on classic science fiction themes.)

Like the previous Bachman novel *Rage* (1977), *The Long Walk* also concentrates solely on young people as its primary characters. The action is seen only through the eyes of adolescents as they experience rude awakenings. *The Long Walk* takes place in an unspecified near future, in a bleak, ultraconservative Amerika (note the spelling, a then-popular representation of America as a fascist state). The country seems to have fought and lost a major energy crisis and the democracy has been replaced by a police state.

King never states precisely why or how these events have come to pass, but it is clearly a parallel world in which joy and hope have long been lost, along with most of our customary constitutional rights. Given the similarities to the future world presented in *The Running*

*Man,* we posit that the future presented in both books is simply the dark future of the more contemporary world of the Bachman novels. Thus, it is feasible to conclude that they all take place in the same reality, at different times.

To buoy the sagging spirits of the citizenry, the powers that be have created a pseudo-spectacle/sporting event called the Long Walk, a grueling 450-mile trek through the state of Maine. One hundred of the nation's best young men (with one hundred alternates) are selected to enter the marathon through a national lottery. Whoever wins the race—there can be only one champion—will be rewarded with whatever his heart desires for the rest of his life.

For reasons of which he is not certain, sixteen-year-old Ray Garraty enters the contest. To win, all he has to do is complete the Long Walk. Unfortunately, there are no stops, no rest periods, no breaks of any sort. If you want to eat,

> *The fact that* The Long Walk *is dedicated to three of King's teachers at the University of Maine (Jim Bishop, Burt Hatlen, and Ted Holmes) was a major clue in uncovering the indentity of Richard Bachman.* The Running Man *is the only Bachman novel not to carry a dedication.*

you must do so while walking. If you need to eliminate your body waste, you have to do it while walking. Plus, there's a simple incentive to obey the rules once the race begins. Those who do not keep up with the pack are given three separate warnings by the soldiers/observers accompanying the Walkers. After issuing the third warning, the soldiers are authorized to shoot to kill. No excuses. No exceptions. No mercy.

Obviously a crude allegory about the military selective service carried to the extreme, King's tale is grimly compelling, if undeniably narrow, in its vision. Like *The Running Man* (1982), there are several elements to *The Long Walk* that were likely inspired by television game shows. For instance, nearly every chapter opens with epigraphs from a host or creator of a classic television game show, including *Jeopardy, Let's Make a Deal,* and most tellingly *You Bet Your Life.* Perhaps the book's most explicit quote is attributed to *Gong Show* creator Chuck Barris at the opening to chapter 4, in which he states, "The ultimate game show would be one where the losing contestant was killed."

*The Long Walk* is a game of winner-take-all, with a live audience of thousands of bystanders cheering from the sidelines in every town the Walkers pass through. These spectators are just as thrilled to watch the carnage that befalls the contestants who lag behind. In this future, King suggests that human nature has changed very little since the era of the ancient Romans, when slaves were fed to the lions in the barbaric games played out in Colosseum. Even though Garraty wins the marathon, it's hinted that he's been driven insane by the experience and thus is unable to enjoy his spoils. The cruel satire is that there is really no point to participating in the Long Walk—everyone loses in the end.

As he did in *Rage,* King's alter ego posits a much grimmer world than readers might expect from the average Stephen King novel. Except for the science fiction element of the lethal race, *The Long Walk* focuses on human beings under extreme pressure, detailing the horrors that can occur when people are pushed to their limits. Like the author's other early works, *The Long Walk* is extremely linear in its focus, with no major subplots or digressions from its main narrative. There is little diversion from the hopeless situation of one hundred young men who have been selected to live and die on their fateful journey through Maine. The narrative radiates an unrelentingly angry and pessimistic worldview. As with *Rage,* the young author was writing during a period in his life when the literary cliche of "angry young writer" more than likely applied.

Much of the novel's extreme pessimism is a product of the era in which it was written, an era in which King and his contemporaries faced the grim prospect of being drafted to fight in the Vietnam War. After one went off to the trenches, it was largely fate that dictated whether a soldier would survive his tour of duty without being grievously wounded or killed. Many people of King's generation believed that the Vietnam War—indeed, *all* wars—made no sense and served no meaningful purpose. Similarly, the government-run Long Walk serves no purpose other than to ensure that the young men involved suffer horrible and violent deaths.

We never learn exactly why the Long Walk is so important to the interests of this parallel Amerika. It's never suggested that women become involved in the Long Walk, though one can safely assume that the futuristic premise was undertaken before the integration of women into the military had begun. It is also hinted by the Walkers themselves that it's possible *no one* truly wins the Walk. Whoever survives the marathon is ultimately rewarded by being taken behind a building and shot in the head. In this Amerika, it doesn't matter if you support or oppose the conservative politics of the nation. Either way, you are just so much target practice for the Establishment.

King makes several veiled references to Shirley Jackson's classic short story "The Lottery" (1948) in furthering a major theme of *The Long Walk:* that life is unfair. At the chilling climax of Jackson's story, an innocent person is sacrificed by a crowd of people simply because someone *has* to die—and this unfortunate woman just happens to be the one who "wins" the lottery. That victim could be any one of us. No one denies that the system is unfair, but it's a system that works for those in control, for those who make the rules.

In *The Long Walk,* King's young victims—who sometimes cry out "It's not fair!" before being shot—could be any innocent person chosen in the national lottery of the government's selective service process. Forced to embark on a deadly journey of self-discovery, they hope against hope that they can somehow reach the end of their tour of duty—their long walk—without being shot by nameless, faceless enemies.

*The Long Walk* fits well into the Stephen King universe in that it reveals King's long-standing distrust of the government, and how little control most of us have over our own lives, even in a free society. No matter what Garraty's fellow competitors say or do to protest their impossible situation, after three warnings they are snuffed out by soldiers obeying the men who control the country.

## PRIMARY SUBJECTS

*RAY GARRATY.* Walker No. 47, Ray is only sixteen years old. He isn't sure why he didn't try to get out of participating in the trek, even though he had several chances to do so, and considering that his father has already been taken away for speaking against the ghastly practice. At one point in the grisly marathon, he goes out of his way to embrace his mother and his girlfriend, and the action nearly costs him his life. Despite the odds, Ray somehow completes the Long Walk, emerging as its sole winner (and survivor). Ray's whereabouts in the Stephen King universe are unknown. It is strongly suggested that he has been driven insane by his harrowing experience.

*JIM GARRATY.* When Ray's father, Jim, dares to speak out against the inhumane Long Walk, he is taken away in the middle of the night by one of the government's special squads. His current whereabouts are unknown, but he is presumed dead.

*PETER McVRIES.* Walker No. 67 and one of the very last to fall, Peter gets to know Ray more intimately than any of the other Walkers. The two young men repeatedly save each other's life before all their warnings from the soldiers are used up. Unfortunately, Peter receives his final "ticket" just as the end of the Long Walk is in sight.

*STEBBINS.* Stebbins, Walker No. 88, almost makes it to the end of the Walk before being terminated. Possibly gripped by madness, Stebbins claims the mysterious Major, an important member of the oppressive governing body, is his father, and that he is one of his many illegitimate sons.

*THE MAJOR.* The mysterious military man in charge of the Long Walk, the Major never appears in public without wearing reflective sunglasses. At the beginning of the Walk, he tells the young participants how proud he is of them and wishes them all luck, then disappears for most of the remainder of the arduous contest. He may or may not be Stebbins's father. Before the squads took him away, Ray Garraty's father called the Major "the rarest and most dangerous monster any nation can produce, a society-supported sociopath."

*THE DARK FIGURE.* At the very end of the Long Walk, Ray Garraty spies a figure who seems to be taunting him to keep on walking. This nameless figure may be the specter of death, but its obscene actions suggest it may instead be a pawn, or may be yet another incarnation of the dark man, Randall Flagg.

# 49

## *Roadwork*

---

CERTAINLY ONE of the bleakest, if not *the* bleakest of the Richard Bachman books, the argument could be made that *Roadwork* (1981) is truly the darkest of all Stephen King's writings. Created at a time when the author was enjoying considerable success, the decidedly mainstream novel was written between *'Salem's Lot* (1975) and *The Shining* (1977), a depressing time in U.S. history. It was also composed a year after the author's mother had died painfully from cancer.

King has expressed mixed feelings about this book over the years. In the introduction to the first omnibus edition of *The Bachman Books* in 1985, King states, "I suspect *Roadwork* is probably the worst of the lot simply because it tries to be good and to find some answers to the conundrum of human pain." However, in his second, new introduction to a later edition of *The Bachman Books*, issued in 1996, King says it is "my favorite of the early Bachman books." Whether it is the best or the worst is still open to debate. But like *Rage*, it remains one of the few books by King where not a hint of the supernatural nor the bizarre is to be found—the horrors of everyday life are more than enough to drive some of us mad.

The novel tells of the imminent destruction of one man's life. Barton George Dawes has spent all of his adult life living in the same average house, living on the same ordinary street, married to the same plain woman, working for an undistinguished company, the Blue

Ribbon Laundry. All of that is about to change as the state government decides to build a freeway extension in his small city that will pass through the laundry's current location, but also through Dawes's neighborhood. Everything that has held Dawes's life together will be plowed under and covered over—in others words, methodically erased.

Barton Dawes isn't going to let his world be taken from him without a fight. He decides to do everything in his power to prevent the freeway extension from being constructed. It doesn't matter that the cards are stacked completely against him, that whatever he does to hinder the roadway, the extension *will* be built. Dawes single-mindedly pursues his goal even when he knows it's hopeless. He firebombs the construction site, burning down the construction hut and damaging most of the heavy equipment. Later, turning on the evening news, he learns to his utter disbelief that the project is going to be delayed only by a few months at most.

> *The Blue Ribbon Laundry chain also figures prominently in the short story "The Mangler," from Night Shift.*

*Roadwork* starts on a shrill note of unwanted change and doesn't let up until Dawes's entire world dissolves in a nerve-shattering wail of loss, mistrust, and pain. Subtitled *A Novel of the First Energy Crisis,* the majority of the plot occurs between November 20, 1973, and January 20, 1974, the time of the United States' nationwide energy shortage brought on by the Middle East oil crisis. In that brief time span, we witness Dawes's rapid disintegration as he loses first his livelihood, then his marriage, and finally his cherished home.

> Roadwork *is the only Bachman novel to have a subtitle* (A Novel of the First Energy Crisis). *It was not carried over for the later omnibus editions.*

Distraught, Dawes concludes he has no other choice than to literally go out in a blaze of glory. Realizing he can't stop the freeway extension, he instead wires his empty home with explosives, arms himself with high-powered weapons, and waits for the police—and the bulldozers—to arrive. His home is the last part of his special world that he can exist safely within; if he can't live there, he won't live anywhere.

Tellingly, King makes a point of never saying precisely what small city or state Barton Dawes calls home (although one could make an educated guess that the story is set in the Midwest, probably lower Wisconsin). His point? That this could happen anywhere, to anyone. Never has King written a more earnestly mainstream novel. There are no fantasy or supernatural elements whatsoever in *Roadwork* to soften the blows, and yet it becomes quickly surreal in the sense that everything that befalls Dawes is like a personal solar eclipse. Everything gets increasingly blacker and blacker until he is finally totally consumed by the darkness around him. There are no joyful sequences to balance the unremitting series of small catastrophes that are steadily burying Dawes alive, one brick at a time. The nation, rocked by an energy crisis, is still licking its psychic wounds from the recent end of the Vietnam War, and no one seems to know what tomorrow may bring.

> *On the back cover copy of the original paperback edition of* Roadwork, *the main character is misidentified as George Bart Dawes.*

No heroes are to be found in *Roadwork*. Most of the characters introduced are unlikable, untrustworthy, or immoral. Oddly enough, one of the few relatively likable figures is a small-time Mafia hood. In *Roadwork*, decent people die in senseless car accidents, or drop dead in supermarkets of a brain hemorrhage, or are fired from their jobs for no good reason. Dawes's only child, Charlie, dies of a brain tumor that his doctors can't explain.

Dawes himself feels he is dying of "soul cancer" and thus believes his criminal actions are his only way of striking back against a world that has so terribly wronged him. Yet King never allows us to do more than pity Dawes, as we only see his dark, obsessive side. His obsession with maintaining his rapidly disappearing lifestyle cannot have any other outcome than to ultimately lead to his violent and meaningless death.

King tells us time and again in *Roadwork* that life is not fair, that it doesn't matter how hard you try to live your life honestly. We are all going to die sooner or later, and when we do, it probably won't be at the right time, and it probably won't be pleasant. Most frightening of all, it's likely that no one else is going to notice your passing, or care if you were ever here in the first place.


## PRIMARY SUBJECTS

*BARTON GEORGE DAWES.* Dawes is a middle-aged, low-level businessman who has worked all his adult life for a local laundry firm. He is married to Mary Dawes, who, even though she loves him, leaves him as his behavior becomes increasingly erratic. Desperate to stop the progress of a freeway extension that is slated to go through his home, Dawes goes to a local used-car salesman who is actually a criminal, and purchases explosives. After first temporarily halting construction by firebombing a work site, Dawes uses the explosives to wire his home. After being cornered by the police during a violent shootout, Dawes puts himself out of his misery by setting off the dynamite.

*MARY DAWES.* A local woman who has lived her life through her husband, Barton Dawes. She has given birth to two children by him, both with tragic results. The first was stillborn, while the second, Charlie, later dies from an inoperable brain tumor. She leaves her husband when she realizes he is too inflexible to cope with any further hard blows from life. Mary Dawes's current whereabouts are unknown.

*CHARLIE DAWES.* The young son of Barton and Mary Dawes, Charlie dies of a brain tumor—a cancerous growth about the size of a walnut, according to his doctor—leaving his parents childless and alone. Charlie's middle name is Freddy. Before he kills himself, Barton frequently holds imaginary conversations with his dead son.

*OLIVIA BRENNER.* A native of Portland, Maine, Olivia is a twenty-one-year-old woman who is hitchhiking her way to Las Vegas when Barton Dawes gives her a lift. Although he deeply regrets the act later, Barton gives in to temptation and sleeps with the attractive young stranger. Later, using money from the sale of his home to the city, he sets up a trust fund for her. She apparently uses it to get her life together and enrolls in business school, an achievement Dawes never lives to see.

*SAL MAGLIORE*. A local criminal who operates a used-car lot as a cover for his extralegal activities, Sal is an obese, vulgar, and unattractive individual who has the ability to get anything for anyone for the right price. Although he at first refuses to sell Barton Dawes the explosives he asks for, he later decides to do so out of a grudging respect for him. Sal realizes that Dawes, crazed though he clearly must be, is operating out of his own code of honor. As such, the criminal finds himself perversely drawn to the doomed man despite his better judgment.

*DAVE ALBERT*. A reporter for the local WHLM television station, Albert first encounters Dawes when both attend the official groundbreaking for the highway extension. By a quirk of fate, Albert is also the first journalist on the scene when Dawes makes his last stand in his home. After giving the reporter an exclusive, Dawes advises him to leave the scene before it is too late. Dawes says the reporter will probably earn a Pulitzer Prize for being in the right place at the right time, and as fate would have it, that's precisely what happens.

*THE BLUE RIBBON LAUNDRY*. The small family business where Barton Dawes has been employed for many years. It is taken over by a company that has no need for anything but the bottom line.

# 50

## *The Running Man*

---

AN EARNEST ATTEMPT at writing a sparse, fast-paced novel squarely set in the science fiction genre, *The Running Man* (1982) was also King's second work, after *The Long Walk* (1979), to be directly inspired by television game shows. In the epigraph that opens chapter 4 of *The Long Walk,* game show creator Chuck Barris is quoted as saying: "The ultimate game show would be one where the losing contestant was killed." Clearly, that statement was the trigger for this grim satire of a North American police state where there is no hope for the masses except to watch and bet on the ultraviolent games shown continuously on "free-vee." As in *The Long Walk,* the setting is an even more corrupt vision of an ultraconservative police state.

The action takes place in the year 2025, when the most popular game show on the planet is *The Running Man.* It is also the most deadly: if a contestant successfully eludes police and specially trained government hunters for thirty days, he wins the game. Of course, no one has survived lived long enough to collect the staggering $1 billion prize.

But Ben Richards, a sullen outsider whose stubborn independence and relatively high intelligence keep him from accepting the status quo, decides to take that suicidal risk and becomes a contestant. He feels he has no other options: he is chronically unemployed, his wife has to work as a prostitute to support the family, and their only child may die unless they get the necessary finances to secure the proper medical care.

Of course, the game is rigged, and it's all but impossible for any-one to last for more than a few harrowing days. Portrayed as a killer and a thief to millions of television viewers by the program's unscrupu-lous producers, Richards finds the odds stacked against him. Perceived as a ruthless criminal, it seems only a matter of time before he is spot-ted by one of his fellow citizens and turned in for a monetary reward.

With the aid of the members of a small underground movement (seemingly the only ones aware of how the Establishment is poison-ing the very air the common citizens must breathe), Richards manages to stay one step ahead of the hunters, at one point kidnapping a wealthy citizen to deter the police from firing on his car. After a har-rowing cross-country chase, he ends up at an airfield in Derry, Maine. Pretending he has a bomb, he hijacks an aircraft and has it flown toward the city where the Games headquarters is situated.

In the meantime, the powerful men who run the game decide it would be better for the government if, instead of killing Richards, they fake his demise and give him a fresh identity and a new job as their new chief hunter. They make their proposal to Richards, informing him that his wife and child have been murdered by "vandals." Devastated, Richards decides to strike back at his tormentors by crashing the huge aircraft directly into their headquarters. Hopefully, the act may inspire the masses to rise up against their oppressors. Then again, maybe no one will even notice.

According to King's own note in *The Bachman Books* omnibus, issued in 1985, "*The Running Man*, for instance, was written during a period of seventy-two hours with virtually no changes." It was con-ceived over a long weekend in 1971, shortly after King wrote the first draft of *Carrie*. King's belief at the time was that *The Running Man* was a more commercial prospect than his tale of a high school misfit endowed with paranormal abilities. He submitted it to both Doubleday & Co. and Ace Books (a leading paperback publisher of science fiction and fantasy), and both promptly passed on it.

The reasons for the rejection may have had to do with the dark tone of the novel. The novel is unrelentingly bleak—Ben Richards is presented as a doomed figure, someone who is selected from the masses to provide a few hours of entertainment on "free-vee" and then trashed. Richards knows he is a marked man, and the way he deals with the individuals who are hunting him can be resolved in only one of two ways: through their violent termination or his own.

Although written several years after *The Long Walk*, *The Running Man* shares many themes with that novel. Both Ben Richards and Ray Garraty of *The Long Walk* enter a government-controlled game in which both know from the outset that they have a very small chance of winning—or even surviving. Both men, when they realize they are going to win, no longer care about the outcome. In spite of their great ordeal, their ultimate fate is meaningless. Just because you survive doesn't mean you're safe. Life still remains horribly unfair, and hopelessness is the status quo.

In both novels, King presents us with grim dystopian societies where, no matter what the final scorecard might say, there are never any real victors. You might survive the games imposed on you by the government, but you will never leave any lasting mark on the rest of the world. That doesn't mean that the battle is not worth fighting. In the Stephen King universe, there will always be a Ray Garraty or Ben Richards who will try to overcome the seemingly impossible odds.

## PRIMARY SUBJECTS

*BEN RICHARDS.* Richards is the longest-surviving contestant ever to play the national game the Running Man. Twenty-eight years old, he has no family save for his wife and child. Essentially a loner, Richards has never believed in any causes or shown allegiance to any political movement. He was fired from his last six jobs due to gross insubordination.

Tired of living in abject poverty, and in need of money to pay for his sick child's medication, he takes the suicidal risk of becoming a contestant on the government-sponsored game show *The Running Man*. While traveling across the country in the run of his life, Richards realizes that the government is purposely keeping the majority of the population downtrodden and ill. After hijacking an airplane, he directs the craft into the game's headquarters in Co Op City, sacrificing his life to make his first and last political stand.

*SHEILA RICHARDS.* The wife of Ben Richards, Sheila is among the millions of citizens kept in poverty by the government. Just as

Richards's mother had done, Sheila is often forced to sell her body to help put food on the table. She is murdered by persons unknown shortly after her husband becomes a participant in the Running Man.

*CATHY RICHARDS.* The eighteen-month-old infant child of Ben and Sheila Richards, Cathy is very ill with the flu. Because medicine is prohibitively expensive, her father becomes a contestant on the game show *The Running Man* to win money to purchase the necessary drugs. She is murdered with her mother by persons unknown, though these nameless intruders may have been under the employ of the Games Authority.

*DAN KILLIAN.* Executive producer of *The Running Man,* Killian is the puppet master, the man who controls everything that goes out over the airwaves. Ben Richards hates him from the moment they meet. Killian later tries to convince him to stay on as the new chief hunter, but his offer is refused. Killian presumably dies when the aircraft carrying Richards crashes directly into the game's headquarters.

*BOBBY THOMPSON.* The on-air host and emcee of *The Running Man.* It is Thompson's job to incite the studio audience—and the millions of people watching at home—to turn against Ben Richards. He dies in the explosion and fire caused when Richard's aircraft smashes into the game's headquarters.

*EVAN McCONE.* The unflappable chief hunter, McCone is aboard the aircraft that Ben Richards uses against the Games Authority. Before he dies, he learns the Authority is quite willing to let Richards kill him and replace him as the new chief hunter. He expires in a shootout with Richards on the plane, even though Richards has no intention of ever taking his place on *The Running Man.*

*ELTON PARRAKIS.* An automatic vending machine serviceman, Parrakis is instrumental in assisting Ben Richards in his cross-country flight. Part of an underground movement trying to inform the public that the government is killing them with unchecked environmental pollution, he is shot to death by the police after a car chase.

*AMELIA WILLIAMS.* The well-to-do woman whom Ben Richards kidnaps near the end of his fateful journey. Because she is clearly a member of the upper class, the police and those hunting Richards are afraid to eliminate him while she remains his prisoner. Also, her innocent death would be seen by millions on the global television system and would not be good for ratings. Although she is terrified by Richards and all that he represents, Amelia inexplicably finds herself going along with the desperate man's requests. Amelia survives Richards's suicidal act of defiance when her captor allows her to parachute from the plane shortly before impact.

## ADAPTATION

Released in 1987, the film version of *The Running Man* was the first screen adaptation of a Richard Bachman novel. King reportedly insisted that the credits read "Based on the novel by Richard Bachman" despite the fact that the world already knew who Bachman was. It is interesting to note, though, that the film rights to the story were purchased *before* it was known that King was Bachman.

In terms of just the basic plot, the movie is faithful to the source material. If Ben Richards (Arnold Schwarzenegger) and his reluctant companion, Amber (Maria Conchita Alonso), can escape a band of professional stalkers, he will win the grand prize on the planet's most popular television game show, hosted by the flamboyant Dan Killian (Richard Dawson). It's a futuristic version of the classic short story "The Most Dangerous Game," with a man on the run from a pack of vicious hunters.

Schwarzenegger's presence influenced the final version, as the story was extensively revamped to serve as a vehicle for the international action star. Rather than a sullen, desperate man trying to win the merciless competition to purchase medicine for his sick child, Ben Richards is now a rogue policeman who has been betrayed by the corrupt government. There really isn't much suspense, as viewers are never in doubt that Richards will ultimately triumph in the end. Schwarzenegger capitalizes on the larger-than-life roles he had already played in *The Terminator* (1984) and *Commando* (1985). The script even has the brutal one-liners that were to become a signature part of his career. (For example, after he cuts one of his foes in two with a chainsaw, Arnold remarks wryly, "He had to split.")

To increase the odds against Richards, screenwriter Stephen E. de Souza created a group of professional hit men—cartoonlike villains called Stalkers—for him to dispatch in imaginative and darkly humorous ways. The actors in these bizarre roles are appropriately larger than life: professional wrestlers Jesse "the Body" Ventura, Professor Toru Tanaka, and athlete-turned-actor Jim Brown, among others. Richard Dawson—himself a longtime television game show personality—clearly has the most fun as the ruthless yet jovial game show host Killian.

This extremely violent, R-rated feature shares little in common with the book other than the title and basic concept. Perhaps King was wise to let the world remember it as a movie based on an early work by Richard Bachman.

# 51

## *Thinner*

---

**T**HE PUBLIC AT LARGE learned the true identity of King's Richard Bachman pseudonym shortly after the publication of *Thinner* in fall of 1984. Ironically, King had at one point considered issuing the book under his own name. This is not surprising in hindsight, given that *Thinner* reads very much like an archetypal King novel. It is a chilling, exquisitely wrought tale of supernatural horror.

The work remains true to the spirit of previous Bachman titles in that it is exceedingly bleak and downbeat. None of the characters is particularly likable, and their ultimate fates are not particularly pleasant. From the very first page there is a sense of dread, of inevitability, that gives the reader the impression that the author wants to show us humanity at its worst and most vengeful. *Thinner* grapples with the themes of guilt, responsibility, justice, and retribution. If revenge is truly a dish best served cold, then nearly all the characters in *Thinner* get their fill.

Billy Halleck is an attorney who resides in suburban Connecticut and practices law in New York City. At age thirty-six, he has it all: a successful career, a pretty wife, and a wonderful daughter. His one flaw is that he enjoys eating too much—he is fifty pounds overweight and has been warned by his doctor that he is at risk for a heart attack if he doesn't cut back.

Billy's girth ceases to be an issue after he accidentally hits and kills an old Gypsy woman, Susanna Lemke, with his car. Taking advantage of his good standing in the community and of his close ties with the local police and judge, he gets off with the proverbial slap on the wrist. Enraged by this miscarriage of justice, the Gypsy woman's father, Taduz Lemke, places a curse on Billy. As Billy is leaving the court-house, Lemke whispers a single word: "Thinner."

From that day forward, Billy loses two pounds every day. At first overjoyed, he later turns fearful as it appears he can do nothing to reverse the process. Judge Cary Rossington and Police Chief Hopley, both of whom helped Billy escape punish-ment, are also victims of Gypsy curses, suffering terribly from unknown and incurable afflic-tions that are rapidly disfigur-ing their bodies. These curses are metaphors for the terrifying maladies that can inflict themselves on us at any time in our lives: cancer, heart disease, even mental illness.

> Thinner *was the first Richard Bachman title to be published in hardcover and given strong promo-tion by its publisher, New Ameri-can Library.*

The fact that nearly two out of every three Americans have a weight problem makes Billy Halleck's dilemma easy to relate to. The eating disorder anorexia nervosa was just becoming known to the gen-eral public at the time of the book's publication. In *Thinner,* the cruel irony is that although being overweight can kill you, being under-weight can do the same.

King delights in showing us the numerous ironies inherent in the lives of these characters. He explores the thin line between hate and love, between justice and vengeance, between ignoring and accepting responsibility. With the exception of ruthless gangster Richard Ginelli, a former client Billy hires to put "the curse of the white man from town" on Taduz Lemke and his family, none of the characters in *Thinner* chooses to accept responsibility for what he or she does. Unlike Billy, Ginelli has no problem dealing with the possibility that his illegal actions might lead to his violent death. What is important to him is that he remains true to his own personal moral code, and that he live up to his promises.

King has always displayed a grudging admiration for gangster and Mafia types. He has demonstrated this in several early stories ("The

Man with a Belly," "The Wedding Gig," "The Fifth Quarter") and, most significantly to the world of Richard Bachman, in the character of Sal Magliore in *Roadwork* (1981). In that novel, only Magliore perceives the futility of the protagonist's actions to halt the inevitable. Ginelli can also see "the big picture," that no one is going to win this blood feud. Ginelli may be an unsavory character, but at least he has a defined moral code that clearly distinguishes black from white.

Whether "white" always represents good and "black" always represents evil is not the question. What matters is that Ginelli's actions are carried out through a sense of moral responsibility. He alone can accept that in this lawless situation, the only code is an eye for an eye. But justice—whether that of the "white man from town" or the Gypsy's—is not achieved in the end. As occurs so often in the Stephen King universe and in the world of Richard Bachman, everyone loses. Life is not fair and we can do nothing but accept that fact.

> *The original title for* Thinner *was* Gypsy Pie.

Ginelli carries out a campaign of terror against Lemke and his family, forcing the old man to lift the curse. Lemke does so, but the power of the curse is strong. The old man temporarily transfers the curse to a pie and tells Billy he must get someone else to eat a piece of it, so that the curse will be felt by another person. Otherwise it will revert back to Billy. Angry with his wife for her actions during his ordeal, Billy decides to offer a piece to her. He later repents, but only after both his wife and daughter eat the cursed pie. Realizing that the only people he loves are now cursed because of him, Billy resignedly cuts himself a piece and sits down to eat it. The circle of vengeance is complete: everyone remotely involved with the accidental death of the old Gypsy woman is dead or will soon perish.

## PRIMARY SUBJECTS

***BILLY HALLECK.*** A successful lawyer whose main problem is his tremendous appetite. When he accidentally hits and kills a Gypsy woman with his car, the leader of her clan puts a one-word curse on the man: "Thinner." Billy begins to lose two pounds each day. After ruling out cancer and a host of other, equally terminal illnesses, he eventually comes to realize that he is the victim of a supernatural curse.

Billy learns that the only way he can be free of the curse is by passing it on to someone else. Suspecting that his wife has been unfaithful to him (at one point she tries to have him committed to an asylum), Billy tricks her into eating a piece of strawberry pie, which holds the essence of the curse. Unfortunately, his beloved daughter also has a piece, dooming her to a nasty death. In the end, Billy realizes there is no escape from the Gypsy's vengeance, and he also partakes of the deadly dessert.

*HEIDI HALLECK.* Billy's devoted wife, Heidi, is partially responsible for the automobile accident that leaves a Gypsy woman dead (Heidi was performing oral sex on her husband while he was driving). Heidi comes to believe Billy is starving himself out of guilt and at one point tries to have him institutionalized. Rumors abound that she is having an affair with the family doctor, but they are never proven. In her husband's growing paranoia, he believes she is against him, and so brings home a cursed pie for her to eat. She presumably dies a horrible death soon afterward.

*LINDA HALLECK.* Billy and Heidi's only child, Linda is an attractive fourteen-year-old who suffers as she watches her parents' marriage deteriorate. Her father leaves when his weight loss becomes too much for him to handle. Linda is later thrilled to learn he is coming back home to stay. Eager to take his revenge on his wife, however, Billy asks Linda to go to a friend's home for a few days until he can patch things up with Heidi. Returning home unexpectedly, Linda joins Heidi in a midnight snack, eating part of the cursed pie. Like her mom, she will die a painful and totally undeserved death.

*SUSANNA LEMKE.* The Gypsy woman who dies after stepping out from between two parked cars and getting hit by the vehicle driven by Billy Halleck.

*TADUZ LEMKE.* The elderly leader of the Gypsy clan who places a curse on Billy Halleck and his associates. Official records state his age at well over one hundred. Possessed of supernatural powers, he takes revenge on all who were responsible for the death of his daughter, Susanna, including Billy, the police chief who looked the other way, and the judge who has a long-standing hatred of all Gypsies. Taduz's current whereabouts are unknown, but presumably he is still traveling with extended family somewhere along the coast of New England.

*RICHARD GINELLI.* The small-time gangster who succeeds in getting the curse lifted from Billy Halleck. Billy had been successful in the past in keeping Ginelli out of prison, and the gangster feels he owes the attorney a personal debt. When Billy decides to put "the curse of the white man from town" on the Gypsy clan that had targeted him, he employs Ginelli as his dark angel of vengeance. Ginelli mounts a campaign of terror against the Gypsies, leaving messages that they must lift the curse off Billy. Although he succeeds, it is at the price of his own life. Billy finds Ginelli's head in the front seat of the gangster's car.

*POLICE CHIEF DUNCAN HOPLEY.* Hopley investigates the accident in which Billy Halleck struck and killed the Gypsy woman. A friend of Billy's, he has no trouble seeing to it that the attorney is rendered blameless in the death of the old woman. Taduz Lemke curses Hopley, creating a worsening skin condition that transforms the police officer into a hideous freak. Unable to cope with the suffering, he commits suicide with his own service revolver.

*JUDGE CARY ROSSINGTON.* An old friend of Billy Halleck's, Rossington is in charge of the court case involving the attorney's automobile accident. An elitist and a racist, he hates the Gypsies who occasionally pass through his district. At the civil hearing regarding the accident, Rossington wastes no time clearing Billy of any possible liability. The judge is touched by Taduz Lemke, who speaks one word to him: "Lizard." Immediately afterward, Rossington develops a spreading skin growth that rapidly transforms his skin into lizardlike scales. He visits the world-famed Mayo Clinic, but to no avail. Like the police chief, he kills himself to end his suffering.

## ADAPTATION

In spite of the novel's success, the film adaptation of *Thinner* did not appear until more than a decade later, perhaps due to the dearth of likable characters or to an inability to create convincing special effects. Despite the fact that Michael McDowell's and director Tom Holland's screenplay

> *In the film version, Stephen King has a cameo role as a pharmacist.*

is remarkably faithful to the plot of the original novel, the ultimate result was similar to that of *Firestarter*. The plot and characters were all there, but little of the spirit or mood of the author's original vision was successfully translated.

Although Robert Burke *(Robocop 3)* and Joe Mantegna do a credible job of portraying Billy Halleck and Richard Ginelli, nothing about any of the characters encourages the viewer to care about their fate. Considering how petty and self-centered everyone is, little sympathy develops for anyone the audience meets.

> *The unabridged audio adaptation of this novel was read by Joe Mantegna, who also starred in the movie version.*

# 52

## Desperation

I N  A D D I T I O N  to the serial novel *The Green Mile*, 1996 saw another unique publishing event devised by Stephen King: the simultaneous publication in late September of two mammoth hardcover novels, *Desperation* and *The Regulators*. Companion novels, the two share interlocking cover art (an unforgettable piece created by Mark Ryden), a nasty villain (an ancient demon named Tak) and a shared cast of characters who exist in parallel realities. The hook is that *Desperation*, published by Viking, was written by King, and *The Regulators*, published by Dutton, was written by King's alter ego, Richard Bachman.

In *Desperation*, King returns to themes first visited in *The Stand* (1978), namely man's relationship with God and his divine intervention in human events. The God reflected in both books resembles the God of the Old Testament who worked through intermediaries such as Moses to achieve his agenda. Like that God, King's deity seems content to sit on the sidelines and observe, unless forces beyond human ken come into play. In *The Stand*, it is Randall Flagg; in *Desperation*, it is the ancient demon Tak.

*Publishers Weekly* reported that the idea for *Desperation* came to King in 1991. Driving across the Nevada desert in daughter Naomi's car, the author passed through the apparently abandoned town of Ruth. King's first thought was, *They're all dead*, followed by *Who killed them?* At this point, the internal voice King has often written about (his muse, perhaps) shot back, "The sheriff killed them all."

The book's opening scene sets the eerie tone for the rest of the novel. Peter Jackson, an English professor at New York University, has recently published a scholarly article, "James Dickey and the New Southern Reality." The title is ironic in light of what subsequently happens to Peter and his wife, Mary (think *Deliverance,* only in the desert). Traveling on Interstate 50 through the Nevada desert, the couple get their first hint that something is wrong when they spy a cat nailed to a speed-limit sign on the outskirts of a town called Desperation. Soon thereafter, they are pulled over and arrested by a cop who stands six feet five inches tall and weighs 300 pounds. Indeed, the policeman seems literally to be bursting out of his skin.

> *To solemnize the merging of King and Bachman, and as a way of thanking his Constant Readers for purchasing* Desperation *and* The Regulators, *the author had his publishers include a small, fifty-nine-page excerpt from the yet-to-be completed* Wizard and Glass *in each book as a complementary gift. The miniature paperback is now a collector's item.*

Expertly playing on the fear many of us have of authority, King raises the tension notch by notch. Like Mary and Peter, readers quickly discern that the cop is not quite right. As he reads the Jacksons their rights, the unfortunate couple see just how out of the ordinary their persecutor is: "You have the right to remain silent. If you do not choose to remain silent, anything you say may be used against you in a court of law. You have the right to an attorney. I'm going to kill you. If you cannot afford . . ."

The officer is Collie Entragian, whose body has been possessed by the demon Tak. When Mary and Peter are taken to the police station, Tak shoots and kills Peter. The Carvers—Ralph, Ellen, Kirsten, and David—are also forced to stop on Interstate 50 just outside of Desperation when their RV runs over a carpet of nails left in the road by the marauding policeman. They are approached by Tak, who makes them his prisoners. The Carvers endure much tragedy over the next few hours. First, young Kirsten is brutally murdered by Tak, who throws her down the jailhouse stairs. Ellen dies also, but only after being possessed by Tak. Ralph is terminated as he, David, Mary

Jackson, and another intended victim, John Marinville, descend into the China Pit mine. Ralph is executed by Tak, who has now been forced to occupy the body of a vulture.

In this world, God acts indirectly through human vessels such as young David Carver and *The Stand*'s Mother Abagail. But despite his active role in events, God remains a mystery; both his part in the universe and his motivations are unknown.

Biblical allusions abound in *Desperation*. Wondering why they were chosen while others were killed, the survivors conclude that they were selected by Tak, who was acting like the angel of death in Egypt, only in reverse. David Carver's battle with Tak is reminiscent of the conflict between David and Goliath in the Old Testament. Plus, Carver's first encounter with God recalls Moses on Mount Horeb. When he asks, "Who are you?" God replies, "Who I am."

In a flashback to the early days of his religious conversion, David recalls the story of Daniel in the lion's den. Marinville later cites the phrase "And a little child shall lead them." David also performs miracles: He gets Steve's cell phone to work in the midst of a vicious sandstorm. Later, he feeds his unfortunate band much as Jesus fed the multitude with loaves and fishes. Like Jesus, David pleads with God to lift the burden placed on his shoulders.

The parallels to *The Stand* go beyond the religious. For instance, David's speech in *Desperation* to the rest of the Collie Entragian Survival Society echoes the words Mother Abagail speaks to the members of the Free Zone. David tells his friends that "if we leave Desperation without doing what God sent us here to do, we'll pay the price." In other words, God wants them to take a stand. When the evil is dispatched in *The Stand*, Tom Cullen witnesses the fist of God in the sky over Las Vegas. In *Desperation*, Tak's passing is marked by a gigantic cloud of dark gray dust: "It hung in the sky, still connected to the [China] pit by a hazy umbilicus of a mountain rising into the sky like poisoned ground after a nuclear blast." The cloud takes the shape of a giant wolf.

Let's not forget the book's connections with *The Regulators*, which become clearer in the next chapter. Kirsten Carver is wearing a *MotoKops 2200* T-shirt when Tak kills her (*MotoKops 2200* is a popular TV show in both realities). The Carver family hails from 248

Poplar Street, Wentworth, Ohio, the setting of *The Regulators*. Several supporting characters bear the same names as leading characters in *The Regulators*, among them Jim Reed, Brad Josephson, and Cary Ripton.

Finally, *Desperation* has links to the overall Stephen King universe. Ellen Carver is described as preferring novels with titles like *Misery in Paradise*. Cynthia Smith, a supporting character from *Rose Madder*, shows up in *Desperation*, providing Steve Ames with a capsule version of the events of that novel.

> *The audio version of* Desperation *was read by actress Kathy Bates, who won an Academy Award for the film* Misery.

## PRIMARY SUBJECTS

**DESPERATION.** A small mining town located off Interstate 50 in Nevada, Desperation was inhabited by approximately 260 people. When an ancient evil living beneath the earth's crust is released, the citizens are wiped out and Desperation quickly becomes a ghost town, haunted by its lone surviving resident, police officer Collie Entragian. Collie has been possessed by the evil entity, a demon named Tak. Tak likes his new host but knows he can't use him indefinitely and thus is looking for another. Having slaughtered the entire town, Tak takes to pulling people off the highway, seeking an adequate vessel to contain his essence.

**TAK.** The ancient evil entity that possesses police officer Collie Entragian, Tak, or Can Tak, is a "big god" (a translation of *Can Tak*). Tak has lived under the earth, near the vicinity of the mine called the China Pit, for eons. At first, David Carver tells his friends that Tak is a deity. Later, he believes the being is more like a disease than something ethereal like a demon or spirit. As to where Tak actually lives, David is vague. The creature is referred to as an outsider, existing somehow beyond the reality we know. David manages to seal Tak in his tomb, where he remains to this day, presumably waiting for a chance to rise again.

*CAN TAH*. The little gods, minions of the demon Tak. They inhabit small stone carvings of wolves, coyotes, snakes, spiders, rats, and bats found inside the China Pit mine. Merely touching one of these carvings is enough to drive a human crazy with lust and hate.

*THE CHINA PIT*. Also known as Rattlesnake Number One, the China Mine, the China Drift, or the old China Shaft, the pit has been home to Tak and the Can Tah for thousands of years. In September 1859, a group of fifty-seven Chinese and four white miners broke into a cave containing thousands of small stone carvings of the Can Tah. When the miners picked up these statues, they went insane. Before they could escape and spread their evil, the mine was sealed by the heroic efforts of the Lushan brothers. The mine remains sealed until a fateful day in 1996, when employees of the Desperation Mining Company accidentally reopen it, unleashing Tak and his minions on the town.

*COLLIE ENTRAGIAN*. The big, blond police officer possessed by Tak, who decimates the population of Desperation, then proceeds to collect new candidates to host his essence. Tak uses Collie up, then casts his ravaged body aside like a child would toss away a candy wrapper.

*PETER and MARY JACKSON*. Driving a borrowed car across Nevada, this unfortunate couple is pulled over by Tak, as Entragian, and arrested. Arriving at the Desperation police station, Peter is fatally shot by the lawman. Mary is imprisoned along with the Carver family and another victim, Tom Billingsley. Tak leaves Entragian's body and moves into that of Ellen Carver. Tak tries to possess Mary but is foiled when she escapes from the makeshift prison deep in the China Pit mine. She is last seen driving away from Desperation, accompanied by David Carver. Her present whereabouts are unknown.

*RALPH, ELLEN and KIRSTEN (PIE) CARVER*. The members of the Carver family are the first victims of Tak after he wipes out the population of Desperation.

*DAVID CARVER.* Some say you cannot petition the Lord with prayer, but don't tell that to young David Carver. A year before the events in Desperation, David faces another tragedy—his best friend, Brian, is critically injured after being struck by a drunk driver. Near death, Brian lies in the hospital as his distraught friend wanders the streets. For some reason, David is drawn to the Bear Street Woods, where he and Brian often played. While walking in the woods, David hears the voice of God. At first scared, David begs God to help his friend, promising to be God's servant in return. Shortly thereafter, Brian emerges from his coma.

David receives guidance from God through prayer, and the faith instilled in David on the day Brian returns to health becomes deeper with each passing day. God instructs the boy to seek out the Reverend Martin, the Methodist minister who eventually becomes

> *The words David uses to describe Tak recall those King employed to describe It in the 1986 novel of the same name. Tak is also referred to as an outsider, the same word used to describe an evil being from beyond our reality that merges with the spirit of Sara Tidwell in* Bag of Bones *(1998).*

David's spiritual guide. Martin tells David he has been chosen by God. David feels God is preparing him for something, but he has no idea what.

When David's family is captured by Tak, he quickly realizes it is no accident—God has sent him to do his work. After Tak kills David's sister and imprisons his family, a divinely inspired David wriggles free from his cell and releases his fellow inmates. Later, David informs them that God has chosen them to battle Tak.

David mistakenly believes God has called him to be the main architect of Tak's defeat; he later learns John Marinville is actually the chosen one. Surviving his encounter with Tak, David is left without family but with the conviction that his God is indeed a loving one, not the cruel, pitiless deity he has always perceived him to be.

David is last seen leaving Desperation in a car driven by Mary Jackson. His present whereabouts are unknown.

*JOHN EDWARD MARINVILLE.* Marinville is winner of the National Book Award and author of the novels *Delight* and *Song of the Hammer.*

This Norman Maileresque bad boy is touring the United States on his motorcycle, searching for material for his new nonfiction book (working title: *Travels with Harley*). Passing Desperation on Interstate 50, Marinville stops to relieve himself by the side of the road. He looks up to find a giant cop waiting for him at the top of the gulley. At first fawning over the famous author, Tak soon reveals his true nature. He beats and arrests Marinville, then throws him into jail with Mary Jackson, town veterinarian Tom Billingsley, and the Carvers.

After David Carver frees the group, Marinville struggles with his inherently selfish nature and eventually emerges as a strong leader. Not a religious man, Marinville is contemptuous of David, referring to him at one point as "the Jesus Scout." Needless to say, he is overwhelmed when he himself receives a message from God instructing him that he must be the one to destroy Tak. The scales fall from the writer's eyes as he suddenly realizes he has been a part of God's plan ever since a near-death experience he had in Vietnam.

During that interlude, he actually spoke with David in a sort of limbo, giving the boy instructions as to how to dispatch Tak. Marinville accepts God's will. Entering the China Pit, he detonates enough explosives to reseal the mine, giving his life to save the others, a selfless act of redemption for a man who, until then, had rarely thought of anyone but himself.

*STEVE AMES.* Steve is hired by John Marinville's publishers to guard the writer during his tour. The Texan follows Marinville at a discreet distance, and thus is not close by when Marinville is abducted by Tak. Marinville does contact Steve briefly on his cell phone and Steve eventually tracks the writer to Desperation. Accompanied by hitchhiker Cynthia Smith, Steve links up with Tak's prisoners. Steve survives the encounter with Tak. He is last seen in the company of Cynthia Smith, driving down Interstate 50. His present whereabouts are unknown.

*CYNTHIA SMITH.* Cynthia is hitchhiking home for a reunion with her parents when Steve Ames picks her up just outside Ely. Present when Steve gets a garbled message from John Marinville, Cynthia becomes embroiled in the trouble plaguing the town of Desperation. Cynthia survives and departs with Steve Ames for destinations unknown.

*AUDREY WYLER*. Visiting Desperation shortly before Tak's killing spree, Audrey unwittingly falls under Tak's power. Posing as the last survivor in town, Audrey makes an unsuccessful attempt on David Carver's life. Consumed by the power of a Can Tah, Audrey dies from injuries sustained in her struggles with the Collie Entragian Survivors Society.

*TOM BILLINGSLEY*. A retired veterinarian, Tom is one of the last survivors of Desperation. Tak throws him in a holding cell, then goes out to look for other potential hosts. Tom tells the group of the demon's rampage through town. He is killed by a panther sent by Tak to distract the group while Audrey Wyler makes an attempt on David Carver's life.

# 53

## The Regulators

---

A S MENTIONED in the previous chapter, *The Regulators* (1996) has several connections to its companion novel, *Desperation* (1996). Some of the characters from the latter appear in major roles in *The Regulators;* others do not. People survive the events of one novel, die in the other, expire in both, or survive in both. Some appear as children in one book and adults in the other. One book's shining hero may be tarnished in the other. The interplay is fairly complex: both texts are salted with inside jokes and pieces of similar-sounding dialogue, providing much for King enthusiasts to debate.

According to various published interviews with King, the idea for *The Regulators* came to him near "the three quarter mark on *Desperation.*" He jotted down the idea, which consisted of a single word, on a scrap of paper: *regulators.* At the time, he knew only that the idea had something to do with "toys, guns, TV, and suburbia."

Soon thereafter, another thought burst forth. King decided to take some of the characters from *Desperation* and place them in *The Regulators,* using them "like the members of a repertory company acting in two different plays." As the idea evolved further, King realized that what worked with the characters might work with the plot as well; that is, he could use many of the elements of *Desperation* in a different configuration, creating a kind of mirror world in the new book.

One last hurdle existed. Even though the books shared many elements, he didn't want to create the impression that the same writer wrote both works. Then it occurred to King that he'd had the answer all along—his alter ego, the pseudonymous Richard Bachman, could write *The Regulators*. There was only one problem: King had already declared that Bachman had died of "cancer of the pseudonym" in 1985, shortly after the publication of Bachman's breakthrough novel, *Thinner*.

*King's office bookshelf* | BETH GWINN

King's solution was rather ingenious. An editor's note at the beginning of *The Regulators* states that the manuscript was found in Bachman's effects by his widow, Claudia Inez Eschelman. The manuscript was then validated by Bachman scholar Douglas Winter, Elaine Koster at New American Library, and Carolyn Stromberg, editor of the earliest Bachman novels. After making minor changes to correct for anachronisms (for example, substituting the name of younger actor Ethan Hawke for that of actor Rob Lowe in the first chapter), E. P. Dutton editor Charles Verrill pronounced it fit for publication.

The tongue-in-cheek publicity materials state: "Stephen King, who had an advance look at *The Regulators* manuscript, said: 'The most interesting thing about *The Regulators* is that Bachman and I must have been on the same psychic wavelength. It's almost as if we were twins, in a funny way.'" King continued to say that he had found similarities between *The Regulators* and his upcoming novel *Desperation*. "It's a little bit like the similarities between *Alice in Wonderland* and *Through the Looking Glass*. It's like everything's been turned on its head."

The two books benefited from all the publicity their combined $2 million marketing budget could buy. One of the gimmicks was a "limited" (200,000-copy) edition two-for-one gift pack in which both volumes were shrink-wrapped together with a "keep-you-up-all night" book light. *The Regulators* itself had a 500-copy limited edition (selling at $325) published by Dutton, available on a first-come, first-serve basis via phone order. Each copy contained a fake check signed by the nonexistent Bachman and made out to a friend or associate of King's or one of his fictional characters. (One check was made out to the Overlook Connection, an independent bookseller specializing in "all things King." Another was made out to Quitters, Inc., the antismoking organization immortalized in King's short story of the same name.) The book came in a cloth-covered box featuring artist Alan M. Clark's conception of a Power Wagon, the vehicle driven by the Regulators.

*The Regulators* is dedicated to two "legendary shadows," hard-boiled novelist Jim Thompson and groundbreaking film director Sam Peckinpah. Although Thompson, author of *The Grifters* and *The Getaway*, certainly influenced the Bachman style, he doesn't cast a large shadow over *The Regulators* (he does, however, influence *Desperation*,

> *The King-imagined film* The Regulators, *which is mentioned in the novel, is also referred to in the author's 1999 release,* Hearts in Atlantis.

> *Tak's use of creatures whose appearance is based on characters from film and television recalls the same sort of activity by* It *(from the 1986 novel of the same name). Both beings are revealed as outsiders, indicating they are likely a related breed of extradimensional monster.*

which certainly nods to the Thompson classic *The Killer Inside Me*). *The Regulators* does, however, owe a deep debt to Peckinpah. The novel had its genesis in *The Shotgunners*, an original screenplay King wrote specifically for Peckinpah. Unfortunately, the film was in preproduction when Peckinpah passed away in 1984 and was never made.

It seems King was also influenced by Peckinpah's classic western *The Wild Bunch* (1969), which may have inspired King's fictional western film *The Regulators*, which plays a key role in the plot of the novel. *The Wild Bunch* gained almost instant notoriety for its bloody, almost poetic action scenes. Set in 1913, the film's plot centers on a group of aging outlaws who, realizing that time is passing them by, decide to retire after one last score. *The Regulators* features a character named Major Pike, after the role played by William Holden in *The Wild Bunch*.

> The Regulators *contains a script excerpt from a* MotoKops 2200 *episode titled "The Force Corridor," a segment Seth is particularly enamored of. The script is penned by Alan Smithee. Movie aficionados know that that name is a Hollywood in-joke. When directors wish to disassociate themselves from a film or TV program, they substitute that name for their own.*

Another fictional precursor is Jerome Bixby's classic 1953 short story, "It's a Good Life," a tale adapted for both *The Twilight Zone* television show (in 1961) and for the feature film *Twilight Zone— The Movie* (1983). This narrative, about a small boy who controls reality, is evoked within *The Regulators* when suburban Poplar Street is transformed by Seth Garin into a surreal western landscape, a panorama that resembles a child's cartoon-influenced perception of the Old West.

*The Regulators* is also a sly commentary about "the god of suburbia, television." King was most assuredly commenting on the influence television has on children, especially commercially geared phenomena like *The Mighty Morphin Power Rangers* and *Teenage Mutant Ninja Turtles*, which were extremely popular when the book was published. In this case, the analog is *MotoKops 2200*, an ultraviolent cartoon that captures young Seth's imagination.

The novel begins innocently enough. It's summertime, and as the old lyric goes, the living is easy. On Poplar Street, a paperboy delivers this week's edition of the *Wentworth Gazette*. People are barbecuing, washing their cars, throwing Frisbees. But up the street, right where Poplar intersects with Bear Street, sits a futuristic-looking red van with what looks like a radar dish on top. Soon it will start its deadly journey down Poplar Street, changing the lives of its residents forever.

## PRIMARY SUBJECTS

*POPLAR STREET.* Poplar Street is located in Wentworth, Ohio. It's abutted on its northern end by Bear Street and by Hyacinth Street to the south. There are eleven houses and an E-Z Stop convenience store on the street. Odd-numbered houses are on the west, even-numbered on the east. On the afternoon of July 15, 1996, Poplar Street is cut off from the rest of the world and transformed into a surreal killing ground. In a way, it becomes the Old West as it appears on TV and in movies. The houses change into log cabins and adobe haciendas. Buzzards, wolves, and wild boars, looking as if they were created by a child, roam through backyards. It becomes a place called the Force Corridor, which exists only in a TV cartoon version of the twenty-third century. Poplar Street returns to normal after the death of Seth Garin, whose young body serves as a vessel for an ancient demon named Tak.

*CARY RIPTON.* Cary is the local paperboy and the first to fall victim to the Regulators on the fateful day of July 15, 1996. Cary is shot-gunned to death by the occupants of a red van.

*THE GARIN FAMILY.* A family of five, the Garins are the victims of a senseless drive-by shooting while vacationing in San Jose, California. Killed in the July 31, 1994, incident were William Garin, his wife, June, and two of their three children, John and Mary Lou. The only survivor is six-year-old Seth, who was playing in a sandbox when the shooting took place. Witnesses reported seeing a red van in the vicinity shortly before the assault, with what looked like a radar dish on the roof.

*SETH GARIN.* At the age of six, the autistic, telepathic Seth is possessed by a demon named Tak, who, sensing the boy's hidden abilities, lures him to an abandoned mine located in Desperation, Nevada.

After Tak kills his family (see above), Seth goes to live with his aunt and uncle, Audrey and Herb Wyler, at 247 Poplar Street. Tak has an odd kind of symbiosis with Seth, both augmenting and feeding off the little boy's latent powers. Tak also seizes on the boy's love of animated cartoons, combining Seth's devotion to *MotoKops 2200* with his own love of Westerns to create the futuristic Regulators, who terrorize the Poplar Street residents. This symbiosis is not total, however. Tak, disgusted by the boy's need to void its bowels, departs his unwilling host whenever the boy goes to the bathroom.

Beneath his autistic shell, Seth has a more "normal" personality, one that is considerably more alert and mature. Able to communicate with his aunt Audrey on a psychic level, Seth conspires with her to rid himself of the demon, an act they accomplish at the cost of both their lives. Although his body is dead, it appears that Seth's and Audrey's spirits live on, inhabiting a gazebo at the Mohonk Mountain House in New York State.

*BRAD and BELINDA JOSEPHSON.* Owners of the house at 251 Poplar, the Josephsons are the only African-American family on the street. Brad is gored by Seth's cartoon version of a wild boar, but both he and Belinda survive the Regulators' attack. It is presumed that they still reside at 251 Poplar Street.

*JOHN MARINVILLE.* Owner of the house at 250 Poplar, Johnny Marinville, winner of the National Book Award for his adult novel *Delight,* got rich in the 1980s writing children's books about a character named Pat the Kitty-Cat, a feline private detective, before "retiring" to Wentworth. Johnny is the first resident of Poplar Street to put together the clues, realizing that Seth, a wild fan of *MotoKops 2200,* must somehow be behind the strange events. Johnny is at the home of Audrey and Herb Wyler when Tak is defeated. It is presumed that he still lives at 250 Poplar Street.

*GARY and MARIELLE SODERSON*. Thought of as the Poplar Street Bohemians, the Sodersons of 249 Poplar are an odd couple. Gary is a helpful soul, though he drinks too much. Marielle loses an arm in one of the Regulators' early attacks and later dies from the trauma. Gary is killed by a cartoonlike Gila monster later that same day.

*THE CARVER FAMILY*. Residents of 248 Poplar, the Carver family is composed of David and Kirsten "Pie" Carver; their daughter, Ellen "Ellie" Margaret; and her little brother, Ralph. Ellie and Ralph are orphaned by the Regulators. Their present whereabouts are unknown. Their father, David, is killed in the Regulators' second attack. Their mother, Kirsten, is wounded in a subsequent assault and expires shortly thereafter.

*AUDREY and HERB WYLER*. The Wylers live at 247 Poplar. Audrey takes in her nephew, Seth Garin, after his family is slaughtered in a drive-by shooting. Audrey and Herb, who come to love Seth as if he were their own child, conclude something is desperately wrong with him as Tak emerges from hiding. First, Tak drives their neighbors, the Hobarts, from Poplar Street. Then he takes control of their lives, forcing Audrey to injure herself and draining the life force from Herb as if he were a human battery.

Herb eventually commits suicide, leaving Audrey at the mercy of Tak. Although Tak keeps her alive (Seth won't let him eliminate her), he makes her life a living hell. Audrey retains her sanity by mentally retreating to the past, when she and a friend visited the Mohonk Mountain House in New Paltz, New York. Audrey is killed when Cammie Reed fires on Seth, whom Audrey is holding at the time. Audrey's spirit lives on, however, and is often seen haunting a gazebo at Mohonk. Audrey is not alone. She is accompanied by a little boy, presumably the spirit of Seth.

*TOM BILLINGSLEY*. Owner of 246 Poplar, Tom, a retired veterinarian, is the only one who can treat Poplar Street's wounded, but he is largely ineffective due to the severity of their traumas. Tom survives the onslaught, but it seems unlikely that he remains a resident of Poplar Street.

*THE REED FAMILY*. Residents of 245 Poplar, Charlie and Cammie Reed have twin sons, Jim and Dave. Although Charlie is not present on the fateful day of July 15, 1996, his wife plays a key role in the action. During a lull in the carnage, Cammie sends her two sons for help from the outside world. While on this trek, a shaky Jim accidentally shoots and kills Collie Entragian. The distraught Jim subsequently kills himself, an action precipitated by Tak. Cammie tries to avenge his death by shooting and killing Seth. Robbed of his host, Tak tries to possess Cammie, but her body is not strong enough to contain the power of his life force. Unable to hold Tak's enormous power, her body literally explodes.

Charlie and Dave Reed's present whereabouts are unknown. It seems unlikely that they still live on Poplar Street.

*THE GELLER FAMILY*. Residents of 243 Poplar, Frank and Kim Geller have one child, Susi. Frank is not present the day the Regulators attack. Kim is killed in the Regulators' final assault. Frank and Susi's present whereabouts are unknown.

*PETER and MARY JACKSON*. Residents of 244 Poplar, Peter Jackson is a professor at Ohio State University and his wife, Mary, is an accountant. Returning from an adulterous rendezvous, Mary is rear-ended by a futuristic yellow van at the beginning of the Regulators' second assault. Leaving her car, she is gunned down by the van's occupant. Peter Jackson is murdered by Tak, who sucks the life force out of his victim after forcing him to watch Seth's video of the movie *The Regulators*.

*CYNTHIA SMITH*. A clerk at the E-Z Stop, Cynthia is one of a small group who survive the Regulators' bloody assaults.

*STEVE AMES*. Driving his rented Ryder truck down Poplar Street, Steve witnesses Cary Ripton's death at the hands of the Regulators. Acting instinctively, he and Cynthia Smith protect Ellie and Ralph Carver from injury during the Regulators' first attack.

*COLLIE ENTRAGIAN*. Owner of 240 Poplar and an ex-cop, Collie is fired from the Columbus Police Department after testing positive for cocaine and heroin. Collie believes he was framed, since he never took either drug. He tries to restore order after the Regulators' first attack but is later shot and killed by Jim Reed.

*MOTOKOPS 2200.* A popular Saturday morning cartoon, *MotoKops 2200* chronicles the interstellar adventures of Colonel Henry, Snake Hunter, Bounty, Major Pike, Rooty the Robot, and Cassandra Styles as they battle archenemies No Face and Countess Lili Marsh. Each character pilots a futuristic Power Wagon, essentially vans equipped with fold-up wheels and stubby extendable wings. Colonel Henry's vehicle is the yellow Justice Wagon, No Face's is called the Meatwagon. Snake Hunter, Rooty the Robot, and Cassandra Styles battle in the red Tracker Arrow, the silver Rooty-Toot, and the "Mary Kay" pink Dream Floater.

*THE REGULATORS.* Premiering in 1958, this American-International Pictures release starred John Payne, Ty Hardin, Karen Steele, and Rory Calhoun and was directed by Billy Rancourt. The movie, based on a screenplay written by Craig Goodis and Quentin Woolrich, tells the story of a Colorado mining town that is terrorized by vigilantes who appear to be supernatural beings but turn out to be post–Civil War baddies "of the Capt. Quantrill stripe." According to reviews, the film includes some scenes and effects that are "surprisingly gruesome for a late-fifties oat opera."

*THE REGULATORS.* Tak's kill squad, the Regulators represent a strange blend of characters from the 1958 Hollywood movie of the same name and the *MotoKops 2200* cartoon. Also among Tak's hit squad are characters from classic TV westerns such as *Bonanza* and *The Rifleman.*

# 54

# Related Tales

---

ALTHOUGH KING has never stated that *all* his crime stories were composed while in a Richard Bachman frame of mind, several seem to have been written in that mode. The following stories certainly *feel* like Bachman stories, even though published under King's name. Also, none of them is specifically connected to the prime reality. Thus, we have taken the liberty of assigning them to the world of Richard Bachman. The discussions below reveal why each was deemed more appropriate for this section.

## "THE FIFTH QUARTER"

### from *Nightmares & Dreamscapes* (1993)

Reminiscent of Donald E. Westlake's pseudonymous Richard Stark novels featuring professional criminal Parker, this hard-boiled crime story was first published in *Cavalier* magazine in 1972 under the byline John Swithen, the only time to date the author has used this particular pseudonym. King himself states in his notes to *Nightmares & Dreamscapes* that this story was written in his Richard Bachman mode.

### PRIMARY SUBJECT

*JERRY TARKANIAN.* An ex-con (he did time in Shawshank prison) out to avenge the death of a comrade known only as Barney,

Tarkanian accosts Barney's double-crossing partners Sarge, Jagger, and Keenan. He is seeking their pieces to a map showing where their loot has been stashed.

## "THE LEDGE"

### from *Night Shift* (1978)

A tennis pro who has fallen in love with a mobster's wife is forced by the mobster to take a bet. If he can walk around the windswept, five-inch-wide ledge of his building, he will receive a pile of money and the freedom to leave with the gangster's wife, or go to prison on trumped-up drug charges. This short story originally appeared in *Penthouse* magazine in 1976, and was later part of the motion picture anthology scripted by King, *Cat's Eye* (1985).

## PRIMARY SUBJECTS

*STAN NORRIS*. A tennis pro and ex-con, Stan meets and falls in love with Marcia Cressner. Much to his misfortune, Marcia is already married to a man tied to the Mob. Stan accepts Cressner's wager and manages to make it around the building, inching along the dangerous ledge, only to discover that Cressner has had Marcia murdered in the meantime. In revenge, he makes Cressner walk the ledge. When last we see him, Stan is waiting for Cressner to fall or finish the walk, but intends to kill him in either case. The final outcome has yet to be revealed at the story's end.

*CRESSNER*. An organized-crime figure who loses his wife to Stan Norris, then has her killed. When last seen, he is out on the ledge. His eventual fate is unknown.

*MARCIA CRESSNER*. After Marcia has an affair with Stan Norris, her husband orders a killer in his employ to take her life.

## "QUITTERS, INC."

*from Night Shift* (1978)

A man wants to quit smoking and inquires about a new program, only to discover that its methods are far more than drastic—they are violent and ultimately for keeps. "Quitters, Inc." was also part of the anthology film *Cat's Eye*, with James Woods effectively portraying Dick Morrison.

### PRIMARY SUBJECTS

*DICK MORRISON.* When Dick first visits Quitters, Inc., he is unaware that he is going to be forced to quit smoking through the use of threats against his own well-being, as well as the safety of his wife and his mentally challenged son. He does, however, kick his cigarette habit.

*VICTOR DONATTI.* An employee of Quitters, Inc., Donatti is in charge of Dick Morrison's treatment. He torments Dick and tortures Dick's wife, but he does gets results.

*JIMMY McCANN.* An old friend of Morrison's, it is McCann who first recommends that Dick try Quitters, Inc., saying, "They'll cure you. Guaranteed."

## "MAN WITH A BELLY"

(1978)

Published in 1978 in *Cavalier* and never reprinted in any of King's short-story collections, this is a bleak crime tale dealing with unpleasant gangster figures and a twisted sense of revenge.

### PRIMARY SUBJECTS

*JOHN BRACKEN.* A ruthless hit man for the Mafia, Bracken is summoned by crime lord Don Correzente to perform a most unusual service. He is to rape the don's wife, who has a serious gambling habit and is humiliating him because of it.

*DON CORREZENTE.* The elderly crime lord who holds his honor above all. He is a "man with a belly," that is, someone who has an iron will. Although John Bracken carries out the Don's instructions to rape his wife, the Don will ultimately be the biggest loser.

*NORMA CORREZENTE.* Don Correzente's beautiful trophy wife, Norma is raped by John Bracken at her husband's request. To get revenge, she hires Bracken to have sex with her repeatedly until she becomes pregnant—with his child, not the Don's.

## "THE WEDDING GIG"

### from *Skeleton Crew* (1985)

This decidedly hard-boiled crime story—and a period piece to boot— first appeared in *Ellery Queen's Mystery Magazine* in 1980.

## PRIMARY SUBJECTS

*THE NARRATOR.* A musician, the nameless narrator tells of a jazz band invited to play at the wedding of Maureen Scollay, sister to Mob boss Mike Scollay. Extremely overweight and homely, Maureen is an easy target for unflattering jokes and comments. A loving brother, Mike wants her wedding to be perfect. Things don't go according to plan, however. One of Mike's rivals, the Greek, sends a lackey to the wedding to deliver an insulting message to the bride. An enraged Mike storms out of the wedding reception and straight into a deadly ambush.

*MAUREEN SCOLLAY ROMANO.* Mike Scollay's sister, who is married to Rico Romano. After her brother's murder, which was arranged by the Greek, Maureen seizes the reigns of his operation and builds it into "a prohibition empire that rivaled Capone's." Rumors abound that Maureen later took revenge on the Greek by sticking a piece of piano wire through his eye and into his brain, killing him as he begged for mercy.

## "MY PRETTY PONY"

*from Nightmares & Dreamscapes (1993)*

According to King's note in *Nightmares & Dreamscapes,* this story is part of an unfinished Richard Bachman novel about a hit man named Clive Banning. "My Pretty Pony" represents a flashback to the memorable day in 1961 when Clive's grandfather instructs him on the "plastic" nature of time. The story originally appeared in 1989 as a separate limited edition from the Whitney Museum of Art. Each of the 150 copies retailed for $2,200, making it the most expensive limited-edition King book ever.

### PRIMARY SUBJECTS

*GEORGE BANNING.* The seventy-two-year-old grandfather of Clive Banning, George instructs his grandson (George never gives advice, he instructs) on the importance of time and what it means in a person's life. He dies in his sleep a month after the lesson.

*CLIVE BANNING.* A young boy who lives in the rural town of Troy, New York. Clive learns a great deal from his grandfather on the importance of time in a person's life, and that it is time that owns a person—a person does not own time.

## "DOLAN'S CADILLAC"

*from Nightmares & Dreamscapes (1993)*

This vivid tale of revenge in the Nevada desert is an update of Edgar Allan Poe's classic tale "The Cask of Amontillado." For this story, King received technical advice on how to bury a Cadillac from his older brother, David, "a child prodigy with a tested IQ of 150." "Dolan's Cadillac" originally appeared in issues 2 through 6 of *Castle Rock,* a subscription-only monthly newspaper that featured news on the author and his works in all mediums. The short-lived newspaper was the only effort of this type ever authorized by King. A revised version of "Dolan's Cadillac" was published as a limited edition by Lord John Press in 1989.

*Dave King (Stephen's brother)* | DAVID LOWELL

## PRIMARY SUBJECTS

***DOLAN.*** Mobster Dolan has Robinson's wife, Elizabeth, killed to keep her from testifying against him. Dolan falls victim to Robinson's revenge; he is buried alive inside his Cadillac beneath a section of Interstate 71 in Nevada.

***ROBINSON.*** Robinson blames Dolan for his wife's murder. After years of meticulous planning and preparation, Robinson traps Dolan's Cadillac in a car-sized hole and buries him alive.

***ELIZABETH ROBINSON.*** Robinson's wife, Elizabeth was "at the wrong place at the wrong time" and accidentally witnessed Dolan engaging in a criminal act. She goes to the authorities and agrees to testify against Dolan. Although promised protection, Elizabeth is killed by a car bomb.

# SECTION EIGHT

## Tales from Beyond

### Further Parallel Realities

O MATTER HOW CAREFULLY one analyzes the numerous definite, probable, and possible connections between parallel realities in the Stephen King universe, a few threads are left dangling. They are the handful of stories that stand alone. In each of them, King posits a reality—often postapocalyptic—that exists for that tale alone. Even so, all of them share a similar theme: protagonists believing they are in control of their world, only to realize they have no control and are likewise losing contact with the rest of the "real" world.

# 5 5

# Further Parallel Realities

---

SEVERAL OF THESE stories are difficult to place because they deal with people who are alienated or cut off from reality. "The Mist" deals with a group of characters who suddenly find themselves in a world in which they are increasingly cut off from reality as we define it. "Trucks" focuses on another small group of individuals who find that in their world, man is no longer in control, but sentient machines are. "Home Delivery" takes place in a battered world dominated by zombies. In each story, humans are the hunted, not the hunters.

Three of these stories have no overlapping connection with any other parallel realities, unless one imagines that the breach between worlds that takes place in "The Mist" is a "thinny" as conceived in the reality of *The Dark Tower*. "Beachworld" is a futuristic tale of doomed space explorers. "The Jaunt" presents another futuristic vision, while "The End of the Whole Mess" is yet another grim examination of how the world might someday end.

## "TRUCKS"
### from *Night Shift* (1978)

A group of people are trapped in a diner after all the world's trucks (and possibly planes as well) take on a mind of their own and start to randomly murder, then systematically enslave, the human race.

## PRIMARY SUBJECTS

*THE STORYTELLER.* The nameless main character of the story is the one who tries to keep the people inside Conant's Truck Stop and Diner from going insane or getting themselves killed. Several individuals die before he and the other remaining survivors realize they are at the mercy of the trucks. Their bondage begins as they are forced to pump gas around the clock to feed their new masters.

*THE COUNTERMAN.* Another survivor, he is the short-order cook at Conant's before being enslaved by the trucks.

*JERRY.* Jerry dies in a heroic attempt to protect those in the diner.

## "THE JAUNT"

### from *Skeleton Crew* (1985)

A tribute of sorts to two classic science fiction novels, Alfred Bester's *The Stars My Destination* (1957) and Robert A. Heinlein's *The Door into Summer* (1956), "The Jaunt" is a futuristic tale of the discovery of a teleportation device capable of sending people and objects to other planets.

## PRIMARY SUBJECTS

*THE OATES FAMILY.* Mark, his wife, Marilys, son, Ricky, and daughter, Patricia, make up the Oates family. While preparing for their teleportation to Mars, Mark tells his family the history of jaunting—the teleportation process—focusing on the trials and tribulations of its inventor, Victor Carune. Mark emphasizes that they must be asleep during the jaunt. Ricky, however, holds his breath when the attendant administers the sleep gas. By being secretly awake during the jaunt, young Ricky is unfortunately driven mad.

*VICTOR CARUNE.* The inventor of jaunting. Lionized for his discoveries, Carune, a "rather peculiar man who showered perhaps twice a week and changed his clothes only when he thought of it," is remembered by the public at large as a "combination of Edison, Eli Whitney, Pecos Bill and Flash Gordon."

# "THE MIST"

*from Skeleton Crew (1985)*

One of King's most popular novellas, "The Mist" first appeared in *Dark Forces: New Stories of Suspense and Supernatural Horror* (1980), an outstanding volume of original works that many critics believe was *the* seminal anthology of the decade. The story of two universes colliding, "The Mist" reflects King's distrust of technology, a theme he would develop more explicitly in *The Tommyknockers*.

"The Mist in 3D Sound" was produced in 1987, with a script written in part by acclaimed author Dennis Etchison. Created using an audio technology called Kunstkopf ("artificial head") binaural sound, this dramatization does have the unique quality of seemingly placing the listener in the midst of the action. Mother Carmody emerges as a truly fearsome personality in this version, lending credence to David Drayton's decision to face the horrors outside rather than deal with the monsters inside the store.

## PRIMARY SUBJECTS

*THE ARROWHEAD PROJECT.* This project is possibly the cause of the accident that unleashes the Mist. The group of people in the supermarket theorize that the military may have created a door into another reality, allowing the creatures that live there to cross over to Earth.

*DAVID DRAYTON.* The narrator of the tale, Drayton tells of the coming of the Mist and its frightening aftermath. The Mist comes rolling across Long Lake, Maine, shortly after a terrific storm devastates the town. Accompanied by his son, Billy, and his neighbor, Brent Norton, David leaves his wife, Steffy, at home and travels into town for supplies. Once there, they become trapped in a Federal Foods Supermarket when hideous creatures emerge from the Mist (which by now has engulfed the town) and begin to slaughter those outside the store. After spending two days in the supermarket, David realizes he and Billy are no longer safe inside, as some of their number have clearly descended into madness. Along with several companions, David braves the Mist and finds his Jeep. When last seen, David and Billy are driving across the apocalyptic landscape toward Hartford, Connecticut, hoping to meeting up with other survivors. It seems unlikely that he does.

*STEFFY DRAYTON.* Mother of Billy, wife of David, Steffy is presumed dead, most likely killed by the creatures that live in the Mist.

*BILLY DRAYTON.* David Drayton's son, Billy survives the siege on the supermarket. He is last seen in the company of his father, traveling toward Hartford, Connecticut.

*BRENT NORTON.* David Drayton's neighbor, Brent leads a group into the Mist. Before they leave the store, David asks one member of the group to tie a rope around his waist, and tie the other end to something secure. After those who remain in the store hear screams, the rope suddenly goes slack. They pull it in and see that the blood-soaked end of the rope has been chewed through. Brent is never seen again, and he and his followers are presumed dead.

*MOTHER CARMODY.* Proprietor of the Bridgeton Antiquary, Mrs. Carmody is famous for her "gothic pronouncements and folk remedies" (which are always prescribed in God's name). Trapped in the supermarket, Mrs. Carmody begins preaching that the end of the world is at hand; not too surprisingly, she wins some converts. But when she begins to preach that a human sacrifice is needed to appease God, David Drayton takes it as a sign to leave and search for other possible survivors.

*MRS. REPPLER.* A third-grade teacher, Mrs. Reppler joins David and Billy Drayton in their quest to find other survivors beyond the supermarket. Mrs. Reppler, a practical woman, battles the creatures that emerge from the Mist with weapons as varied as bug spray and a tennis racket.

*MRS. TURMAN.* Billy Drayton's babysitter, she takes charge of the boy as David, his father, deals with the situation inside the supermarket.

*AMANDA DUMFRIES.* Seeking comfort in the midst of chaos, Amanda becomes David Drayton's lover. Amanda is the only one in the supermarket who is carrying a weapon—a gun she keeps in her pocketbook.

## "BEACH WORLD"
### from *Skeleton Crew* (1985)

Set in the future on a far-flung desert planet, this brief but effective science fiction/horror hybrid would not have been out of place in the EC Comics King enjoyed as a child.

### PRIMARY SUBJECTS

*SHAPIRO and RAND.* Crew members of a spaceship that crash-lands on a desert planet, killing one of their fellow passengers. By the time a rescue ship arrives, Shapiro is ready to leave, but Rand is not. Rand is insane, having been consumed by—and having consumed—the sentient sand of which the desert world is composed.

## "THE END OF THE WHOLE MESS"
### from *Nightmares & Dreamscapes* (1993)

King's note mentions that readers will "find reflections" of his brother, David, in Bobby Fornoy, Howard's genius brother. "The End of the Whole Mess" is a cautionary science fiction tale, once again dealing with the dire consequences that face anyone possessing special powers or paranormal talents.

### PRIMARY SUBJECTS

*HOWARD FORNOY.* The narrator of the story, Howard describes growing up with his genius brother, Bobby. He opens his narrative with, "I want to tell you about the end of war, the degeneration of mankind, and the death of the Messiah." Shortly after injecting himself with the wonder drug discovered by his brother, Howard tells the tale of Bobby's quest for world peace. His story is told in a series of diarylike entries, which become increasingly incoherent as the story progresses.

**BOBBY FORNOY.** Howard writes, "People like my brother Bobby come along only once every two or three generations, I think—guys like Leonardo da Vinci, Newton, Einstein, maybe Edison." Bobby *is* a genius, but instead of pursuing wealth, he seeks a cure for man's inhumanity to man. Bobby finds a cure in an aquifer near Waco, Texas, and arranges to distribute it to the whole world. In an ironic twist of fate, the genius overlooked one thing: the water that pacifies people also causes a precipitous drop in their IQs. In essence, Bobby turns the entire world into passive idiots.


## "HOME DELIVERY"

### from *Nightmares & Dreamscapes* (1993)

This tale of homicidal zombies was originally commissioned for a 1989 theme anthology titled *Book of the Dead* and purposely set in writer-director George A. Romero's *Night of the Living Dead* (1968) universe. It takes place on Little Tall Island, the setting of *Dolores Claiborne* (1993) and *Storm of the Century* (1999). Clearly, however, this is *not* the Little Tall Island of the prime reality, but a nightmarish mirror image from some parallel dimension. Though focused on the ordeal of Maddie Pace, it's a story of the stubbornness and sheer gumption of "Mainers" never to give up without a fight, no matter how horrifying the odds.


### PRIMARY SUBJECTS

**MADDIE PACE.** Widowed after her husband falls off a fishing boat and drowns, Maddie is pregnant with their child. When zombies attack, Maddie and the other citizens of Little Tall are determined to do whatever it takes to save their island, even if it means combating deceased family members and loved ones.

*JACK PACE.* Jack, Maddie's late husband, returns from the dead as a hideous zombie and seeks to make her his next victim. Although she had once truly loved Jack, she knows this monster is not her husband. To save herself and their unborn child, Maddie takes an ax and hacks Jack into little pieces.

## "THE DOCTOR'S CASE"

from *Nightmares & Dreamscapes* (1993)

This story was King's contribution to a 1987 anthology titled *The New Adventures of Sherlock Holmes,* a group of original stories written in honor of the great Sir Arthur Conan Doyle, creator of the legendary detective.

## PRIMARY SUBJECTS

*SHERLOCK HOLMES, DR. WATSON, LESTRADE.* If you don't know who these three gentlemen are, you have clearly failed Great Literary Characters 101. Suffice it to say that King indulges in a bit of role reversal here, allowing Dr. Watson to solve a mystery instead of master sleuth Holmes.

# APPENDIX A

## *A Stephen King Chronology*

———————

**1947.** Stephen Edwin King is born September 21 in Portland, Maine, at Maine General Hospital. He is the son of Donald Edwin and Nellie Ruth (Pillsbury) King. The couple had previously adopted an older son, David, in 1945.

**1949.** Donald Edwin King separates from Ruth, then deserts the family and is never heard from again.

**1954–1958.** Stephen King begins first attempts at writing stories, inspired by the science fiction films and books he reads. Early influences include the films *The Creature from the Black Lagoon* (1954) and *Earth vs. the Flying Saucers* (1956).

**1959–1960.** Finds a box of science fiction and horror books that had belonged to his father. Obtains first typewriter and begins to actively submit stories to genre magazines.

**1962–1966.** Attends high school in Lisbon Falls, Maine. Writes his first novel-length manuscript, "The Aftermath." Also starts work on "Getting It On," which would later be published as *Rage* (1977) under a pseudonym of Richard Bachman.

**1965.** Publishes his first short story, "I Was a Teenage Graverobber," in *Comics Review*, a fanzine.

**1966–1970.** Attends the University of Maine at Orono, graduating with a B.S. in English. Writes a regular column for the university newspaper titled "King's Garbage Truck."

While working at the university library, he meets Tabitha Jane Spruce (b. 1949), an aspiring poet and short-story writer.

451

Makes his first professional sale in 1967, with the story "The Glass Floor" in the pulp magazine *Startling Mystery Stories*. Also makes sales to various men's magazines (most notably *Cavalier*) of his short fiction. Completes two novel-length manuscripts, "The Long Walk" and "Sword in the Darkness." The former would later be published as a Bachman title, while the latter would never see print.

*1971*. Marries Tabitha Spruce.

*1971–1973*. Teaches high school English at Hampden Academy in Hampden, Maine.

Completes a manuscript for "Getting It On" but is unable to sell it. Writes "The Running Man" over the course of a long weekend but is unable to sell it. Begins work on a short story called "Carrie," which his wife encourages him to complete as a short novel.

*1973*. Sells *Carrie* to Doubleday & Co. for a hardcover advance of $2,500.

*1974*. Writes "Roadwork," which will later see print as a Bachman book.

*Carrie* is published in hardcover by Doubleday. Paperback rights are sold for $400,000, of which Stephen King receives half, the other share going to the hardcover publisher.

King's mother, Ruth, dies of uterine cancer before the publication of *Carrie*.

*1975*. *'Salem's Lot* is released by Doubleday.

*1976*. Movie version of *Carrie*, released by United Artists and directed by Brian De Palma, becomes a surprise summer hit. The movie tie-in paperback edition of the novel becomes a bestseller.

*1977*. *The Shining* is published by Doubleday. Though it is only his third published novel, the dust-jacket copy proclaims King "the undisputed master of the modern horror story."

In October, *Rage*, the first novel published under the name of his alter ego, Richard Bachman, is published by New American Library, King's paperback publisher, as a mass-market paperback original.

Travels with his family to England. There he develops what would become a lifelong friendship with horror and suspense novelist Peter Straub, with whom he would later collaborate on *The Talisman* (1984).

*1978*. His first collection of short stories, *Night Shift*, is published by Doubleday.

The first version of *The Stand* is published by Doubleday. The "complete and uncut" edition would not appear until 1990.

Serves as writer-in-residence and instructor at the University of Maine at Orono.

**1979.** Attends the Fifth World Fantasy Convention in Providence, Rhode Island, as a guest of honor.

*The Dead Zone* is published by Viking Press after contract dispute with Doubleday. It is his first book to go to the No. 1 position on the *New York Times* bestseller list.

*'Salem's Lot* is adapted as a miniseries for network television on CBS, directed by Tobe Hooper.

The second Bachman novel, *The Long Walk,* is released by New American Library without fanfare as a paperback original.

**1980.** *Firestarter* is published by Viking Press.

*The Shining,* adapted and directed by Stanley Kubrick, is released by Warner Bros.

**1981.** *Danse Macabre,* King's nonfiction study of horror in the mass media, is published by Everest House.

*Cujo* is published by Viking Press.

*Roadwork,* the third Bachman novel, is published by New American Library.

Receives Career Alumni Award from the University of Maine.

**1982.** *Different Seasons,* a collection of original novellas, is published by Viking Press.

*The Dark Tower: The Gunslinger* is published in a limited run by Donald M. Grant Publishers. It becomes an instant collector's item.

*Creepshow,* a collection of graphic stories done in the style of the infamous EC Comics of the 1950s, is published by New American Library.

*The Running Man,* the fourth Bachman novel, is published by New American Library as a mass-market paperback original.

*Creepshow,* based on previously published short stories, is released as a motion picture by Warner Bros. Directed by George A. Romero, it is the first film produced from a Stephen King screenplay.

**1983.** *Christine* is published by Viking Press.

*Pet Sematary* is published by Doubleday.

*Cycle of the Werewolf* is released by Land of Enchantment, a specialty press, in a limited edition.

*The Dead Zone,* directed by David Cronenberg, is released by Paramount.

*Cujo,* directed by Lewis Teague, is released by Taft Entertainment Company.

*Christine,* directed by John Carpenter, is released by Columbia Pictures.

**1984.** *The Talisman,* co-authored with Peter Straub, is published jointly by Viking/ G. P. Putnam's Sons.

*Thinner,* the fifth Richard Bachman novel, is published by New American Library. Unlike previous Bachman titles, it is issued in an original hardcover edition and heavily promoted at the American Booksellers Association convention that year.

*Children of the Corn,* directed by Fritz Kiersch and based on the short story of the same name, is released by New World Pictures.

*Firestarter,* directed by Mark L. Lester, is released by Universal Pictures.

**1985.** After years of successfully denying it, King admits to a local newspaper that he uses the pseudonym "Richard Bachman."

King writes and directs the feature *Maximum Overdrive,* based on his short story "Trucks," for Dino De Laurentiis in Wilmington, North Carolina.

*Cat's Eye,* directed by Lewis Teague, is released by MGM/UA. It is the second film produced from a King screenplay.

*Skeleton Crew,* his second major collection of short stories, is published by G. P. Putnam's.

*The Bachman Books,* an omnibus collection of the first four Bachman titles, is published by New American Library in simultaneous hardcover and trade paperback editions.

*Silver Bullet,* directed by Daniel Attias and based on the book *Cycle of the Werewolf,* is released by Columbia-EMI-Warner. King also wrote the screenplay.

**1986.** *IT* is published by Viking Press.

*Maximum Overdrive,* the first movie both scripted and directed by King, is released by De Laurentiis Entertainment Group.

*Stand by Me,* directed by Rob Reiner and based on the novella "The Body," is released by Columbia Pictures.

**1987.** *Misery* is published by Viking Press.

*The Eyes of the Dragon* is self-published by King's own Philtrum Press. A revised version is published by Viking Press.

*The Tommyknockers* is published by Viking Press.

*Creepshow 2,* directed by Michael Gornick with a screenplay by George A. Romero, is released by New World Pictures.

*The Dark Tower II: The Drawing of the Three* is published by Donald M. Grant Publishers.

King writes an original teleplay called "Sorry, Right Number" for George A. Romero's syndicated television series, *Tales from the Darkside.*

*The Running Man,* directed by Paul Michael Glaser, is released by Taft Entertainment. The credits read "based on the novel by Richard Bachman."

**1988.** *Nightmares in the Sky,* a collection of photographs by "f-stop fitzgerald," for which Stephen King writes only the introductory text, is published by Viking Press.

*Carrie* is transformed into a Broadway musical, opening at the Virginia Theater. It closes after only five regular performances.

**1989.** *The Dark Half* is published by Viking Press.
*Pet Sematary,* directed by Mary Lambert from a screenplay by King, is released by Paramount Pictures.

**1990.** *The Stand* (complete and uncut version) is published by Doubleday.
*Four Past Midnight,* a collection of original novellas, is published by Viking Press.
*Misery,* directed by Rob Reiner, is released by Castle Rock Entertainment.
*Stephen King's Graveyard Shift,* a feature film directed by Ralph S. Singleton and based on the short story of the same name, is released by Columbia Tri-Star.
*Stephen King's IT,* directed by Tommy Lee Wallace, airs on ABC as a television miniseries.

**1991.** *Needful Things* is published by Viking Press.
*The Dark Half,* adapted and directed by George A. Romero, is released as a motion picture by Orion Pictures.
*Golden Years* airs on CBS as a seven-part television series. Most of the episodes are written by King.
*Sometimes They Come Back,* based on the short story of the same name, airs as a made-for-television feature on CBS, directed by Tom McLoughlin.
*The Dark Tower III: The Waste Lands* is published by Donald M. Grant Publishers.

**1992.** *Gerald's Game* is published by Viking Press.
King performs with his celebrity-author rock band, the Rock Bottom Remainders, at the American Booksellers Association convention in Anaheim, California.
*Sleepwalkers,* with an original screenplay by King and directed by Mick Garris, is released by Columbia Pictures.
*The Lawnmower Man,* directed by Brett Leonard, is released by New Line Cinema. It bears so little resemblance to King's story that the author successfully sues to have his name removed from the credits.

**1993.** *Nightmares & Dreamscapes,* King's third major collection of short stories, is published by Viking Press.
*Dolores Claiborne* is published by Viking Press.
*Needful Things,* directed by Fraser Heston, is released by Columbia Pictures.
*Stephen King's The Tommyknockers,* directed by John Power, airs as a miniseries on ABC.

**1994.** *Stephen King's The Stand* airs as a miniseries on ABC, with a teleplay by King and directed by Mick Garris.
*Insomnia* is published by Viking Press.
*The Shawshank Redemption,* directed by Frank Darabont, is released by Columbia Pictures. It is based on the novella "Rita Hayworth and Shawshank Redemption," which originally appeared in *Different Seasons* (1982).

**1995.** *Rose Madder* is published by Viking Press.

*The Mangler,* directed by Tobe Hooper and based on the short story of the same name, is released by New Line Cinema.

*Dolores Claiborne,* directed by Taylor Hackford, is released by Columbia Pictures. It stars Kathy Bates, who had previously won an Academy Award for her performance in *Misery.*

*Stephen King's The Langoliers,* directed by Tom Holland and based on the novella that appeared in *Four Past Midnight,* airs as a miniseries on ABC.

**1996.** *Desperation* is published by Viking Press. *The Regulators* (credited to Richard Bachman) is published simultaneously by Dutton.

The first installment of *The Green Mile,* a serial novel, is published by New American Library.

"The Man in the Black Suit" receives the O. Henry Award for best American short story. It was originally published in 1994, when it won a World Fantasy Award.

*Thinner,* directed by Tom Holland, is released by Paramount Pictures.

On September 15, King has six books on the bestseller list, earning him a place in the *Guinness Book of World Records.*

**1997.** *The Dark Tower IV: Wizard and Glass* is published by Donald M. Grant Publishers.

*Quicksilver Highway,* directed by Mick Garris, an anthology movie that includes "Chattery Teeth," is broadcast as an original television feature on FOX.

*Six Stories* is published in a limited edition by King's own Philtrum Press.

*Trucks,* based on the story of the same name and directed by Chris Thomson, is broadcast as an original television feature on USA Network.

*Stephen King's The Shining,* directed by Mick Garris, airs on ABC as a miniseries, with a teleplay by King.

**1998.** *Stephen King's The Night Flier,* directed by Mark Pavia, is briefly released as a theatrical motion picture by New Line Cinema. It had premiered on HBO.

King writes "Chinga," an original teleplay for *The X-Files,* which was subsequently rewritten by series creator Chris Carter.

*Apt Pupil,* directed by Bryan Singer and based on the novella that originally appeared in *Different Seasons,* is released by Paramount Pictures.

*Bag of Bones* is published by Scribners.

**1999.** *Storm of the Century,* the script for "an original novel for television," is published by Pocket Books. The miniseries of the same name, directed by Craig Baxley, airs on ABC, with a teleplay by King.

*The Girl Who Loved Tom Gordon* is published by Scribners.

*Hearts in Atlantis* is published by Scribners.

On June 19, King is seriously injured in an automobile accident near Center Lovell, Maine. It takes him many months to recover.

*Blood and Smoke,* a collection of three stories, is published as an audiobook by Scribners.

*The Green Mile,* adapted and directed by Frank Darabont, is released by Warner Bros. It is nominated for four Academy Awards.

**2000.** "Riding the Bullet," a never-before-published tale, is sold by King on the Internet, bypassing the use of "traditional" publishing methods, though in conjunction with a traditional publisher, Simon & Schuster.

In 2000, King began to serialize his novel *The Plant* online at his own Web site. The novel had begun many years earlier as an annual Christmas event for friends and family, a chapter per year. King sold the serial book on an honors system online, but the percentage of customers who took the material for free began to grow over the course of the year. On November 29th King announced that he was, at least temporarily pulling the plug on the online serial novel in order to focus on the sequel to *The Talisman (The Black House)* and the rest of the Dark Tower series. King assured his constant readers that he would return to *The Plant* eventually.

*On Writing: A Memoir of the Craft,* a nonfiction work, is published by Scribners.

*Rose Red* goes into production as an original miniseries for ABC.

The film version of *Hearts in Atlantis* starts production, with Anthony Hopkins slated to play Ted Brautigan.

**2001.** Begins work on *The Dark Tower V: The Crawling Shadow* (tentative title).

A sequel to *The Talisman, The Black House,* again in collaboration with Peter Straub, is published by Scribners.

*Dreamcatcher,* a novel, is published by Scribners.

The film version of *The Girl Who Loved Tom Gordon,* written and directed by George A. Romero, goes into production.

Production begins on *Desperation,* directed by Mick Garris. *The Sun Dog* is released as an Imax film.

*The Talisman* starts production as a miniseries for ABC.

# A P P E N D I X   B

## The Fiction of Stephen King

---

The following chronological list does not include King's individually published short stories or e-published works.

*Carrie* (1974)

*'Salem's Lot* (1975)

*The Shining* (1977)

*Rage* (as Richard Bachman, 1977)

*Night Shift* (collection, 1978)

*The Stand* (1978)

*The Long Walk* (as Richard Bachman, 1979)

*The Dead Zone* (1979)

*Firestarter* (1980)

*Roadwork* (as Richard Bachman, 1981)

*Cujo* (1981)

*Creepshow* (1982)

*The Running Man* (as Richard Bachman, 1982)

*The Dark Tower: The Gunslinger* (1982)

*Different Seasons* (collection, 1982)

*Christine* (1983)

*Pet Sematary* (1983)

*Cycle of the Werewolf* (1983)

*The Talisman* (with Peter Straub, 1984)

*Thinner* (as Richard Bachman, 1984)

*Skeleton Crew* (collection, 1985)

*Cat's Eye* (original screenplay, 1985)

*IT* (1986)

*The Dark Tower II: The Drawing of the Three* (1987)

*The Eyes of the Dragon* (1987)

*Misery* (1987)

*The Tommyknockers* (1987)

*The Dark Half* (1989)

*Four Past Midnight* (collection, 1990)

*Needful Things* (1991)

*Stephen King's Golden Years* (original television series, 1991)

*The Dark Tower III: The Waste Lands* (1991)

*Sleepwalkers* (original screenplay, 1992)

*Gerald's Game* (1992)

*Dolores Claiborne* (1993)

*Nightmares & Dreamscapes* (collection, 1993)

*Insomnia* (1994)

*Rose Madder* (1995)

*The Green Mile* (1996)

*Desperation* (1996)

*The Regulators* (as Richard Bachman, 1996)

*The Dark Tower IV: Wizard and Glass* (1997)

*Six Stories* (collection, 1997)

*Bag of Bones* (1998)

*Storm of the Century* (original television miniseries, 1999)

*The Girl Who Loved Tom Gordon* (1999)

*Hearts in Atlantis* (1999)

*Blood and Smoke* (collection, 1999)

*Dreamcatcher* (2001)

# APPENDIX C

## Recommended Reading

---

At last count, some forty-odd (including some *very* odd) books have been published about Stephen King and/or his work in the United States alone, of which *The Stephen King Universe* will certainly not be the last word. Below are fourteen titles that we feel are the most useful to both the casual fan and the serious scholar. These are listed in order of their original publication. Many have since been reprinted in both hardcover and paperback editions by other publishers, often in revised form.

Although some of the titles are currently out of print, they may be obtained through the usual services that handle out-of-print and used books. We recommend Betts Bookstore (207-947-7052 or e-mail bettsbooks@aol.com) in Bangor, Maine, owned by Stuart Tinker, which handles "all things King" right in King's backyard. We also heartily recommend a search of the Overlook Connection (770-926-1762 or e-mail OverlookCN@aol.com), owned by Dave Hinchberger, which has been dealing in all things related to King since 1979. This online bookstore carries many King rarities and oddities.

*1.* Stephen King, *Stephen King's Danse Macabre.* New York: Everest House, 1981. This remains the most personal and in-depth look at King's thoughts, feelings, and opinions on the subject of horror. Encouraged by editor William Thompson to write a nonfiction study so that King would never have to answer interviewers and fans about the topic again, King reluctantly but enthusiastically took on the task. (The fact that what he had already said about horror filled no less than two volumes of interviews may also have had something to do with the undertaking.) As King explains in his introduction, "Writing this book has been both an exasperation and a deep pleasure, a duty on some days and a labor of love on others." As engaging and moving as his fiction, *Danse Macabre* remains an affectionate yet perceptive look at how horror in the mass media and the arts has affected our popular culture in general—and one little boy from Maine in particular.

**2.** Chuck Miller and Tim Underwood, eds. *Fear Itself: The Horror Fiction of Stephen King.* Columbia, Pa.: Underwood-Miller, 1982. The first major collection of essays on King, written by such contemporaries as Fritz Leiber, Chelsea Quinn Yarbro, and Douglas E. Winter, with an introduction by Peter Straub and an afterword by George A. Romero. In the introduction to "Stephen King: A Bibliography," the compilers boldly observe: "It has been stated that Richard Bachman is a pseudonym of Stephen King. This is not the case. Mr. Bachman lives in Bangor, Maine, and Stephen King has never used this name as a pseudonym."

**3.** Douglas E. Winter, *Stephen King: The Art of Darkness.* New York: NAL, 1984. The first and only authorized biography/overview/critical examination of Stephen King, written by noted critic and horror authority Douglas E. Winter. The first book to turn to when one wishes to know more about the man and his writings. An expanded and updated edition appeared in 1986, detailing the previously concealed subject of the Richard Bachman pseudonym. A further revised edition is long overdue.

**4.** Michael R. Collings, *The Many Facets of Stephen King.* Mercer Island, Wash.: Starmont, 1985. The first of many critical guides to the novels, short stories, and films of Stephen King by Professor Collings. Although all of Collings's studies to date have been issued by academic or specialty publishers and therefore are not widely available to the general public, Collings has become the most prolific critical writer on the subject at hand. He has authored or co-authored more than half a dozen volumes on King. This initial volume is a comprehensive overview of the author, his work, and his critics.

**5.** Michael R. Collings, *The Annotated Guide to Stephen King.* Mercer Island, Wash.: Starmont, 1986. The first comprehensive bibliographic study. The author later expanded and updated the volume for Borgo Press as *The Work of Stephen King: An Annotated Bibliography & Guide.* Although a new and further updated edition is reportedly in the works from Overlook Connection Press, the current revised volume may certainly be considered, to date, the definitive bibliographic study.

**6.** Don Herron, ed., *Reign of Fear: The Fiction and Films of Stephen King.* Columbia, Pa.: Underwood-Miller, 1988. The third collection of original essays compiled by critic Heron for editors-publishers Underwood and Miller, who had previously released a second volume of essays titled *Kingdom of Fear: The World of Stephen King* in 1986. This third volume is notable mostly for the fact that although most of the essays look on the work of King charitably and favorably, the editor himself does not.

**7.** Chuck Miller and Tim Underwood, eds., *Bare Bones: Conversations on Terror with Stephen King.* Columbia, Pa.: Underwood-Miller, 1988. The first collection of interviews, compiled from various sources and organized by theme. Nearly one-fifth of the book's contents is taken from interviews conducted by Stanley Wiater. Also published as a trade hardcover by McGraw-Hill (New York) in 1988.

**8.** Chuck Miller and Tim Underwood, eds., *Feast of Fear: Conversations with Stephen King.* Columbia, Pa.: Underwood-Miller, 1989. A second collection of interviews, compiled from various sources and organized by theme. Also published as a trade hardcover by Carroll & Graf Publishers (New York) in 1992.

**9.** George Beahm, ed., *The Stephen King Companion.* Kansas City, Mo.: Andrews and McMeel, 1989. The first collection of articles, interviews, appreciations, and reviews to be issued by a major publisher. An interesting mixture of both new and reprinted material, compiled by a recognized popular culture authority. (Beahm also edited *The Unauthorized Anne Rice Companion* for the same publisher.) A revised edition was issued by the same publisher in 1995.

**10.** Stephen J. Spignesi, *The Shape Under the Sheet: The Stephen King Encyclopedia.* Ann Arbor, Mich.: Popular Culture Ink, 1991. A monumental work that reportedly took more than four years to write and compile. The book is both a companion volume (interviews, articles, reviews, fiction) and a concordance to everything (and we do mean everything) that King had written up until that time. A noted popular culture authority, Spignesi is also the author of two quiz/trivia books on King, and most recently 1998's *The Lost Work of Stephen King* (Secaucus, N.J.: Birch Lane Press), described as "a guide to the unpublished manuscripts, story fragments, alternative versions, and oddities." An updated edition covering the past decade would be welcomed.

**11.** George Beahm, *The Stephen King Story.* Kansas City, Mo.: Andrews and McMeel, 1991. A literary profile of the author, with emphasis on the manner in which King has become a celebrity and a worldwide publishing phenomenon. Given the rate at which King produces new work, the volume was revised and updated for its 1992 appearance in paperback. A newly updated edition would be appreciated.

**12.** Ann Lloyd, *The Films of Stephen King.* New York: St. Martin's, 1994. A heavily illustrated if woefully slender volume first published in England in 1993, it still remains the most accessible and entertaining of all the books written on the subject. For the record, there have been no less than *three* other volumes written covering the same territory: *Stephen King at the Movies* by Jessie Horsting (New York: Starlog Press, 1984), *The Films of Stephen King* by Michael R. Collings (Mercer Island, Wash.: Starmont, 1986), and *Stephen King Goes to Hollywood* by Jeff Conner (New York: NAL, 1987). Even so, the definitive book on this vital aspect of the author's career has yet to be published.

**13.** George Beahm, *Stephen King from A to Z : An Encyclopedia of His Life and Work.* Kansas City: Andrews and McMeel, 1998. An earnest attempt to look at the life and work of King through the format of an encyclopedic compilation, with entries ranging from "Ackerman, Forrest J." to "ZBS Productions." According to the publisher, the volume is "the only book of its kind. Illustrated with seventy-five photos and twenty-six illuminated letters, the book includes hundreds of entries covering everything you wanted to know about King . . . but were afraid to ask."

*14.* George Beahm, *Stephen King Country.* Philadelphia: Running Press, 1999. Subtitled *The Illustrated Guide to the Sites and Sights that Inspired the Modern Master of Horror.* A fascinating collection of photographs and text presenting the world of Stephen King from two viewpoints. First, the locations in Maine that show the "real" world of King, such as his home, the laundry where he once worked, and his old high school. Also contains original photographs showing the actual sites, buildings, and locations that reportedly inspired corresponding locales in his fiction. These include the Shiloh Church in Durham, which may have inspired the Marsten house in *'Salem's Lot* (1975), and the Stanley Hotel in Estes Park, Colorado, the inspiration for the Overlook in *The Shining* (1977).

# APPENDIX D

## *Recommended Web Sites*

---

Literally hundreds of Web sites are devoted to the world's most popular author. We have chosen thirteen sites that we feel are the most useful—and the most entertaining—to the devoted Stephen King fan. On most of these you will find book reviews, movie reviews, the latest news about King as an author and a celebrity, trivia games, discussions between fans, and so forth.

### OFFICIAL

*1.* The Official Stephen King Page
(www.stephenking.com)
As the title says, the only Web page authorized by King and maintained directly from his office.

### UNOFFICIAL

*2. Skemers*
(www.skemers.com)
Launched in 1995, this is the largest King fan club for those wanting to discuss and chat about their favorite author online.

*3.* The Stephen King Cover Gallery
(http://home5.swipnet.se/~55592/gallery.htm)
An incredible site, fan Anders Jackson has scanned in more than a thousand different editions of Stephen King book covers from around the world.

*4.* The Stephen King Web Site
(www.utopianweb.com/king/)
A comprehensive, well-done site.

5. David's Stephen King Page
(www.lisp.com.au/~davidth/king/king.html)
A comprehensive site, more informal and purposely entertaining than most.

6. The Stephen King Page
(http://malakoff.com/sking.htm)
An entertaining page, this site includes a Randall Flagg homepage and a Richard Bachman homepage.

7. The Last Gunslinger
(www.geocities.com/Area51/Dimension/1004/gunslinger.html)
An impressive, visually dazzling site devoted exclusively to the *Dark Tower* epic.

8. The Unofficial Stephen King Website
(www.stephenking.net)
A well-designed and respectful site maintained by fan Ian Richardson, which has been in service since 1996.

9. Stephen King Information Site
(www.eddog.com/sk/)
One of the oldest and most reliable sites out there, run by hardcore fan Ed Nomura.

10. Charnel House, The Stephen King Site for the Discerning Reader
(http:/members.tripod.com/~charnelhouse/)
A full-service information source for "all things King."

11. SkingWeb—Stephen King Fun and Information
(http://skingweb.virtualave.net/)
As the title indicates, this is part of the "official" series of Stephen King sites in the Stephen King Web ring.

12. IMDB—Stephen King
(http://usidmb.com/Name?/King,+Stephen)
The International Movie Data Base listing of all movies associated with King. Complete and factual, but without any visuals to accompany the reams of data.

13. Stephen King's Movies
(http://moviething.com/king/)
An entertaining and well-illustrated guide to films based on the works of King.

# Index

Names listed in boldface refer to characters.

Page numbers in boldface refer to character biographies.

466

# ABOUT THE AUTHORS

*STANLEY WIATER* has been interviewing and writing about Stephen King for more than two decades. He has been called "the world's leading authority on horror filmmakers and authors" *(Radio-TV Interview Report)* and "the master journalist of the dark genres" *(World of Fandom)*. Wiater has recently begun production, as both writer and host, on a television series inspired by his award-winning Dark Dreamers books.

His first collection of exclusive interviews, *Dark Dreamers: Conversations with the Masters of Horror,* received the Bram Stoker Award for superior achievement from the Horror Writers Association. A companion volume, *Dark Visions: Conversations with the Masters of the Horror Film,* was a Bram Stoker Award finalist. *Comic Book Rebels: Conversations with the Creators of the New Comics,* co-authored with Stephen R. Bissette, was both an Eisner Award and Harvey Award nominee. *Dark Thoughts: On Writing,* a "best of" compilation, also received the Bram Stoker Award. A collaboration with acclaimed photographer Beth Gwinn led to a unique collection of photographs and interviews in *Dark Dreamers: Facing the Masters of Fear.* Wiater's first published short story, "The Toucher," was the sole winner of a 1980 competition judged by none other than Stephen King.

Wiater was born and raised in Massachusetts, where he still lives with his family. He graduated from the University of Massachusetts with a degree in writing and cinema. He is presently completing work on a study of the films of Wes Craven. Please visit him at www.stanleywiater.com.

*CHRISTOPHER GOLDEN* is the award-winning, bestselling author of *Buffy the Vampire Slayer: The Watcher's Guide, Buffy the Vampire Slayer: The Monster Book,* and *CUT! Horror Writers on Horror Film,* for which he received the Bram Stoker Award. As a journalist, his work has appeared in such publications as *Disney Adventures,* the *Boston Globe, Billboard,* and *Hero Illustrated.* For several years he wrote a regular column for the international service BPI Entertainment News Wire.

Golden's teen thriller series, *Body of Evidence,* was recently optioned by Viacom Television, and he is currently developing a second series for teens with Pocket Books. His novels include *Strangewood, The Shadow Saga* trilogy, and *Straight on 'til Morning,* as well as *Hellboy: The Lost Army.* He has also written or co-written nine *Buffy the Vampire Slayer* novels.

As a comic-book writer, Golden's work has included *Batman Chronicles, Wolverine/Punisher, The Crow, Spider-Man Unlimited, Angel, Blade, Buffy the Vampire Slayer,* and the creator-owned *Thundergod.*

Before becoming a full-time writer, he was licensing manager for *Billboard* magazine in New York, where he worked on FOX Television's *Billboard Music Awards* and *American Top 40* radio, among other projects.

Golden was born and raised in Massachusetts, where he still lives with his family. He graduated from Tufts University. Please visit him at www.christophergolden.com

*HANK WAGNER* is a prolific and respected critic and interviewer. Among the publications in which his work regularly appears are *Cemetery Dance, Horror, Wetbones, Nova Express,* and the *New York Review of Science Fiction.* Wagner also writes for such online trade magazines as *Dark Echo* and *Hellnotes,* and is a regular contributor to Barnes and Noble.com and the Overlook Connection. He lives in New Jersey with his wife and four daughters. Wagner graduated from the University of Notre Dame in 1982, received his J.D. from Seton Hall University in 1985, and earned an L.L.M. in taxation from the New York University of Law in 1991.